Citizen Spielberg

Citizen Spielberg

LESTER D. FRIEDMAN

UNIVERSITY OF ILLINOIS PRESS

Urbana, Chicago, and Springfield

∞ This book is printed on acid-free paper.

Library of Congress Cataloging-in-Publication Data
Friedman, Lester D.
Citizen Spielberg/ Lester D. Friedman.
p.   cm.
Filmography:
Includes bibliographical references and index.
ISBN-13: 978-0-252-03114-4 (cloth : alk. paper)
ISBN-10: 0-252-03114-8 (cloth : alk. paper)
ISBN-13: 978-0-252-07358-8 (pbk. : alk. paper)
ISBN-10: 0-252-07358-4 (pbk. : alk. paper)
1. Spielberg, Steven, 1946—Criticism and interpretation.
I. Title.
PN1998.3.S65F75   2006
791.4302'33092—dc22   2005035191

This book is dedicated to Delia Temes,
for thirty-nine years
the most generous reader and best friend imaginable.

We shall not cease from exploration
And the end of all our exploring
Will be to arrive where we started
And know the place for the first time

—T. S. Eliot, "Little Gidding"

Contents

Acknowledgments   ix

Introduction: The Elephant in the Center of the Room   1

1. "I'm Sorry I Didn't Tell You about the World":
   Spielberg's Science-Fiction and Fantasy Films   11

2. "They Don't Know What They've Got There":
   Spielberg's Action/Adventure Melodramas   63

3. "Objects in the Mirror Are Closer Than They Appear":
   Spielberg's Monster Movies   119

4. "The World Has Taken a Turn for the Surreal": Spielberg's
   World War II Combat Films   180

5. "Whoever Tells the Best Story Wins": Spielberg's Social
   Problem/Ethnic Minority Films   244

6. "Control Is Power": Imagining the Holocaust   290

Filmography   325

Works Cited   333

Index   347

Acknowledgments

Writing this book was a long and often frustrating journey, one that began in upstate New York, meandered through Chicago, and ended back in upstate New York. I was fortunate, as always, to have the support of my family during this trek: my parents, Eva and Eugene Friedman; my children, Marc and Rachel Friedman; my daughter-in-law, Jessica Friedman; and my stepdaughter, Allison Kavey (who helped shape my thoughts on *A.I.*). Most important, my wife, Rae-Ellen Kavey, provided loving encouragement and compassionate understanding during my worst days. I also owe a debt of gratitude to my students in Spielberg courses at Syracuse and Northwestern Universities for their comments and challenges. In particular, I appreciate the insights and assistance of Tom Antonellis, Mike French, Larry Knapp, Leslie Lewis, Jeremy Schipp, and Dan Silver. At the University of Illinois Press, I was fortunate to have the patient persistence of Joan Catapano, as well as the considerable professional skills of Rebecca Crist and Matthew Mitchell. John Ferrance at Hobart William Smith Colleges worked diligently to supply needed bibliographic information. I also wish to thank two of my gracious colleagues and sympathetic friends, David Desser and Murray Pomerance, whose thoughtful suggestions made this a far better book. For help obtaining stills and publicity materials, I would like to thank the following sources: Amblin Entertainment, Columbia Pictures, DreamWorks Pictures SKG, HBO Film, Jerry Ohlinger's Movie Material Store, Lucasfilm, Tristar, United Artists, Universal Studios, and Warner Brothers. Finally, I want to acknowledge the immeasurable acts of kindness and skill provided by Delia Temes, who edited this book as it was being created.

Citizen Spielberg

The Elephant in the Center of the Room

"How very Steven Spielberg."
—Angels in America

Beyond the Page

This project did not begin as a labor of love. I was not one of those awestruck viewers mesmerized as the mothership harmonized with humankind, sobbing when E.T. finally left for home, or cheering as Indiana Jones rode off into the sunset. It began when students requested a course on Spielberg and, much to my surprise, I could not find a single comprehensive scholarly study of his films. While many of those currently on the market contain pockets of intelligent analysis, most are primarily concerned with other matters: biography (McBride, Mott and Saunders, Taylor, Yule, Baxter, Sanello), interviews (Friedman and Notbohm), behind-the-scenes revelations (Perry, Freer, Gottlieb, Brode, Rubin), and general commentaries for fans (Clarke, Slade and Watson). Closest to what I had in mind was Charles Silet's collection of previously published essays, though these wildly disparate pieces offer no coherent vision of Spielberg's works over time, and Yosefa Loshitzky's collection of provocative essays on *Schindler's List,* an in-depth study of Spielberg's Holocaust film. Considering that my academic field traditionally welcomes a panoply of media and cultural topics and each year greets an impressive array of books that range from rare silent films, to arcane theoretical subjects, to popular social phenomena, I could not understand why scholars had ignored Steven Spielberg, arguably the most important figure in screen culture over the last three decades.

The answer came after reading academic articles in a range of journals and periodicals. For most scholars, Spielberg is the New York Yankees of the film world: he is the man they love to hate because he fields the best players, controls the biggest budgets, draws the largest crowds, reaps the most profits, and wins far too often. When his movies garner awards, the applause barely dies down before the whispered accusations of unfair advantages arise. Equally important, academics often prefer to wield their analytical skills in the service of undervalued creative artists whom they can "discover" and present to the world, not directors who sit atop immense financial empires and command princely budgets for their projects. As Frank Manchel wryly observes, "Film is a medium where the more successful you are commercially, the less acceptable you are to the critical community—at least until you are dead" (85). Like Alfred Hitchcock, who was not recognized as a great visual artist until relatively late in his career, Spielberg's cinema seems too filled with earthly pleasures, too stuffed with things that go bump in the night, and too reliant on emotional manipulation to command favorable attention from those who see themselves as guardians of culture maintaining the barricades against hordes of encroaching barbarians.

The standard scholarly view resolutely positions Spielberg as little more than a modern P. T. Barnum, a technically gifted and intellectually shallow showman who substitutes spectacle for substance and emotion for depth. Read any extended account of his work, and you will quickly recognize the party line echoed by most academic writers: Spielberg (along with his pal George Lucas) is responsible for two of the greatest sins in modern cinema history—the Blockbuster mentality that permeates the commercial film industry, and the infantalization of contemporary movies. The former, they claim, leaves little room for intellectually challenging cinematic works that may lack widespread audience appeal, and the latter encourages wham-bam action flicks accentuating multiple explosions rather than significant subjects. For most cinema-studies scholars, Spielberg embodies the excesses and the ideology of mainstream American filmmaking; he has "become a synonym for Hollywood itself . . . an incarnation of Hollywood's large-scale, world-conquering ambitions" (Scott 60, 63).

My subsequent experiences confirmed my initial observations—and fears. When I told my colleagues at a Society for Cinema and Media Studies conference that I intended to write a book examining Spielberg's entire film output, one friend laughingly suggested that doing so was the academic equivalent of appearing in a porn movie: how would I ever regain scholarly legitimacy? Suddenly, I did feel quite naked. Another greeted my news by describing himself as an "anti-Spielbergian," a curious phrase, since I have never heard anyone label themselves an "anti-Wellesian" or "anti-Tarantinoist." Most just raised an eyebrow, uttered an elongated "hmmmmm," and moved elsewhere in the room—presumably to find more enlightened company. The most daunting moment came when a respected colleague drew herself up and sneered, "Spielberg. Well, he does have a lot to apologize for, doesn't he? See that you make him do so. He is, after all, the antichrist!" Hmmmmm. I should have known right then that *Citizen Spielberg* would be harder to write than I initially anticipated.

Within these pages I willingly engage in ongoing dialogues, in what I hope are respectful conversations, with Spielberg's harshest critics, not ignoring the flaws and failures in his artistic canon but also reclaiming ignored elements of value and significance. I contend that his films are worthy of more careful and nuanced study by film scholars and that the director demands more respect for his particular accomplishments and the overall quality of his work. This has taken longer to complete and entailed more frustration than any of my previous works. The difficulty was neither the breadth nor the depth of the subject matter. It was a question of finding my voice. For the first time in my career, I heard the reviews in my head before I typed a single word. I heard the dismissals by my colleagues that I was not appropriately rigorous in my analysis. I heard commentators outside the field complaining that my prose contained far too much jargon and extraneous dissection. Frankly, I am not sure what shook me out of this stagnant phase, though my wife's insistent prodding certainly made it necessary either to move forward or abandon ship. Without (I hope) sounding too pretentious, I remembered the lessons in Thomas Carlyle's *Sator Resartus,* as his bedeviled Professor Diogenes Teufelsdrockh struggles to find his way out of "the Everlasting No" by first confronting his fears and then resolving that "whatsoever thy hand findeth to do, do it with thy whole might."

Moviemaker and Mogul

As a cinema studies teacher interested in contemporary American films, I thought I was quite aware of Spielberg's various endeavors, not only his commercial productions but his role in the business of filmmaking. I knew, for example, that he was the most financially successful director in Hollywood history: six of his movies remain among the top twenty-five box-office hits of all time, while five were included in the American Film Institute's best hundred films in history. Along with Jeffrey Katzenberg and David Geffen, he founded a new studio, Dreamworks SKG, in 1994. (In 2005, the partners sold Dreamworks to Viacom for a reported $1.6 billion.) He had a hand in producing successful television series such as "E.R.," "Band of Brothers," and

"Taken," joined GameWorks entertainment centers in an Internet venture, and developed projects involving theme restaurants, toy lines, and amusement parks. Not surprisingly, Spielberg often holds the number-one spot on *Forbes* magazine's annual list of the highest-paid entertainers.

And damn if his face didn't keep showing up in the strangest of places. There he was carrying the Olympic flag (representing culture, no less) into the arena at the Salt Lake City Winter Games, strategically preceded by a commercial touting the re-release of *E.T.* Here he was peering out from the covers of *Modern Maturity* (March–April 2003) and *Business Week* (July 13, 1999), being named by *Time* as one of the hundred most important people of the twentieth century, and receiving a National Humanities Medal from President Clinton (September 30, 1999). Snippets in tabloids revealed that he is the godfather of Gwyneth Paltrow's daughter, that he finally earned his undergraduate degree from California State University–Long Beach in June 2002, that the art photographer Gregory Crewdson was influenced by *Close Encounters of the Third Kind,* that the budding filmmaker (James Van Der Beek) in "Dawson's Creek" idolizes him, that his first public appearance after having a kidney removed was to receive the Vanguard Award (February 16, 2000) from the NAACP, that he spent eight hours talking to Fidel Castro during the Havana festival of his films, that his racehorse (Atswhatimtalknbout) finished fourth in the Kentucky Derby, that he played air guitar with Mick Jagger, and that he was saluted by the American Film Institute (May 27, 1995). If you want more, just go to any of the twenty or so Steven Spielberg Web sites and drown yourself in the trivia.

The point is this: Whether you know it or not, you have probably been touched by Steven Spielberg's ubiquitous hand in our contemporary culture. No other artist has matched his uncanny ability to tap into the collective imagination while simultaneously displaying a business acumen usually reserved for CEOs of Fortune 500 companies. (For example, he will collect 2 percent of the grosses from Universal's two theme parks in Florida for life.) He is truly Citizen Spielberg, the consummate popular artist and industry mogul:

> Depending on the context, to call something "Spielbergian" is to say either that it is wondrous and full of feeling or that it is pushy, pandering, and manipulative; the word refers equally to the exaltation of the cinema as a popular art form and its debasement. (Scott 62)

Spielberg is the most influential filmmaker since the 1960s, someone who not only produces megahits at the box office and gives popular culture beloved (and not-so-beloved) figures and phrases but whose films have transformed the way Hollywood does business. In effect, he has become a brand name. His movies become events that rivet the nation's attention on a diverse series of subjects, from UFOs, to marine biology, to genetic engineering, to Holocaust history and World War II, to future fears. In so doing, they interact significantly not only with American cinema but with larger issues in American culture.

Starting after Ending

Like many authors, I am writing this preface after having completed the rest of the book. For those of you who want the Cliff Notes version, I offer the following thoughts, in no particular order, about the films of Steven Spielberg.

COUNTERNARRATIVES

Spielberg is a far more complex, sophisticated, and wry filmmaker than most mainstream critics and academic scholars appreciate. Their static assumptions derive from a variety of sources, but here I will explore only one facet of this dynamic. More than any other American filmmaker, Spielberg's reputation suffers from the practice of naive criticism that equates the director's point of view with the ideological positions of his protagonists. I want to make the radical claim that some Spielberg films protest against what they reveal, that they parody rather than advocate or affirm a particular set of values held by his protagonists. To assume that Spielberg uncritically condones Roy abandoning his family in *Close Encounters,* believes that Pete is right not to express his feelings for Dorinda in *Always,* or approves of Frank's deceptions in *Catch Me If You Can,* to cite only three examples, seems gullible and simplistic. As he matures as a filmmaker, Spielberg's camerawork increasingly offers uneasy counterpoints to his protagonists' worldviews, as I will discuss at length in chapters examining *Empire of the Sun,* the *Indiana Jones* trilogy, and *Minority Report.* Instead of a direct correlation between the characters' and the viewers' perspectives, Spielberg makes alternative options available to his audience, consistently allowing for an ironic distance from events as they unfold before us. Far from the lock-step, fascist aesthetic his detractors attribute to him, Spielberg's cinema is filled with opportunities to contest and even contradict the attitudes of his characters, and his visuals consistently propose counternarratives to those recognized and ultimately espoused by them.

SPIELBERG'S CHARACTERS

In his discussion of Spielberg's "Man-Boys," Murray Pomerance observes that this figure undoes the social order "in the name of something more important, and indeed permits the suggestion that something more important than social order can really exist" (151). He rightly notes that these Man-Boys often disrupt the established and conventional social order, as do his Boy-Men (Elliott in *E.T.,* Jim in *Empire of the Sun,* David in *A.I.,* Short Round in *Temple of Doom,* and Frank in *Catch Me If You Can*) and Woman-Girls (Celie in *The Color Purple*). Spielberg's protagonists are almost always dreamers, defined by their desire for something different, something more, than they have at the present time. Sometimes, these characters harbor illusions of an idyllic past, as in *The Sugarland Express, E.T., The Color Purple, Empire of the Sun, Hook, Amistad, Minority Report,* and *Catch Me If You Can,* that make their present life seem dull or fragmented. Other times, they become almost monomaniacal, driven by a singular goal that comes to define their lives, such as in *Duel, Jaws, Close Encounters, 1941,* the *Indiana Jones* trilogy, *Hook,* the *Jurassic Park* films, *Schindler's List, Saving Private Ryan, A.I., The Terminal,* and *War of the Worlds.* All, to one degree or another, lose control of their lives or are forced to relinquish the illusion that they control their lives in the first place.

All of Spielberg's characters must leave or are forced to forsake seemingly safe locales and venture into unstable environments where the standard rules of civilized behavior no longer hold sway: oceans, skies, highways, deserts, war zones, and concentration camps. Even when they inhabit conventionally safe areas—amusements parks, airport terminals, shopping centers, beaches, costume parties, laboratories—the social order breaks down, and they are reduced to primitive survival instincts. These contacts with unruly forces, often represented by their worst nightmares, ripen Spielberg's characters emotionally, if not chronologically: they force boys to become men, girls to become women, and men to become boys. Chief Brody (*Jaws*) must venture onto the water, Indiana Jones (*Raiders of the Lost Ark*) must get past snakes, Peter must face the pirate captain (*Hook*), Alan Grant must deal with children after dinosaurs (*Jurassic Park*), Celie (*The Color Purple*) must stand up to Mister, Stern (*Schindler's List*) must outwit the Nazis, Miller (*Saving Private Ryan*) must outfight the Germans, Anderton (*Minority Report*) must overcome blindness, and Ray Ferrier (*War of the Worlds*) must survive the attack of the space invaders—and these are only the physical dangers. Equally compelling, Spielberg's characters face daunting emotional and psychological challenges when forced to defend themselves and protect those they love, and overcoming these challenges allows them to truly emerge into adulthood.

COME FLY WITH ME

Flight, most often in airplanes, is one of the most sustained leitmotifs in Spielberg's films. For him, flying is "synonymous with freedom and unlimited imagination" (Friedman and Notbohm 153). It is his personal signature, akin to Hitchcock's cameos in his films, though some historical settings (such as *Amistad*) won't allow for its inclusion. Aircraft appear in almost every movie, sometimes simply as part of the backdrop (*Jaws, Saving Private Ryan, Raiders of the Lost Ark*) but more often as central metaphors for freedom or the lack of it (*Jurassic Park, Catch Me If You Can, A.I., 1941*). Flying forms the centerpiece of *Empire of the Sun* (where Jim longs to fly but can only watch others do it), *Always* (where Pete must teach others to fly properly), and *E.T.* (where flight means both escape and home), while an airport is the setting for *The Terminal*. Most clever is Spielberg's oblique incorporation of flight in *The Color Purple*. Nettie, teaching Celie to read, tapes words written on paper around the house, posting "sky" on the screen door and saying the word aloud. Instead of responding in kind, as she has done previously, Celie says, "Mister. M-i-s-t-e-r. Period," as his image appears in the doorframe, aptly demonstrating how this man will blot out her dreams to rise above her earthbound station in life.

MALE ANGST

Contrary to conventional criticism, which sees the director as simply reaffirming masculine dominance with a traditional nuclear family structure, Spielberg's male characters are filled with fears about their masculinity in an evolving society where gender roles keep shifting. From *Duel* to *War of the Worlds,* every one of the director's men—including the supposed embodiment of rugged American masculinity, Indiana Jones—struggles with his actions as a father, husband, son, or lover. The result is a cinema suffused with male anxiety, as Henry Sheehan aptly observes ("Spielberg II" 69), in which macho aggressiveness is balanced with awkward uncertainty. At the center of any of his films you will find a man who is never quite sure how to interact with his parents, his children, his wife, or his lover. Only when faced with physical challenges or forced by uncontrollable events to alter his life radically does he move forward with any degree of assurance or authority. Otherwise, he fumbles around his emotions, unsure whether to kiss the girl, hug the child, or embrace the father—or even if he wants to. Take, for example, the trio of men in *The Color Purple*: Mister, Harpo, and Old Mister. Each son is afraid to appear as a weakling in front of his father and, as a result, berates and beats his wife. Each father fears losing control of his son and affects a macho pose to deflect that concern. The result is a cycle of mistrust, fear, and domestic violence. While critics dismissively cite Spielberg's obsession with home and family, his male figures usually appear most comfortable defending their homes far away from them on foreign soil, islands, highways, oceans, and battlefields. Their rose-colored visions of domesticity are illusions based on how family life should be, manufactured fantasies often directly contradicted by the facts of their lives as they are.

FEMALE TROUBLES

For a man so adept at all the technical and narrative aspects of filmmaking, Spielberg, even at his best, seems incapable of creating complex female figures. His mothers usually appear oblivious to their surroundings and to the suffering of their children, and they rarely provide much in the way of comfort or sustenance. His romantic partners seem more like fun-loving pals than sexual lovers, tomboys instead of mature women. Almost all of his female characters are secondary figures, many of whom disappear for long stretches of time in the movies, and most can be summed up in snappy casting-call phrases: smart, plucky scientist (*Jurassic Park*), wisecracking sidekick (*Always*), disloyal partner (*Catch Me If You Can*). Sometimes women are barely present at all (*Empire of the Sun, Amistad, Saving Private Ryan, War of the Worlds*). In most of the other movies, women function more as narrative devices than as full-bodied creations; they remain necessary for the men to progress (*Minority Report*), present stumbling blocks for them to overcome (*Indiana Jones and the Last Crusade*), or serve as rewards for a job well done (*Schindler's List*), but rarely are their concerns central to the story. Only in *The Color Purple* does Spielberg convey a sense of female strength and complexity beyond these superficial portraits.

A Note on Methodology

I have relied predominantly on two basic critical methodologies—genre study and auteur criticism—to undergird my exploration of Spielberg's films, though it grows out of my broad conception of cultural studies as well. By grouping his works into genre categories, I have sacrificed a chronologically determined analysis that would have highlighted his development as a filmmaker, but I hope readers will have some sense of that evolution as I move through the various, often hybrid, genre categories. My postmodernist colleagues will no doubt dismiss my methodology as retrograde theories to describe a retrograde director. I have little desire to defend my choices beyond noting that the demise of auteurism and genre criticism never made it far beyond ivy-covered barricades. As Roberta Pearson recently quipped, Barthes may have declared the death of the author, but few outside academica attended the funeral. The majority of people continue to discuss films in terms of directors and genres. I recommend the following texts for those inclined to understand the appeal and reconfigurations of these categories. 1) On authorship: John Caughie (*Theories of Authorship*), David Gerstner and Janet Staiger (*Authorship and Film*), and Virginia Wright Wexman (*Film and Authorship*); 2) On genre: Nick Browne (*Refiguring American Film Genres*), Barry Keith Grant (*Film Genre Reader II*), Steve Neale (*Genre and Contemporary Hollywood*), and Wheeler Winston Dixon (*Film Genre 2000*).

Still Standing

Looking at the gallery of saints and sinners who comprise the last great era of American filmmaking, the "Raging Bulls and Easy Riders" of the 1970s, only two still function at the height of their powers: Martin Scorsese and Steven Spielberg. Others from that generation still plow the fields, but their labors evoke little of the excitement and anticipation that greets each new film by Scorsese and Spielberg. None match their breadth and consistency, and of the two, I would argue that Spielberg has been the more daring in selecting his projects in recent years. While earlier films like *Close Encounters of the Third Kind* and *E.T.* emerged from deeply personal needs and obsessions, his latest productions turn toward broader social concerns such as racism and prejudice (*Amistad* and *Schindler's List*), historical and cultural memories (*Saving Private Ryan*), humanity's place in a technological world (*A.I.*), governmental intrusion (*Minority Report*) and restriction (*The Terminal*), invasion and annihilation (*War of the Worlds*), and personal identity (*Catch Me If You Can*). While all these films contain Spielberg's trademark fixations and demonstrate his skills as a narrative filmmaker, they are primarily concerned with moral issues rather than roller-coaster narratives or adolescent fantasies. Ironically, it is Steven Spielberg, the child of the studio system, who has become America's truly "independent filmmaker, able to do his work with minimal creative interference and with very little budgetary constraint" (Scott 63). Often, he has used that power to challenge himself and to make films where others fear to tread, such as *The Color Purple, Amistad, Schindler's List,* and *A.I.* Surprising his detractors, Spielberg has evolved into a director of thought and spirit as well as spectacle and style, demonstrating a sustained intellectual growth and emotional maturity that was once impossible to imagine.

Note: Though I wrote this book before the release of *Munich* in 2005, the themes of Spielberg's movies outlined in the previous pages and discussed in the subsequent chapters can be directly applied to that film. Familiar hallmarks of Spielberg's work are recognizable: the continuing obsession with male angst seen in Avner's (Eric Bana) confusion about his role as a husband and father (his own father a dominating but absent figure); the conceptualization of home—though here more complicated than idealized—when Avner is called upon to defend his country, but ultimately chooses to exile himself and his family from it; and the turn toward broader issues of social concern by engaging in the debate that underlines the Arab-Israeli conflict.

1

"I'm Sorry I Didn't Tell You about the World": Spielberg's Science-Fiction and Fantasy Films

Science-Fiction and Fantasy Films

Science-fiction and fantasy films reveal more about the cultures that spawn them than the imaginary worlds they ostensibly describe. By extending contemporary societal problems far into the future, or by inserting fantastical elements into present-day environments, these movies encourage viewers to contemplate disruptive communal questions made less volatile by the mediating distance of time, the remoteness of space, and the illusion of supernatural encounters. Fanciful creatures (such as aliens, ghosts, or pixies) interjected into ordinary life, or diverse life forms confronted by human beings in galaxies far, far away, become representatives of "the cultural other," allowing filmmakers to explore current dilemmas of ethnic, racial, sexual, and gender differences freed from the confinements typically associated with depicting daily life. Similarly, films about the problems of futuristic societies set on remote planets reflect social realities and ethical dilemmas on earth. The science-fiction and fantasy genres grant their practitioners license to ponder complex moral and cultural questions, while they simultaneously provide fertile opportunities for dazzling visual spectacles, imaginative creations, and inventive narrative structures.

Although each chapter in this book opens by broadly defining the genre into which various Spielberg films fit, these segments provide only limited space to consider complex definitions and broad historical questions, certainly not enough room to examine them fully. Here, it is necessary to note the general distinctions film scholars make between science-fiction and fantasy films before discussing Spielberg's individual works within these genres. Because films iconographically identified with one genre inevitably poach narratives, ideas, and stock characters from other genres, critics often struggle when attempting to make clear distinctions between film categories. Commentators who investigate the boundaries between science-fiction and fantasy films, for example, usually cite the intimate relationships between them, noting how they often spring from similar sources. A fundamental narrative pattern ties these two genres together: supernatural occurrences disrupt comfortable daily routines and challenge characters' conceptions of reality. Ordinary people with whom the audience can identify find their lives irrevocably altered by encounters with supernatural situations that force them to reconfigure their conceptions of the world and their place within it.

The Fantasy Film

In his classic book *The Fantastic: A Structural Approach to a Literary Genre,* Tzvetan Todorov asserts that three narrative structures constitute fantasy fictions: the marvelous (events that involve the supernatural or spiritual), the fantastic (events that question common reality), and the uncanny (events produced by the unconscious). *Always* fits nicely as a "marvelous" narrative and *Hook* as a "fantastic" or an "uncanny" one, depending on whether Neverland is conceptualized as an alternative reality or a mental projection. Building on Todorov, Wade Jennings argues that the only "indispensable element in a fantasy is a central situation that defies rational or even pseudo-scientific explanation. . . . The chief distinction between fantasy and science fiction is that in science fiction the drive is toward explanation, toward resolution of the mystery and its attendant problems, whereas in fantasy the situation cannot be explained; it must simply be accepted" (249). Classic fantasy films, as diverse as *The Wizard of Oz* (1939), *Lost Horizon* (1937), *Mary Poppins* (1964), and the *Lord of the Rings* trilogy (2001–3), rarely explain how their strange worlds and exotic characters were created: instead, they provide the complex pleasure of allowing us to "believe without really believing" (Todorov 56). We watch these movies knowing that they defy the laws of common reality, giving ourselves up to the delight of accepting them on their own terms.

Fantasy films often invoke a perilous quest that necessitates an equally significant internal journey of personal understanding and self-realization. Protagonists in fantasy films discover or rediscover joy and freedom and eventually comprehend that rational knowledge alone is insufficient to survive the arduous tests they must pass. Fantasy worlds are commonly populated by three general character types: 1) the superman with powers beyond ordinary beings; 2) the child hero who battles evil armed with natural innocence and goodness; and 3) the supernaturally wise mentor to the human hero (Jennings 252–53). The initially dislocated protagonists must find a new place for themselves in these fantasy realms, choosing either to stay within the new environment or return to their old worlds, forever altered by the lessons they have learned. They are forced to examine "their values and decide under what circumstances they can live freely and happily given those values" (251). The question of "what constitutes home" (251), therefore, lies at the deep center of most fantasy films. Given this fact, it is not surprising that Steven Spielberg, a director whose characters perpetually search for sites of emotional stability, reciprocal love, and sustained acceptance, would be drawn to this genre. In one sense, his works from 1971 onward represent a sustained quest to discover exactly where his figures belong, where they might call home.

Spielberg's Fantasy Films

Ironically, critics almost never recognize that both of Spielberg's fantasy films focus on the need to discard childish illusions and accept adult responsibilities. The maturity levels that accompany the cultural demarcations of "child" or "adult" in these movies are determined more by the emotional states of the protagonists than by their chronological age. In *Hook* (1991), Peter Banning (Robin Williams) returns temporarily to boyhood but ultimately chooses fatherhood over "never growing up," while in *Always* (1989), Pete Sandrich's (Richard Dreyfuss) death forces him to assume as a spirit the mature burdens of care and protection he recklessly spurned in life. Such shifts allow Spielberg to explore the intimate tangles between past events and present actions, between what we believe was once ours and the challenge of dealing with its absence. Banning and Sandrich lose what is most dear to them; to recapture it, they must accept obligations that entail personal sacrifices. They struggle to accommodate their lives to their memories and losses; they attempt to put things back together as they once were (Banning) or to find new ways to enrich a present that cannot possibly duplicate the past (Sandrich). Each character confronts an amalgam of past and present losses and gains within his individual life and family life to create a successful future. Growth in *Always* and *Hook* necessarily involves emotional pain; to mature, Sandrich and Banning must put away the lavish dreams of childhood and place the needs of others before their own desires for youthful pleasures.

ALWAYS

Spielberg's remake of Victor Flemming's *A Guy Named Joe* (1943) was clearly a labor of love. The film had greatly moved him as a struggling adolescent growing up in Phoenix; it was "'a story that touched my soul . . . the second movie after *Bambi* that made me cry'" (qtd. in McBride 406), and he admired the movie enough to reference it on the television screen in his script/production of Tobe Hooper's *Poltergeist* (1982). Spielberg's crucial decision was to update the original's World War II combat pilots into modern-day flyers dumping chemical retardants on forest fires in the Pacific Northwest. He chose not to make it a period piece because he worried that contemporary audiences might think, "That's how people thought back in the old days; people don't feel that way in modern times" (Royal, "*Always*" 146). And therein lies a basic problem. Flemming's film resonated during a wartime environment for two fundamental reasons: It provided reassurance and comfort to hometown audiences struggling with the pain of losing loved ones in the war, allowing them to understand their private sorrow as a necessary sacrifice required for the public good, and it alleviated "the guilt of women who found new men after their husbands or boyfriends had been killed" (Greenberg, "Raiders" 116). But the transition from battling Nazis to dousing forest fires makes Pete's reckless flying feats narcissistic and selfish rather than heroic and noble. Libby, Montana (the film's shooting location), and even the majestic Yellowstone National Park (where Spielberg's crew captured footage of actual fires), hardly compare to the drama and carnage of Omaha Beach or the Battle of the Bulge.

The selfless heroism and military romanticism common in wartime films seemed hopelessly outmoded in 1989. The flight base tucked into the mountains is weirdly anachronistic; despite its prop-engine planes, macho bantering, old-time music, and obsolete phrases ("You big lug!"), it lacks the desperate urgency of a World War II setting. This awareness is self-consciously alluded to several times in the film, most overtly when Pete nearly crashes his plane after running out of fuel. Trying to convince him to take a safer job instructing younger pilots in Colorado, his best friend Al (John Goodman) explicitly makes the analogy that dooms the film:

> What this place reminds me of is the war in Europe, which I personally was never at, but think about it: The beer is warm, the dance hall's a quonset hut, there's B-26's outside, hotshot pilots inside, an airstrip in the woods. It's England, man. Everything but Glenn Miller. Except we go to burning places and bomb 'em until they stop burning. You see, Pete, there ain't no war here.

This is why they don't make movies called *Night Raid to Boise, Idaho,* or *Fireman Strike at Dawn.* And this is why you're not exactly a hero for taking these chances. You're more of what I would call a dickhead.

One can certainly feel sympathy with a dickhead, can laugh with or at him and even admire his actions; but a dickhead can't be a hero in the same mold as a World War II fighter pilot, no matter how skillful his airborne maneuvers or how many fires he drenches. The stakes are simply not the same. Ultimately, Pete's rash decisions seem driven more by an internalized masculine code than by widespread external danger; in effect, he chooses indulgence and bravado over personal happiness, the needs of his ego over his commitment to Dorinda (Holly Hunter). Even Pete's own comment after he dies strikes a self-deprecating, dickheadish note: "What a jerk I turned out to be."

This self-confessed "jerk" is the romantic lead in *Always,* a rare Spielberg film that focuses primarily on a love relationship between adults. Pete adheres to the typical American-movie image of rugged men with deep feelings they remain incapable of expressing: John Wayne (called up by Ted's poor imitation), Gary Cooper, or Henry Fonda. For such iconic images of masculinity, the voicing of emotions was deemed a weakness, a concession to the "feminine" vulnerability. These men always did "what they had to do," but they did it laconically, and they never overtly confessed their feelings to the womenfolk. In *Always,* Dorinda begs Pete several times to say that he loves her, to speak aloud the words she longs to hear. Sadly, he does so only before his final flight and—with the engines roaring—a retreating Dorinda never hears him say it. He can only make up for this failing by returning as a spirit to help another man say the words that he could never summon the courage to express.

Pete is sent back to earth not only to liberate Dorinda emotionally, so she can love another man, but also to do penance for his macho stance, which Spielberg overtly critiques. "The love we hold back," Pete tells Dorinda when he releases her to embrace Ted, "is the only pain that follows us here." As Spielberg put it in an interview:

> It's a story about a man who had a chance to say everything important to the one person he loved and didn't say it until it was too late. And now that he's gone, his mission—so to speak—is to come back and say all the things he was never able to say as a living human being. (Royal, "*Always*" 146)

By demonstrating how Pete breaks free of typical masculine stereotypes only after he is dead, and how deeply he regrets his inability to do so while still alive, *Always* undermines the code of manly conduct validated in those 1940s films Spielberg so dearly loves, aptly illustrating how conventional standards of emotional suppression, stoicism, and silence create a lonely and chilling gap between men and the women they love. As we will see, the director's ability to undercut narrative stereotypes is extensive and almost totally ignored by sympathetic commentators and hostile critics alike.

In detailing the female partner in this adult love relationship, *Always* offers a confusing melange of ideas. In the film's most consistently criticized scene, Pete brings Dorinda some "girly clothes" for a birthday present. Beaming with delight, she tells him, "It's not the dress; it's the way you see me." She quickly changes into the outfit and, when she reappears, turns the rough-and-tumble, grease-smeared firefighters into befuddled little boys rushing to wash their hands before they dance with her. David Denby summed up the general response in *New York* magazine when he wrote that Dorinda's entrance is "'the most purely sexless moment in Spielberg's long, long career as a boy, and it made me realize to what extent sex in his movies is a matter of dreams and idealization'" (qtd. in McBride 408). Dorinda is a mosaic of mixed messages. She is a tough-talking, clever-bantering Hawksian heroine who flies a plane to show her displeasure with Pete and rescues trapped firemen to save Ted. Yet she is also a severe mother figure who threatens to leave Pete unless he gives up the thing he loves most: fighting fires from the air. Dorinda attempts to clip the wings of the main character, simultaneously agreeing to forego her own aerial ambitions and to "ground myself and be your girl."

And now things get curioser and curioser. Most American romance movies reward audiences by having the man and the woman—whom viewers know are right for each other from their first introductions—recognize their mutual attraction and ultimately merge in a blissful union. In *Always,* to the contrary, the people meant to be together must learn to live without each other forever. In fact, Pete prepares Dorinda to love another "big lug." The film's emotional movement runs totally against traditional genre conventions; instead of figuring out how to be together, Pete and Dorinda must learn how to let go of each other: he by abandoning his jealousy, and she by opening herself up to new romance. "Anything you do for yourself," counsels Pete's celestial guide, Hap (Audrey Hepburn), "is a waste of spirit." While we may recognize and applaud Spielberg's efforts to twist genre expectations, which he does far more frequently than commonly recognized, the temporal setting thwarts his intentions. Audiences could accept that Rick must send off Ilsa to be with Victor Laszlo in *Casablanca* (1942) because wartime responsibilities demanded such noble self-sacrifices; but the director,

Michael Curtiz, never forces viewers (or more importantly, Rick) to watch Victor and Ilsa—the less-than-ideal couple—in a passionate embrace, as Spielberg does in *Always,* creating an incredibly uncomfortable scene that transforms Pete into a distraught voyeur. Ultimately, however, he evolves from the childish daredevil to the mature surrogate father who guides Ted ("That's my boy!") into becoming an expert pilot and a suitable match for Dorinda ("That's my girl!").

Why is *Always* the "most forgotten film" of Speilberg's career (Freer 190)? Financially, it ranks substantially below even his other generally acknowledged critical and popular failures: compared with *1941* ($90 million) and *Hook* ($119 million), *Always* grossed $43 million in its stateside theatrical release—a reasonable figure for any director not named Spielberg. The theme of love lost, a foundation for high tragedy as well as bodice-ripping romances, is not inherently antithetical to popular tastes. A year after *Always,* Jerry Zucker's *Ghost* (1990) racked up box-office records and Academy Awards with a similar premise, although the buff Patrick Swayze comes back from the dead to protect Demi Moore, not to prepare her for another man. Joseph McBride contends that the film can be best understood "as about Spielberg's acceptance of loss" (406), that the director's affection for his source material blinded him to its "irrelevance for contemporary audiences" (406), and that it flopped because of the "wide disparity between the sophistication of its craftsmanship and the relative shallowness of its romantic relationships" (409).

Other elements also contribute to the film's problems. Spielberg modernizes the setting while attempting to duplicate the feel of the World War II combat films, creating a discordant tone. His undercutting of the masculine codes that infused those earlier movies substantially diminishes his hero (no one would dare call John Wayne a dickhead!). He frustrates the audience's romantic expectations. Mostly, however, I think audiences did not anticipate Spielberg's ambivalent and melancholy attitude toward love, his growing understanding (perhaps as a result of his recent divorce from Amy Irving) that love can be detrimental as well as nourishing, dangerous as well as uplifting. Perhaps audiences went to the film expecting a gentle *E.T.*-like cascade of emotions; instead, they found a film that, for all its invocations of heavenly spirits, playful banter, and divine inspiration, plunges viewers over a waterfall by focusing primarily on the irrevocable surrendering of true love. Exploring such a painful topic, *Always* became a unconventional genre piece that never found an audience, a romantic fantasy film swathed in darkness.

HOOK

Whereas *Always* revolves around the pain of lost love, *Hook* focuses on the consequences of lost time. Most of Spielberg's biographical critics agree that he decided to film his version of the Peter Pan myth too late in life: "*Hook* mostly serves to demonstrate the middle-aged director's overwhelming sense of boredom with Peter Pan, the Lost Boys, and all they represent about the anarchic spirit of childhood. . . . He no longer felt comfortable with mere celebrations of childhood innocence, but now was concerned about the death of innocence and the coming of manhood" (McBride 409). The director admits as much in response to questions about why he didn't do the movie earlier:

> My son [Max] was born, and I lost my appetite for the project. Because suddenly I couldn't be Peter Pan anymore. I had to be his father. That's literally the reason I didn't do the movie back then. . . . In a way, my son took my childhood away from me. But he also gave it back to me. When he was born, I suddenly became the spitting image of my father and mother. . . . I guess now I can appreciate even more who my parents were. (Bahiana 152–53)

Given Spielberg's basic orientation, it is not surprising that *Hook* totally reverses Sir James Barrie's classic tale about children without parents, making it a story about a father who—at least metaphorically—leaves his children. No longer able to connect with Barrie's fierce and eternal youth, Spielberg relates more to Peter Banning's myopic preoccupation with his work: "I have even experienced it myself when I have been on a very tough shoot and I've not seen my kids except on weekends. They ask for my time, and I can't give it to them because I'm working" (Bahiana 154). To underscore the importance of lost time, Spielberg's mise-en-scène contains an almost numbing variety of timepieces, from postcard-perfect shots of Big Ben, to the intimate pocket watch Peter gives his son Jack (Charlie Korsmo), to Hook's (Dustin Hoffman) emblematic museum of broken clocks.

In *Hook*, Spielberg emphasizes the fleeting fragility of time. Banning mishandles time by ignoring his children, even yelling at them to "shut up and leave me alone!" Not visiting Wendy (Maggie Smith) even once in the last ten years, he concentrates on mergers and acquisitions. He "blows any resistance out of the water," an excited Jack tells his grandmother, who wryly notes that Peter has become a pirate. (Later, the Lost Boys tell Peter, "Grownups are pirates," perhaps because they steal time away from children.) Peter commits one of the cardinal sins within Spielberg's world: he ignores his children, talking on his cell phone throughout Maggie's (Amber Scott) school play and sending an office flunky to videotape Jack's baseball game. "My word is my bond," he tells his son after missing the contest he promised to attend. "Yeah, a junk bond," responds the hurt and angry boy. Seeing precious time slipping away, his wife, Moira (Caroline Goodall), reminds Peter:

> Your children love you. They want to play with you. How long do you think that lasts? Soon Jack may not even want you to come to his games. We have a few special years with our children when they're the ones who want us around. After that, you're going to be running after them for a bit of attention. So fast, Peter. It's a few years, then it's over. You are not being careful. And you are missing it.

By foregrounding the relentless passage of time, *Hook* forces viewers to reconsider and take responsibility for how they allot their limited portion in their daily lives.

Only late in the film does Peter Banning remember that he accepted the responsibilities of the temporal world—and gave up being the eternally youthful Peter Pan—for a reason: "I wanted to be a father." That decision to put others before himself kills the child-hero and replaces him with the fallible man. Far from being about remaining a boy forever, as most critics interpret it, *Hook* demonstrates the necessity to grow up, to choose external obligations over personal pleasures. To vanquish Hook and regain his children, Banning must learn to balance his childhood memories with his adult responsibilities, to keep one from overwhelming the other. Peter "can't stay and play" in Neverland after he rescues his children; indeed, the happy thoughts that finally allow him to fly are not about his adventures with the prepubescent Lost Boys, games with the free-spirited Tinker Bell (Julia Roberts), or battles against Hook's nefarious pirates, but about his children and, by extension, his parental obligation to love, nurture, and protect them. Hook, intuitively understanding that his permanence depends on the existence of Peter Pan, seeks to generate a timeless frieze: the perpetual boy endlessly fighting his unchanging adult adversary. After all, great heroes and villains need each other to guarantee their immortality. "What would the world be like without Captain Hook?" asks the pirate. The answer, as every parent knows, is that Hook's flamboyant wickedness pales in comparison with the genuine dangers, potential disasters, and real evils that threaten the safety and happiness of those they love. Beyond the childhood borders of Neverland, Hook is irrelevant.

In the end, Peter Pan must return to being Peter Banning, though he will carry the memory of being "the Pan" with him forever. As another artist addicted to childhood, the poet William Wordsworth, so poignantly observes, "nothing can bring back the hour / Of splendour in the grass, of glory in the flower" ("Ode: Intimations of Immortality," ll. 177–78). Instead of the carelessly thrilling and exuberantly selfish pleasures of youth, Wordsworth's lost "visionary gleam" (l. 56), Peter finds a deeper pleasure in fulfilling his familial responsibilities. The lessons he learns from his return—and final—voyage to Neverland are basic truths: time can never be halted, and it moves far too fast. We each carry with us precious memories from our childhoods, those times of "trailing clouds of glory" (Wordsworth l. 64) behind us, but we cannot reproduce them as adults because we travel "daily farther from the east" (l. 71) and drift into "the light of common day" (l. 76). The play of an adult self-consciously assuming various disguises remains necessary for Spielberg—after all, filmmaking is an exaggerated and expensive form of fun and games—but it can never duplicate the natural, spontaneous, and impulsive joys of childhood. In this sense, *Hook* is an elegy for, rather than a celebration of, impulsive childhood and youthful innocence. "All children, except one, grow up" in *Peter Pan*. "And even he must do so," concludes Steven Spielberg in *Hook*.

In stressing these ideas, Spielberg creates a startling deviation from Barrie's original work. The scene begins as a rejuvenated Peter flips open the ornate face of the grandfather clock that houses Tinker Bell, its hands frozen at X and XII and its cobwebbed face glowing in the silent darkness. Literally encircled by time as his face replaces the clock dial, Peter Pan finds a melancholy Tinker Bell sitting amidst relics from Peter Banning's former life: driver's license, gold Master Card, box of Certs, and BMW keyholder—symbols of the daily obligations he has forsaken. When Peter tells Tink that he returned to Neverland "to always be a little boy and have fun," she reminds him that this is not true, that he came back to save the children he barely remembers. Shattering the arrested time tower she inhabits, Tinker Bell transforms herself into a full-sized woman, dressed in a soft blue, off-the-shoulder evening gown, and gives Peter a "real" kiss and tells him that she loves him. "Moira. I love Moira. Jack and Maggie," he says haltingly, breaking the momentary spell and devising a plan for their rescue. But Tink realizes the painful truth embedded in this tenderly ambivalent moment. "When it's all over, you'll leave and never come back again." In rejecting this stylized adolescent romance bathed in shimmering blue light for the mature marriage with Moira and his duties as a father, Peter accepts the joys and sorrows of emotional adulthood.

This acceptance of time's passage brings with it the sobering acceptance

Flights of childhood fantasy clash with adult responsibilities for Peter Banning (Robin Williams) in *Hook* (1991).

of death. Ironically for a film ostensibly concerned with eternal childhood and directed by a man most critics attack as a perpetual adolescent, Spielberg stuffs *Hook* with a startling amount of talk about dying; it even portrays the death of a child, Rufio (Dante Basco), a rare moment in Spielberg's work that actualizes his worst fears. Both main characters discuss death at crucial moments in the movie. Peter reveals to Tinker Bell that he ran away from home to avoid getting older "because everyone who grows up has to die some-day." A depressed Hook attempts suicide, albeit comically, telling his first mate Smee (Bob Hoskins), "I want to die. There's no great adventure here. Death is the only great adventure I have left." Before their duel commences, Hook warns Peter to "prepare to die." "To die would be a great adventure," responds Pan, speaking a line absent in the Disney cartoon version and most subsequent iterations of Barrie's far darker story. For the second time, Hook answers that "death is the only adventure." Yet for all his bravado, Hook fears death more than any figure in the movie. His museum of broken clocks, each one having "ticked its last tock," testifies to his dread of time passing and his inching closer to death. By encouraging Jack to destroy Peter's watch, "to make time stand still," Hook attempts to sever the relationship between a father "who's never there," a crying child who feels that his dad "didn't even try" to save him, and their home filled with "broken promises."

Hook's demise comes at the jaws of his tenacious nemesis, the fearsome creature who devoured his hand and now stands as a stuffed-croc clock in the town square. In the climactic duel scene, the pirate tries to slit Pan open with his hook but, with Tink's help, Peter jams the weapon into the crocodile's hide. The puncture forces the clock face to slide from the beast's mouth and crash onto the ground. A frightened and retreating Hook trips over it (literally stumbling over time), the straps holding the animal snap, and the reptile falls forward onto Hook, who disappears without a trace inside its mouth. Time has finally caught up with the captain. But Hook's symbolic end comes earlier in his battle with Pan. Encircled by the Lost Boys—each holding malevolently ticking clocks—a terrified Hook hears Peter taunt him: "Tick tock, tick tock, tick tock. Hook's afraid of an olden clock. Hook's afraid of time ticking away." Flicking off Hook's elaborate black wig with his sword, Peter reveals the old, balding, and rather pathetic man hidden underneath it. The humiliated Hook begs the triumphant Pan, "Give me my dignity." Peter hands back the hairpiece and heeds his children's plea to spare his enemy and return home. The start of time, however, is the end of Hook's futile struggle to halt the relentless march of minutes, and he knows it. When boys become men, they leave Captain Hook behind.

Like all of Spielberg's films, *Hook* explores how men struggle to fulfill the cultural expectations of generically masculine roles. Henry Sheehan, one of the most perceptive readers of the director's work, makes a particularly insightful point when he asserts, "Although Spielberg's films are usually described as warm or even exhilarating and euphoric, their most prevalent temper is anxiety" ("Spielberg II" 69). Spielberg's male figures consistently grapple with their culturally constructed roles as sons, husbands, boyfriends, and fathers. In Peter Banning, Sheehan sees a figure genuinely uncertain of his own manhood and lacking the "rough-and-tumble masculinity" ("PAN-ning" 54) of the pirates and the "potent masculinity" ("Spielberg II" 71) embodied in Hook. Peter's (re)learning to fly allows him to integrate his past and his present; he can now rescue his children because he achieves a "more secure and emotionally open masculinity" ("PANning" 54). In many ways, this is the goal of almost all of Spielberg's male figures, from the submissive David Mann (*Duel*), to the bullied Clovis (*The Sugarland Express*), to the cowed Brody (*Jaws*), to the beleaguered Neary (*Close Encounters*), to the infantalized Mister (*The Color Purple*), to the dutiful Viktor Navorski (*The Terminal*), to the desperate Ferrier (*War of the Worlds*), to the emotionally stunted Indiana Jones.

Sheehan's two essays on Spielberg—a lone voice arguing for *Hook* as a film of "astonishing beauty" and "eloquent resonance" that established the director as a "legitimate aspirant to greatness" ("PANning" 54)—were published in 1992, before some of the director's most intriguing works were released. I would situate *Hook* as a building block for Spielberg rather than the seminal work Sheehan describes in his essays; but I have the advantage of knowing what followed it. Sheehan's observations remain valid for the important male figures in Spielberg's subsequent movies, despite their genres. At the center of each, a man strives to reconcile his personal, and often selfish, feelings with the broader roles and demands imposed by society. Much more than is apparent from standard critical perceptions of the film as a "deeply regressive experience with a hero who retreats from the adult world" (Frayling 220), *Hook* insists that men, as differentiated from boys, must learn to put their self-indulgent pasts behind them, to subordinate childhood memories to adult commitments.

These masculine anxieties adumbrate more sophisticated depictions and perilous situations in Spielberg's subsequent films, which often shift their focus from the roles of mothers to those of fathers. So, for example, Peter's consternation about losing his children's love escalates into fathers' or surrogate fathers' fears about actually allowing harmful forces to destroy those for whom they are responsible: the Nazis to exterminate Oskar's Jews, the dinosaurs to devour Tim and Lex, the Feds to shoot Frank, the German soldiers to kill Ryan, the aliens to kill Robbie and Rachel. Most disturbing of all, two fathers actually forfeit their sons, one by choice in *A.I.,* and one by carelessness in *Minority Report.* Kidnapped children represent a persistent threat in Spielberg films, from *The Sugarland Express* early his career, to *Indiana Jones and the Temple of Doom* at the height of his popularity in the 1980s, to *Empire of the Sun* as he shifts to more mature themes, to his social-problem films like *Amistad* and *The Color Purple,* and even within his science-fiction works like *Close Encounters* and *Minority Report.*

Hook was a critical flop, even though it garnered far bigger domestic ($119 million) and worldwide ($288 million) profits than most movies. McBride observes that it became a symbol of the "runaway excess in Hollywood in the 1990s," suggesting that Spielberg overdid its special effects and "fell off the wagon of fiscal responsibility" (411)—an ironic charge, given that the film is all about accepting adult accountability. The pervasive sense of strained artificiality that permeates the film engenders feelings of overstuffed claustrophobia rather than liberating freedom. Particularly in the Neverland sequences, the movie feels like a donut stuffed with candied jelly, drenched in maple syrup, and rolled in powdered sugar. The director ultimately recognized his own failures: "'From the beginning of the picture to when Peter flies out of the window in Kensington is, I think, some of my best work. For some reason, the moment he gets to Neverland it sort of becomes children's theatre'" (qtd. in Freer 203). He is right. Like *Always, Hook's* best moments are its most intimate. The essentially unadorned scene where Moira's lost children jump from beneath their covers to hug and kiss their worried mother remains one of the film's most emotionally powerful scenes, far surpassing anything that occurs in Neverland.

Part of the problem stems from Spielberg's original conception of *Hook* as a musical with Michael Jackson in the Peter Pan role—another attempt to satiate the director's craving to direct a musical. Prior to production, John Williams teamed with the lyricist Leslie Bricusse to write ten songs, three of which appear in the movie: "Pick 'em Up," "We Don't Wanna Grow Up," and "When You're Alone" (Freer 199). To capture the enclosed theatricality of a traditional musical, Spielberg hired the renowned Broadway set designer John Napier (*Les Miserables, Cats, Miss Saigon*) as a visual consultant and shot *Hook* totally on sound stages previously used to film such classics as *The Wizard of Oz* and *Singin' in the Rain.* It remains the only one of his movies constrained by interior constructions, though he did assemble elaborate camera housings for more fluid movement in the action scenes. He also had lots of room to play. According to Doug Brode, the immense sets covered nine sound stages at Sony's Culver City studios, with *Hook's* gigantic (thirty-five-foot-wide, 170-foot-long, seventy-foot-high) Jolly Roger alone covering one of them (203). The film also contains disconcerting cameos, often from thinly disguised performers like Glenn Close, David Crosby, Jimmy Buffett, Quincy Jones, George Lucas, Phil Collins, and Carrie Fisher. (A then-unknown Gwyneth Paltrow plays the young Wendy.)

Perhaps audiences simply expected too much from this film that Spielberg seemed destined to make from the time he began shooting movies but probably waited until too late in his life to direct. In some ways, he had already made his Peter Pan from the perspective of a lost boy: *E.T.* (in which the mother actually reads the story to her daughter). In retrospect, *Hook* can best be situated as a transitional piece, like far better films such as *The Color Purple* and *Empire of the Sun,* that demonstrates Spielberg's evolving maturity as a thinking filmmaker concerned with personal problems and social issues. Though it may, as Sheehan argues, pull together "the many different thematic strands, visual motifs, and character types that had been haphazardly scattered through his first 15 years of work" ("PANning" 54), *Hook* ultimately sinks under its own bloated weight, a victim of too much money and too little imagination. With *Schindler's List* already in mind, Spielberg could hardly find Captain James Hook the ultimate symbol of evil; he knew full well that in the world of death camps and sadistic Nazis, little boys and girls didn't live forever.

It is more fun to talk about *Hook* and *Always* than to watch them. Neither offers a sustained sense of pleasure or the complexity of Spielberg's finest works. That is not to say that sparks don't light up the screen at times; Spielberg simply has too much visual flair and technical expertise to make a consistently dull film. The sequence in *Always* when an unseen Pete (Richard Dreyfuss) dances with Dorinda, without touching her, to the strains of "Smoke Gets in Your Eyes," is painfully moving and flawlessly executed. So, too, when Al tells Dorinda that Pete is dead, Spielberg shoots the scene silently from outside her window, relying on acting rather than showy special effects or editing to convey the sorrow. Peter Banning's intimate moments with his children during his quest to regain their affections are far more effective than the overblown fight scenes. The first time Banning flies, as the rejuvenated Peter Pan, Spielberg makes us partners in his jubilant exultation, as he does in the aerial sequences in *Always*. But these are isolated islands in a sea of competent but hardly exceptional filmmaking that must be judged as basic craftsmanship without passion within the context of Spielberg's overall output.

The Science-Fiction Film

Science-fiction movies, as distinct from fantasy films, base their plots within plausible or at least possible situations, sometimes stretched to their breaking point. Vivian Sobchack defines science-fiction films as incorporating elements of science (actual and speculative), empirical reasoning, magic, and religion within social contexts "to reconcile man with the unknown" (*Screening* 63). They are concerned with how scientific research and discovery alters relationships between groups of people, and between people and their environments, rather than how a particular event changes a particular character. This emphasis on the public sphere rather than on private enlightenment represents a pivotal demarcation between science-fiction and fantasy films. J. P. Telotte argues that, characteristically, the science-fiction genre has three pervasive "fascinations":

> 1) the impact of forces outside the human realm, of encounters with alien beings or other worlds;
> 2) the possibility of changes in society and culture wrought by our science and technology;
> 3) technological alterations in and substitute versions of the self. (12)

In utilizing this classification, I would put *Close Encounters of the Third Kind* (unless otherwise noted, I refer to the initial theatrically released version) and *E.T.* into the first category, *Minority Report* into the second, and *A.I.* into the third.

Rather ironically, science-fiction films consistently challenge the advancement of science. They provoke "a type of intellectual terror" that emerges from conceptualizing scientific accomplishments more as a threat than as a promise: "[T]he element of fear arises from knowledge that the technology contains within itself the seeds of disastrous possibilities no expert could foresee, and that therefore no preparations have been made to control the technology" (Solomon 118). Scientific research in the form of applied technology inevitably creates subtle cultural modifications and even dramatic transformations. Mirroring the cultural anxieties inherent in these alterations, the dilemmas central to science-fiction narratives often question how fully technological achievements should be embraced, contested, or repudiated by society. In these films, therefore, the "most ingrained contemporary mistrust of the intellect is visited . . . upon the scientist-as-intellectual" (Sontag, "Imagination" 217); they embody a palpable and broad apprehensiveness about how scientific advancement necessitates troubling changes to our sense of how we understand ourselves and our place in the world.

This inherent mistrust of the intellectual/scientist is equally evident in the depiction of frightening alien creatures who radically disrupt the serene lives of American citizens. A now commonplace critical assumption regarding the vast proportion of movies composing the genre's first golden age, the 1940s and 1950s, reads them as visual allegories of intense national phobias inspired by a stringent cold-war, anticommunist ideology and defined by a conservative isolationist rhetoric. In essence, any contact with aliens—visually represented as having physical characteristics notably different from middle-class Americans—was ultimately deemed perilous. The only good aliens were dead aliens. This attitude is abundantly evident in science-fiction classics such as *The Thing* (1951), *Invaders from Mars* (1953), *This Island Earth* (1955), *Forbidden Planet* (1956), and *Invasion of the Body Snatchers* (1956). The most remarkable exception to this widespread xenophobia, *The Day the Earth Stood Still* (1951), presents a benign attitude toward aliens that Spielberg emulates in *Close Encounters* and *E.T.* Science-fiction films remain "one of the purest forms of spectacle . . . the immediate representation of the extraordinary . . . a sensuous elaboration by means of images and sounds" (Sontag, "Imagination" 215, 212). Perhaps more than any other genre, these films encourage spectators to immerse themselves in the voluptuous visual and aural immediacy of the movie. Audiences marvel at the sleek spaceships, recoil from the monstrous aliens, and gape at the lifelike robots.

By inviting viewers to succumb to their visual and auditory pleasures, science-fiction films entice us into their highly constructed worlds. They immerse us in sensations while forcing us to contemplate technological challenges: "[Science fiction] has proven such a popular form in recent years precisely because its particular argot not only provides us with a most appropriate language for talking about a large dimension of technologically inflected postmodern culture, but also because its fundamental themes help us make sense of our culture's quandaries" (Telotte 19). By supplying entertaining narratives and radiant special effects, these films divert us from being haunted by actual fears and standardize our worst nightmares by making them visible and thus less frightening. They intensify and nullify the dangerous world we inhabit by presenting our collective fears as enticing dishes that we consume and vanquish, at least temporarily. The monsters we can see are far less terrifying than the ones we imagine hiding in our closets, not to mention the skies above us. Most science-fiction films have happy endings: the aliens are defeated, the Death Star is destroyed, the earth is saved from imminent destruction, and the captain and his or her crew continue their exploration of "the final frontier." If only life could mirror art.

Spielberg's Science-Fiction Films

Spielberg rarely sets his films in the realistic present, devoting most of his career either to peering into the future, looking back to the past (mainly the World War II era), or stitching threads of fantasy and science fiction into the fabric of contemporary American life. A few films even merge disparate eras, as when dinosaurs roam among the grassy fields of futuristic amusement preserves. To best analyze the director's contributions to the science-fiction genre, I have structured my discussion differently here than in the other sections of this book, except for the segment in chapter 2 dealing with the *Indiana Jones* trilogy. As in my analysis of that series, this organizational pattern demonstrates how particular technical, thematic, and visual striations link these works together in a distinctive manner and style. At their heart, *Close Encounters of the Third Kind* (1977), *E.T. the Extra-Terrestrial* (1982), *Artificial Intelligence A.I.* (2001), and *Minority Report* (2002) are sustained meditations on similar issues that demand an integrated critical approach. While such a structural deviation disrupts the book's systematic construction, it allows me to foreground the numerous crossovers and connections between these movies, an approach based on shared elements rather than distinctions. The one exception to this consolidated methodology, an extended analysis of *Minority Report,* details how this film, while containing many comparable elements, differs substantially from Spielberg's other three science-fiction movies.

Close Encounters of the Third Kind and *E.T. the Extra-Terrestrial* are Spielberg's science-fiction songs of innocence that celebrate, however complexly, the exhilarations of childhood; *A.I.* and *Minority Report* are his songs of experience that understand, however reluctantly, the need to accept adult responsibilities. Like the best makers of science-fiction movies, Steven Spielberg explores contemporary social implications within fantastic plots. Dazzled by his elaborate symphonies of light and music, most critics fixate on his technical expertise and ignore the persistent tension between personal truths and public responsibilities that endow his finest films with compelling strength and enduring power. Concentrating mainly on the resplendent special effects, they overlook the broader social and psychological significance embedded in the works. The wondrous events and remarkable occurrences in Spielberg's movies ultimately have human consequences; they force common people outside the boundaries of their daily routines. Once these revelatory moments occur, his characters can never return to their former lives, no matter how intense the lure of domestic or communal activities. Like Plato's cave dwellers, they recognize the images on the wall as mere shadows, as reflections and not reality. This knowledge brings them profound understanding, because of a new relationship between themselves and the external world, and also intense pain, because they no longer share the common perceptions that bind them to their community. Since they cannot convince others of the truths revealed, such characters are scorned, abandoned, and finally banished from the society of shadow watchers, sentenced to follow a higher calling but often denied the solace of human companionship.

STRUCTURE AND POINT OF VIEW

Each of these four science-fiction films breaks neatly into a classical three-act structure, with act 1 situating the character in a domestic setting, act 2 detailing a serious interruption of the status quo, and act 3 reestablishing order. In *Close Encounters,* the Neary homelife before and after the alien encounter is succeeded by act 2, Roy's quest to reach Devil's Tower, and finally his participation in the alien landing. *E.T.* opens with the life of Elliott and his family before the alien arrives, moves into their struggle to keep the alien's presence a secret and save him from government experiments, and concludes with his tearful departure for home. *A.I.* continues this pattern: It begins by detailing David's life with his family, proceeds with his quest for the Blue Fairy, and ends with his dream fulfilled by the surviving androids in act 3. *Minority Report* starts with Anderton's life following the death of his son, the breakup of his marriage, and his installation as head of the Pre-Crime Unit, followed by his fugitive existence, and ending with him destroying the unit he once led and reuniting with his wife.

In all of these films, Spielberg explores how encounters between humans and nonhuman lifeforms—whether from outer space or futuristic laboratories—drastically alter daily life. These films display a growing darkness in Spielberg's vision of such contacts. In *Close Encounters,* human responses to otherworldly encounters dominate the narrative, as shimmering aliens appear only briefly at the film's conclusion. The assembled humans view these creatures as technologically superior, looking to them for guidance as they cautiously venture into life among the stars. In *E.T.,* which was made five years later, humans and aliens equally share the narrative in scenes that run the gamut from comic, to compassionate, to exploitative, and to potentially tragic. This film posits a relationship between humans and nonhumans that is more equal morally and technologically than in *Close Encounters:* Elliott protects the alien, who at first seems rather like a lost and helpless pet but eventually displays powers far beyond human possibilities. While the scientists in *Close Encounters* approach the space travelers as students eager to learn from and emulate them, those in *E.T.* strive to capture them. Even though he expresses as much excitement as Lacombe (Francois Truffaut) about extraterrestrial life, Keys (Peter Coyote) initially believes that humans have the technological capability, military strength, and moral right to trap, probe, and investigate this cuddly stranger in a strange land, an intellectual arrogance never shared by his counterparts in *Close Encounters.*

In *A.I.*, a robot-child—the clear equivalent of the aliens in the previous two pictures—dominates the narrative. In this case, the humans are technologically superior but morally inferior to the humanoids they create: David faces personal and societal cruelty as an abandoned child, a hunted fugitive, and a frozen supplicant. Indeed, the kindest figures in the film, the mechanical gigolo who befriends him and the androids (called "the Specialists" in Spielberg's shooting script) who appear long after the humans have perished, are the only ones who grant him any consistent peace and fulfillment. Though the resemblance between these figures and the willowy aliens in *Close Encounters* caused some confusion, Spielberg clearly did not intend them to be space visitors. Dennis Muren, Spielberg's special-effects supervisor, says:

> "The idea is that the Specialists have all been manufactured. They are not alive and, apart from a few differences in color, they are all pretty much identical. . . . We were creating a nanotechnology, mixed with a mysterious glow. We wanted to suggest that technology had developed to the point where robots were trying to be as good as humans; so most of the creatures' higher functions were seated inside their glowing heads." (Qtd. in Fordham 92)

Ironically, these mechanical creatures care about David as a sentient being and not—as do their human counterparts—as a replacement for a lost son or as an experiment in robotic engineering. Early in the film, when Dr. Hobby (William Hurt) first proposes "that we build a robot who can love . . . a robot that dreams," one of his associates asks the crucial question: "Can a human love a robot?" In response, Hobby cites "God and Adam" as the apt analogy for such a momentous venture with metaphysical overtones.

Unlike the other three films, *Minority Report* contains no nonhumans. Yet, the Pre-Cogs—children with predictive powers born to drug-addicted mothers—are literally turned into aliens to serve the needs of the state: they are heavily sedated, kept endlessly floating in an antiseptic environment, hooked up to monitors and electrodes, fed as if they were babies, and treated more as machines than as human beings. In fact, the members of the Pre-Crime Unit, whose daily work depends upon the Pre-Cogs, specifically try "not to think of them as human beings," lest a sympathetic response to these imprisoned beings cloud their judgment and make it more difficult to carry out their task of interpreting the clues given them. Early on we wonder how much control the Pre-Cogs have had in this process; they seem to have exercised no free will, and by fulfilling their assigned role, they ensure that others will have none as well: their visions of future crimes are taken as revealed facts and result in concrete actions. We never learn how (or if) the Pre-Cogs freely consent to function as the ever watchful eyes of the government or even if they get paid for their services. Later, however, Spielberg reveals the shifting sand upon which this castle is built: it was a crime itself, a premeditated murder, that made the entire Pre-Crime Unit possible.

Point of view remains a crucial component of Spielberg's thematic focus and audience appeal in these science-fiction movies. In *Close Encounters* and *E. T.* the camera assumes the perspective of the humans who search for and/ or discover the aliens, allowing audiences to imagine themselves in similar roles. Spielberg permits viewers to share the amazement of Elliott and the madness of Roy as they reconfigure personal and communal assumptions that have been shattered by their discoveries of beings from other planets. We speculate how we might react if we were confronted with huge spaceships while driving home from work, or if strange-looking creatures nestled in our garage. Would we pursue them against overwhelming odds and at the expense of our families? Would we cherish and protect them from potentially malevolent forces? In *A.I.,* Spielberg radically shifts the focus. Here, filmgoers experience the world through the consciousness of the "other" and vicariously suffer from the callousness of human beings, starting with the opening forest-hunt sequence that aligns us with the hunted rather than the hunters. All three films force us to consider how our perception of the world would change if we were not alone in the universe. In *Minority Report,* the point of view stays with the Pre-Crime investigator Anderton (Tom Cruise), but it shifts radically as he switches social roles from enforcer of the law to fugitive from the authorities. In assuming this new identity, he forms an alliance with the "other," Agatha (Samantha Morton), who forces him, and viewers as well, to understand her humanity on a level not previously realized when she functioned exclusively as a governmental instrument.

CHILDREN IN THE SCIENCE-FICTION FILMS

As in most of his other genre films, children are at the center of Spielberg's science-fiction productions, from Barry (*Close Encounters*), to Elliott (*E. T.*), to David (*A.I.*), and the kidnapped Sean (*Minority Report*). Spielberg's choice to situate children at the heart of so many of his movies is one of the keys to his continuing popularity among general audiences, but it also provides ammunition for his detractors. Even sympathetic commentators routinely liken the energetic director to Peter Pan or Huck Finn, lumping him with archetypal figures who refuse to grow up. More disparaging writers use such analogies to assail his movies for reifying heedless impulses over mature

An alliance of necessity between the fugitive Anderton (Tom Cruise) and the Pre-Cog Agatha (Samantha Morton) leads to an understanding of their mutual humanity in *Minority Report* (2002).

thoughts; they censure him for presenting childish pleasures as far preferable to adult responsibilities. Peter Biskind, for example, accuses Spielberg of being obsessed with a "sentimental view of our better self as the inner child, the innocent youth we used to be," concluding that he wants to "return the boomers to the sandbox" (*Easy Riders* 363). Such critiques condemn Spielberg for wasting his considerable technical skills on childish stories, for enticing audiences to wallow in sentimental illusions, and for turning the American cinema into an intellectual wasteland of pretty pictures and adolescent fantasies.

A RESPONSE TO THE CRITICS Contentions like Biskind's fail to recognize the complex and nuanced aspects of Spielberg's art. His portraits of children rarely dissolve into maudlin paeans to some idyllic existence. On the contrary, the kids we see in some detail—David (Haley Joel Osment), Barry (Cary Guffey), and Elliott (Henry Thomas)—are not particularly happy.

Their environments often mirror their stressful, chaotic, and lonely lives. David dwells in a sterile home of glass and wood with perpetually shiny floors reflecting muted walls of gray and brown, utilitarian furniture sitting at perfectly spaced angles in every room, where sunlight continuously bathes the space with a fuzzy, diffused glow. Nothing irregular or distinctive interferes with the uniformly bland, cold design. The households of Barry and Elliott overflow with garish pop-culture icons, rooms stuffed to the choking point with the materialistic excess of modern American life. Occupying similar domestic space, the Neary children exist in a cacophonous world of insipid television programs and neighborly snooping. An elaborate system of toy trains, nailed to the top of a stark plywood table, dominates the family room, and the childrens' bedrooms are cluttered with dirty clothes, Humpty Dumpty lamps, and wallpaper imprinted with steam engines. Whether garish or stark, these physical environments reflect the intellectual and emotionally arid settings these children inhabit.

Though detractors indict him for offering a sanitized picture of suburban existence, Spielberg's depiction of middle-class suburban life ranges far beyond familiar cliches. He rarely presents this milieu uncritically. Even a staunch detractor such as Andrew Britton, who positions Spielberg as central to the conservative filmmaking of the Reagan era, compares the director to Flaubert as a creator of petit bourgeois culture, who believes that it is "stupid, anodyne, and oppressive," and whose characters are "motivated . . . by the impulse to transcend it" (35). Spielberg's suburbia is characterized by dissonant chaos, flat landscapes, tract housing, tasteless interiors, battling siblings, mindless television programs, and polyester clothing. Such settings hardly express warmth, creativity, or joy; instead, they debilitate the imaginations of the inhabitants. Even though Spielberg crams his sets with products emblematic of tangible abundance, his films criticize this debasement of the American Dream rather than endorse its cold affluence. Such an existence numbs the innate sense of wonder and adventure. Those characters who struggle to surmount the rigidly enforced superficiality find themselves alienated, isolated, and ultimately shunned by their communities.

CHILDREN: THEIR FATHERS Spielberg's screen children usually discover that father never knows best. Their dads either remain forever distant, forsake the family, neglect their offspring, or run off to pursue goals and people beyond the family unit. Elliott and his brother Mike (Robert MacNaughton) live with their sister, Gertie (Drew Barrymore), in a single-parent home. David's father (Sam Robards) brings him home as an experiment, a sophisticated "toy" to ease his wife's obsession over their cryogenically suspended son. Once domestic difficulties arise, he wants to return him to the laboratory like a defective vacuum cleaner. Near the end of the film, David tells Dr. Hobby, who modeled him after his own dead son, that he was sent away because "Henry did not like me." The Neary children watch in horror as their father disintegrates into a madman before their eyes, throwing dirt into the kitchen window and turning their home into a site for his obsessive sculptures. No dependable Ward Cleavers populate Spielberg's films, and no resourceful Mike Bradys exist for the children to admire and emulate.

Spielberg clearly modeled Roy Neary on the classic figures of that master filmmaker—and popular entertainer—Alfred Hitchcock. Like typical Hitchcock heroes, Roy is thrust into dangerous and strange situations over which he exerts little control but which he must continue to explore: the archetypal ordinary man caught up in extraordinary circumstances. Like numerous Hitchcock protagonists—such as Jeff Jeffries (*Rear Window*, 1954), Scotty Ferguson (*Vertigo*, 1958), and Roger O. Thornhill (*North by Northwest*, 1959)—he finds a blonde companion, Jullian, to accompany him on the perilous journey into a seemingly malevolent world governed by confusing rules and obscure aspirations. Just who are these people, why have they lied to the American public, and what are they waiting for atop that mountain? The sequences that depict Roy's deterioration from his interest in aliens, to his obsession with building the model of Devil's Tower inside the house, to his plunge into lunacy, contain elements of black humor akin to similar scenes in Hitchcock. Most importantly, as with Hitchcock, Spielberg's film remains as concerned with uncovering psychological truths as with presenting exciting dramatic events. But it does rip apart the Neary family.

Spielberg's films are filled with psychologically and emotionally lost boys. The sheer number of missing, consumed, distant, or malevolent father figures makes this motif a striking part of his work, from his earliest to his most recent films. Most commentators cite biographical evidence to explain this recurring pattern. The director's father, Arnold, was a World War II veteran, electronics engineer, and early computer pioneer who paid little attention to his son. In numerous interviews, Spielberg reveals how emotionally distant his father was during adolescence: "'I always felt my father put his work before me. I always thought he loved me less than his work and I suffered as a result'" (qtd. in McBride 41). Spielberg's parents divorced in 1966. This disruptive event directly inspired, sixteen years later, the story of three suburban children unsettled by the absence of their father and brought together by the appearance of an alien. Yet this universe of deranged, absent, or cold fathers creates a strange vision of patriarchal culture, particularly from a director repeatedly censured for his ideologically traditional and patriarchally conservative movies. How do the codes of the father get passed down to the son if the father is not physically present? Some models of masculine behavior can be learned via the media. So, for example, Elliott mimics John Wayne's treatment of Maureen O'Hara in *The Quiet Man* (1952), grabbing and kissing one of the girls in his class just as Sean Thornton captures Mary Kate Danaher in his arms and kisses her. But while defense of the Other reconstitutes the family in *E.T.*, the most conservative of the director's science-fiction films, those in *Close Encounters* and *A.I.* remain permanently fractured, the children never able to recover from being abandoned or rejected by the most important man in their young lives.

In *Minority Report*, Spielberg focuses once again on distraught family members abandoned by those they loved and believed would always remain part of their lives. The film represents yet another account of "trying to get the family back together . . . about loss of family and regaining family," which the director readily admits stems from his parents' divorce, which still "haunts" and "compels" him (Caro 11). Though Agatha represents another of Spielberg's parentless children, John Anderton reverses the director's typical familial alignment: instead of focusing on the child with one or no parent, he concentrates on a man who loses his only son, a childless father. Because of that tragedy, his marriage dissolves. To grasp this fundamental narrative and psychological transformation, imagine Spielberg telling *Empire of the Sun* (1987) from the perspective of Jim's parents desperately searching for their missing son, instead of from that of the lost child. Although he continues to perform his duties as chief officer in the newly created Pre-Crime Division flawlessly, Anderton's personal life degenerates into a morass of intense guilt, persistent insomnia, recycled family holograms, and numbing drugs.

Spielberg adds an additional layer of complexity by making Anderton not only a father but also a son, at least symbolically. His relationship with Lamar Burgess (Max von Sydow), the avuncular director of the Pre-Crime unit, is more a family configuration than a business or professional link. Because circumstances deprive Anderton of masculine roles (father/husband) that are inherently authoritative and responsible, he initially assumes the more deferential identity of a son who trusts the advice of a tragically flawed father figure. Thus, Burgess's treachery affects Anderton as deeply as the loss of his son, and this betrayal violates a trinity of important precepts in Spielberg's moral universe: never abandon the family (Burgess set Anderton up to commit a crime and be captured); never choose public advancement over personal loyalty (Burgess remains head of the unit as it goes national); never sacrifice ethical principles for the supposed good of the many (Burgess commits a murder to save the Pre-Crime system). By the end of the film, Anderton happily reassumes his adult obligations as a husband and future father, as he reunites with his loving and now pregnant wife—a typically Spielbergian "happy" ending, but one that never fully dispels the bleakness that preceded it.

CHILDREN: THEIR MOTHERS But what of Spielberg's mothers? The science-fiction films feature women who possess extremely limited vision. Ronnie Neary (Teri Garr), for example, never fully believes her husband's story and remains more concerned about what her neighbors think than about what Roy may be feeling. "Don't you see what's happening?" she screams at him. "None of our friends call us anymore." When Elliott first tells his skeptical mother (Dee Wallace) about this visitor from outer space, she brushes him off: "It's not that we don't believe you, honey. . . . All we're saying is that, maybe, you probably imagined it." Her son sadly concludes, "Dad would believe me." Even worse, David's adored mother figure, Monica (Frances O'Connor), ultimately abandons him when she can no longer endure the sibling rivalry between him and their biological son. Spielberg's mothers are emotionally and intellectually limited. More importantly, all three commit the worst crime imaginable in the domestic world of Steven Spielberg: they are not available when their children truly need them, either to keep the family together, to believe and defend their children, or to love them in the midst of disruptive family conflicts. Lara (Kathryn Morris) in *Minority Report* is a different type of mother figure: she does not forsake her child; he is taken from her. Divorcing Anderton because "every time I looked at him I saw my son," she returns to rescue him, help him destroy Burgess, and reunite with him to form a new family unit.

Sexuality plays a small role in the lives of Spielberg's mothers. Early in *E.T.,* one of Mike's friends reaches out to touch his mom's backside as she dances obliviously around the kitchen in an orange bathrobe, eliciting an annoyed "stop it!" from her eldest son. Later, she dresses up for Halloween in a tight leopard-print skirt, a sexy outfit that Mike and Elliott greet with confusion, then embarrassment, and finally disapproval. Far from expressing her sexuality, Mary's momentary dress-up is nothing more than a brief, colorful respite from the gray life she is living. Overwhelmed emotionally at the dissolution of her family, the loss of her husband, the additional financial pressures of her new life, and the added burdens of single parenthood, the distracted mother has little time for much beyond her personal grief and immediate concerns. In fact, the emotionally damaged Mary never notices the strange events occurring all around her, such as the extra "thank you" that follows her compliment about their costumes and that the figure under the ghost sheet faints from the glare of the flash bulb. She even misses an intoxicated *E.T.* staggering around the house in her son's bathrobe as she puts away groceries, talks on the phone about Elliott's odd behavior at school, and ignores Gertie's persistent demands that she "meet somebody."

Ronnie Neary, however, does have a romantic moment with Roy. In his bewildered euphoria, he wakes her at four in the morning to join the search for aliens, to participate in this miraculous adventure beyond the constraints of their middle-class existence. "I need you to see something with me," he tells her. "It's really important." Even in the face of her husband's giddy exhilaration about the spaceships he has witnessed, she grounds his experience into mundane, domestic terms: "Was it like a Sara Lee moon-shaped cookie, those crescent cookies?" she asks him, bringing the stars down to the kitchen.

Mothers, like Ronnie (Teri Garr) in *Close Encounters of the Third Kind* (1977), represent the earthbound practicalities of middle-class life in Spielberg's science-fiction films.

Instead of looking upward toward the heavens with Roy, Ronnie focuses nostalgically on their romantic past. "I remember when we used to come to places like this just to look at each other," she tells him, then adds a gentle command, "Snuggle." He absentmindedly puts his arms around her, still peering toward the heavens. She kisses his cheek, turns his face toward hers, and kisses him deeply. For perhaps the last moment of emotional connection with his former life, Roy melts into her embrace—but only temporarily. As the kiss continues, his eyes open and move upward, scanning the skies and foreshadowing his increasing withdrawal from his family. By conjoining Ronnie's sexuality with her earthbound sensibility, Spielberg depicts her feelings as insignificant when contrasted with her husband's transcendent experience. Even Jullian, who could potentially become a substitute love interest as she joins Roy on his quest, functions more as a buddy than a girlfriend.

In almost every aspect of its stylistic and thematic focus, *A.I.* presents a very different picture of sexuality. The Swintons display little overt affection or sexual energy. We never see them hugging or kissing. When David invades their bedroom to cut a lock of Monica's hair, he finds them on different sides of the bed, neither entwined nor even touching. When the two eat supper, they chew deliberately and sit opposite each other, their expressions as placid as the salad they consume. Few words are spoken. Only twice does Spielberg emphasize Monica's sexuality, both times silently and visually. Early in the film, as the couple leaves for a formal dinner, Monica returns to the house to talk with David. The camera actually peers down the top of her strapless dress as the adoring child sits at her feet. Obviously enjoying her attention, particularly since she is supposed to be with Henry at this moment, David prolongs their stolen intimacy as long as possible. Eventually, an annoyed Henry—viewing David as a rival for Monica's affections—breaks their reverie by telling her they are beyond fashionably late and rushing her out of the house.

The film's final sequence is even more disturbing. Throughout the movie David demonstrates the most severe case of obsessive mother-love since Norman Bates in *Psycho* (1960). In fact, his entire quest has been to return to his home, this time as a real boy worthy of his mother's affections. The surviving androids provide David with one joyful day with a virtual image of his beloved mother. Yet Spielberg configures this time together more like a romantic date than a parent with her son. When David wakes Monica in bed, the camera catches her in the warm and gentle afterglow of sleep, her hair spread luxuriously across the pillow. Spielberg shoots the characters from the side, emphasizing the low neckline of Monica's nightgown and the curve of her breast as David sits worshipfully at her feet. Their dialogue could easily be mistaken for intimate words between two lovers. At the end of their time together, David gently tucks her back into her bed. She falls asleep, never to awake again, and he elects to spend eternity lying next to her and holding her hand. The narrator (Ben Kingsley) assures us that "for the first time in his life, he went to that place where dreams are born." Technically, this sequence resembles nothing else in the movie: relatively long takes, only warm colors, the camera moving fluidly, the action underscored with a comforting piano solo, a calming off-camera narrative voice, and everything linked together with a languid editing pace. The narrator intones, "There was no Henry. There was no Martin. There was no grief. There was only David." Just how the son wants it to be, though Freud would undoubtedly have much to say about dreams that involve deleting your sibling, eliminating Dad, and sleeping with Mom.

THE RELIGIOUS COMPONENTS

Many science-fiction film commentators emphasize the preoccupation with realms beyond the earthly and explicate the genre by focusing predominately on spiritual issues. Vivian Sobchack's definition, for example, stresses that science fiction attempts to "reconcile man with the unknown" (*Screening* 63), a statement of purpose that explains religious activity as much as film narrative. Siegfried Mandell and Peter Fingesten also stress this point of view:

> "We see that the new mythology is a subtle point-for-point exchange for religious doctrines.... The spaceship displaces the church as a vessel of salvation.... The pilot leads his community of saints like a savior.... The dashboard paraphernalia and control dials become as potent and dominant as icons and sacraments.... Faith is placed in technical efficiency.... The breakthrough in space, the bursting through gravitational pulls, constitutes a baptism or climactic initiation into the heavenly mysteries." (Qtd. in Sobchack, *Screening* 56)

And this was written in 1955. It should not surprise us, therefore, that critics respond to Spielberg's science-fiction films through a template of religious terminology. His science-fiction pictures have been analyzed with this particular set of conventions more consistently and in greater depth than those of most other directors, though exegesis using this critical lens often produces more heat than light.

In his discussions of *Close Encounters,* for example, Robert Torry claims that the final sequence incorporates New Testament accounts of the Parousia, the culminating event in God's narrative of salvation for the chosen (190). Similarly, Tony Williams argues that Roy's path is "akin to religious conversion," invoking New Testament sayings and the Day of the Pentecost scene in Acts 2 and asserting that Roy abandons his family "to really follow the Savior" (27). Elizabeth Hirschman compares Roy to Moses, who "was called away by God [and] . . . may return to earth as a savior or messiah to share the gifts he has gained with the rest of humanity" (122), while Neil Lerner contends that John Williams's score uses "ancient religious musical codes" to reinforce the film's "authoritarian rhetoric" (104). Going even further, Carl A. Mounteer formulates a genre he labels "spiritual science fiction" and names Spielberg its greatest proponent. He believes that the main religious message of *Close Encounters* is the godlike ability of the extraterrestrials to confer "immortality on worthy humans. . . . The most emotionally powerful and profound promise of Christianity" (56). Stanley Kauffmann's review exclaimed that *Close Encounters* was "not so much a film as an event in the history of faith" (20), while Pauline Kael talked about its "beatific technology—machines from outer space deified" (54).

 E.T. inspired similar responses. The little creature's ability to emerge from and return to the sky, to resurrect himself from the dead, and to heal injuries with a touch of his lighted finger generated a cottage industry of metaphysical interpretations. Andrew Britton's vitriolic essay, "Blissing Out: The Politics of Reaganite Entertainment," notes how "in one of the most vulgar moments of Spielbergian religiosity . . . [he] appears in the back of a truck in the archetypal posture of the risen Christ, and ascends to heaven a few sequences later" (38). Andrew Gordon equates E.T. to a mythological "child god": "As a child who is also a divine being, E.T. ascends to Earth from the heavens and mingles with the sons of men, risking his own life. He is misunderstood, hunted, captured, tormented, dies, and is reborn" (*E.T.* 301). Viewing the alien as a thinly disguised Christ figure, Frank P. Tomasulo argues that the film's "overt representation of Christian iconography and ideology" is a "referent for political rhetoric" that "clothes the state in religious robes to achieve popular acceptance" ("Gospel" 274), an elaborate continuation of his earlier argument that Spielberg's 1980s films functioned as conduits for Ronald Reagan's right-wing social and imperialist agenda. Hirschman characterizes the alien creature as the "new messiah," one of the "divine beings . . . who die in our secular society, or are killed by our culture [and] can be brought back to life by divine intervention" (166). These selected comments represent a small but representative portion of the vast amount of criticism attaching religious symbolism to the film.

Yet Spielberg's two earlier science-fiction movies spotlight spectacle more than scripture. One stumbles into treacherous terrain by lashing specific scenes directly to particular sections of the New or Old Testament and, from there, extrapolating religious messages. If anything, the spiritual sensibility in these Spielberg movies partakes of the ecumenical culture of American vernacular religion, the prevailing belief in some higher presence beyond ourselves that intersects with our daily lives.

Consider how the director himself talks about the relationship between science fiction and the spiritual: "'Science fiction does not have to go very far to connect with the spiritual. Science fiction is about the pure imagination, about dreaming. And imagination and dreaming are as close to basic beliefs as anything we can cherish'" (qtd. in Abramowitz 7). In other words, for Spielberg, spirituality springs from the imagination and dreams. Those creative sources, in turn, form our most cherished beliefs. There is no mention of God here, no invocation of a higher power other than intuitive, human faculties that beget artistic creations.

In this sense, Spielberg's notion of spirituality equates so-called sacred texts with products of the secular imagination: the writings of St. Paul are no more or less "spiritual" than those of Dostoyevsky. To put it another way,

E.T. the Extra-Terrestrial (1982) demonstrates how Spielberg's science-fiction films recast the ecumenical culture of American vernacular religion into temporal mythmaking.

Spielberg's strategy creates analogies, not allegories. In *Close Encounters* and *E.T.*, he invokes readily available religious motifs to add emotional depth to his stories and, by incorporating commonly recognized symbols, directs the viewer to events beyond the temporal—but not necessarily toward one-to-one interpretations that in some readings turn the cinematic texts into visual re-creations of biblical events. Such readings do a substantial disservice to Spielberg's broader and more inclusive artistic impulses. To shoehorn his films into neat parables that fit preexisting modes of western religious expressions robs them of their particular power. Instead of simply recapitulating religious motifs, Spielberg's pictures do something far more interesting and more daring: they suggest—and at times directly invoke—the transcendent without necessarily embracing biblical divinity. I am not arguing that critics must restrict themselves to what Spielberg says about the religious aspects of his films, should he even admit such aspects exist, but Spielberg should not be tied down to this or that religious event. His work is not doctrinaire; it is broader, more general, and more diffuse that most conventionally religious readings would allow.

This whole issue of religion in Spielberg's films—what Tony Williams characterizes as "an infiltration of religious codes into a popular cinematic genre to the point of saturation" (27)—raises a more general and complex question: can transcendence be communicated visually without resorting to traditional religious symbolism? *Close Encounters* and *E.T.* demonstrate that things—and beings—exist outside the bounds of our limited understanding without necessarily having anything to do with God or traditional religious doctrines. Spielberg incorporates common and widely recognized Christian tropes into his narrative in decidedly secular ways to shake his audience out of its complacent routines, to sharpen its sense of possibilities beyond commonly accepted truths. Events that might be viewed as religious, as evidence of God's power and majesty, here become secular tales of technological wonder and individual imagination. They function not as authentic expressions of a deep religious faith or a mature spiritual consciousness but as readily available sets of preinscribed codes that contextualize his narratives and heighten their ethereal qualities.

Close Encounters of the Third Kind and *E.T.* admire and even celebrate technical achievement, but they never deify scientific accomplishments. Even more importantly, these wondrous technological achievements spring from inspired human endeavors, not divine intervention; they result from hard and persistent labor, not prayer and penitence. Everything within Spielberg's narrative frames can be explained rationally, and the stories demand willing suspensions of disbelief rather than fervent leaps of faith. No events turn the central figures toward God. A few scattered mentions of God appear, as does a formal prayer before the astronauts journey into space in *Close Encounters,* but these are formalized, stock expressions rather than sincere affirmations of religious conviction. Belief resides not in deities but in the potential of human progress over time and beyond current limitations. Rather than genuflect in the face of traditional Christian doctrines, the films strive to expand our imaginations about what is possible within the genius of humankind. *Close Encounters* and *E.T.* represent fascinating examples of temporal mythmaking that have more in common with the Brothers Grimm than with the Gospels.

A.I. presents viewers with an altogether different type of religious situation than *Close Encounters* or *E.T.* Early reviewers such as Mark Caro, who claims that "David's journey is a parallel to Man's never-ending quest to obtain proof of God's love," and David Kerr, who notes that in going from the Flesh Fair to the underwater sequences Spielberg "swaps his Jewish metaphor for a Catholic one" (9), continue the religious speculation. But things have changed in the director's life. Making *Schindler's List* profoundly altered Spielberg as a man and a visual artist. Numerous interviews and articles relate how deeply this project affected him: it made him more conscious of his religious heritage and "shook up [his] life in a good way" (Schiff 176). Because this picture marked a distinct and dramatic shift in Spielberg's personal and artistic life, it is reasonable to conclude that the director would treat religious motifs and images differently in the two science-fiction films he made after it than he did in the two he directed before it.

If Spielberg uses conventional religious imagery and motifs in *Close Encounters* and *E.T.* as a convenient way of reflecting American religious mythology and accessing the popular imagination, *A.I.* displays a different sensibility, particularly in the segment where David goes to Manhattan ("the city at the ends of the earth") to find the Blue Fairy who will turn him into a real boy. He pilots his helicopter under the water, through the entrance to the submerged Coney Island, into the Storyland section devoted to Pinocchio, and comes face-to-face with the Blue Fairy, though still separated by the glass of the aircraft window. Trapped by collapsing structures, and then frozen by drastic climate changes, he "prays" to the figure who is "always there, always smiling," and, as the voice of the authoritative narrator reveals, "two thousand years pass." Finally freed by kindly androids, he gingerly inches toward the statue accompanied by angelic choir music. Initially, it seems like the buildup to yet another overly sentimentalized Spielbergian moment, an emotional apex that reaffirms faith and fortitude. As David finally touches the object of his veneration, the music swells, but shockingly, the statue cracks and shatters into millions of crystalline pieces.

The statue of the Blue Fairy, drawn from the Pinocchio fable popularized by the Disney cartoon, merges two narrative realms that often rely on supernatural events: folktales and religious stories. While physically resembling David's revered mother, the Blue Fairy represents the magical female figures integral to numerous folk legends. In addition, given how Spielberg pictorializes her and the language the narrator uses to describe events, the Blue Fairy also functions as a religious icon, most obviously the Madonna. By using her image to conflate magic and miracles, enchantment and dogma, Spielberg equates religious faith to superstition, demonstrating the inability of both traditions to aid David: childhood beliefs are false, and adult worship is useless. Thus, David's prayers become the futile gestures of terrified and desperate children lost in the woods, Hansel and Gretel crying out for protection against the witch. Never answered, he remains in suspended animation—much like his cryogenically preserved "brother" earlier in the film. That this statue shatters upon his gentle touch renders the film's Christian iconography an expression of empty fantasies that temporarily soothe our fears but offer only illusionary protection against harsh realities.

Such a cynical position would be unthinkable in the pre-*Schindler* Spielberg films. Perhaps his renewed sense of Jewish identity inspired a reevaluation of basic Christian doctrines, particularly their formative role in the centuries-old anti-Semitism that culminated in the Holocaust. Maybe Spielberg's study of the Third Reich, extensively documented in various interviews he gave at the time of the film's release and afterwards, convinced him that Christian theology played a pivotal role in the destruction of European Jewry, a position taken by some influential Holocaust scholars such as Dennis Prager and Joseph Teluskin (*Why the Jews?*) and Charlotte Klein (*Anti-Judaism in Christian Theology*). After making *Schindler's List,* Spielberg hinted at basic artistic and personal reconsiderations beyond the level of mere characterization. It is therefore plausible to conclude that working on the film made it impossible for him naively and uncritically to incorporate such religious iconography, as he had done in *Close Encounters* and *E.T.* But if the old values no longer hold, what replaces them? Where is the moral center of *A.I.?*

One way to answer this vexing question is to examine how David finally achieves his mother's love and acceptance. Strangely, in this film the human desire for an emotional bond can be fulfilled only via technology. The Specialists use their sophisticated power to scan David's mind for his memories and, joining into a circle, pass those images from machine to machine. Rapidly moving scenes from his past jump from the face of one mechanical being to the next, forming a virtual movie of his life stretched around the ring and shared by all members of the interpretive community. Memory preserved by technology; memory filtered through technology; memory as technology. Ironically, this robot boy who desperately wants to become a flesh-and-blood child remains the only creation who actually saw and touched the human progenitors. He possesses unique, experiential knowledge of the species that first invented robots and then sought their destruction: "They made us too smart, too soon, and too many." Human beings become the ghosts in the machines, new works of art in the age of mechanical reproduction, with David the only apparatus capable of accessing remembrances of Orgas past. The film directly renders "popular uncertainty regarding core questions about origins and futures, and mediated representations themselves" (Williams, "Real-Time" 160); it "affords a reflexive perspective on the anxieties about digital culture, though with an emphasis on the component process of subjectivity itself" (Williams 168). In this sense, "popular uncertainty" seems a polite way of talking about a crisis of faith.

The central section of the film provides a transition from the human to the android world. In particular, Gigolo Joe (Jude Law), a robot designed for women's pleasure (one of the few times overt sexuality appears in Spielberg's films), evolves from a mechanical device to a moral agent. While he is not programmed for such responsibilities, he demonstrates that creations may become ethically superior to those who created them.

Like Jim (*Empire of the Sun*), another child forced into a cruel and unfamiliar world after losing his parents, David needs protection and guidance. His Orga parents abandon him, but his Mecha father shelters him. Joe demonstrates far more human qualities than any people in the film by befriending David, educating him, and aiding him on his quest. In *A.I.*, technological creations possess a conscience beyond the imagination of their makers and a sense of moral responsibility that outstrips the cold experiments of Dr. Hobby, the jealousy of brother Martin (Jake Thomas), the distant curiosity of Henry, and the tearful betrayal of Monica. That the robots can transcend their programming to act as surrogate parents makes even more horrific their violent destruction at the Flesh Fair, accompanied by the cheers of frenzied humans.

Minority Report is the least overtly religious of Spielberg's science-fiction films. The Pre-Cogs inhabit a room called the "temple," and Agent Witwer (Colin Farrell) compares their work to that of priests rather than law-enforce-

Gigolo Joe (Jude Law) evolves from a mechanical device into a moral agent in *A.I. Artificial Intelligence* (2001), protecting David (Haley Joel Osment) when his human parents abandon him.

ment personnel, but Anderton forcefully rejects this notion as an inappropriate description of their responsibilities. Ironically, he fails to recognize that his absolute faith in the Pre-Cogs' visions of the future amounts to a zealous defense of a particular belief system. As will be demonstrated repeatedly throughout the movie, Anderton must go blind before he can see; he must lose his way in the darkness before he can find a light that will lead him to personal redemption and political reality. The film posits that uncritically trusting in any system inevitably leads to disastrous consequences. When Anderton becomes a criminal in the eyes of the state, he finally understands that truth is subjective, always vulnerable to manipulation and abuse. Skepticism rather than doctrinaire conviction provides the only appropriate safeguard against human frailty and desire. One can choose to accept (or reject) a particular formulation of belief in a higher power or the construction of the state itself, but doctrinaire coercion creates oppression, not freedom. In *Minority Report,* salvation rests in the reconstitution of the individual consciousness, not in the power of the state or in any sort of superior being or consciousness.

A Note on Spielberg and Kubrick

It might be argued that this shift from the optimism of *Close Encounters* and warmth of *E.T.* to the darkness of *A.I.* and *Minority Report* has more to do with Spielberg's collaboration with Stanley Kubrick than any fundamental alteration in his own psyche or worldview. Many articles published at the time of *A.I.*'s release stressed this connection. Spielberg and Kubrick first met in England in 1979, when Kubrick was finishing *The Shining* (1980) and Spielberg was just starting *Raiders of the Lost Ark*. They got together about a dozen times in Kubrick's large estate in Hertfordshire and continued their growing friendship via extensive transatlantic phone calls and faxes. In 1985, during a four-hour conversation, Kubrick told Spielberg his idea for a film in which humans treat robots like slaves and asked for his help with the special effects. Basing the film on Brian Aldiss's short story about a robot child and his mechanical teddy bear, "Super-Toys Last All Summer Long," Kubrick hired the illustrator Chris Baker (who creates fantasy book covers and writes graphic novels under the pseudonym Fangorn) to draw fifteen hundred black-and-white storyboards; then he shot some test footage of oil rigs in the North Sea to be used in the underwater shots of New York city and wrote a ninety-page treatment.

It was 1994 before Kubrick first proposed that Spielberg direct *A.I.* and that he produce it. "'Don't you think people would come to see a Stanley Kubrick production of a Steven Spielberg film?'" he asked the stunned director (qtd. in Abramowitz 5). When they set about the work, Kubrick, famous for his paranoia, swore Spielberg to an oath of secrecy and insisted he install a fax machine in his bedroom so that the reclusive director could send him thoughts no matter what the time of day or night. The two men even drew up and almost finalized a deal with Warner Brothers. But Spielberg ultimately backed out of the project, concluding, "'I didn't want Stanley to be robbed. . . . I felt like I was taking something away from him. I was sort of a safety net, and if I took the net away, he would do it himself'" (qtd. in Abramowitz 5). After Kubrick died of a heart attack on March 7, 1999, his widow, Christiane, and her brother, Jan Harlan, convinced Spielberg to complete the aborted project. For Spielberg, a director whose films obsess about absent father figures and who speaks in interview after interview about his own distant father and the pain of his parents' divorce, finishing Kubrick's film must have seemed like an act of artistic respect and filial devotion.

It is enticing to speculate about what initially drew together these strikingly different filmmakers whose personalities, production methods, artistic goals, imagistic constructions, potential audiences, commercial aspirations, and worldviews seem overtly at odds. Although both were middle-class Jewish boys who loved technology and felt severely alienated from their childhood environments, the austere and coldly intellectual Kubrick, seemingly oblivious to audience expectations and bringing an uncompromising intellectual rigor to his films, would seem to have little in common with the hyperkinetic and viscerally emotional Spielberg, who desperately wants filmgoers to like his work and goes to extraordinary lengths to seduce them. Even their way of working is totally dissimilar: Kubrick would shoot in continuity at a glacially slow pace, while Spielberg would film setup after setup, far faster than most Hollywood directors. Though both loved the mechanical aspects of filmmaking and exercised strict control over their images, their few similarities fall within the technological rather than thematic or stylistic spheres. Even their forays into similar genres, for example science-fiction films (*2001: A Space Odyssey*, 1968; and *Close Encounters of the Third Kind*), historical costume dramas (*Barry Lyndon*, 1975; and *Amistad*, 1997), or war epics (*Full Metal Jacket*, 1987; and *Saving Private Ryan*, 1998), result in radically different movies on almost every imaginable level. This odd coupling of "the Prince of Bleak and the Emperor of Ice Cream" (Arthur 22) seems akin to Woody Allen finishing a film started by Sam Peckinpah. The question is, Whose movie is this, anyway?

It is probably accurate to say that Kubrick's ghost hung over the production of *A.I.* After all, he did labor on the project, on and off, for fifteen years. Dennis Muren, the special-effects director from Industrial Light and Magic who worked with Kubrick and Spielberg on the production, thought of *A.I.* as "'Stanley's story'" and "'Steven's film'" (qtd. in Fordham 93). Ample evidence exists that Kubrick's presence was felt before, during, and after the production as well. Jude Law reported that "'Stanley was talked about every day.'" The producer Bonnie Curtis claimed that the picture is "'Steven's interpretation of what Stanley was trying to do,'" that Spielberg used roughly six hundred of Baker's original storyboards, and that the director struggled "'to get as much of what Stanley wanted upon the screen as possible'" (qtd. in Abramowitz 2). Spielberg even played music from the *2001* soundtrack to help establish the mood during the production. Yet Spielberg wrote the screenplay, produced the piece, supervised the shoot, oversaw the editing, and directed the picture. He did not channel Kubrick. In fact, as he told Rachel Abramowitz, he fought hard to cast off his anxiety of influence and make the picture his own, even though at first,

> "Stanley was sitting on the seat behind me, saying, 'No, don't do that!' I felt like I was being coached by a ghost! I finally just had to kind of be disrespectful to the extent that I needed to be able to write this, not from Stanley's heart, but from mine. . . . I can't know what Stanley knew. I can't be who Stanley was, and I'll never be who Stanley might have been." (6)

Although inspired and tinted by Kubrick, *A.I.* is—as it says it is—a Steven Spielberg film.

A Dystopic Vision

Unlike the largely negative popular and critical response to *A.I.*, *Minority Report* struck a responsive chord with critics and audiences, garnering excellent reviews and quickly crossing the hundred-million-dollar box-office mark. The same director that critics had earlier disparaged for creating the blockbuster mentality and infantalizing the cinema was now hailed for going "against the grain" by challenging "the big fluff of summer" and offering "a counterpoint to . . . the dumbed-down standard for summer fare" (Lyman 17). Amidst a summer season stuffed with car chases and explosions, pale sequels and comic-book heroes, Spielberg emerged as the thinking man's filmmaker for adapting Philip K. Dick's 1956 short story into an engaging and intelligent film. Dick spent most of his life in obscurity and desperate poverty, his works attaining popular acclaim only after the success of Ridley Scott's *Blade Runner* (based on Dick's 1968 novel *Do Androids Dream of Electric Sheep?*), released soon after the author's death at age fifty-three. Dick's bleak, intense, and often paranoid visions inevitably focus on the complexities of human memory and psychology rather than on technological gadgetry and flamboyant aliens: the brain, not the computer, remains the focus of his futuristic thrillers. In particular, his consistent motif that humans beings and machines are becoming increasingly interchangeable, and that in such a world surface appearances inevitably prove to be bewildering deceptions, becomes a primary theme in *Minority Report.*

As a self-described "fictionalizing philosopher" (Edelstein 17), Dick's work falls more in the tradition of Kafka than most mainstream science-fiction writing; his concerns are with "the technology of the soul" (Dick ii), not that of spaceships. Like its literary source, Spielberg's foreboding, expressionistic film starts with an engaging plot premise—the social and personal repercussions that occur when people are convicted of murders before they commit them—and expands the concept into a political warning and ultimately a compelling meditation on the ancient question of whether human action is predestined or the result of free will. The film features Dick's tortured central character, a futuristic cop psychologically wounded from the loss of his own child, addicted to illegal drugs, and assigned to prevent crimes before they happen. While wrapping itself in the genre trappings of science-fiction and chase movies, *Minority Report* explores the potentially disastrous misuses of modern technology, particularly how digital manipulation can destabilize visual images and abuse them for ideological reasons. The movie functions on at least three interwoven levels: the personal, the political, and the philosophical, each accompanied by an interlocking set of visual motifs.

Stylistically, Spielberg cites the influence of master directors of film noir like John Huston, Howard Hawks, and Sam Fuller and emulates their classic techniques to produce an ominous landscape composed of complex, overly cluttered spaces that swallow up figures; stark and opposing areas of light and dark that contain uncertain points of refuge and danger; undiffused, low-key lighting that harshly illuminates characters; extreme depth of field that keeps most frame elements in focus; distorting and disorienting camera angles; suffocating close-ups that chop off parts of the anatomy; and irregular spacing between objects and characters that creates discomfort (see Place). Such techniques allow him to capture what Spielberg characterizes as "the photo-realism of film":

> "We decided to put the film through a process called bleach bypass, which essentially takes all of the technicolor out of your face and makes your face much more pale. What it does is take those happy, delightfully rosy skin tones away from people that are naturally that way and washes everything out. Then we shot some of the scenes on 800 ASA film stock, which creates a kind of graininess that makes it feel more like an old film noir." (qtd. in Lyman 26)

These film-noir elements create "a visually unstable environment in which no character has a firm moral base from which he can confidently operate" (Place 338). By entering this threatening sphere where, as Dr. Hineman (Lois Smith) advises Anderton, "You shouldn't trust anyone," Spielberg creates an ideologically equivocal and inherently treacherous atmosphere that remains more personally tangled, politically duplicitous, and morally relative than in any of his previous films.

THE PERSONAL

The characters in *Minority Report* remain trapped within this morally ambivalent world. As an intriguing contrast between anxious urban and contemplative rural life, images of water in various contexts suggest meditative creation and psychological destruction. The film is virtually awash in spoken references to and visual images of water. To cite only the most obvious, Agatha and the other Pre-Cogs transmit their visions of future crimes while floating in pools of nutrient-enhanced water; the sprinkler in the front lawn rotates throughout the initial crime sequence, when a man tries to kill his unfaithful wife; the disreputable part of the city (called the Sprawl) is filled with puddles and often seen through rain showers; the hologram image of Anderton's wife urges him to "watch the rain" with her; Anne Lively (Jessica Harper) is drowned in a lake; when Anderton seeks to escape the invading mechanical spiders, he immerses himself in a bathtub filled with ice water; the Burgesses have a lake house, as does Anderton's ex-wife; Anderton and Agatha leave the shopping mall in a downpour; Dr. Hineman waters her exotic plants as she converses with the frustrated Anderton; Anderton and his pregnant wife watch the rain outside their windows in their final scene; and the freed Pre-Cogs eventually live in a cabin beside the water. Most crucially, Anderton loses his son Sean (Spencer Treat Clark) while playing underwater. In an ironic reversal of traditional baptism symbology, he emerges from the pool a different man, reborn not into spirituality but into emotional pain.

THE POLITICAL

Spielberg taps into a sensitive communal nerve with *Minority Report*. Conceived, shot, and edited before the current crisis in domestic security spawned by the attack on the World Trade Center and Pentagon, *Minority Report* hit movie screens while an ongoing debate was being stimulated by questions about how much personal liberty Americans were willing to sacrifice for the promise of public security. Can we trust government agencies to exercise appropriate restraints if given greater power to patrol our lives? Will they monitor only those who endanger our safety and not those who hold unpopular opinions? Will such agencies actually prevent violent activities or routinely engage in a frenzied search for pre-crimes? Does prevention justify the surveillance? This is also a time when ethicists debate the ramifications of the latest scientific findings about genetic predispositions and prisons are holding people who have been arrested because the government suspects they would have committed future crimes. *Minority Report* offers a sobering scenario of how dangerous it is to exchange individual freedoms for governmental assurances.

At the heart of *Minority Report* rests a dire warning: because human beings create and control the machines, as well as the system that employs them, no safeguards can infallibly shield citizens from violence. Even more importantly, any mechanism, however sophisticated and refined, remains vulnerable to human interpretation, and such devices are therefore inherently susceptible to corruption and misuse. The cynical Witwer misjudges his true enemy, but he understands that "the flaw is always human," as he tells Anderton about the Pre-Crime system. Spielberg beautifully illustrates this fatal flaw by way of layered visual constructions that mesh with his narrative. The Pre-Cogs, called "pattern recognition filters" by one officer, project images of future crimes, drawn from their tortured consciousness, onto a tripartite, screenlike apparatus attached to the ceiling of their "temple." From there, the images are transferred to a transparent video screen, where Anderton, using specially designed sensor gloves, manipulates the colliding image fragments, orchestrating them (to the strains of Schubert's Unfinished Symphony) into a coherent narrative. Thus, the Pre-Cogs function as authors—or at least transmitters or channelers—of the text, throwing up images that Anderton, as the reader, fashions into a coherent story, identifying the scene and setting himself up to prevent a crime.

Because the meanings of the Pre-Cog-initiated narratives inevitably shift from reader to reader, as Spielberg demonstrates throughout the film, governmental actions based on those constructed patterns rest on a shaky foundation of selection and interpretation. The images flash so quickly onto the screens that an accurate understanding of their meaning is never possible. Only after slowing down the rapid images and rearranging them into a seemingly logical narrative configuration of cause and effect does the government take action. Also open to question is whether or not each Pre-Cog projects the same scenes as the other two: does each see identical angles, events, sequences, and outcomes simultaneously? (Viewers finally discover that they do not, since "minority reports" provide alternate endings.) Thus, the apparently precise montages sutured together by Anderton prove inherently ambiguous, a series of actions open to competing interpretations despite their ostensible clarity. As numerous theorists have demonstrated, a viewer's subjective positioning always colors his or her reception and interpretation of visual images: we habitually see what we have been trained to understand and, sometimes, what we want to see (as does Anderton's nemesis Witwer). All the variables that constitute one's personal and social identity determine how, and even what, one sees. Furthermore, we are left to wonder, if the unit ever goes national, could these three beings alone possibly "predict" all the crimes throughout the United States? Alternatively, do other Pre-Cogs exist in this perpetual government servitude?

Anderton initially places total faith in the system before learning its limitations by becoming its victim. The Pre-Cogs project a scenario of him killing a man: Anderton points his gun, fires at close range, and blasts a man out of the window, all while being watched by a third man from outside of a high-rise building. But when the murder actually occurs, a set of previously unrecognized circumstances change Anderton's (and the viewer's) perception of the event: the man looking from outside the building is actually a painted figure on a billboard, not a witness; the crime scene turns out to be a false setup designed to enrage Anderton; the man is not the kidnapper of Anderton's son but a criminal who agrees to be killed so that his family can get insurance benefits; Anderton chooses not to pull the trigger, and it remains uncertain who does. Therefore, the scenario reconstructed from the Pre-Cogs' original vision and deemed sufficiently accurate to arrest Anderton and send him into the Hall of Containment for the remainder of his life, ultimately documents serious discrepancies between the reassembled interpretation and the actual events. These revelations force speculation about how many other "criminals" may have suffered because of false readings: incarceration by misinterpretation. Given that viewers, watch these two "movies" with sometimes more and sometimes less information than the characters on the screen raises crucial questions about the complexities of spectatorship, the shifting truth of images, and the inherent subjectivity of visual information. On a metavisual level, nothing "real" ever happens, because everything the theater audience views in *Minority Report* is an elaborate illusion, literally pieces of celluloid passing in front of a light source that our imaginations endow with power and meaning.

From its first blurred image that slowly evolves into a distorted kiss between two unidentified characters, *Minority Report* fundamentally questions our sight: How do we see? What do we see? How do we understand what we see, or think we see? Not surprisingly, the film's imagery pattern primarily involves the eyes. As with the leitmotif of water, the film incorporates a vast array of spoken references to, and pictorial emphasis on, eyes. In the opening sequence, for example, the "precriminal" Howard Marks (Arye Gross) returns home for his glasses ("You know how blind I am without them"), only to find his wife (Ashley Crow) in bed with another man. Earlier, his son plunges a pair of scissors through the eyes of a cardboard picture of Abraham Lincoln, the same instrument Howard later attempts to drive into his unfaithful wife's eyes. A drug dealer who sells Anderton narcotics has no eyes, so he cannot be identified. "Can you see?" Agatha asks Anderton several times throughout the film, a physical as well as metaphysical question. "The eyes of the nation are upon us," Lamar Burgess tells Anderton in warning him about the upcoming vote on the Pre-Crime Unit. When the cops search for Anderton and Agatha, they "have got their eyes on them." One set of exotic flowers in Hineman's greenhouse are called "Doll's Eye," and, most importantly of all, the "mother of Pre-Crime" informs Anderton that "in order to see the light, you have to risk the dark."

The entire population in the year 2054 undergoes repeated retinal scans, a sophisticated verification procedure functioning as surveillance apparatus and consumer inducement: a citizen's identity is checked numerous times throughout the day, while manufacturers personally target him or her (through the eyes) to buy an array of products. In the future, the eyes are less the window to the soul than the path to the checkbook—or to jail. Such intrusions merely refine devices now routinely used at airports and received via e-mail. Spielberg, however, takes them to oppressive levels, especially in the visually stunning spider-hunt scene: when government agents search for Anderton, they release swarms of tiny, robotic spiders that leap onto the faces of innocent citizens and force them to endure retinal scans. The camera initially looks steeply downward into all the compartments of the tenement building and then, dipping and darting, it dashes along with the spiders from room to room as they visually interrogate its helpless inhabitants: frightened children, a couple making love, another man and woman fighting, an old man sitting on the toilet. Even in their most private moments, none can find sanctuary from the government's intrusive, and ultimately oppressive, tactics.

On a more literal level, Spielberg incorporates macabre humor within various scenes involving eyeballs. In an extended, creepy sequence, Anderton hires an unsavory criminal surgeon (Peter Stormare) to remove his own eyeballs and replace them with a set that will allow him to pass undetected through the ubiquitous retinal scans. Tied down, drugged, and with eyes clamped open in a scene that overtly references Kubrick's *A Clockwork Orange* (1971), a terrified Anderton belatedly realizes that his vision rests in the grimy hands of a once prominent plastic surgeon he sent to prison for setting his patients on fire so he could repair their burns. Blindfolded after the operation, able to feed and relieve himself only by pulling on ropes that lead to rancid food and a filthy toilet, the detective faces the prospect of literal blindness to accompany his metaphorical state. In a weirdly comic moment, Anderton desperately chases after his removed eyeballs as they careen down a hallway, only to watch one fall through a grate. Although he survives, Anderton never looks at the world in the same way again: the veil of certainty that surrounded his blind faith in the Pre-Cogs has been ripped away, replaced by a tattered and uncertain cloth that reveals the world as a more ambiguous and less trustworthy place. In a literal sense, and with a pun on the film's title, Anderton's view of the world is a "minority report," a picture from the perspective of a racial outsider—Mr. Yakamoto, the Asian whose eyes have been substituted for his own.

THE PHILOSOPHICAL

The repeated use of eye imagery throughout *Minority Report* leads to the film's philosophical level. Narrative events raise the ageless argument about whether human beings possess free will or are predestined by some higher power. Such debates are as ancient as *Oedipus Rex* (the drug dealer with empty eye sockets seems a modern counterpart of Tiresias, Sophocles's blind prophet) and as modern as the controversies swirling around the Human Genome Project. They are found in virtually every religious conceptualization, play a significant part in great and small literary works, and rest at the heart of endless philosophical speculations. Spielberg gives voice to this debate in an extended dialogue between two of his central characters, Anderton and the Justice Department agent Ed Witwer, the man sent to investigate the Pre-Crime Unit and, if it goes national, to replace Anderton. Initially, Anderton defends the fundamental philosophy of stopping crime before it happens, while Witwer asserts, "It's not the future if you stop it." Does knowing what the future holds automatically change it? As the plot progresses, both men shift their positions on this question. Witwer sees the Pre-Cogs' images of Anderton murdering a man and goes after him solely on that basis, never realizing that his interpretation arises from what he wants to see rather than what actually transpires. His lack of clear vision causes his death. Anderton learns that external events always have multiple interpretations.

In answering this conundrum about free will versus predestination, Spielberg has it both ways. "You can choose," Agatha the freed Pre-Cog tells Anderton as he faces Crow (Mike Binder), the man he thinks kidnapped his son. Yet the future acts projected by the Pre-Cogs do transpire: Anderton doesn't assassinate anyone, but a man still dies. Events remain the same, but the revelation of the conditions surrounding them alters how we read and understand them. The interpretations various characters draw from these physical facts contradict each other; more crucially, conclusions about Anderton's guilt result in incarcerating an innocent man and allowing the murderer to remain unpunished, at least for the time being. Ironically, Anderton's decision to overcome his rage and refrain from killing—arguably the most profoundly ethical action in the film—results in his moral rebirth, but not in any alteration of the predicted concrete actions. Since the forfeiture of individual freedoms inevitably leads to personal abuse, miscarriages of justice, and ultimately social repression, surrendering our liberties in a quest for public security is seen as far too high a price to pay. Ultimately, *Minor-*

ity Report warns us that even during times of widespread public anxiety, the motto of the Pre-Crime unit—"That which keeps us safe also keeps us free"—must be reversed: that which keeps us free also keeps us safe.

Spielberg as a "Fascist" Filmmaker

Commentators persist in labeling Spielberg's science-fiction movies as conservative. In one sense, this charge is understandable. Take *Close Encounters of the Third Kind* as an obvious example. From our current perspective, it strikes a jingoistic American chord: the kindly aliens choose the United States as a landing place; the only lost pilots brought back to the present are American; and a white, middle-class midwestern male represents the entire earth. The scientific team is headed by a Frenchman, but this hardly restrains the overwhelming emphasis on American culture and technological prowess celebrated in the film; in fact, it seems primarily an homage to the revered director Truffaut and the French New Wave, a movement and moviemaker Spielberg honored, rather than an attempt at multinationalism. When nonwestern cultures are depicted, such as the old Mexican who first sees the ship or the Indians who point upward in unison, they are hastily sketched, often unable to communicate without interpreters, and play decidedly small roles in the unfolding events.

Significantly, *Close Encounters* came into being during America's bicentennial celebration, a time awash in patriotic fervor and national pride. Yet for all the celebrations and commemorations, the country was still trying to assess what had gone wrong in the rice paddies of Vietnam. How could the most powerful nation in the world lose a war to a bunch of shoeless peasants in black pajamas? Given this historical moment, Vivian Sobchack astutely argues that the era ushered in by *Close Encounters* entailed "the revisioning of America's history of failure and guilt in Vietnam" ("Science" 228). At its center, therefore, the film reaffirms America's historical sense of Manifest Destiny, substituting space for the western frontier. The film clearly reconnects American culture to the lofty sense of national purpose that characterized, at least in retrospect, the Kennedy era: the challenge of putting men on the moon and the communal glory that supersedes petty differences. *Close Encounters* wraps itself in the flag; it identifies itself with the lunar landing in 1969 and not the assassinations and riots of 1968, with Neil Armstrong the astronaut and not Abbie Hoffman the revolutionary. Yet, *Close Encounters* offers the potentially liberating prospect of accepting variation and valuing distinction.

E.T., however, presents an even more ideologically conservative and circumscribed vision of difference than the earlier film. For all its overt attempt to confront "the Other," here pictured as a cute brown alien trapped on earth, Spielberg constructs otherness as essentially sameness: We have met the Other, and he is just like us. Indeed, E.T. wants nothing more than to "phone home" and ultimately return to his native soil. He is here on a temporary visa, not looking to become a citizen.

Spielberg never includes anything about life on E.T.'s planet and how it contrasts with that on earth. What are the political structures, social values, and cultural variations there? Do multiple species coexist peacefully? Are there class or gender differences? What do E.T. and his friends do for fun? Is the ability to heal with the touch of a finger a natural gift shared by all members of his species? Is it a learned skill, the result of a mechanical implant, or a native endowment? What do they eat? Do they like Jerry Lewis? Ultimately, E.T. is as funny, endearing, and nonthreatening as the stuffed animals among which he hides. The movie eases our fears by projecting an alien who, at least on the surface, seems more vulnerable to us than we are to it. As such, it never illuminates a true sense of variation or, for that mat-

A circumscribed view of difference: the alien Other as cute, cuddly, and socially acceptable minority in *E.T. the Extra-Terrestrial* (1982).

ter, strains our level of acceptance beyond mere recognition of emotional similarities beneath external differences.

Vivian Sobchack aptly describes the conservative nature of this narrative strategy in her discussion of *E.T.*:

> Articulation of resemblance between aliens and humans preserves the subordination of "other worlds, other cultures, other species" to the world, culture, and "speciality" of white American culture. We can see this new "humanism" literally expand into and colonize outer space, making it safe for democracy, multinational capitalism, and the Rolling Stones. (*Screening* 297)

Whereas Sobchack consistently lumps *E.T.* and *Close Encounters* together, however, seeing both as "nostalgic" and "conservative," I would argue that *Close Encounters* is the more ideologically progressive of the two. While some of the iconography remains the same in each film, from the visual inclusion of American fast-food franchises to the childrens' bedrooms stuffed with products of modern consumer culture, the films display more significant thematic differences than she allows in her argument. As one obvious example, whereas E.T. appears defenseless and survives more by guile than force, Spielberg depicts the aliens in *Close Encounters* as more technologically advanced, and hence more powerful, than their human counterparts: E.T. is greeted mainly with affection, the aliens with respect.

A far more strident note is struck in pieces by Tony Williams, Frank P. Tomasulo, Robert Entman and Francie Seymour, and Andrew Britton. In one of the harshest condemnations of Spielberg, Robert Kolker cites Leni Riefenstahl's Nazi documentary *Triumph of the Will* (1935) as the structural paradigm for *Close Encounters* and labels it "a quasi-fascist solution to society's problems" (140–41). Drawing heavily on Susan Sontag's famous essay "Fascinating Fascism," Kolker calls the movie an "example of fascist form" that keeps the audience "submissive" for its duration, "dehumanizes" the filmgoer, reduces viewers to a "function of the sound and images confronting them," and culminates in "the yearning to yield to something more exciting than the merely human that will relieve us of responsibility" (143). Such an attack on Spielberg in general, and *Close Encounters* in particular, provides an intriguing example of how commentators treat the most financially successful director in Hollywood history far differently from others who proffer the same essential vision in less profitable works.

Kolker's assault comes in the midst of a generally astute and significant auteurist study of Spielberg and four other American directors: Arthur Penn, Stanley Kubrick, Martin Scorsese, and Robert Altman. It is part of his extended defense of *2001: A Space Odyssey*, a film assailed by Sontag for its "fascist aesthetics ... [that] glorifies surrender, exalts mindlessness, [and] glamorizes death" ("Fascinating" 40). Kolker mounts his defense of Kubrick's film, and consequently his denigration of *Close Encounters*, by arguing that *2001* "does not create the kind of insistence, the rhythmical structuring ... that is part of the fascist model" (127) and that Spielberg's picture "creates a formal pattern of assent and submission" in its very design (128). Let me harken back to Sontag's initial definition in defending the film: *Close Encounters* does precisely the opposite of glorifying surrender, exalting mindlessness, or glamorizing death. In his all-consuming quest to understand his profoundly disturbing experience, Roy Neary chooses to rebel against the strictures of middle-class family life, to defy the threats of the military forces, and to challenge the men of science leading this expedition. He stands outside the worlds of military power and space research, and his actions isolate him from the relative safety and social values of his suburban community. In essence, he resists acceding to some of the most powerful forces in our society: the lure of the family, the arm of the government, and the authority of professional expertise. It is also crucial to remember that Neary is only one of two "civilians" who reach Devil's Tower and the only one invited aboard the spacecraft. That he willingly goes is not, as many critics would have it, a moment of mindless surrender but one of deliberate choice.

Such actions represent a defiant resistance to personal and social pressures, not submissive behavior or, as Sontag describes it, "the turning of people into things ... the orgiastic transition between mighty forces and their puppets" ("Fascinating" 40). Neary refuses to become a puppet of the state. Indeed, the aliens likely select him and not the government-sponsored representatives—who resemble Nazi storm troopers, in contrast to Neary's rotund figure and nonmilitary bearing—because he embodies the individual revolutionary impulse, that spark of stubborn dissent that ignites an unwillingness to embrace socially acceptable alternatives. Far from embodying Sontag's fascist aesthetic that "exalts ... egomania and servitude" (40), Roy Neary fits within a long line of distinctively American literary and film characters whose obsessive individualism evolves into the madness of rare and singular purposes, figures such as Ahab (*Moby Dick*), Ethan Edwards (*The Searchers*), Thomas Dunson (*Red River*), and even Norman Bates (*Psycho*). These men never secure a comfortable space in society because the demons that drive them allow for no peace, no love, and no contentment. They remain fixated on a vision so strong and narrow that it obliterates any other possibilities. Ultimately, Neary is vindicated. Unlike Ahab and Bates, whose obsessions destroy them, or Edwards and Dunson, who reach a sad accord with them, he finds himself headed for the stars, a triumph of rugged persistence over common sense and state control.

On a basic narrative level, therefore, Neary's actions directly counter Sontag's definition of fascist art, which Kolker dutifully echoes to denounce *Close Encounters*. But what about the film's visual structure and thematic implications? Kolker claims that "the viewer is allowed as little free will as the characters," that a series of expertly crafted cinematic techniques effectively works to "reduce the spectator to an accepting position," and that the film provides "no place to move emotionally and no place to think" (142). His assertions rest on the rickety assumption that viewers react uniformly to the film when, as cinema theorists persuasively argue and audience demographers aptly demonstrate, filmgoers read even overtly didactic visual messages in widely divergent ways, mainly due to their individual backgrounds and particular psyches. By insisting that his judgment of *Close Encounters* is the only possible response, and contending that the film itself permits only that reaction, Kolker practices criticism the way he indicts Spielberg for making movies: not allowing the possibility of diverse thoughts and opinions. In addition, using Alfred Hitchcock (whom Kolker himself quotes as saying how satisfying it is to use cinematic art to achieve "mass emotion" [143]) to defend a Kubrick film and then attacking Spielberg for creating a "submissive" viewer strikes me as somewhat perverse. One could not find two more manipulative filmmakers, two cinema artists who more possessively control every aspect within and between the frames, than Stanley Kubrick and Alfred Hitchcock.

Returning to Kolker's main critique, let me focus on his discussion of Spielberg's techniques. He cites the following elements as primarily responsible for creating "submissive" viewers and claims that they are derived from Riefenstahl's infamous propaganda film: "Extremes of dark and light, a predominance of low-angle shots and rapid dollies toward figures and objects, the incredible size of the space paraphernalia" (142). While I fully agree with Kolker's contention that "no work of cinema . . . is ideologically innocent and Spielberg is responsible for the formal construction of the film" (142), his implicit assumption that specific techniques result in particular, and seemingly one-dimensional, viewer responses remains questionable. An expansive, low-angle shot that fills the screen with a huge spacecraft passing overhead may well inspire awe; it might also stimulate claustrophobia, anger, admiration, confusion, fear, or nothing at all. Context is all in films. The way images connect and bounce off each other, sometimes within the same frame and certainly between frames, establishes meanings that vary with different viewers.

I am not arguing for a reception theory that allows any and all interpretations simply by virtue of the fact that we are all individuals with unique histories. However, the same techniques used in different films can render disparate emotions and even contradictory themes, whether by accident or design. It is well known, for example, that Nazi filmmakers cut and edited scenes from Hollywood films (like *The House of Rothschild* [1934]), which portrayed Jews positively, to convey their anti-Semitic philosophy visually. Similarly, and in a deliciously ironic transposition, the director Frank Capra inserted scenes from *Triumph of the Will* in *Why We Fight* (1943) to illustrate the evils of Hitler's totalitarian regime—certainly not what Riefenstahl planned when she filmed them as a paean to Hitler's greatness. To argue, therefore, that technical choices such as lighting, shot selection, camera angles, and other elements restrict viewer reactions to singular responses ignores, on the basic level, the decisive results of editing and, on a broader scale, the multiplicity of possible outcomes. It presupposes that any given text has limited inherent meanings, that even widely disparate viewers have little choice but to interpret ideas similarly, and that multiple and often contradictory readings cannot occur as viewers watch the same scene. Kolker's argument therefore conflicts with much contemporary thought on film analysis and interpretation, especially persuasive notions about the inherently polysemic nature of all texts.

Contrary to the contentions of Kolker and other critics who malign the director as a fascist filmmaker and cite *Close Encounters* as evidence, Spielberg's film represents a radical departure from the antagonistic attitude toward difference embedded deeply in the traditions of the science-fiction film genre. Judith Hess Wright remarks that the 1940s and 1950s science-fiction films clearly "build on fears of intrusion and overpowering and thereby promote isolationism" (48). This observation seems universally accepted by film historians and scholars. Yet these same commentators usually ignore how radically Spielberg cuts against the grain of this xenophobia. Particularly in *Close Encounters,* he transforms the persistent distrust of elements foreign to American culture into an acceptance and respect for deviations. Though most commentators characterize it with words such as "conservative," "regressive," and "nostalgic," *Close Encounters* presents a more progressive, tolerant, and even cosmopolitan vision of the universe than the vast majority of the science-fiction films preceding it.

Even more importantly, Spielberg's depiction of aliens (not "spacemen," as Kolker calls them, for they are neither human nor gendered) dramatically reverses the paranoia and cold-war fears typically found in previous features about outer-space creatures: "The other, however strange and alien, had at least some significant relation to those massed hordes of Communists foisted on the American people by such venomous Red-baiters as Joseph McCarthy, Richard Nixon, and Billy Graham" (Wright 46). Since *Close Encounters* militates precisely against these right-wing attitudes, one wonders why critics disparage rather than embrace Spielberg for fashioning a liberal, humanistic vision of respect and acceptance that effectively overturns the genre's ideological conservatism. The film's popular success profoundly influenced the way the general public perceived and future filmmakers treated interactions with aliens. By moving beyond parochial concerns to offer endorsement—and even reverence—for fundamental differences, *Close Encounters* welcomes the mysterious, embraces the distinctive, and sanctifies the unconventional.

*   *   *

Spielberg's science-fiction films offer a surprising range of perspectives, from the ideologically orthodox (*E.T.*), to the liberally humanistic (*Close Encounters*), to the radically unconventional (*A.I.*), to the morally dystopic (*Minority Report*). The indisputable fact that *Close Encounters* and *E.T.* resonated deeply within the American psyche, that *A.I.* has become one of the most controversial films of its time, and that *Minority Report* proved politically prophetic demands close scrutiny beyond explicating the secrets of their special effects, detailing their box-office receipts, revealing events during their creation, and marking their biographical connection to Spielberg. While such approaches can be worthwhile and certainly have their place within cinema studies, their domination in books and articles about these films neglects significant aspects of them. Reception of *Close Encounters, E.T., A.I.,* and *Minority Report* by a vast moviegoing public, in the United States and around the world, calls for sustained, scholarly analysis of their emotional power, their narrative constructions, their visual artistry, and ultimately, their thematic insights.

2

"They Don't Know What They've Got There": Spielberg's Action/Adventure Melodramas

The Action/Adventure Melodrama

Although few critics discuss Spielberg's films as melodramas, almost all of them could aptly be classified as family-based narratives that center on the tensions, fissures, and breakdowns within domestic relationships. It is worthwhile, therefore, to review the cardinal tenets of the melodrama genre, noting how it connects to the action/adventure format commonly associated with Spielberg throughout his career. Traditionally, the film melodrama focuses on either an individual (usually a woman) or a couple "victimized by repressive and inequitable social situations, particularly those involving marriage, occupation, and the nuclear family" (Schatz, *Genres* 222). Its emphasis on the family, an individualized unit simultaneously bound to and defined by broad issues of cultural demarcation and signification, endowed the melodrama with the potential for social commentary made palatable to middle-class viewers by its commonplace and communal settings. However, just beneath the entertaining surface of these highly emotional but seemingly escapist trifles lies a deep and consistent tension between supporting the ideology that nurtured its existence and criticizing its fundamental assumptions

The melodrama, therefore, remains a genre of frustration and fulfillment, a "paradoxical view of America, at once celebrating and severely questioning the basic values and attitudes of the mass audience" (Schatz, *Genres* 223). It often disparages entrenched social values in its narrative flow, while its resolution "invariably reaffirms, however implausibly, the cultural status quo" (238). In the hands of sophisticated directors like Douglas Sirk, Vincente Minnelli, and Nicholas Ray, Hollywood melodramas (particularly in the 1950s) emerged as incisive if submerged critiques of American family life and, by extension, of dominant American values: "[T]he tensions of seeming and being, of intention and result, register as a perplexing frustration . . . that has turned the American dream into its proverbial nightmare" (Elsaesser, "Tales" 378). By forcing audiences to recognize and then measure the distance between the everyday world as they know it and the ideal world of their imaginations, the best melodramas reflect on the cultural expectations and social constructions that forge our personal and communal identities.

The heroes and heroines of melodrama suffer for our sins; their torment caused by the intolerance, rigidity, and repressive codes of the conventional social order establishes and confirms them as innocent victims worthy of our compassion and admiration. Thus, melodramatic characters attain moral status chiefly through their suffering. We are forced to share their perspectives, feel their pain, and understand their plight: "[T]he victim-hero gains empathy that is equated with moral virtue through suffering" (Williams, "Melodrama" 66). Like players in a Greek tragedy, these victim-heroes battle against powerful social forces beyond their control; but ultimately they must either resign themselves or be crushed, not by the ancient gods but by the ladies of the local PTA. Audiences share their suffering, reacting (some critics say overreacting) with a spontaneous flow of strong emotional responses. "The capacity to shift very rapidly from one extreme feeling to another . . . to arouse direct and immediate emotion in its audience" (Cawelti 264) remains a key element in melodramas and, not coincidentally, plays a crucial role in the immense popularity of Spielberg's most successful films.

On first glance, yoking the melodrama (dominated by women, emotional situations, and domestic issues) with the action/adventure film (dominated by men, physical escapades, and external conflicts) would seem implausible. After all, the action cinema inevitably locates its adventurous hero far from the concerns of everyday life, often in the romanticized past or an exotic location, while the melodrama situates its conflicted heroine securely in the mundane world of hearth and home. Yet the two share some tantalizing connections. Extreme physical and violent actions are not inherently antithetical to melodrama; they generate the suffering crucial for strong, empathetic viewer responses. The action hero also suffers, and often bleeds profusely, whether he is John McClane (Bruce Willis) in the *Die Hard* series, Sylvester Stallone as Rocky or Rambo, Ripley (Sigourney Weaver) in the *Alien* series, or Harrison Ford as Indiana Jones. While the action/adventure film incorporates physical exploits as one of its key ingredients, the real focus of the narrative is "the character of the hero and the nature of the obstacles he has to overcome" (Cawelti 40). As we will see, action/adventure cinema is really about the hero's moral education, about how events test his physical courage and ethical imagination and force him to alter his perspective radically from the beginning of a film to its ending.

The melodrama and the action/adventure film share intense suffering and fundamental dynamics of intensified feeling and motion. As Linda Williams astutely notes, "The climax revealing the moral good of the victim can tend in one of two directions: paroxysm of pathos or channelled into the more virile and action-centered variants of rescue, chase, and fight" ("Melodrama" 58). The difference is that protagonists of the melodrama must bear whips and arrows imposed by representatives of a vast social network of values, while the action/adventure heroes endure suffering as a necessary prelude to glorious deeds of bravery and valor. Melodrama shows a communal punishment for challenging the prevailing social mores; action/adventure displays an individual victory by overcoming tremendous personal odds. Thomas Schatz splices many of the best action/adventure films and melodramas together when he identifies their narrative-thematic core as "a metaphoric search for the ideal husband/lover/father who, as American mythology would have it, will stabilize the family and integrate it into the larger community" (Schatz, *Genres* 235). Such a search inevitably turns up in Spielberg's films, even in those action/adventure movies that may seem simply like nostalgic, escapist entertainments. Thus, melodramas often incorporate crucial elements of the adventure/action genre, while action/adventure films rely on characteristic melodramatic ingredients, though most critics rarely acknowledge this hybridization in Spielberg's works.

Spielberg's Action/Adventure Melodramas

"I don't think I've ever *not* made a melodrama," Spielberg told an audience in June 1988 at the American Film Institute's Center for Advanced Film and Television Studies (Spielberg 13). His films fuse intense feelings to spectacular actions, yoking the physical and the emotional. In any particular segment of a Spielberg movie, either emotion or action may take precedence, but his uncanny ability to merge masterful action sequences with increasingly developed character progressions is crucial to his sustained success. His films that failed to find an audience, such as *1941, Hook,* or *Always,* arguably are overloaded with either action or pathos, the director paying too little attention to one or the other side of the equation. Conversely, his more popular films such as the Indiana Jones cycle, despite their seeming dependence on rapidly edited and thrillingly scored chase-catch-lose-chase set pieces, reflect the skillful wedding of action to feeling, a combination that is also evident in *The Sugarland Express* and *Catch Me If You Can*. All of these films infuse deep family emotions into externalized action occuring mainly on the road, constructed as an extended series of escalating chase sequences but really representing all-consuming psychological drives.

Unlike standard adventure movies, the compelling motivations for these journeys in *The Sugarland Express* and *Catch Me If You Can* radiate not from the characters' desire for external goals (such as money, fame, or escape) but rather from domestic obsessions: a mother and son's struggle to reconstitute their shattered families. Each yearns to acquire the unobtainable. Lou Jean believes that capturing her infant will recoup her lost domestic equilibrium, while Frank Abagnale Jr. embarks on his crime spree to reunite his parents. In the throes of maternal and filial sufferings, these compulsive figures veer far beyond the white lines of socially (and legally) acceptable behavior, and ultimately both are cruelly deluded. Their quests for secure households, which each nostalgically and unrealistically idealizes, result in permanent domestic disintegrations. Lou Jean causes the death of her husband and never regains custody of Baby Langston. Frank lands in prison in France and then America, his mother remarries, and his father dies. Thus, two of Spielberg's most realistic features about contemporary American life conclude not with joyous reconciliation scenes so common in his fantasy movies but rather with irreparably demolished families whose members remain incapable of enduring emotional stability.

The Sugarland Express: Beyond the Screen

Spielberg's first theatrically released feature was *The Sugarland Express,* a film inspired by an Associated Press story in the May 2, 1969, issue of the *Hollywood Citizen-News.* Under a provocative headline proclaiming a doomed Texas couple, Bobby and Ila Faye Dent, the "New Bonnie 'n' Clyde," Spielberg discovered a tantalizing slice of Americana he later characterized as "'a tragic fairy tale'" (qtd. in McBride 178). The plot follows the skeletal outline of events described in that enticing article: a young Texas couple, renamed Lou Jean (Goldie Hawn) and Clovis (William Atherton) Poplin, kidnap and hold hostage an inexperienced highway patrolman, Maxwell Slide (Michael Sacks). In exchange for his release, they demand a reunion with their baby son, recently adopted by foster parents because of the Poplins' criminal record. Their quest to retrieve Baby Langston progresses from an initially comic misadventure into a progressively more disastrous tragedy, the hapless couple traveling across the bleak Texas landscape trailed by a phalanx of police vehicles under the direction of an alternatingly sympathetic and exasperated Captain Tanner (Ben Johnson).

Looking back at *The Sugarland Express* in light of Spielberg's subsequent career, one can isolate basic thematic elements that recur throughout his more mature and better-known movies. At its uneasy center, the director paints a disturbing portrait of a disintegrating American family and the fragmented culture that surrounds it; a frayed and splintered family unit seeks personal reconciliation and redemption. On a broader level, a young couple battles a father figure representing society's authority to sacrifice dissenters on the altar of communal justice. While the film's setting and characters diverge from the middle-class milieu so effectively manipulated in his later works, Spielberg pinpoints the disruption of natural bonds between parents and their children as symbolic of the overall collapse of contemporary culture. Thus, *Sugarland*'s basic structure counterposes an intimate story within and against public events, each commenting upon and often contradicting the other—a narrative device common in his subsequent films.

Spielberg's interviews around the time of the film's release reveal a director far more concerned with public issues than with private psychodrama. He described the movie as "highly political" and a "terrible indictment of the media" for fostering this "circus on wheels" in which people seek to make themselves famous "by doing the smallest, most simple, neurotic act" (Helpren 6). Contrary to what one might expect from a mid-seventies film undertaken by a young director in the midst of the turbulent countercultural revolution, Spielberg's inherent sympathies lay not with the alienated couple but with the police, whom he characterizes as "the heroes of the picture" (Helpren 5). Equally interesting for a man who was eventually to become the most broadly popular and commercially successful moviemaker in history, Spielberg remains extremely wary of the adoring masses, the faceless throng of autograph seekers and back-slappers who track Lou Jean and Clovis, whom he identifies as the film's "villains" (Helpren 6).

VISUAL ANALYSIS

On the technical side, *Sugarland* demonstrates Spielberg's emerging visual dexterity. His cinematographer, the Hungarian-born Vilmos Zsigmond, had already gained recognition as a skilled visual artist from his work with directors such as Robert Altman (*McCabe and Mrs. Miller* [1971] and *The*

Long Goodbye [1973]) and John Boorman (*Deliverance* [1972]). Zsigmond's aesthetic sensibility and European training clearly influenced the film's documentary quality; he often used available lighting and ambient sound to fashion a distinctly non-Hollywood texture that Spielberg achieved again only with *Schindler's List* and in the beach-landing segment of *Saving Private Ryan*. Zsigmond also employed one of Altman's favorite techniques, zooming and panning simultaneously to shift the audience's perspective with smooth and subtle, rather than abrupt and disconcerting, movements. In addition, the film's visual construction benefited greatly by the arrival of a newly developed camera, the highly mobile and almost silent Panaflex, which allowed Spielberg and Zsigmond to execute highly innovative and technically complicated maneuvers inside and around the speeding vehicles driven by the Poplins and the police.

As William S. Gilmore Jr., the film's unit production manager, notes with evident admiration:

> "We shot a 360–degree pan inside a car with dialogue. That had never been done before. It was the first film that had a dolly shot *inside* a car moving from the front to the back seat. We did a dolly shot into the back seat at thirty-five miles per hour." (Qtd. in McBride 218)

Though Zsigmond and Spielberg frequently clashed, each ultimately gained enormous respect for the other. Spielberg claimed that they "were almost brothers on our movie" (Bobrow 22), and Zsigmond said, "'I can only compare him to Orson Welles'" (qtd. in McBride 218). *The Sugarland Express* also marked Spielberg's first collaboration with the composer John Williams (who scored all of his pictures except *The Color Purple*) and the editor Verna Fields (a crucial collaborator on *Jaws* who was replaced by Michael Kahn in his subsequent films).

One shot provides ample evidence of Spielberg's consummate grasp of visually communicating drama, emotion, and meaning. Adumbrating the justly famous beach sequence in *Jaws,* he fuses a dolly and zoom shot late in the picture, when Clovis, Lou Jean, and Officer Slide finally arrive at the house that they erroneously believe holds Baby Langston. Gilmore aptly describes this striking moment: "'The foreground and background were juxtaposed, with the people in the car and the sharpshooters in the same relation to each other. With two tools fighting [the zoom and dolly] against each other, he literally froze time'" (qtd. in McBride 218). That a young director could even conceive of, much less flawlessly execute, such a technically complex shot is astounding, but it functions as more than a flamboyant stylistic flourish. By constructing this capsule of suspended animation, Spielberg fuses the hunters and the hunted into an eerie nexus of intense desire and fatal deception. In so doing, he shuts down time and makes the audience hold its breath: we recognize that Clovis is about to die, hope something will appear to avert this tragedy, and at the same time know that nothing can be done to prevent it. Such a clash of intellect and emotion, of concurrently realizing what must happen and hoping it won't, shows Spielberg at his most skillful and most manipulative.

It is tantalizing to speculate about the direction Spielberg's career might have taken if *The Sugarland Express* had been more widely successful; if it, rather than *Jaws*, had resulted in his initial triumph. Pauline Kael, for one, recognized something special. She noted the presence of a "natural entertainer" who could become "a new generation's Howard Hawks," understood that "composition seems to come naturally to him, as it does to some of the young Italians," and declared that "this film is one of the most phenomenal debut films in the history of the movies" (Kael 559). But worrying that Spielberg may be "so full of it [movie sense] that he doesn't have much else," the *New Yorker* critic paid him a decidedly backhanded compliment: "[H]e's one of those wizard directors who can make trash entertaining" (559). If *Sugarland* had been a resounding hit, Spielberg might have veered toward social commentary rather then escapist fantasy. His visual style might have continued as a uniquely American version of neorealism, emphasizing natural locations and lighting, episodic plots, and working-class characters facing common events. Though such conjectures seem perverse when discussing the most commercially celebrated filmmaker of all time, it is important to recognize that, for Spielberg, *Sugarland* represents a road not taken.

Catch Me If You Can: Beyond the Screen

Most critics, and even the filmmakers themselves, consistently describe *Catch Me If You Can* as a bouncy, frothy work, a mental furlough for Spielberg after the brutal, dark dramas of *A.I.* and *Minority Report*. As Spielberg puts it on the bonus features disc accompanying the DVD, "I thought this would be a breath of fresh air for me. I enjoy that whiplash sensation of going from a film like *Jurassic Park* to *Schindler's List*." Summing up his feelings about the film, the director uses phrases such as "a dessert of a movie" and "pure, unadultered fun." On that same disc, the cinematographer Janusz Kaminski characterizes the visual approach as bubbly: "Let's have fun. Let's create a world that's . . . not too serious. The lighting reflects that. It's like a glass of champagne." Despite its superficial cleverness, breezy tone, and colorful exteriors, however, *Catch Me If You Can* clearly falls within the parameters of the action/adventure melodrama, particularly in its emphasis on the family and sense of movement, its consistent interrogation and ultimate reaffirmation of the status quo, its suffering hero battling overwhelming social forces, its focus on the protagonist's moral education, its intensified feelings and emotion, its intrinsic structural anxiety, and its engaging visual pleasures.

THE DARK SIDE

For all its superficially diverting charms, *Catch Me If You Can* explores the dark side of the American Dream of financial success and familial stability. In the film's first flashback, a dirty, disheveled, and desperately sick Frank Abagnale Jr. (Leonardo DiCaprio) lies spread-eagled on the floor of a Marseille prison on Christmas Eve 1969, looking up sadly at FBI agent Carl Hanratty (Tom Hanks) and pleading with his long-time adversary to help him "go home." But his memory of Christmases past draws him back six years to a smoky New Rochelle Rotary Club Meeting, where his father is inducted as a lifetime member. Introduced by the club's president (James Brolin), Frank Senior (Christopher Walken) strides to the podium amidst a standing ovation by the roomful of middle-aged men—dressed identically in dark suits, white shirts, and dull ties—and proceeds to thank his loving wife Paula (Nathalie Baye) and his beaming son seated at the table in front of the dais. He launches into a story that he has repeated many times before, one that will become an ironic metaphor for the entire film:

> Two little mice fell in a bucket of cream. The first mouse quickly gave up and drowned. The second mouse wouldn't quit. He struggled so hard that eventually he churned that cream into butter and crawled out. Gentlemen, as of this moment, I am the second mouse.

Spielberg shifts from this triumphant moment, capped by father and son embracing, to a picture-perfect suburban house with a new white Cadillac sitting majestically in front, statues of Joseph and Mary and baby Jesus adorning the lawn—a snapshot that encapsulates how financial achievement and religious practice have become equated in American society. Ultimately, we come to see that Frank Abagnale Sr., drunk on fantasies of post–World War II prosperity, is cut from the same tattered cloth as Willy Loman, another sorrowful dreamer who exists "out there in the blue riding on a smile and a shoeshine" (Miller 105), a tainted legacy both men pass on to their sons.

Cut to a close-up of a vinyl record spinning on the turntable. The silky strains of Judy Garland singing "Embraceable You" drift through the tastefully decorated living room, its fireplace decked with colorful lights and red stockings, a shimmering Christmas tree in the window, and glowing candles set on tables and walls. We hear Paula's voice offscreen telling her son, "You're a better dancer than your father, Frankie." Though the father, hanging his treasured Rotary award on the wall, gently disagrees, he proceeds to repeat the narrative of how he first met his wife, another tale the son can repeat word for word. Spinning around with a glass of red wine in her hand, Paula accidently spills some drops on the beige rug, sending Frankie for a towel to blot out the stain. When he returns, he sees his parents dancing elegantly around the room. "Whenever I dance for you I get in trouble," Paula playfully chides her husband as they step on the dark wine stains, embedding them deeply into the carpet. An admiring Frankie watches as his father gracefully dips his tipsy mother but keeps his eyes directly on his son. It is a moment of male bonding and eroticism—as the father teaches his son how to sweep women off their feet by using his mother as the model—and an idyllic portrait of the All-American family frozen in time: the prosperous father, the adoring mother, and the respectful adolescent primed to emulate his dad.

But it is a moment carved in sand, a tantalizingly cruel illusion of security and stability that the rest of the film will splash away. The father proves an inept hustler and a failure, the mother betrays him by having an affair with and then marrying another man, and the son becomes a notorious counterfeit-check forger hunted by the FBI. Frank Senior's debonair dance on the drops of wine that soil the carpet becomes an apt metaphor for his failure to clean up life's difficult problems: instead of acknowledging their presence, he performs charming but meaningless gestures that leave permanent stains. He believes, and teaches his son, that appearances matter more than fundamental abilities, a philosophy summed up in his second homily: "You know why the Yankees always win, Frank?" Brushing aside his son's logical reply that it's "'cause they have Mickey Mantle," he answers, "It's because the other teams cannot stop staring at those damn pinstripes." Frank Junior spends the rest of the movie clothing himself, figuratively, in pinstripes and avoiding reality. When his parents split up and he is asked to choose between living with his father or his mother, the boy simply cannot make that decision and instead runs off to Grand Central Station to begin his own life of lies.

RUPTURED FAMILIES

Catch Me If You Can offers yet another Spielberg portrait of a ruptured family, echoing a compulsive theme of abandoned children that pervades his cinematic landscape. In this film, as in *Empire of the Sun, Hook, Indiana Jones and the Last Crusade, War of the Worlds,* and *Saving Private Ryan,* the director explores the often fragile relationships between sons and fathers, both biological and adopted. Late in the film, Frank surprises his father in a New York City barroom and invites him to attend his wedding, only to hear the older man congratulate him for his illegal activities. "You got their number," he proudly tells his son. "You got 'em scared. The United States government running for the hills." Frank, uncertain how to respond to this praise, tells him, "It's over. I'm gonna stop now," and entreats his father for some parental guidance or restraint. "Ask me to stop now," he begs. "Ask me to stop." He receives instead another piece of his dad's myopic, inappropriate advice. "You can't stop," he responds, and then embellishes his illusion as his son flees the room: "Where you going tonight? Someplace exotic. Tahiti. Hawaii." Frank Junior actualizes, at least for a time, his father's failed dream of beating, or at least fooling, the government. Once he is caught, he lives out the reality of his father's actual life: in jail, Frank delivers the mail, just as his father did to pay the bills after losing his business.

Frank Junior's first pseudo–father figure, Roger Strong (Martin Sheen), is a more successful version of Frank Senior and a man equally consumed by appearances. He banishes his daughter Brenda (Amy Adams) after his golfing buddy gets her pregnant and she has an abortion, only to welcome her back with open arms when she returns as the fiancée of a doctor-turned-lawyer-turned-Lutheran. Even when Frank attempts to tell him the truth about who he is, declaring, "I am nothing really. Just a kid who is in love with your daughter," Roger insists on seeing him through his own lens as "a romantic," declaring that "men like us are nothing without the women we love. I am guilty of the same foolish whimsy." Frank, eager to join this replacement for his own destroyed family, passes the Louisiana Bar, takes a job with his future father-in-law in the New Orleans district attorney's office, and happily joins the Strongs on the family couch singing along with Mitch Miller to the strains of "Has Anybody Here Seen Kelly?" In a touching scene tinged with regret, Frank gently smiles as, unobserved, he watches Roger and his wife (Nancy Lenehan) sway shoulder-to-shoulder doing the dishes together and listening (as did his biological parents) to Garland's "Embraceable You." Another seemingly idyllic snapshot of family harmony and love, this scene airbrushes out the ugly past and the precarious future for the Strong family—particularly its newest member, whose whole identity rests upon an assortment of glossy deceptions.

If Frank Senior is the permissive daddy and Roger Strong the seductive father, the monochromatic Carl Hanratty embodies the tough-love parent. Earlier, when Frank suavely repeats his father's question about the Yankees during his initial Christmas Eve call to the humiliated agent, Carl responds with a refreshing dose of New England common sense: "The Yankees win because they have Mickey Mantle. No one ever bets on their uniforms." While Frank has lost his father because of a divorce, Carl, in a similar marital upheaval, rarely sees his daughter, Grace. Each man, therefore, needs the other to fill a hole in his emotional life. The dyspeptic Hanratty does not offer Frank the easy cons of his biological parent—"I won't lie to you," he tells the young man, clearly differentiating himself from Frank Senior and the glazed vision of Roger Strong. Instead, he proffers harsh reality: "You're gonna get caught," he tells Frank. "It's like Vegas, the house always wins." He understands that Frank did not seek him out to apologize on Christmas Eve but rather that he has "no one else to call." Ultimately, Carl saves Frank by

"I won't lie to you," Carl Hanratty (Tom Hanks), the tough-love father figure, warns his wayward surrogate son, Frank Abagnale Jr. (Leonardo DiCaprio), in *Catch Me If You Can* (2003).

forcing him to take responsibility for his actions. He obtains permission to extradite him back to the United States, saving him from further deterioration in the French jail, brings him comic books in prison, and helps him obtain a job in the FBI's Financial Crime Unit (the check-fraud division, naturally). Though Carl fully understands that it can be "easier living a lie" than facing the tough, daily realities of life, he offers Frank a realistic alternative to the destructive delusions shared by his father and Roger Strong.

Along with this acceptance comes a concomitant loss of the enticing illusions created and sustained by an incessant flow of media fantasies that throw shimmering images on the walls of the cave. Frank learned how to deceive others by studying fictional doctors and lawyers on television, how to dress by emulating James Bond in *Goldfinger,* how to fit into the Strong family by singing along with Mitch, and how to assume fictional names by reading comic books (*Flash*). In one of the film's most interesting sequences, Spielberg crosscuts between Frank seducing a former *Seventeen* cover girl, Cheryl Ann (Jennifer Garner), and Carl washing his shirts in a late-night laundromat, a pseudo-domestic sphere similar to the one David Mann inhabits for a short time in *Duel.* It begins with a shift in music from the jazzy James Bond theme to Dusty Springfield languidly singing the syrupy Burt Bacharach/Hal David classic, "The Look of Love." Spielberg opens the seduction with a shot of their expensive shoes rather than their expressive faces: her stiletto heels adorned with jewel-encrusted straps, and his highly polished black shoes. As they begin to banter, Spielberg abruptly cuts to a bored Hanratty, arms folded across his chest.

Wedged between two older women, each reading *Post* magazine as the rotating machines drone into the night air, he sits as a brooding presence over the ensuing events. Panning right, the shot ends in a close-up of the soapy, churning wash, as Spielberg dissolves to Frank and Cheryl kissing romantically in his plush hotel room, Springfield's voice again wafting around them. But here Spielberg cynically undercuts the action. Instead of a conventional romantic interlude reminiscent of 1950s movies, he transforms the apparent seduction into a business arrangement. Frank agrees to buy Cheryl Ann for a thousand dollars, pays with a counterfeit fourteen-hundred-dollar check, and gets back four hundred dollars in change. Meanwhile, an exasperated Hanratty pulls his previously white shirts, now pink, from the washing machine, along with a small red sweater that has dyed all of them. Sex and love, like everything else depicted in the movies, is also a media-made delusion, a commodity paid for by those involved. The smiling model on the cover of the wholesome teen magazine has grown up to be a prostitute, selling her body and not only her image to the highest bidder. Real life is filled with little exasperations and few rewards, but trivial truths ultimately prove more sustainable than romantic illusions.

Like many of Spielberg's characteristic movies, *Catch Me If You Can* centers around a threat to the family. In this case, there is only a minimal happy ending, and the actual dissolution of his family sends Frank into his criminal life. He is drawn to Brenda, braces and all, not because of who she is but because he can reunite her with the rest of her family—and find a place for himself as he does so. He relates to Carl because he, too, often finds himself alone on Christmas Eve, bereft of wife and child on that most family-centered night of the year. Spielberg told Jeff Giles that Frank "saw the banks and the IRS systematically break down his father's spirit. It's like a revenge story in a lot of ways. He went out to attack the big corporations, and tried to piece his life and his father's spirit back together" (59–60). He struggles to re-create what has been irrevocably lost, buying Frank Senior a 1965 Cadillac to replace the one he had to sell and telling him, "I'm gonna get it all back, Daddy, I promise. I'm gonna get it all back." Ironically, the only one who does "get it back" is Frank's mother, starting a new life and having another child with her ex-husband's best friend.

When a distraught Frank learns his father is dead, having broken his neck in a fall while trying to catch a train in Grand Central Station, he escapes from Hanratty's custody and makes his way back to his mother's new home, one reminiscent of the one she shared with him and his father. Watching her through a frost-etched window, he comes face-to-face with a little girl who enters the frame within the frame playing a harmonica. When Frank asks, "Where's your Mommy?" she turns and points to the mother they share. A stricken Frank begs Carl, who has arrived with the local police, to "get me in the car, please. Get me in the car." Frank's last glimpse of his mother is accompanied by Nat King Cole singing "The Christmas Song": in the background she stands with her husband and their daughter in their front doorway, set off and enclosed by a semicircle of Christmas lights; in the midground is the blurred hood of the police car; in the bottom foreground a red police light flashes, and at the top, in the rear-view mirror, an image of the stunned Frank Abagnale Jr. floats in space, seemingly disconnected from the world around him. As the scene fades out, the Nat King Cole song continues and, along with it, the stern voice of a judge sentences Frank to twelve years in Atlanta's maximum-security prison. We see him locked into solitary confinement, an appropriate objective correlative for his emotional state.

On the DVD bonus disk, Spielberg says that one of the things that inspired him about *Catch Me If You Can* was that "it shows you can turn your life around and make something better of yourself." But that aspect of the story occupies a relatively short space at its conclusion, another of the many tacked-on happy endings that characterize the director's work. What lingers long after the final credits fade is not that Frank Abagnale Jr. ended up married for twenty-six years, worked for the FBI to capture check forgers, remains one of the world's foremost authorities on bank fraud, designs secure check systems for Fortune 500 companies, and is paid millions for his services. It is not the colorful life he led or even the clever way he insinuated himself into the worlds of aviation, law, and medicine. It is the moments of personal heartbreak, the times when Spielberg explicitly calls into question the siren song of the American Dream, that move the film beyond a formulaic depiction of the "clever rogue": The scene where Frank Senior's voice cracks and his eyes well up with tears as he reveals that his son's mother has remarried; Frank's feeling of betrayal when he understands that Brenda has informed the FBI of their secret meeting at the Miami airport; Frank watching his mother with her new family, finally realizing that some dreams remain forever broken. In spite of the jaunty surface of the film, as well as Spielberg's disingenuous claim that the story was "pure, unadulterated fun," *Catch Me If You Can* clearly reflects the director's dissatisfaction with and critique of middle-class American values.

The Indiana Jones Trilogy: Internal Chronology

Commentators who analyze various aspects of Spielberg's Indiana Jones films customarily situate their analyses within a framework of the trilogy's production and release dates: *Raiders of the Lost Ark* (1981), *Indiana Jones and the Temple of Doom* (1984), and *Indiana Jones and the Last Crusade* (1989). Such a methodology provides clearly defined cultural and historical contexts, an obvious benefit for critics such as Andrew Britton, Patricia Zimmermann, Frank P. Tomasulo, Peter Biskind, Ella Shohat, Robert Stam, and Robin Wood, who castigate the films as archetypal examples of "Reaganite entertainment." Later in this chapter, I will examine these and other attacks on the ideological assumptions within this cycle, but I want to structure my initial, formal analysis around the films' internal narrative chronology. I align them therefore as follows: the opening vignette in *Last Crusade* (1912), *Temple of Doom* (1935), *Raiders* (1936), and finally the main section of *Last Crusade* (1938). My approach shifts the common critical framework; instead of remaining three loosely connected films linked by a common central character, the works coalesce into an integrated narrative, each particular movie spliced to the others in proper sequential order. Using the schema of an evolutionary bildungsroman with Indiana Jones at its core, I want to look at themes and elements that recur in the three films: 1) narrative structure; 2) the costumes worn by Indiana Jones; 3) each film's opening vignette; 4) the objects of his quests; 5) the female figures he encounters; 6) the antagonists who oppose him; 7) the father figures who inhabit the films; and 8) the non-white characters (the "dark Others") who aid and combat him. Following an investigation of these common ingredients, I will turn to the widespread attacks on the films' "retrograde ideology," interrogate the charge raised by numerous critics that Spielberg and George Lucas have infantalized the American cinema, and offer an alternative reading of this series.

NARRATIVE STRUCTURE

Various commentators have discussed the plot of the Indiana Jones films as emulating classical formats. For example, Susan Aronstein sees the series as re-creating the formula of the Arthurian legends, with America standing in for the Court of Arthur, the Third World settings as forests of adventure, and the Nazis/Thuggees as hostile knights to be defeated. All three films, she argues, comprise a typical plot with the knight's entrance into court, his adventures and triumphs (rescuing of maidens), and his movement to spiritual values. Tomasulo relates the plot to the epic mode, citing the classical trajectory of the mythical hero delineated in Joseph Campbell's *The Hero with a Thousand Faces:* separation, trials and victories of initiation, return, and integration with society ("Mr. Jones"). Similarly, Andrew Gordon talks about the "monomythic" pattern of heroic quests for sacred objects that precede Indiana Jones (*Raiders*), and Lane Roth notes how Spielberg employs narrative archetypes outlined in the works of Northrop Frye and C. G. Jung: a journey to the underworld, the motifs of jungles/deserts, and the physical representation (shadows) of the dark side of our nature.

All these observations have some merit, for the series does echo broad patterns of heroic action embedded in our cultural consciousness. Indeed, the three Indiana Jones plots utilize a highly structured narrative pattern that remains basically unchanged from film to film. Each begins with Indiana seeking an object of historical and monetary value: the Sankara Stones (*Doom*), the Ark of the Covenant (*Raiders*), and the Cup of Christ/Holy Grail (*Last Crusade*). Each culminates in a critical moment when Indy must choose between the desired object and a person and, to emphasize his difference from his foe and how much he has learned during his journey, he selects the person and his antagonist the object. In *Temple of Doom*, the evil priest of Kali, Mola Ram (Amrish Puri), is burned by the stone he sought and plunges to his death in the alligator-infested river below, while Indiana climbs to safety and returns the sacred object to its rightful owners. In *Raiders,* Belloq (Paul Freeman) insists on opening the Ark, destroying himself and his Nazi patrons, while Indiana and Marion (Karen Allen) shut their eyes and avoid incineration. In *Last Crusade,* Donovan (Julian Glover) is killed by Elsa Schneider's (Alison Doody) wrong choice of the cup, and she falls into the chasm trying to reach the chalice, while Indiana heeds his father's sage advice.

Within this basic structure, the Indiana Jones films clearly and self-consciously harken back to the early movie serials of a bygone and seemingly simpler era, such as those produced by the low-rent Republic studios featuring Flash Gordon. Scenes where Jones swings from vines into rivers, jumps from horses onto moving objects, slides underneath vehicles, defeats muscular opponents, and performs numerous other daring feats emulate iconic moments in movies featuring the likes of Zorro or Tarzan or Hopalong Cassidy. Yet, unlike his predecessors, Jones does not emerge from his dangerous escapades unscathed. We often see him covered with dirt and fleeing from his adversaries, his clothing shredded, his body beaten, and his spirit shattered. His fear of snakes renders him vulnerable, and he yelps in pain when Marion applies an antiseptic to his cuts. Most importantly, although all the quests begin with his search for riches and fame, they peak in a defining moment when he must select a person over an object, and they conclude with his personal illumination: spirituality over cynicism and communal needs over individual goals. Thus, all three films function as stories of moral education.

In terms of genre expectations, these moral lessons come with a price: the reduction of Indiana Jones's claim to the mantle of rugged individualist. He functions as the center of all three movies, but his individual power shifts from his clear superiority to Willie and Short Round in *Temple of Doom,* to his equal partnership with Marion in *Raiders,* to his dependence on his father (as well as Sallah and Brody) in *Last Crusade.* Indy's status as a lone action hero actually degenerates as the extended narrative progresses. Because the people who surround him literally become the objects of the quest, he must rely on them to accomplish his goals. Whereas the impetus for the initial quest in *Temple of Doom* comes from Indy himself, in *Raiders* it results from the behest of the American government, and in *Last Crusade* he literally follows in his father's footsteps. Ironically, therefore, the more Indiana Jones learns to interact emotionally with others, the less he fulfills the traditional role of the conventional action hero, the man who is usually as alone at the end of the movie as he was when it began. The concluding union of Jones with Willie, Marion, and even his father represents a significant departure from the audience desires typically satisfied in an action/adventure film. As such, it remains the most obvious instance where Spielberg, a director fixated upon reuniting families in almost all of his movies, weaves his personal obsession into the fabric of rigid genre demands and audience expectations.

THE COSTUME

The series is a stylistic pastiche, and Indiana Jones wears a pastiche of articles that bind him to previous cinematic action/adventure heroes and recall earlier, seemingly less fraught times in American history. Indy's adventure costume remains essentially the same from one movie to the next. According to Michael French, webmaster of an Internet site devoted to Indiana Jones (www.Geocities.com/indyfrench/inspire.html), the character's clothing consists of the following items:

1) The hat. A felt fedora inspired by a popular style in 1930s men's fashion and the many adventure film heroes who wore swooped-brim headpieces. French cites Alan Ladd in *China* (1943) and Charlton Heston in *Secret of the Incas* (1954) as prototypes, while Ian Freer references Heston in *The Greatest Show on Earth* (1952), the first movie Spielberg ever saw (Freer 97).

2) The jacket. A bomber style inspired by those worn by A-2 pilots during World War II.

3) The shirt. A safari style, with epaulets and pleated pockets, similar to that worn by Stewart Granger in *King Solomon's Mines* (1950) and by other adventure heroes. As with the hat, these were also common in the 1930s.

4) The pants. Their flapped back pockets and khaki coloring are based on U.S. military uniforms of the period known as "officer's pinks."

5) The boots. Alden 405 walking boots (now trademarked and sold by that company as the "Indy Boot"), an orthopedic ankle boot constructed in the same fashion now as it was in the early twentieth century.

6) The pant belt. A dark brown belt with a buckle modeled on those worn by U.S. naval officers since World War I.

7) The shoulder bag. A green Mark 7 British canvas gas bag that was standard issue to soldiers and civilians during the Battle of Britain and the Blitz.

8) The bullwhip. Indy's trademark weapon is a twelve-plait, Australian-style leather whip whose size varies from eight to eighteen feet in the film's fight scenes and fourteen to twenty feet when used as a swinging rope. Most critics agree that it was inspired by the Zorro and Lash La Rue serials.

9) The guns. In *Raiders* and *Temple of Doom*, a Smith and Wesson Hand Ejector Mark II, a style invented in the early twentieth century and used extensively in World War I. In *Raiders* a second gun is kept mostly in his bag,

a semiautomatic Browning Hi-Power invented in the 1930s. In *Last Crusade,* he carries a Webley Mark VI revolver, a British pistol used throughout World War I and made famous in *Lawrence of Arabia.* His holster is a common flap-style used during World War I.

10) Professorial garb. In his role as a college teacher, Dr. Jones usually dons a three-piece suit and tie, along with eyeglasses that he somehow does not need in his action persona.

The appealing surface features of his clothing, reflective of the films' historical settings, contribute to the films' displacement of disturbing contemporary events with romanticized past triumphs. For Americans in the 1980s, that idealized historical period occurs before the frustrating stalemate of the Korean conflict and the disheartening morass of the Vietnam War: an unquestionably righteous time during World War II when the enemy was clear, the cause explicit, and the violence moral. Indy's armaments augment this comforting vision. On a presentational level, the Indiana Jones films are rough equivalents to English heritage films, sumptuous visual feasts that invite audiences to gaze backwards to a time without moral ambiguities, an era of national pride and achievement. They implicitly juxtapose a nostalgically imagined past with a sadly debased present.

The most unique and unexpected part of Indy's carefully constructed outfit is the now-famous bullwhip. Viewers see his face for the first time when he wheels around, cracks the whip, and flicks the gun from the hand of a traitor about to shoot him in the back. This intimate weapon can be used only for face-to-face fighting, individualized tests of courage. Unlike mechanized instruments of war, like rumbling tanks or spitting machine guns, the whip never distances a fighter from his or her opponent and never depersonalizes the pain and death it inflicts. A direct equivalent to the knight's sword, the whip harkens back to fighting situations defined by personal bravery, honorable actions, and codes of behavior far removed from the detached napalming of rice paddies and the deafening roar of helicopter blades. By using the bullwhip, Indiana Jones assumes the mantle of those individualistic heroes of the past whose wit, valor, and daring represented a collective national image of gallant Americans fighting the evil Axis powers.

OPENING VIGNETTES

The opening vignettes function similarly in all three films. They quickly capture the audience's attention by providing thrilling mini-adventures, teasers with truncated but definable beginnings, middles, and endings. More importantly, they establish Jones's philosophical and psychological attitudes at that particular moment in his cinematic life, a pattern of actions based on beliefs that subsequent events inevitably force him to reevaluate and finally to reject. In *Temple of Doom,* for example, he moves from a selfish desire for personal wealth—which almost costs him his life in the opening nightclub fight scene—to an understanding of communal responsibility evident in the final sequence, where he reunites Indian parents with their children. Similarly, in *Raiders,* he converts from an isolated religious skeptic who steals exotic artifacts for profit into a chastised academic who accepts the power of God and the love of a woman he once abandoned. Keeping the internal chronological structure in mind when exploring the opening vignette in *Last Crusade,* however, demonstrates not only that it presages events in this particular episode but, in retrospect, establishes basic patterns for understanding aspects of Indiana Jones throughout the entire series: as Wordsworth famously put it, "The child is the father of the man."

The first artifact Indiana Jones attempts to capture (because "this should be in a museum") is the Cross of Coronado, a present to the Spanish explorer from Cortez. Trekking deep into John Ford country with his ragtag Boy Scout troop, the teenage Jones (River Phoenix) chances upon a mercenary archeologist (Richard Young) unearthing the Cross to sell for a handsome profit. The cave where it is hidden remains a common location in all the Jones films, which often move from dark underground spaces to open bright landscapes. The ensuing chase aboard, inside, beneath, and atop the Dunn and Duffy circus train provides the intrepid, if naive, adolescent with accoutrements and attitudes that will remain part of his costume and character into adulthood: the bullwhip he grabs to defend himself against a lion permanently scars his chin when he first ineptly cracks it, and his fear of snakes springs from accidentally landing in the reptile car. Later, at the moment of defeat, the rogue archeologist ruefully places on the crestfallen boy's head a well-worn fedora that will continue to remind him of this first loss.

Indiana Jones (named for George Lucas's Malamute Huskie) experiences the stark dichotomy between these equally seductive approaches to the past and its secrets. For Professor Henry Jones (Sean Connery), a sedentary medievalist, the rigorous study of ancient texts provides keys to spiritual enlightenment. His fascination with the enigmatic words etched on the fragile page before him, "May he who illuminated this illuminate me," characterizes his conceptualization of the past as a source of sacred wisdom rather than marketable commodities. Conversely, the unnamed archeologist whose facial scar resembles the one now permanently engraved on Indiana Jones's chin tells him: "You lost today, kid, but that doesn't mean you have to like it," an admonition that forms a crucial part of Indiana's credo as a man. Throughout these films, Indiana Jones is torn between these antithetical ideas of how modern men should relate to ancient objects, beliefs, and societies. *Temple of Doom* starts with his emulation of the mercenary archeologist, as Indiana loots sacred relics for individual profit and fame. By the film's end, however, he accepts a moral obligation imposed by social responsibility. In the opening of *Raiders,* he ignores the spiritual significance of the religious artifacts he seeks to obtain and sell, as well as their sacred importance to the people who worship them. By its conclusion, he accepts the presence and power of divine forces beyond his comprehension. *Last Crusade* begins with Indy's penchant for placing ancient objects in glass cases but finishes with an emphasis on personal reconciliation rather than professional codes and abstract principles.

OBJECTS OF THE QUESTS

HISTORICAL SIGNIFICANCE Although the objects that ostensibly motivate Indiana's quests have distinct historical significance, their value as salable commodities initially entices the archeologist, since he remains skeptical of their religious importance. The objects associated with these ancient societies retain value solely as museum pieces on the open market. What price will be paid by those who will put them inside glass cases? Early in *Raiders,* Belloq chides Indy for seeking cultural products upon which time, not intrinsic value, bestows worth. Holding up a cheap watch in a seedy Cairo bar, he quips: "Look at this. It's worthless. Ten dollars from a vendor in the street. But I take it, I bury it for a thousand years, and it becomes priceless. Men will kill for it. Men like you and me." Indiana Jones has devoted his life to securing ties to ancient cultures, elusive conduits to knowledge about the past. Part of their allure is the adrenalinized competitions they inspire between Jones and his clever antagonists, a duel that represents competing worldviews about how to best preserve these pieces of time and, as the films progress, how to utilize their potentially destructive power. Their historical value becomes less central as the films highlight their ties to supernatural forces and their personal resonances for Indiana Jones.

RELIGIOUS SIGNIFICANCE The objects of Jones's quests have clearly defined historical importance as vital links to ancient civilizations, but they are also sacred representations of hallowed religious traditions: Hinduism (*Temple of Doom*), Judaism (*Raiders*), and Christianity (*Last Crusade*). In this sense, each film functions as an encounter between the secular and the sacred.

"The search for the Cup of Christ is the search for the divine in all of us," Marcus Brody proclaims early in *Last Crusade,* and the same can be said for the Stones and the Ark. Early in all three movies, Jones disdainfully dismisses any notion of their transcendent power, mocking their supposed connection with higher forces with disparaging phrases like "ghost stories" (*Temple of Doom*); "magic," "superstitious hocus pocus," and "the bogey man" (*Raiders*); and "bedtime stories" and "an old man's dreams" (*Last Crusade*). But supernatural power channeled through these objects has been convincingly demonstrated by the conclusion of the films: the Stones' energy to generate good or evil, the Ark's strength to destroy those who view it, and the Cup's ability to bring back the dead. Each film reaffirms that these sacred objects embody knowledge and strength that, if used properly, could benefit mankind but, if perverted, could destroy us as well. (In *Raiders,* ironically, the Ark the Nazis desperately seek belongs to the tradition of a people they undertake to annihilate.) Those who perish seek secular gain, whether monetary profit, governmental dominance, or personal power. Jones and his allies survive because they ultimately recognize the power of the divine within the artifacts. Although Indiana fails to retain possession of these objects, he finds personal fulfillment and spiritual illumination.

Last Crusade, in particular, forces Indiana to take a literal leap of faith. He must step onto a bridge that remains invisible to nonbelievers and is manifest only to those with true faith and understanding. "Believe, boy," his father whispers as Indiana contemplates the chasm beneath him, "Believe." In the face of such overwhelming evidence, Jones moves from dubious nonbelief to acceptance of divinity in the universe. Doug Brode sees this progression as Spielberg's rejection of "jaded sophistication" for "enlightening simplicity," contending that these films show how "contemporary men must unlearn modern nihilism by rediscovering old-fashioned faith" (174). Along the same lines, Susan Aronstein views the series as a modernization of chivalric romances in which, as a means to recuperate and reaffirm America's cultural identity, Indiana moves toward "spiritual values . . . moral understanding [and] . . . an acceptance of a higher force" (15). Other critics remain far less enraptured by Indiana's acceptance of a higher power, interpreting it as reactionary neoconservativism in line more with Reaganite politics than spiritual values.

PERSONAL SIGNIFICANCE The objects of Jones's quests also spark personal resonances for the archeologist and mark his individual evolution. The Sankara Stones, for example, demonstrate his growing understanding of his communal responsibilities. Initially in *Temple of Doom,* Indiana appears relatively unconcerned with the plight of distraught Indian villagers who cite the theft of the Stones as the reason for their barren land, their crushing poverty, and their missing children. He seeks the Stones only for their monetary value. Yet as the film progresses, he comes to perceive that they must be given back to the villagers, in spite of the high price he can sell them for. His moral vision shifts from individual goals to community needs, from the mindset of the mercenary to that of the ethical scientist. In *Raiders,* the scope of his social action enlarges to encompass a whole country. He goes to work for the American government to deprive the Nazis of a powerful weapon. As with the Stones, Indiana comes to understand the Ark as having importance far beyond his own desires or, for that matter, even the demands of the government that employs him. This change dramatically appears in the moment when he threatens to blow up the Ark: "I don't want the Ark, I want the girl," he tells Belloq, aiming his bazooka as a palpable threat. But Belloq convinces him that, while he and Indiana are "passing through history," the Ark "is history." At this point, Jones evolves beyond his wish for personal gain, beyond his love for Marion, and even beyond his duty to the American government. He is, in fact, responsible to history, to those who came before him and those who will follow.

Finally, in *Last Crusade,* the Holy Grail becomes more important as a connection to Indy's father than as a religious or historical relic. At the start of the film, Jones is even not interested in seeking the Grail until he learns that his father is missing; near its conclusion, when the knight asks, "Why do you seek the Cup of Christ? Is it for His glory or yours?" Jones answers, "I didn't come for the Cup of Christ. I came to find my father." While some commentators interpret this response as referring to the Heavenly Father as well as Henry Jones Sr., it seems clear that Indiana is conscious only of the latter. In fact, he must learn to think like his father to save him. He can succeed only by performing a literary exegesis guided by his father's intellectual and spiritual example. As Aronstein argues persuasively, "Indiana's search for his father is more than the search to find and retrieve him. It is, as he must learn, the search both to accept him and, in a very real way, to emulate or become him" (21). To drive home this point visually, Spielberg crosscuts between Indiana and his father as Indiana struggles to solve the riddles associated with the breath of God, the word of God, and the path of God. No bullwhip here. No pistols or knives, nor any flesh-and-blood figures who can be vanquished by weapons or fists. Indiana Jones stands alone facing an intellectual challenge and a spiritual commitment. All he has to guide him are his father's words, erudite scribblings in a diary that marked his lifelong obsession with the Holy Grail. When victory is finally secured, it is not through force or guile, as in the earlier films, but by virtue of Indiana learning the lessons taught by his father.

FEMALE FIGURES

The action/adventure genre is not a particularly hospitable environment for women, especially the serials of the 1930s and 1940s that inspired the Indiana Jones trilogy. Spielberg inherited a tradition of creaky female stereotypes from his original source materials, much as he did the outmoded attitudes toward dark Other and ethnic characters examined later in this chapter. The so-called damsel-in-distress motif accounted for a substantial part of the early movie serials' appeal. Lashed to a railroad track in the path of an onrushing locomotive or chained to a log headed for a saw blade, she allowed the hero to achieve mythic proportions by fighting her captors and saving her—in the nick of time—from disaster. But defenses based on "original source materials" do not fully exculpate Spielberg from charges of sexism and racism. Nor does the plea for historical accuracy. Any director setting his or her film in the past faces the dilemma of choosing either to allow objectionable elements prevalent in that time period to remain intact or to modify them to avoid offending modern sensibilities. Since the Indiana Jones series makes no pretense of binding its plot or characters to realism and facts, Spielberg cannot be granted a pass by appeals to historical verisimilitude. That said, he actually modernizes the perpetually quivering, often hysterical female victims who populate these earlier films, particularly in *Raiders* and *Last Crusade,* yet his female figures remain a decidedly underdeveloped aspect, as in most of his other films as well. Willie in *Temple of Doom,* to Marion in *Raiders,* to Elsa in *Last Crusade* represents an evolution from the overwrought burdensome female, to the attractive sidekick, to the intellectual equal. Looking at how these women abet Indy's three quests, it is fair to conclude that Willie often hinders his progress, Marion helps him the most, and Elsa provides a formidable antagonist.

WILLIE SCOTT The weakest and most disturbing of Spielberg's trio of women is the slinky chanteuse Willie (Kate Capshaw), an irony not lost on those who comment upon Spielberg's subsequent marriage to Capshaw and note that the character has the same name as the director's cocker spaniel. At times, the film juxtaposes its relentless action with elements of screwball comedy, complete with a battle of the sexes, an innocent (and interrupted) seduction scene, and a final reconciliation between the warring parties, who are attracted to each other despite their differences. One of Spielberg's harshest critics, Andrew Britton, castigates the director for what he characterizes as overt sexism, which he finds particularly repugnant in *Temple of Doom*: "The film's subject, at this level, is the formation of a misogynistic homoerotic bond between father and son, consummated through imitative violence and the systematic degradation of the heroine . . . the focus of intense and anti-feminist animus" (41–42). I agree with Britton's basic assertions, though Spielberg is not so much antifeminist as disappointingly juvenile when depicting women. His inability to fashion a mature relationship between a man and woman in any of his films, even his later and more sophisticated works, will be explored later in this book.

Brode offers the most sympathetic interpretation of this figure, claiming that she is "a variation of . . . the gold digger, a sleek, self-serving blonde who cares about nothing except money" (135). Such a characterization seems appropriate when, dressed in a figure-hugging gown of glittering red sequins, she crawls around on her hands and knees searching for a diamond in the Club Obi Wan, ignoring hired killers and the antidote necessary to save Indiana's life. But Brode's statement hardly accounts for her subsequent actions, and throughout the rest of the film the director uses her as a typical damsel in distress. In a fleeting but disturbing early moment, Indiana holds Lao Che (Roy Chiaq), the Shanghai gangster, to his bargain by threatening to harm Willie, ominously poking a fork into her slightly exposed right breast. For him, she is merely meat on the hoof. Mostly, Spielberg derives humor at Willie's expense by taking this ultrafeminine figure accustomed to fine clothes and good food out of her civilized element and into the jungle. "I hate the outside," she tells Indiana.

Basically, Jones treats her like a hindrance, an annoying irritation thrust upon him that he wearily accepts. "The biggest trouble with her," he complains, "is the noise!" As if to prove his assertion, Willie cries and yells and screams and shrieks and simpers and babbles incessantly throughout the movie. Even their potential sexual encounter is filled with argumentative banter. When Indiana finally decides to go to her room, he is attacked by a Thuggee goon and almost strangled, considerably cooling his ardor. Only once does Spielberg allow Willie some modicum of heroic competence, but even as she rescues Indy and Short Round (Ke Huy Quan) he undercuts her: conquering her fear of bugs to save her companions from being crushed in a room equipped with spikes and a descending ceiling, she obsesses about a broken fingernail. Willie is present merely for Indy to save and embrace at the film's conclusion. Even their long-delayed joining, however, entails more laughs than passion: a playful elephant sprays the couple, and Short Round covers his eyes as they kiss for the first time to end the film.

MARION RAVENWOOD Unlike Willie's frilly sexuality or Elsa's professional maturity, Marion Ravenwood (Karen Allen) begins *Raiders* as the girl next door, the tomboy who climbs trees and hangs out with the guys. In her first sequence, Marion wears pants, runs her own bar in Nepal, chainsmokes cigarettes, and outdrinks a burly local peasant. Her first act after Indiana "walks through her doors" is to slug him in the jaw and spit out how much she hates him. During the ensuing fight scene with the sadistic Toht (John Dietrich) and his mercenaries, she matches Indiana's toughness, hitting a thug over the head with a burning log and shooting another with a Mauser pistol to save Indy's life. After her bar goes up in flames, she boldly declares, "Until I get my five thousand dollars, I am your goddamned partner." This early Marion seems modeled on the spirited female characters in the films of Howard Hawks, one of Spielberg's heroes: an independent, feisty woman who matches tough talk, witty banter, and bold action with the macho men who populate her cynical world. This image does not last. Once she partners with Indiana, her autonomy diminishes and then vanishes. She trades her pants for a series of dresses, an act Tomasulo interprets as Spielberg's "nostalgia for a pre-feminism America" ("Mr. Jones" 334) and Zimmermann as a "resurgence in the ideology of the traditional nuclear family" (37). The costume change attests to her growing vulnerability and emerging sexuality. In the market abduction scene, she hits an attacker with a frying pan, a symbol of her newfound domesticity, and when borne off in a basket she cries out meekly: "You can't do that! I am an American!" Though she does attempt to rescue herself from Belloq, the scheme requires a retreat to seductive feminine wiles.

The most uncomfortable part of the Indiana/Marion relationship is the events that happened before the opening of the film that are alluded to several times. How old was Marion during her original affair with Indiana, when he was still Abner Ravenwood's graduate student? At the very least, Indiana's seduction of his academic father figure's daughter creates the impression of "symbolic incest" (Gordon, *Raiders* 263). Even more disturbingly, could the dashing Indiana Jones actually be a pedophile? Such possibilities bother even the reliably sympathetic Doug Brode: "Their confrontation is a classic case of an adult male engaging in sexual activity with an underage young woman, then claiming he isn't responsible because he saw a flicker of desire in her eyes" (94). We have no information about when the affair started or how long it continued, only that it destroyed the close relationship between Indiana and Abner and that it was not a one-time occurrence. It remains clear that this liaison profoundly affected Marion, though Indiana seems to feel the loss of Abner more than he does his daughter:

> Indiana: I never meant to hurt you.
> Marion: I was a child. I was in love. It was wrong, and you knew it.
> Indiana: You knew what you were doing. I did what I did. You don't have to be happy about it, but maybe we can help each other now.
> Marion: Do you know what you did to me and my life?
> Indiana: I can only say I'm sorry so many times.
> Marion: Everybody's sorry for something.

With such a cavalier attitude about his past transgressions, one fully understands why Marion's first act is to punch him.

As many commentators have noted, Marion gets conflated with the Ark throughout *Raiders*: "Marion, like the Ark, is a prize . . . and surrounded by taboo. . . . They are both treated as valuable prizes, objects of barter, constantly stolen and recaptured, passing from the hands of one man to another" (Gordon, *Raiders* 263). They become interchangeable at several points in the movie, "twin objects of the hero's search for harmony . . . [and] competing nationalist male desires" (Shohat and Stam 152). In the Well of Souls, for example, she literally replaces the Ark, and later Belloq removes Marion and the Ark from the *Bantu Wind,* leaving the ship and taking them both to the island. Early in the film, Spielberg visually solders their connection as he crosscuts between Indiana's attempt to unearth the Ark and Belloq's attempt to seduce Marion. At the film's conclusion, Indiana must content himself with walking arm in arm with the now totally domesticated Marion, yet again unable to obtain the original object of his quest, now lodged (and forgotten) in a cavernous U.S. government warehouse.

For Indiana and Belloq, therefore, Marion becomes almost as much a prize as the Ark itself, though each abandons her at various points in the film either to capture or preserve the Ark. In one of the film's most disturbing scenes, Indiana sneaks into the Arab camp and, instead of rescuing a bound and gagged Marion, leaves her to face Belloq and the Nazis, which could mean torture, rape, and perhaps even death. This decision shatters the typical action/adventure hero mold. Would Flash Gordon leave Dale Arden to fend for herself against Ming the Merciless? Indiana forsakes Marion because he realizes that saving her would endanger his mission to obtain the Ark, his primary quest at this point in the film. Later, he is lashed to a pole with Marion as the

Ark-opening ceremony commences. His command to "shut your eyes; don't look at it" hardly constitutes the stuff of action heroes, particularly for the modern heir to fabled exploits or, as some critics would have it, the contemporary version of classical myths and Arthurian feats of daring.

DR. ELSA SCHNEIDER Elsa Schneider is the most complicated woman in the series and quite a different character from the one-dimensional female figures who precede her in *Temple of Doom* and *Raiders*. For one thing, Indiana actually has sex with her, as does his father. "I'm as human as the next man," the slightly chagrined Henry tells his son. "I *was* the next man," comes the tart reply. Given that Elsa is not the friendly colleague she pretends to be, the estranged father and son share a nearly fatal lapse in judgment and character assessment, which initially disconcerts but ultimately impresses the other: they literally sleep with the enemy. None of the coy interruptions seen between Indy and his previous leading ladies exist in *Last Crusade*. Elsa is a mature and, at times, sexually aggressive woman, experienced and willing to use her considerable physical charms to seduce Indiana and his father on multiple levels.

Dr. Elsa Schneider (Alison Doody), the most complex female character in the Indiana Jones trilogy, snares father (Sean Connery) and son (Harrison Ford) in *Indiana Jones and the Last Crusade* (1989).

She is also Dr. Jones's professional and intellectual equal, unlike the defenseless Willie or the tomboy Marion. Like Belloq in *Raiders of the Lost Ark,* Elsa willingly joins forces with readily available sources of power (Nazis) and money (Donovan), no matter their pernicious ideology or objectives, to obtain the historical objects she desperately seeks, immoral alliances that ultimately doom her.

To say that Elsa is the most complex and demanding of the three female figures in this series is to damn with faint praise. Like all of Spielberg's female characters, she is the Other, defined predominately in relation to the masculine figures, particularly Indiana and his father. Deriving her importance solely by what she provides them, she bridges their initial hostility toward each other, splicing them together through her sexuality and allowing each to gain a clearer perception of the other through her negative example. Like the Cup of Christ itself (and similar to Marion and the Ark), Elsa becomes a shared object between two men, centering an imbroglio of pride, conquest, and mortification. She enables each to complete his emotional journey to gain the affection and respect of the other and to forsake the ostensible object of their quest. Only after she perishes can Dr. Jones, the elder, call Dr. Jones, the younger, by his chosen first name rather than continually addressing him as "Junior," an unmistakable sign of the father's acceptance of his son's emergence into adulthood. Even though Indiana ends the film with a snappy "yes, sir," he and his father attain a new level of maturity, a mutual realization of each other's strengths and acceptance of each other's weaknesses, a psychological balance impossible to achieve without the initial seduction and eventual death of Elsa.

As with all the villains in the series, Elsa's actions function mainly as object lessons for Indiana Jones, negative moral behaviors he must avoid to survive and mature. Although most critics chastise her for selecting the wrong chalice, a closer look at this scene yields an alternative reading that demonstrates her calculating intelligence. Elsa purposely selects the wrong vessel to destroy Donovan and gain the prize for herself. Her quick selection of the object provides the first hint of this cold decision. She takes only a few seconds to decide which cup, among the rows of goblets, is the authentic Holy Grail, hardly the act of a well-trained and prudent archeologist. After handing the golden chalice to Donovan, she exchanges a quick and knowing look with Indiana, her tight smile silently communicating her satisfaction and superiority. Even more obviously, she displays neither surprise nor emotion when Donovan convulses after drinking from "the Cup of the King of Kings," which he supposes will provide "eternal life," breaking into screams only when his writhing skeleton seeks to crush her. "*He* chose poorly," the knight drily observes after Donovan's demise, absolving Elsa of blame for selecting the wrong object. Instead of being blinded by the glittering exterior of the golden chalice, as most commentators interpret this scene, Elsa selects quite purposefully. "It would not be made out of gold," she tells Indiana following Donovan's collapse, knowing that a poor carpenter would never own such an expensive item.

Yet Elsa's cunning hastens her own death. One can reasonably assume that obtaining the Cup of Christ would bestow an academic legitimacy denied her in the male-dominated discipline of archeology, a strong motivation to seek the grail of professional success. Like her predecessors, she remains unwilling to release her emotional obsession; she cannot free herself from the lust for secular accomplishments and accept the divine wisdom embodied in the Holy Grail. By crossing the specified boundary with the Grail, a literal representation of women who transgress tightly guarded male domains of power and prerogative, her audacity and selfishness cause the world to collapse around them. Spread-eagled on the ground, her body literally bisected by a widening chasm, she is temporarily saved by Indiana grasping both her hands. But seeing the Grail on a ledge just below her, Elsa frees one hand and stretches for her elusive prize. "I can reach it," she tells Indiana, smiling maniacally in the throes of her obsession while Indiana pleads with her to hold onto him with both hands. But dreams often crush their dreamers. Slipping out from her glove, she utters one last scream as she plunges into the cloudy pit, punished for her perfidy, rebelliousness, and ambition.

Immediately following Elsa's death, Indiana finds himself in the same dire position as his adversary moments before, dangling precariously above an immense crater as the earth cracks wider apart. He moves from potential rescuer to victim, his father's tenuous grasp on his wrist temporarily forestalling his death. "Junior. Give me your other hand," the elder Jones plaintively implores his offspring. "I can't hold on." Momentarily ignoring him and struggling to capture the chalice, Indiana echoes Elsa's words: "I can get it. I can almost reach it, Dad." And then the moment of recognition, of understanding between father and son that transcends any material, or even sacred, object sought for contemplation and display. Both men must abandon their obsession with the cup to survive. "Indiana, Indiana. Let it go," says the father to his son. A look of comprehension passes between them, flickering in their eyes and dancing on their lips. Each perceives that he is far more important to the other than the quest that brought them to this perilous moment. Their personal tie as father and son outweighs their professional status as medieval scholar and archeologist. Indiana gives both hands to his father, an act of trust that cements mature acceptance over past transgressions and paves the road toward a new relationship between them.

THE ANTAGONISTS

Because I have already discussed Elsa and consider Mola Ram below, this section will focus on Indiana Jones's antagonist in *Raiders of the Lost Ark:* the clever, suave, and unscrupulous French archeologist Rene Belloq. As with many other elements in these three movies, Spielberg draws upon a history of stereotypes deeply embedded within the serial action/adventure format to fashion his villains. Yet, as Indiana Jones deviates from strict adherence to masculine codes of conduct, the relationships between the hero and his adversaries often subvert their conventional roles. All of Indy's foes represent corrupt exaggerations of fundamental elements within his own personality and psyche. A little push here, a bit of a pull there, and Indiana Jones may well have tread a far more shadowy path. In facing Belloq—a doppelganger who shares his obsession for ancient objects and his drive to obtain them, his academic expertise and his practical cleverness, his adventurous daring and his romantic worldliness—Indiana comes closest to confronting the darkness inside himself.

Up until *Raiders'* grisly conclusion, Belloq appears far superior to the hero. Several crucial scenes reveal the personal rivalry that looms so large between the rugged American and his urbane European competitor. Following the thrilling opening vignette in which Indiana captures a golden Aztec statuette, Belloq removes it from his grasp, contemptuously telling him, "Dr. Jones, again we see there is nothing you can possess which I cannot take away." Later in the film, as he stands gloating above Indy at the Well of Souls, Belloq repeats a similar line: "So, once again, Jones, what was briefly yours is now mine." The viewer's visual introduction to these figures provides significant contrasts and telling insights into their personalities. Indiana appears scruffy and unkempt, his face raspy with days-old stubble, his clothing soiled with mud stains and dry sweat, his rumpled hat dripping with cobwebs and dead leaves. The clean-shaven Belloq looks fresh and well-groomed, as if he just had a shower and dressed to meet Indiana: his pristine beige outfit, shiny knee-high leather boots, and jaunty safari hat mark him as a civilized man who consciously coordinates his outfit and makes certain not to soil it.

Though they seek the same object, their methods are dissimilar: Indiana works essentially alone, obtains relics by virtue of his own skill and cleverness, engages in sustained physical action, and uses force to subdue his treacherous enemies; the more refined Belloq speaks native languages (as well as English, French, German, and Hebrew), employs armies of workers to dig for artifacts, and commands others to overpower his foes. Though he gives orders for Indiana's destruction, he never fires a pistol, wields a sword, punches anyone, or snaps a bullwhip. Their differing response to their initial confrontation is revealing. Upon securing the golden idol, Indiana merely smiles, repositions his hat on his head, and lightly tips its brim, a sign of professional achievement and relief. Belloq demonstrates his personal megalomania and colonialist mentality by holding the statue above his head in exhilarated victory, as the subjugated natives drop to their knees before him. Not coincidentally, this heady moment of power allows the humiliated Indiana to slip away, Belloq's triumphant laughter echoing through the dense jungle foliage as his defeated foe races for his life, just steps ahead of the pursing Hovitos.

As Roth and Gordon have noted, the key scene between these two fierce, yet intimately linked, competitors occurs in a hazy Cairo bar immediately following Marion's apparent death in a fiery truck explosion. It opens with a direct homage to *Casablanca* (1942): the frame's visual construction mimics the famous late-night scene in which the drunk and distraught Rick (Humphrey Bogart) bemoans Ilsa's (Ingrid Bergman) reappearance. A similarly despondent Indiana Jones sits absent-mindedly playing with Marion's pet monkey on the bar's sun-drenched balcony, the bustling marketplace behind him, and a nearly empty bottle of whiskey on the table in the foreground. Suddenly, two German thugs appear and hustle him inside the bar. Employing an over-the-shoulder shot from Belloq's point of view, Spielberg shows Indiana inside the bar as his antagonist, waiting like a coiled cobra, measures his actions, smoking from a hookah with his left hand and dangling a watch in his right. Again, the physical contrast is striking. In the midst of his grief, the disheveled Indiana wears a rumpled hat and sweat-stained shirt carelessly draped onto his body. Belloq, as usual, looks far more stylish in a white suit and matching hat, a dark tie and crisp white shirt. Spotting Belloq, Indy moves threateningly toward him. "I ought to kill you right now," he mutters. "It wasn't I who brought the girl into this business," Belloq calmly reminds him. "Sit down before you fall down." Sipping genteelly from his glass of whiskey, Belloq also has a bottle on the table, but his remains almost full. Then the verbal jousting begins.

"How odd it should end this way for us," Belloq muses. "After so many stimulating encounters I almost regret it. Where shall I find a new adversary so close to my level?" Jones sneers and then growls out, "Try the sewer," engendering a chuckle from his nemesis. At this point, Belloq explicitly marks the connections between them. Spielberg shoots this crucial scene in deep focus, keeping Belloq fully lit in a facial close up, with Indiana dominating the darkened foreground on the left side of the screen in an even more extreme close-up of his eyes, nose, mouth, and chin:

> You and I are very much alike. Archaeology is our religion. Yet we have both fallen from the purer faith. Our methods have not differed as much as you pretend. I am a shadowy reflection of you. It would take only a nudge to make you like me. To push you out of the light. You know it's true. How nice.

Spielberg never cuts away during this soliloquy, maintaining tension and keeping Indiana (and the viewer) uncomfortably trapped within the frame and forced to contemplate the truth of Belloq's assertions. Throughout this speech, Indiana stares straight ahead, refusing to look directly at Belloq, as if to deny that he represents this murky part of himself.

Narrowing his subject to the Ark, the Frenchman again equates himself with his American counterpart, claiming, "Men will kill for it. Men like you and me. It's a transmitter, a radio for speaking to God. And it's within my reach." Indiana, driven by his guilt and pain over Marion's presumed fate, responds to this arrogance with suicidal nihilism: "You want to talk to God.

"I'm a shadowy reflection of you," Rene Belloq (Paul Freeman) tells a distraught and drunken Indiana Jones (Harrison Ford) in *Raiders of the Lost Ark* (1981).

Let's go see him together. I've got nothing better to do." For the first time in the film, Belloq seems genuinely frightened as Indiana pushes back the table and reaches for his gun. But he is still one step ahead of Jones. The seemingly random, innocent-looking Arabs surrounding their table are actually heavily armed mercenaries under his control and willing to kill Jones where he sits. Before Indiana's pistol can clear its holster, he finds himself encircled by their cocked rifles and readiness to gratify his suicidal wishes. Only the sudden appearance of Sullah's sons and daughters clamoring around "Uncle Indiana" like human shields protects him. "Next time we're together," Belloq ominously warns Jones as the youngsters hustle him out of the bar, "it will take more than children to save you." This scene emphasizes the "moral ambiguity" shared by Indiana and Belloq (Gordon 262).

In *Raiders* and *Last Crusade,* the Nazis are the muscle, the manpower, and the money behind Belloq, Elsa, and Donovan. Spielberg has remarked that, after making *Schindler's List,* he could never again use them as prefabricated cardboard villains: "'The bad guys are more out of Clampett and Jones than Sturm und Drang'" (qtd. in Sheehan, "Spielberg II" 67). They are cartoon heavies who reinforce our sense of nationalistic pride by harkening back to America's glorious military past. The Nazis, at this point in Spielberg's film career, provide him with a host of serial film caricatures: the sadistic SS man, the muscle-bound goon, the heartless military man—all stock characters implanted in our cultural consciousness as "icons used as a kind of visual shorthand for signifying evil" (Prince, *Visions* 73). Only in one scene does Spielberg migrate beyond these stereotypes: surreptitiously entering Berlin to recapture the Grail diary, Indiana and his father witness members of the Third Reich destroying the works of great artists and writers, an orgy of anti-intellectualism and patricide that causes even Elsa to cringe with disgust. Dressed in a Nazi uniform, Indiana inadvertently finds himself standing in front of Hitler (Michael Sheard), who, seeing the book in his hand, assumes that one of his soldiers wants his autograph. Spielberg depicts Hitler as a charismatic celebrity, the focus of frenzied adoration by the fawning masses; in Spielbergian terms, and particularly within a film overtly about parent/child relations, this embodiment certainly represents the ultimate incarnation of the bad father.

FATHER FIGURES

No matter the genre, father figures—good and bad, dependable and unreliable, genetic and assumed—pervade Spielberg's movies, and commentators employ a variety of critical frames to explore this fact. Biographical critics build their readings upon accumulated grains of personal information, sifting through the director's strained relationship with his emotionally distant, often physically absent, father, whose divorce from Spielberg's mother opened sizable wounds their son evidently still nurses. Other interpreters view his artistic creations through the lens of psychoanalytical theory, contending that Spielberg's works express unresolved Oedipal tensions that strike responsive chords because they mirror the viewer's own emotional development. Myth critics see the presence of such figures as conforming to ritualistic narrative patterns, while those invoking religious archetypes explicate them as a desire to reaffirm spiritual faith in heavenly fathers. More ideologically driven writers cite this obsessive thematic strain as further evidence of the director's conservativism, particularly his sustained reconstitution of the traditional nuclear family, his adoring genuflection before strong masculine characters, and his adolescent aspiration for a dominant male role model. Political authors make these claims more specific: Ronald Reagan becomes the embodiment of strong father figures envisioned by Spielberg in his movies. Whatever the varied and complicated reasons why Spielberg fills his cinematic world with an assortment of father figures, the Indiana Jones cycle provides a particularly fertile site to explore this fixation.

The surrogate and biological father figures in these films range from supportive to critical, from loving to openly hostile, and from destructive to restorative. But no matter their expression, these powerful characters play significant roles in all three movies. Mola Ram, the abductor and enslaver of children in *Temple of Doom*, functions as a truly sinister father figure, forcing Indiana to drink human blood during a cruel sacrificial ceremony and transforming him into a drugged abuser of Short Round. McBride argues that Indiana can only fully understand his fatherly responsibilities, to Short Round and the kidnapped village children, by undergoing a "purifying test of character" (357) and being "freed from his murderous trance . . . by his surrogate son (358). Significantly, it is not the lure of adult love, embodied in the figure of Willie Scott, who has the power to call him back to his former self, but only Short Round's plaintive "I love you, Indy," that breaks the spell cast upon him. As Brode aptly observes, "In the world according to Spielberg, the parent-child bond is more basic, potent, and positive than the man-woman bond" (143), and the most formidable and influential attachment of all is between fathers and their literal and figurative sons.

Raiders begins with a brusque and cavalier acknowledgment that Indiana has betrayed his academic father figure, Abner Ravenwood, by sleeping with his teenage daughter. Such apparent disloyalty, not to mention its dramatic

The surrogate family: Indiana Jones (Harrison Ford), Willie Scott (Kate Capshaw), and Short Round (Ke Huy Quan) in *Indiana Jones and the Temple of Doom* (1984).

toll on Marion's life, seems to have made little lasting impression on Indiana's subsequent progress as either Professor Jones or Indy the adventurer. Abner's replacement, Marcus Brody, remains a lightly drawn, if idealized, substitute, though his role as museum curator marks him as part of Indiana's academic life rather than his action quests. Until Brody reappears as part of a trio of father figures in *Last Crusade,* he remains confined to securing money for Indy's fieldwork, paying for the objects he obtains, and citing the religious significance of the Ark. The Ark is the physical manifestation of the Heavenly Father, whose power, dramatically displayed once Belloq opens it, transcends human comprehension. The metaphorical father–son relationships in *Temple of Doom* and *Raiders of the Lost Ark* demonstrate Indiana Jones's susceptibility to the roles of both father and son, the tug-of-war between his reluctance to take on adult responsibilities and his childlike acceptance of higher authority. The ambivalence between these two culturally conditioned roles becomes the centerpiece of the final film in the series.

Last Crusade foregrounds the dysfunctional father–son relationship between Henry Jones Jr. and Sr. (The Abagnales also share the same name in *Catch Me If You Can,* as well as a similarly dysfunctional father–son relationship.) Spielberg was always clear on this issue: "'I wanted to do Indy in pursuit of his father, sharing his father's dream, and in the course of searching for their dreams, they rediscover each other'" (qtd. in McBride 401). Throughout the film, the rugged figure whose hypermasculinity has often been cited as his most distinguishing characteristic dwindles into an inept little boy in his father's intimidating presence. Though he continually rejects the label "junior," the son is reprimanded for not being more like the father at crucial moments. When, for example, he gives Elsa the Grail diary against his father's admonitions, she accepts it and then says with a smirk: "Thank you, but you should have listened to your father." In many ways, the film's most surprising moment occurs when Indiana's father slaps him across the face after he says "Jesus Christ," angrily telling him, "That's for blasphemy!" What the son takes as a convenient epithet to express frustration and anger, the father takes as an insult to God, a lack of proper respect. In this one brief action and reaction, we witness Henry's strict and unforgiving demands on his son, as well as the chasm between their approaches to the sacred: Henry sees their quest for the Grail as "a race against evil," while Indiana sees it as an archeological expedition.

As the film progresses, each becomes more like the other: the father engages in daring action, and the son in cerebral sleuthing. The crucial transformation in the father–son relationship occurs when Henry thinks that Indiana, trapped in a Nazi tank, has plunged over a steep cliff and perished while telling Sullah to "save Dad." Henry rushes to the lip of the precipice and cries out an anguished "Junior!" as he looks down at the smashed vehicle on the canyon floor far beneath him. Then, distraught and in close-up, he speaks: "Oh, God. I've lost him. And I never told him anything. I just wasn't ready, Marcus. Five minutes would have been enough." Though one wonders what could possibly have been imparted in those fleeting five minutes, our attention immediately shifts to a battered Indiana climbing up the far side of the cliff wall, eventually joining the three men staring down at the tank. When his father belatedly realizes that his son is standing next to him, he smiles and impulsively hugs him, the first genuine sign of affection between the two men in the movie. "I thought I'd lost you, boy," he tells Indiana, close to tears. "I had too, sir," sighs his son, smiling contentedly in his father's embrace and accepting—at long last—its comfort and warmth. "Well done," says Henry, recovering his composure. Though he chides Indiana for "sitting there resting when we're so near the end," Henry's playful tone lacks the critical bite and disparaging disappointment so evident in early remonstrations. The ice jam has been broken. For the remainder of the film, father and son act as equals, culminating in the climactic sequences when each saves the other's life: Indy secures the Cup of Christ to preserve his father, and Henry dissuades Indy from reaching for the Holy Grail and plunging to his death.

In his biography of Spielberg, Joseph McBride argues that *The Last Crusade* treats "some of his most cherished psychological obsessions within the framework of genre conventions . . . [and] conducting creative experiments" (399) that would lead him to more mature films, such as *Schindler's List,* a few years down the road. Such a reading is appealing, particularly during this acknowledged and well-documented period of intense stress and emotional turmoil in Spielberg's life, as he suffered through a disintegrating marriage to Amy Irving that ended in divorce one month after the film's release. How could his new conceptualization of himself as a divorced father not affect his artistic work, as had his resentment toward his own father earlier? How could he not critically reexamine the acute friction between career and family that drove such a deep rift between husband and wife in his own marriage, as it had that of his parents? Perhaps Spielberg's desperate need to see himself as a good father, in spite of the impending divorce, provided him with a new vantage point from which to reassess his relationship with his father, to see Arnold Spielberg with more compassion than had previously been possible as an angry and damaged young boy. "The depth of Spielberg's involvement in his characters' neuroses in these transitional films," claims McBride, "makes them resemble cinematic Rorschach inkblots" (400).

Peter Biskind sees the initially dysfunctional connection between father and son in this film as relating directly to the evolution of America's Baby Boomers, as metaphorically encapsulating their increasing understanding of and empathy with their own fathers as they reached a similar stage of parental responsibility. "If *The Last Crusade* begins with the don't-trust-adults lessons of the sixties, it ends with a lesson of the eighties: generational reconciliation" ("Blockbuster" 138). Pushing this inevitable realization that if Dad didn't always know best, at least he tried to do the best he could, Biskind argues that such a personal recognition of masculine good intentions and human frailties was directly translated into the political sphere as well: "The renegade adults of the Nixon era became the avuncular, benevolent authority figures of the Reagan-Bush era" (138). Such a reading, of course, places Spielberg securely into the camp of the neoconservatives who found their thirst for strong fatherly support quenched by drinking in the philosophy and persona of Ronald Reagan, the actor-turned-politician who projected a renewed image of American power and determination as he faced down the Soviet Union (the "evil empire" that threatened America's well-being). The *Newsweek* reporter Bruce Bawer cemented the nationalistic consensus between real-world events and reel-world adventures by conflating the fictional film character's appeal with the president's manly mystique, coining the phrase "Indiana Reagan" (14).

DARK OTHER AND ETHNIC FIGURES

As with most of the other basic elements in the Indiana Jones series, Spielberg's pictorialization of dark Other and ethnic characters springs from well-established action/adventure genre conventions. Yet while he often refracts other conventional characterizations to offer surprising nuances or even counterbalancing tendencies, his depiction of ethnic types demonstrates a disturbing recycling of offensive stereotypes. Because he modifies many aspects of the action/adventure serial in all three films, Spielberg's dark Other and ethnic stereotypes cannot be defended by citing cinema precedents or by arguing that, in attempting to be true to the spirit of these earlier works, the director could not adhere to contemporary values. Even a sympathetic biographer like Joseph McBride severely reprimands Spielberg for this "mindless carryover from the mentality of old-style adventure movies . . . when colonial attitudes still prevailed . . . [and] uncritically imitating antiquated Hollywood conventions" (318). The swarming throngs of Indian religious fanatics and gangs of oily Chinese gangsters in *Temple of Doom,* the tribe of painted South American savages and treacherous Hispanic double-crossers in *Raiders,* and the exaggerated Arab mercenaries and slave laborers in *Raiders* and *Last Crusade* all sustain formulaic dark Other and ethnic cliches that were part of Hollywood's unsavory history. Their unalloyed presence in one of the most popular series of all time reinforces denigrating typecasting, particularly when these dark Other and ethnic characters are negatively contrasted with the titular white, American hero: "[T]heir unthinking perpetuation for the purposes of mass entertainment constitutes . . . an insidious form of racial insult" (McBride 318).

Let me quickly note that outward indications in Spielberg's personal life argue against labeling him a racist, including his adoption of multiracial children. It also seems plausible that the director who made *The Color Purple* and *Empire of the Sun* between the second and third Indiana Jones movies was quite conscious of how his dark Other and ethnic stereotypes would be viewed. He did, after all, reject a storyline Lucas suggested for the series that was set in Africa, even after Chris Columbus wrote a tentative screenplay about an African Monkey King (half man/half monkey) for that adventure. Perhaps to mitigate the anticipated criticism, Spielberg does include positive alternatives to these negative dark Other and ethnic portraits. Sullah, for example, functions as such a figure, evolving from the excitable lackey in *Raiders* to one of the three potent father figures in *Last Crusade*. Short Round, in *Temple of Doom,* not only becomes Indy's diminutive sidekick but also fulfills the crucial role of making him aware of his parental and social responsibilities. But such isolated characters do little to stem the flood of hackneyed dark Other and ethnic stereotypes that inundates the Indiana Jones series.

Temple of Doom presents the most egregious examples, though all three films indulge in these representations. Spielberg got a preview of the criticisms he would face when Indian government officials in Rajasthan refused to grant him permission to film in the Rose Palace of Jaipur because they viewed the script as racist; he was forced to relocate to Sri Lanka. Here indigenous people, seen mainly as either impoverished villagers or extravagant potentates, are essentially infantalized, needing a white outsider to save them from their evil countrymen and to rescue their children from servitude. The dinner served at Little Maharajah's (Raj Singh) Pankot Palace contains an array of disgusting dishes, such as sheep's eyeball soup and monkey brains, which "the locals" consume with finger-licking delight while the westerners recoil in disgust. Mola Ram represents the most excessively heinous caricature imaginable, ripping hearts out of chest cavities, imprisoning and torturing children, and threatening the political and religious foundations of western civilization: "The British in India will be slaughtered," he tells Indiana, outlining his grand domino scheme. "Then we will overrun the Moslems. Then the Hebrew God will fall. Then the Christian God will be cast down and forgotten." His religious zealotry leads his followers to condone sadistic fanaticism.

It should not be surprising, given this fundamental orientation toward Third World cultures and traditions, that religious elements are treated simplistically in *Temple of Doom*. In the other two films, Judaism and Christianity never appear as inherently evil, although their physical representations (the Ark and the Grail) can be used for nefarious purposes, and the films perpetuate stereotypical images of the wrathful Old Testament God and the restorative New Testament savior. Here, however, Spielberg depicts the worshippers of Kali Ma as a heinous cult. By selecting the fierce goddess who, adorned with skulls, eternally intertwines unimaginable horror and abundant bliss, the sacred spark of creation and the certainty of death, Spielberg

Mola Ram (Amrish Puri), Spielberg's most racist caricature of Third World villains, in the xenophobic *Indiana Jones and the Temple of Doom* (1984).

emphasizes her frightening aspects rather than her powerful energy. In truth, the worship of and reverence for Kali Ma, a complex amalgamation of feminine strength and rage, remains widespread throughout contemporary India, but in this film she becomes simply the cause of human sacrifice, barbaric rituals, and enslavement. *Temple of Doom* becomes a textbook example of cinematic xenophobia, its repellent images demonizing Third World people, making them obedient supplicants of westerners, showing them as passive, and depicting them as ineffectual or cruel.

Any armchair psychiatrist worth his or her cigar will note the disturbing, decidedly un-Spielbergian images that inundate *Temple of Doom* and contend that they reflect the director's inner turmoil: physically abused children, hearts ripped out of chests, men burning alive, and human sacrifices. In fact, this film's violence (along with the Spielberg-produced *Gremlins* [1984]) was instrumental in motivating the Motion Picture Association of America to institute the PG-13 rating ("some material may be inappropriate for children under thirteen"). Spielberg himself added the figure of Short Round, named for a character in Sam Fuller's *The Steel Helmet* (1951), to the Gloria Katz and Willard Huyck script and changed the film's more brutal working title, "Indiana Jones and the Temple of Death," to the more cartoonish "Temple of Doom." Despite the director's claim that it was "'too dark, too subterranean, and much too horrific. . . . There is not an ounce of my personal feelings in *Temple of Doom*'" (qtd. in McBride 355), the rescue fantasy of Indiana saving scores of Indian children, following his incarnation as the evil Dr. Jones who must be rescued by Short Round, seems to spring directly from personal nightmares.

A specific nightmare debilitated Spielberg during the production of *Temple of Doom,* one of the most depressing periods in his life. The disaster on the set of *Twilight Zone: The Movie* (1983; Spielberg co-produced and directed the second segment of the four-part anthology) made him "sick to the center of his soul" (McBride 350). The actor Vic Morrow and two Asian-American children—six-year-old Renee Shin-Yi Chen and seven-year-old My-Ca Dinh Le—were killed in a helicopter accident on July 23, 1982, during the shooting of John Landis's segment. Though Spielberg was not on the set when the fatal accident occurred and was never charged with criminal actions, he was involved in the multimillion-dollar civil court settlements won by the families of the victims: the children were nonprofessional performers hired illegally, and Landis violated child-labor laws by having them work late at night. Spielberg claimed to have no knowledge of this situation, and investigators never directly linked him to these activities. Ultimately, Landis was charged with involuntary manslaughter, acquitted on May 29, 1987, and reprimanded by the Directors Guild of America soon thereafter. The two men never spoke again, and Spielberg altered his original plan to make "The Monsters Are Due on Maple Street," a story of suburban bigotry, as his contribution to *Twilight Zone* and instead made "Kick the Can," a far gentler tale about magic and rejuvenation.

Rather than agreeing with those critics who characterize the film as revealing Spielberg's "unremitting stridency, compulsiveness, and hysteria" and
as exposing "the system of values and assumptions whose harsh outline is
softened in less desperate works by an appearance of charm and geniality"
(Britton 41), I would conceptualize *Temple of Doom* as mirroring various
components of the director's state of mind at a particularly despondent point
in his life. Such a reading does not excuse the film's excesses, but it helps to
contextualize them, to see this particular work within the overall spectrum
of his other movies and thereby to help us judge whether it represents part
of a consistent pattern or stands apart as an aberration.

Because all three Indiana Jones films display a disdain for indigenous
people, we rarely question Indiana's right to take their precious artifacts,
even though he never condescends to learn their language or study their
culture. As Shohat and Stam aptly summarize, *Raiders* "assumes a disjunc-
ture between contemporary and ancient Egypt which only the Western scientist can bridge, since he alone can grasp the full significance of the ancient
archeological objects . . . reducing the Egyptian people to ignorant non-enti-
ties who happen to be sitting on a land full of historical treasures" (151). The
most obvious flash of this inherent contempt for local peoples is the famous
marketplace scene where Indiana nonchalantly shoots the scimitar-wielding
Arab swordsman. Remembering that this moment appeared in the wake of
American frustration over the Iranian hostage crisis and the government's
impotence to rescue its citizens, one understands why audiences responded
with cheers and laughter to Indiana effortlessly dispatching this menacing
figure. It bespeaks not only a pride in American technological superiority
but also a braggadocio that, in the midst of furious impatience, warns, "If
we really wanted to, we could go over there and pulverize you guys."

Given this historical context, Indiana Jones's tag line in *Last Crusade,*
"That belongs in a museum," takes on added and not particularly positive resonance, as does the word "crusade" in the title. Both foreground
a western sense of arrogance and acquisition, an implicit superiority that
claims to understand and appreciate the values of other cultures better than
those people who are heirs to that tradition. This series scrutinizes ancient
cultures with equal measures of awe and suspicion because they can access
forces beyond the understanding and control of modern western man. Biskind puts it provocatively when he observes that in each film the idea of the
primitive is "associated with dangerous, out-of-control power, [and] also
stands in for the unconscious, the id, and in the same way that sexuality has
to be repressed, so does the unconscious which, by extension, happens to be

the Third World" ("Blockbuster" 139). To contain these potentially disruptive elements, as concretized in objects that represent the most sacred and powerful forces in ancient cultures (the Ark, Sankara Stones, Cup of Christ), westerners must entomb them behind glass cases and store them safely in museums; they must become objects of passive viewing rather than conduits to dynamic action.

SPIELBERG AND LUCAS

Because of their personal friendship dating back to a UCLA student film festival in 1967, through early box-office successes in the 1970s (*Jaws* [1975] and *Star Wars* [1977]), domination of the 1980s film market, creations of multimedia conglomerates, and collaboration on one of the most commercially successful series in the history of moviemaking, Steven Spielberg and George Lucas have often been lumped together, as reflected in the memorable term "Lucasberger" (Mott and Saunders 101). Here, however, I would like to examine the charges against Spielberg in connection to his association with Lucas and to argue that these directors should not be conjoined at the hip. Their friendship aside, the careers of Spielberg and Lucas demonstrate how different they are from each other.

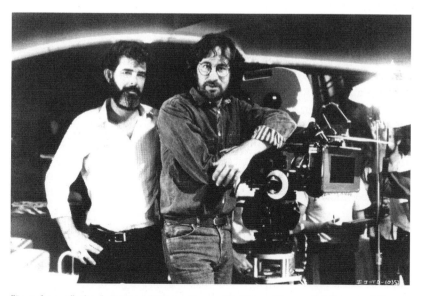

"Lucasberger": the derisive nickname given to the films of Steven Spielberg and George Lucas by critics who accuse them of infantalizing American cinema.

In his essay "Twenty-Five Reasons Why It's All Over," Wheeler Winston Dixon lists at number fifteen "the malign influence of Steven Spielberg and George Lucas" (361) and moans that "the emptiness of Lucas and Spielberg has been embraced by the public, and their films have thus become emblematic of late twentieth- and early twenty-first-century cinema: visuals over content, excess before restraint, spectacle rather than insight" (361). Dixon is no lone voice crying in the critical wilderness; his statements reflect the majority opinion among film scholars about these two men. Larry Gross, for example, claims that Spielberg and Lucas formulated "commercial cinema's discourse as we inhabit it today" (7) by elevating B-movie plots, reducing narrative complexity, and allowing technology to dominate over narrative. All this has culminated in the dominance of the "Big Loud Action Movie," which has become a "central economic fact, structuring all life, thought, and practice in Hollywood since the late 70s" (3). To their everlasting discredit, Spielberg and Lucas "realigned the creative atmosphere in Hollywood, shaping the release and slate of all the major studios and virtually crushing the European art cinema" (Gross 8).

The two have frequently been attacked not only for the conservative ideology of the Indiana Jones series but more generally for what Peter Biskind calls their "aesthetics of awe," which "infantalize" viewers by 1) overwhelming them with sound and spectacle; 2) attacking spectatorship within their films; 3) punishing cynicism; 4) eliminating or suppressing elements that contribute to irony and critical self-consciousness; 5) excluding camp; 6) attacking and discrediting adults; and 7) valorizing children and childlike qualities, particularly innocence ("Blockbuster" 124–25). It is not surprising that when David Thomson asked rhetorically, "Who killed the movies?" his answer was Spielberg and Lucas. His attack ranges from how the pair changed the industry, the crass merchandizing and spinoff deals from their movies, their betrayal of the ideals put forth in the New Hollywood cinema of the 1970s, their inability to risk tough endings, their reliance on special effects, their mentality as child-artists, the anonymity of their work, and their stress on fantasy. All in all, says Thomson, "I fear the medium has sunk beyond anything we dreamed of, leaving us stranded, a race of dreamers. This is more and worse than a bad cycle. This is something like the loss of feeling, and I blame Spielberg and Lucas" (56).

Various commentaries have discussed the intertwining connections between these extraordinarily popular filmmakers, particularly in the Indiana Jones series. Typically, such pieces emphasize their apparently conservative and simplistic nature: "The Spielberg-Lucas productions of the 1980s

... set out to reassure their audiences with comforting narratives of virtue rewarded and evil defeated, stories about the need to submit to benevolent authorities who will take care of us as parents take care of children" (Prince, *Visions* 22). Less noted is the fact that Spielberg was essentially an employee of George Lucas when they collaborated on *Raiders of the Lost Ark.* When they hatched the idea for Indiana Jones while building sandcastles on the beach of the Mauna Kea Hotel in Hawaii, Spielberg was at a low ebb in his career following the critical drubbing and financial failure of *1941.* The shaken director had to convince industry powerbrokers that he could still control a large-scale production, stick to a timetable, adhere to a budget, and fashion a commercial hit. Accordingly, he received only a quarter as much as Lucas in salary and percentage points for directing *Raiders* and ceded final-cut privileges to his friend. Lucas handled the majority of the pre- andpostproduction duties, directed some of the footage in Tunisia, and left Spielberg to work with the actors and accomplish on-location shooting.

Mindful that his reputation—and possibly the direction of his career— was on the line while making *Raiders,* Spielberg used the film "as a form of professional rehab" to prove that "he could make a movie responsibly for a relatively medium budget that would appear to be something more expensive" (McBride 310). The extensive advertising campaign for the first Indiana Jones movie harkened back to past accomplishments, inviting moviegoers to see "the new hero from the creators of *Jaws* and *Star Wars.*" Despite this yoking, Spielberg always claimed that his vision of Indiana Jones was at odds with his co-creator's view: he wanted a shabby, scruffy alcoholic protagonist modeled on the smarmy Fred C. Dobbs (*Treasure of the Sierra Madre* [1948]), while Lucas conceived of Indy as a more of a James Bond–like playboy, "'a suave Cary Grant type who used the riches from his expeditions to fund a penchant for top hats, the finest champagnes, and the slinkiest blondes'" (Spielberg qtd. in Freer 96). Spielberg always maintained that the series was "'more in George's vein'" and that he took it no more seriously than "'a barrel of buttered popcorn'" (qtd. in McBride 317–18), but he still consciously or unconsciously incorporates fundamental elements found throughout his other works into this series.

Critics who lump Spielberg and Lucas together ignore crucial distinctions between them. Although both directors clearly love technical devices, share an affection for traditional genres, and seem reluctant to explore issues of adult sexuality, their creative and business paths have diverged to the point where only rough similarities remain. While Lucas reluctantly went back behind the camera to extend the *Star Wars* franchise, he displayed little desire to move the series beyond its original outlines. Spielberg, however, has consistently pushed himself to explore deeper and more complex issues, often working on starkly different films simultaneously, such as *Jurassic Park* and *Schindler's List*. Even after critics panned his attempts to do so, as was the case with *The Color Purple*, Spielberg continued to wrestle with complicated questions of ethnicity (*Schindler's List*), history (*Saving Private Ryan*), racism (*Amistad*), human identity (*A.I.*), and technology (*Minority Report*). If anything, his darker side became more prominent, though he never totally surrendered to cynicism and despair. Bad things happen to good people in his movies, but ultimately E.T. gets to go home, Oskar saves his Jews, David spends the day with Mommy, Anderton gets back his wife and a new child, Ferrier protects his children, Jim reunites with his parents, Neary goes into space, Brody kills the shark, and Celie joins her kids.

Most of the criticism hung on Spielberg fits far more comfortably around the neck of George Lucas, particularly the reliance on special effects and computer-generated technology, the lack of complex figures, the obsession with heroic myths, and the emphasis on rescue fantasies. *Star Wars* remains a more obviously prototypical example of the traditional male action film than any of Spielberg's movies, including the Indiana Jones series. Whereas Spielberg consistently modifies and even subverts genre conventions, Lucas uses them simply as recurring narrative devices: "[T]his emphasis on plot over character makes a significant departure from classical Hollywood films, including *The Godfather* and even *Jaws,* wherein plot tended to emerge more organically as a function of the drives, desires, motivations, and goals of the central characters" (Schatz, "New Hollywood" 23). Even basic visual differences exist between the two filmmakers: Spielberg characteristically employs inventive camera manipulations, as evident in his earliest films (*Duel* and *The Sugarland Express*) as well as his later efforts (*Minority Report* and *Catch Me If You Can*), while Lucas's wooden camera movement does little besides basic tilts and pans throughout his career.

But the majority of critics still refuse to see these distinctions and progressions. Take as a recent example the comments of Jon Lewis, who insists that Lucas and Spielberg are "almost exclusively post-production directors, experts in sound and special effects and action editing" ("Perfect" 19). Such a broad claim leads him to the erroneous conclusion that the artistic signatures of Spielberg and Lucas "intersect so often and in so many ways that it just isn't useful to distinguish them" (21). But Lewis goes further. He compounds this common misunderstanding by failing to distinguish between Spielberg the director and Spielberg the producer, attempting to prove his case by citing a film (*Who Framed Roger Rabbit?*) created by one of the director's protégés, Robert Zemeckis, rather than referring to the director's own movies. The fact that a host of critics still characterize Spielberg primarily as a postproduction director—a condescending label belied by a close examination of his visual skills, creation of mise-en-scène, or direction of actors—aptly demonstrates that a superficial conception of him still reigns as critical orthodoxy.

RETROGRADE IDEOLOGY

One of the most consistent attacks on the Indiana Jones series contends that it encapsulates and propagates a conservative political and social philosophy characterized by a "nostalgic desire for authority, the return of the father, and an ideological support of the agenda of the New Right that reinstated the privileged position of the white male hero" (Aronstein 25). Citing the historical concurrence of the Reagan–Bush presidential era (1981–89) and the release dates of the Indiana Jones films (1981, 1984, 1989), this body of antagonistic criticism basically fuses the one with the other: these films were so commercially successful during a decade dominated by conservative governmental and cultural policies because they skillfully mirrored the era's essential values, camouflaging a retrograde ideology within seemingly innocuous entertainment packages. Hostile critics conflate Reagan's ideology and the film's themes, vehemently maintaining that Spielberg implicitly endorses "the new Reagan administration's policies in the Middle East, Central and South America, as well as the new regime's positions on women's rights, laissez-faire capitalism, CIA covert operations, the Moral Majority, and America's renewed stature in the world of nations" (Tomasulo, "Mr. Jones" 331–32). Putting it more bluntly, if hyperbolically, Biskind claims that "Lucas and Spielberg helped make the world safe for Reagan" ("Blockbuster" 148), and Jon Lewis goes so far as to suggest that the Indiana Jones films "anticipated and then helped define Reaganism and did so in a particularly accessible and attractive package" ("Perfect" 22).

The Indiana Jones films struck responsive chords in the collective American psyche still battered by aftershocks from the traumatic Vietnam War, divisive cultural conflicts, disheartening generational divisions, and overheated political rhetoric. "Sex, drugs, and rock 'n' roll" may have been the rallying cry for those who celebrated the Age of Aquarius, but each element in that trio contained revolutionary potential that frightened and alienated as many people as claimed it for their mantra. Add to this the national anxiety caused by an irritating oil embargo, a humiliating hostage crisis, and the seething Watergate hearings, and one readily understands why many feared that the country would rip apart from internal dissention or fall prey to external enemies. In the midst of this confusion, the Indiana Jones films gratified a deep yearning for two-hour furloughs, a nationwide nostalgia for simpler times and easily identifiable heroes and villains. *Raiders of the Lost Ark* came to be seen as the "perfect film to mark the beginning of the Reagan era" (McBride 318).

Two critics offer potent and representative critiques of the Indiana Jones films: Patricia Zimmermann ("Soldiers of Fortune: Lucas, Spielberg, Indiana Jones, and *Raiders of the Lost Ark*") and Andrew Britton ("Blissing Out: The Politics of Reaganite Entertainment"). While scrutinizing the films from leftist vantage points, these commentators provide examples of the sustained and often vitriolic critical attack leveled at the series, a decidedly negative point of view shared by other film scholars such as Ella Shohat and Robert Stam, Robert Kolker, Stephen Prince, David Thomson, Robin Wood, Frank P. Tomasulo, Peter Biskind, and Susan Aronstein, among a host of others. Zimmermann and Britton's key points provide exemplary sketches of why the overwhelming majority of these critics see the Indiana Jones cycle as prototypic commercial products, incarnating the worst elements of this conservative period in American history and filmmaking. In essence, such writers view them as recruiting posters for the Reagan political and social agendas, brightly wrapped packages of crowd-pleasing, mass entertainment that artfully conceal reactionary assumptions—razor blades buried in delicious Halloween treats.

Zimmermann contends that *Raiders'* slick exterior, rapid editing pace, and embrace of spectacle seduces viewers, enticing them to imbibe the film as pure entertainment and to ignore its "reprehensive . . . jingoism, Third World exploitation, . . . and backlash against feminism" (34). Noting that Hollywood was reeling from a sharp economic decline, increasing competition from alternative entertainment sources, and a thirty-month recession, she situates the film within the matrix of the ailing commercial film business, arguing that its publicity strategy frames it as "pure entertainment, free of ideology, and simultaneously erases it as a social practice imbedded within and referring to a current social and historical context" (34). Zimmermann's essay attempts to pull back the curtain, to "unpack how ideas of capitalism, history, male domination, and fantasy . . . are constituted in the exhibition and public discourse of filmic spectacle" (35). She elucidates how a conservative ideology that "poses American muscle, machismo, technology, and cunning as solutions to the complexities of the Third World" (39) fuels the film's narrative, how the figure of Indiana Jones "elaborates a male fantasy

... as adventurous, competitive, and intellectual" (37), and how the press developed a behind-the-scenes scenario that conflated the men responsible for the series (mainly Spielberg and Lucas) with the swashbuckling fictional archeologist who embodied it.

In a longer and more densely theoretical essay, Andrew Britton flogs a wide spectrum of popular 1980s films, including *E.T.*, the *Superman* films, the *Star Wars* trilogy, *Ghostbusters*, James Bond movies, *Dragonslayer*, *Modern Problems*, *An Officer and a Gentleman*, *Poltergeist*, as well as the Indiana Jones series. He concludes that Spielberg creates exemplary instances of what he labels "Reaganite entertainment"—"a general movement of reaction and conservative reassurance in the contemporary Hollywood cinema" (2). A number of characteristics demarcate such films: 1) their highly ritualized and formulaic character; 2) their interminable solipsism (self-celebrating and self-referential; 3) their flattering of the spectator with his or her familiarity with conventional forms; 4) their escapist sensibility; 5) their refusal to challenge the viewer; 6) their overt signaling of how audiences ought to feel; 7) their simplistic resolution of tensions and anxieties; 8) their pleasurable obviousness; and 9) their insistence on their unreality, playfulness, and detachment from real issues. As might be expected, Britton's wrath finds its most prominent target in Steven Spielberg, whose films, while "undoubtedly distinctive," are seen as "ideological deposits" (42). Ultimately, he hopes that "directors will emerge who have more radical sympathies and a greater readiness to contemplate the real conditions of the social present than Lucas, Spielberg," and others who failed to create, during the entire decade, even one certifiable "masterpiece" (42).

The critical positions represented by Zimmermann and Britton merit serious consideration, although the latter's wholesale rejection of an entire decade of films smacks of a rabid elitism at odds with his more egalitarian aesthetics and social sentiments. Both commentators rightly demand a rigorous and skeptical exploration of these much-acclaimed and exceptionally profitable movies, along with a steadfast refusal to accept them as merely charming entertainment or diverting spectacles. I too believe that films always have ideological valances, that critical scrutiny and engagement are always necessary, and that the less transparent the beliefs, the more deeply implanted the values. Spielberg, like any artist, is responsible for the images that he showers upon us. I am persuaded, for example, by claims that in creating his dark Other and ethnic characters, Spielberg relies on "theme park cliches drawn from the orientalist repertoire" (Shohat and Stam 124). Equally distressing, his depiction of women remains fundamentally juvenile and essentially degrading. Within these films Spielberg's obsession with reconstituting families persists, as does his fixation with strong father figures. Even so, the straight line some critics draw from Spielberg's problems with his own father, to his divorce from Amy Irving, to his casting of Sean Connery (James Bond begetting Indiana Jones), to the election and reelection of Ronald Reagan seems overly reductive. Perhaps not surprisingly, many of these critical onslaughts seem motivated as much by the series' hefty box-office receipts, the producer's canny studio deal, the director's percentage points, and the films' merchandizing bonanzas as by their so-called repressive politics. In other words, the astonishing success of the series guaranteed that it would attract a horde of detractors innately distrustful of its mass appeal.

AN ALTERNATIVE READING OF THE INDIANA JONES TRILOGY

In contrast to the standard critical readings of Spielberg's work as encapsulating "regressive values" (Biskind, "Blockbuster" 115), I position the cycle as critiquing rather than celebrating conservative notions of American masculinity and imperialism. A recognition of the significant deviations in the series challenges the nearly monolithic explications of the Indiana Jones figure as emblematic of American manhood and these films as consecrations of nationalistic arrogance, dominance, and power. One could claim that by selecting this highly masculinized and spectacularized genre, or even deciding to work within a genre structure at all, Spielberg embraces a fundamentally conservative approach to filmmaking necessarily founded on stock plots and unoriginal characters. Such a rigid stance, however, ignores the power of narrative filmmaking within prescribed patterns, the attraction of cinematic categories with historical lineage, and the lure of popular artistic achievement. Along with denigrating popular genre filmmakers like John Ford and Alfred Hitchcock, it ignores how creative artists from ancient Greece to Elizabethan England to contemporary America use genre formats and characters to situate their stories within a rich and highly varied context. Those visual artists who best negotiate the tricky terrain of genre formulations manage to fuse their personal themes with collective practices. For them, the discipline of working within genres becomes liberating rather than confining; it provides a series of traditional, communal, historically sanctioned formats within which individual expressions can find structure and latitude.

So it is with Spielberg, who consistently pushes beyond the confining strictures of the action/adventure genre in this series, often subverting its most cherished conventions. Take, for example, the opening of *Last Crusade*, a set piece often admired for harkening back to the revered western classics of John Ford. This sequence satirically comments on these previous works rather than reaffirming their inherent values. Instead of encountering the Seventh Cavalry racing to the rescue of terrorized settlers or kidnapped maidens against the grandeur of Monument Valley, viewers meet a band of local Boy Scouts who can hardly mount their horses without falling. In place of John Wayne–like figures, men who rode tall in the saddle, we get an adolescent hero whose father makes him count to twenty like a little boy, a clear reduction of masculine stereotypes. The archetypal chase sequence occurs only briefly on horseback, and when Indiana tries to jump from an overhanging rock onto the saddle, a traditional feat in westerns, he lands sprawling on the ground. Spielberg even replaces the broad landscape with enclosed spaces on, of all things, a speeding circus train. For all its breathtaking editing pace and bravura traveling shots, this is the stuff of revisionism, parody, and burlesque, not authentic heroism, high adventure, and worshipful homage. Spielberg reduces the fabled West, the traditional site of the classic stories that define American national greatness and masculine ideals, to a playground for children.

All three Indiana Jones films contain such conspicuous deviations from the macho codes that dominate their source materials, the stereotypical matinee serials and conventional adventure movies; in so doing, they call into question the American masculine codes of conduct acclaimed in those movies. While usually ignored by commentators who cast Indiana Jones alongside ancient mythic heroes, as well as those who assail the films' ostensible ideological conservatism, Spielberg challenges simplistic definitions of masculine heroism and offers significant shades of gray within a portrait most critics accuse him of rendering in simple black and white. His unmistakable departures from genre expectations should be foregrounded more explicitly; they show Spielberg conspicuously bending, if not always clearly subverting, genre conventions to encompass characters and narratives with recognizable personal themes that reappear consistently throughout his work. Equally crucial, these variations and alterations demonstrate Spielberg's emerging discomfort with several fundamental aspects of "matinee" moviemaking, particularly the cardboard figures who dominate genre formulas.

For all his rugged charm and daring physical feats, Indiana Jones is an ineffective and largely unsuccessful figure, one not particularly well suited to hoist the banner of American manhood triumphantly aloft. On the most basic level, his dread of snakes, boyish yelps of pain, and inconclusive sexual interludes mark his lack of heroic stature within a genre pumped up with steroidal action heroes or populated with suave super spies. More damning, he rarely captures and never retains what he originally sets out to obtain. The films shift their focus from external treasure hunts to internal psychodramas, not particularly common terrain for previous adventure sagas. Moving from *Temple of Doom* to *Raiders* to *Last Crusade,* Indiana's status as an independent hero actually regresses: he becomes more emotionally, physically, and psychologically dependent, needing others to rescue him from outward dangers and inner degenerations. In film after film, he exercises bad judgment, displaying severe lapses in thought and understanding that almost cost his life and endangering those around him. He is also cruel. His seduction and abandonment of Marion, first deserting her as an adolescent and later leaving her at the mercy of Belloq and the Nazis in the desert, demonstrates careless disregard, blatant insularity, and self-centered superficiality rather than traditional masculine heroism and gallantry.

Ironically, Indiana survives his sternest tests either by failing or by not doing: he doesn't look at the Ark and not does not grasp the Holy Grail. He is more reactive than proactive. Even more tellingly, he never really defeats his antagonist in a one-to-one confrontation; most of the time, he is either one step behind them or at their mercy. Mola Ram, Belloq, Donovan, and Schneider all die because of their own character flaws and obsessions, not because of Indiana's actions. Jones always stays in the contest, but he crosses the goal line only because his enemies have removed themselves from the competition. And he rarely carries and never keeps the game ball. In *Last Crusade,* he impotently confronts Hitler, the ultimate embodiment of evil and dread, mutely accepting his autograph. What red-blooded American hero, even at the cost of his own life, would fail to take a shot at the German leader in the midst of World War II? Given all of these clear deviations, it seems strange that critics and fans alike enshrine Indiana Jones as personifying Reaganist masculine values when he violates some of the most prominent and essential codes for action/adventure heroes. He survives his trials, but Indiana Jones never becomes the "monument . . . to ancient ideals of manhood" claimed by Zimmermann and others (Zimmermann 38). Quite the opposite, he emerges from these films as neither a paragon of traditional masculine values nor an unalloyed heir to the adventure heroes who preceded him.

Spielberg treats big business and governmental institutions negatively throughout the series. In *Raiders,* for example, American War Department bureaucrats hire Jones to obtain the Ark before it falls into the hands of the Third Reich. Described throughout the film as a superweapon, it contains "secrets no one knows," is capable of "leveling mountains and laying waste to entire regions," and remains a "source of unspeakable power." Any "army which carries the Ark before it is invincible," claims the awestruck Brody. Yet such a devastating weapon, whose mushroom-shaped cloud resembles the atomic bomb, is ultimately rendered powerless by a much stronger force: governmental incompetence. Even the daring Indiana Jones, who has defeated a slew of Germans and survived Belloq's treachery, finds himself powerless when confronted with the rigid intransigence of oily, pipe-smoking Washington functionaries. Despite their bland assurances that this relic "of incredible historical significance" is "somewhere very safe" and that "top men are working on it right now," the sacred item for which men have searched "for nearly three thousand years" ends up nailed shut and padlocked inside a wooden crate. Stamped "Top Secret / Army Intel / Do Not Open," this priceless historical artifact and supreme weapon gathers dust amidst countless other similarly inscribed crates in a cavernous, Xanadu-like warehouse, buried not by Egyptian sand but institutionalized ineptitude. If Indiana Jones encapsulates nationalistic pride and simplistic patriotism, how are we to interpret his last words to Marion: "Bureaucratic fools. They don't know what they've got there"? Such caustic sentiments ring antithetical to the jingoism often ascribed to this series.

While American governmental incompetence renders Indiana and the Ark impotent in *Raiders,* avaricious representatives of big business prove among Jones's most intimidating foes throughout the series. Indiana never aligns himself with wealthy collectors, such as the unscrupulous man in the panama hat (Tim Hiser) who takes the Cross of Coronado from him early in the film and later washes overboard in a violent storm. His goal is always to bring objects of antiquity back intact, to study them in museums rather than to use them to gain power over others or to satisfy personal manias. While his stated objectives bespeak cultural insensitivity, an initially imperialist perspective, and even a racist mentality, Indiana's motivations surely fall into a lesser circle of hell than those who would ransack ancient cultures for self-aggrandizement, such as Belloq, Mola Ram, and Dr. Schneider. Walter Donovan, in the *Last Crusade,* most dramatically represents the amoral businessman willing to betray his own country for self-indulgent desires, in this case to gain immortality by drinking from the Cup of Christ. His hideous demise offers little hint that Spielberg sympathizes with the economic policies of an administration dedicated to supporting large corporations.

Finally, there is the most widely held and perhaps most damning criticism of all: Indiana Jones represents a colonialist mentality, and the films support Reagan's imperialist adventures throughout the world. So, for example, McBride severely chastises Spielberg for skillfully manipulating audiences into "identifying with this ruthless figure and finding him heroic," for cynically exploiting him for "purely visceral thrills," for presenting his violence and greed in a "winking tongue-in-cheek style," and for "anesthetizing the audience's moral sense" over a "casually amoral" character who "loots Third World cultures" (317). And that's from a sympathetic biographer. Shohat and Stam offer this summation: "The Indiana Jones series recycled Rider Haggard and Kipling for the Reagan-Bush era, resurrecting the colonial adventure genre with insidious charm" (124). Tomasulo claims that Indiana's theft and exploitation "marks a return to values of gunboat diplomacy and Manifest Destiny" ("Mr. Jones" 333), and Biskind contends that Spielberg "shamelessly revived and relegitimated the figure of the dashing colonialist adventurer who plunders and pillages antiquities from Third World countries for First World collections" ("Blockbuster" 118–19). All of these interpretations posit that, by making Indiana Jones such an attractive figure, Spielberg signals approval of his actions. Consequently, such readings argue that these three films encourage audiences to identify with whatever Indiana Jones does.

While I agree that Indiana Jones always begins his adventures as an imperialistic mercenary devoid of cultural understanding, the films clearly function as moral lessons about how wrong he has been and how he learns to correct his vision—far from reinforcing his initial worldviews. In essence, the three movies utilize the conventions and appropriate the veneer of Hollywood fantasy/adventure movies to censure the western ideology initially personified by Indiana Jones. They do this in two basic ways: by establishing the power of the divine objects he seeks, and by forcing him to accept the wisdom of the ancient cultures he encounters. Indiana begins each film blatantly rejecting any suggestion of supernatural power associated with the Sankara Stones, the Ark of the Covenant, or the Cup of Christ. He arrogantly dismisses their connection with supernatural powers as superstitions or delusions. Yet each film concludes, literally, with a miracle, a dramatic representation of the long-sought artifact's connection with the divine that totally repudiates Indiana's original position: the Sankara Stones destroy the evildoers, the Ark melts the Nazis, and the Holy Grail brings Henry Jones back to life.

Because these hallowed objects actualize mystical powers, the cultures that revere them ultimately emerge as repositories of spiritual wisdom, not as the primitive societies Indiana first perceives them to be. Their collective wisdom surpasses the cynical comprehension of those who inhabit the modern world. Thus, groups of people Indy initially stereotypes as merely ignorant and backward are reconfigured as intimately connected with sacred sources of meaning. Through them, he (and presumably the audience as well) experiences a sense of the transcendent. Such knowledge, forbidden or forgotten in contemporary times, can be both profane and holy; it is capable of salvation and destruction. But it does exist, despite Indiana's dismissive skepticism. Within each film, Indiana Jones moves from ignorance to understanding, from a simplistic and shallow conceptualization of "uncivilized" societies to a deeper grasp of and appreciation for their knowledge. Far from being sympathetic and reassuring portraits designed "to legitimize the colonizer's act of appropriation" (Shohat and Stam 145), the films argue that removing objects from one culture to another is arrogant, dangerous, and destructive, a lesson that Jones must learn and relearn in *Temple of Doom, Raiders,* and *Last Crusade* but that has evaded most of his critics.

Given the role of sacrosanct elements in the ultimate turnaround of the Jones trilogy, critics who assert that Spielberg advocates the looting of native cultures and that the films express "fantasies of American cultural dominance over Third World primitives" (McBride 320) strike me as perversely incorrect. Their interpretations, based on the convictions Indy expresses as the films begin, completely ignore the total repudiation of those opinions by the time the films conclude. One constant refrain in this series is that Indiana Jones learns to respect the traditions of nonwestern cultures. Yet even supportive critics such as Henry Sheehan insist that nothing Indy experiences, "no matter how melodramatic, causes him to undergo any sort of change" ("PANning" 59). Nothing could be further from the truth. At the conclusion of each movie, his initial need for external gratification (fame and fortune) shifts to an inner need for love, understanding, and reconciliation. The callow Indiana Jones who starts each movie becomes the caring Indiana Jones who ends it, a transition made possible only by his perceptions being wiped clean and his acceptance that divinity exists. One could claim, as does Aronstein, that Spielberg's invocation of religious iconography is inherently conservative, a lamentation that "America has failed because it has lost its religious and familial (read patriarchal) values, and its strength will be rediscovered only in an individual rediscovery of these traditions and a return to both transcendent and human fathers" (25). This reading remains plausible if one equates the director's vague sense of vernacular religiosity (see chapter 1) with a right-wing political agenda.

Instead, I would place Spielberg squarely in the tradition of artists who sought to highlight the sublime in the everyday, the sense of wonder and awe amidst the dross of common experiences. In the Indiana Jones movies, he refers directly to specific religious traditions by including objects sacred to Hindus, Jews, and Christians. These objects of desire remind viewers of possibilities beyond the ephemeral and meanings beyond the material. But such thematic consistencies, contrary to the overwhelming majority of critical opinion on this series, does not necessarily situate Spielberg in the same pew with right-wing ideologues, supporters of American imperialism, antifeminists, homophobes, and racists. It merely makes him a man searching for spiritual values in his life and work, a desire shared by a vast proportion of the world's population. By finding memorable ways to express this need for something beyond the transient, something that partakes of the ethereal, Spielberg positions himself within the company of artists who sought to see radiance within the ordinary.

* * *

Spielberg is right: all of his films are essentially melodramas, despite the adrenalin-pumping overlay of exciting exploits and daring escapes that lead many commentators to dismiss him as emotionally manipulative and thematically hollow. This amalgamation of actions and feelings remains a vital component in understanding his popular success and longevity as a filmmaker: audiences thrill to the whirling action sequences replete with technical and dramatic flair, but they also connect with the characters who undergo these trials and survive these adventures. Unlike conventional action/adventure movie characters, Spielberg's figures ultimately discover that their most important quest is for inner knowledge, emotional depth, and psychological fulfillment rather than material gains or public glory. Lou Jean Poplin, Frank Abagnale, and Indiana Jones all seek to reestablish stable family relationships, no matter how skewed their methods. Lou Ann never attains this goal, and her obsession dooms her husband; Frank replaces his charismatic biological father with Carl Hanratty, a steady and socially acceptable if not particularly warm substitution. Only Indiana Jones manages to achieve a level of familial reconciliation as father and son come, at long last, to respect one another as equals.

3

"Objects in the Mirror Are Closer Than They Appear": Spielberg's Monster Movies

The Monster Movie

The monster movie, or horror film, has much in common with the science-fiction and fantasy film genres discussed in chapter 1; all three incorporate elements and creatures beyond ordinary reality. They compel audiences to confront difference, or "otherness," in a wide variety of formulations, whether nonhuman creatures, alien beings, or deranged men and women. Narratively, Robin Wood's basic formula for the horror film, "normality is threatened by the monster," aptly fits films within the three genres. "Normality" might be defined as the status quo at the start of the movie, and "the monster" as the embodied force that seeks to alter or destroy it (Wood 78). Noel Carroll posits the "deep structure of the horror fiction" as a three-part movement from normality, to disruption, to the final confrontation and defeat of the monster (200). Orcs, replicants, and Norman Bates all represent malevolent, destructive deviations from what *Lord of the Rings, Blade Runner,* and *Psycho* posit as acceptable conventions and normative behaviors in their vastly different societies.

Though these genres contain fundamentally similar plot structures, their practitioners generally intend their narratives to evoke different responses from spectators: the fantasy film provokes amazement, the science-fiction film speculation, and the horror film fright. Carroll bases his entire philosophy on the complex series of emotions these "art-horror" movies elicit from the viewer. He argues that while watching these films, "the emotions of the audience are supposed to mirror those of the positive human characters in certain, but not all, respects" (18). The attitudes of the characters, therefore, create dissimilar responses to the monsters in different types of films; so, for example, normative figures in the horror movies usually regard these creatures as "abnormal disturbances of the natural order," while those in fantasy films see their antagonists as evil forces in their everyday worlds that threaten their existence. The result is that the monster in the horror film is "an extraordinary character in an ordinary world, whereas in fairy tales and the like the monster is an ordinary creature in an extraordinary world" (16). While our rational consciousness understands that these are fictional creations with no power to harm us, we share the emotions of the characters trapped within the narrative unfolding before us.

Even though they are filled with dark and terrible creatures, fantasy films are fundamentally playful and quite distant. They overtly foreground their status as make-believe. The most elaborate fantasy films create worlds of such imaginative breadth that few apparent connections exist between our lives and those fantastical scenes enacted on the screen. The space between our world of Happy Meals and sitcoms and their world of incantations and trolls remains too great to substitute one for the other. We cheer the bravery of daring fantasy heroes and recoil from the evil creatures who oppose them, but we never mistake their world for ours—too many stark contrasts exist between the two. This explicit dissimilarity remains the central appeal of fantasy films: they transport viewers to radically alternative realities governed by different rules, exciting adventures, and strange beings. The fantasy film grows out of what we normally categorize as the impossible, defying physical laws and conventional constructions of reality.

Unlike fantasy films, science-fiction movies usually originate from a potentially possible, or at least speculatively imaginable, premise and proceed to ask, "If this is true, then what would happen if [fill in the blank] were to occur?" The critical discourse surrounding these films often questions how much they rely on current scientific data or deviate from or conform to what can and cannot actually be done; in other words, they assess the likelihood that events depicted in the film might actually transpire given the current state of scientific knowledge and technological advancement. Thus possibility, often stretched to its most fragile thinness, remains essential to the appeal of science fiction. Viewers must be convinced that events on the screen remain within the realm of what is (at least remotely) possible outside the theater, and filmmakers strive for levels of realism sufficient for audiences to accept the reel world as roughly similar to the real world. If we do not believe that essential elements in *2001: A Space Odyssey* (1968) or *RoboCop* (1987) are congruent with our understanding of daily existence, then they slip from science fiction into the realm of the fantastic. No matter how outlandish the plots become, or how unrealistic the characters, science-fiction films remain grounded in the possible, exuding a veneer of everyday reality easily recognized as somehow akin to our own.

The most effective monster movies keep this veneer of everyday reality while incorporating supernatural creatures or aberrant human beings. Whereas science-fiction films are usually concerned with future events, monster movies often focus on the present dangers that surround us or those that exist inside ourselves. Consequently, the attitudes toward the unknown that underlie the various films in each genre are distinctly different. The traditional narrative trajectory of science-fiction and monster movies contains confrontations between something unknown and those who seek to understand or are threatened by it. But in science-fiction movies, the impulse to explore the unknown, even if it leads to death, is generally applauded. Such brave acts are necessary for humanity to advance and are considered a noble individual sacrifice for the common good. In monster movies, however, admonitions such as "these things are against the laws of God and nature" or "mankind was not meant to know these secrets" propose limitations to scientific investigation and personal curiosity. Actions meant to penetrate various mysteries result mainly from overweening hubris; the arrogant individual threatens the common good for his or her personal aggrandizement. Thus one genre accepts and even celebrates the dangers inherent in an exploration of the unknown, while the other persistently cautions against transgressing natural, moral, and spiritual boundaries of acceptable behavior.

While commentators such as Bruce Kawin trace the roots of monster movies back to their literary sources in "folklore, mythology, and classical tragedy" (314), the analytic perspective most commonly utilized has been psychoanalysis, particularly the theories of Sigmund Freud and C. G. Jung employed by critics such as Margaret Tarratt, Harvey R. Greenberg, Morris Dickstein, Noel Carroll, and Robin Wood. Wood's classic formulation of the horror movie uses the psychoanalytic concept of "surplus repression" ("the process whereby people are conditioned from earliest infancy to take on predetermined roles within that culture," such as "monogamous heterosexual bourgeois patriarchal capitalists" [71]) to inform his analysis of these movies in the 1970s and 1980s. Following in the footsteps of Freud and Herbert Marcuse, Wood asserts that "all known existing societies are to some degree surplus-repressive" (71), and therefore the monsters in these movies are projections of what is suppressed in society and the individual;

such transgressive threats must be disowned and ultimately annihilated for the dominant ideology to survive:

> One might say that the true subject of the horror genre is the struggle for recognition of all that our civilization represses or oppresses, its re-emergence dramatized, as in our nightmares, as an object of horror, a matter for terror, and the happy ending (when it exists) typically signifying the restoration of repression. . . . Popular films, then, respond to interpretation as at once the personal dreams of their makers and the collective dreams of their audiences, the fusion made possible by the shared structures of a common ideology. (75, 78)

According to Wood, the monster movie reenacts a brutal cycle of cultural subjugation within which society destroys those corruptive, unruly elements that it deems deviant and therefore dangerous to its rigid ideology.

Nearly everyone who writes about monster movies accepts that the disruptive creatures who inhabit them represent dark, primal gushes from beneath encrusted layers of socially acceptable behavior, though exactly what repressed desires creep, crawl, slither, and squirm into our cultural consciousness remains a debated issue. Wood focuses on the surplus repression of sexual energy in various forms (homosexuality, bisexuality, female sexuality, and childhood sexuality) and the closely related concept of "otherness" in intolerant societies and constrained individuals (72–73). Other critics emphasize how various monsters force viewers to confront their fragile mortality; so, for example, R. H. W. Dillard calls these films "pageants of death" (37), Morris Dickstein claims that their ultimate attraction is "the fear of death" (69), and Paul Wells maintains that the genre "is predominately concerned with the fear of death" (10). John D. Denne turns outward, seeing such films as "social problem plays" (125), while Andrew Tudor talks of contemporary movies as hybrids attesting to "the need to express rage and terror in the midst of postmodern upheaval" ("Paranoia" 114). S. S. Prawer asserts that monster movies embody "fears about the rebellion of man's lower instinctual nature" (55) and that "the enlightened, scientific view of the world may not tell us all there is to know" (81).

Whatever the various creatures represent, it remains clear that monster movies force viewers to confront the darker side of human nature and the world surrounding us. One need not look far afield to find the terrors and anxieties that make our hold on rationality fragile and tentative. Daily horrors assault us in an endless stream of sound bites and montages, as close to us as the remote-control button or the house next door. Twenty-four hours a day, news anchors speak in measured tones about the murders of children, the mutilations of women, the ravages of war, the toll of lethal epidemics, and countless other tragic events. We even label these occurrences as "monstrous" and thus liken them to the havoc produced by mythical creatures on our movie screens. That we live in an age dominated by scientific reason provides little comfort amidst the global violence and individual madness that surrounds us; scientific and technological advances cause as much anxiety as elation:

> In the ways that fairytales, folktales, and gothic romances articulated the fears of the "old" world, the contemporary horror film has defined and illustrated the fears of the "new" world characterized by a rationale of industrial, technological, and economic determinism.... It has interrogated the deep-seated effects of change and responded to the newly determined grand narratives of social, scientific, and philosophical thought. (Wells 3)

Effective monster movies, therefore, perform the traditional cathartic function of art. By giving image and voice to deviant desires, frightening nightmares, and depraved emotions, they force us to confront our most dreaded demons. But situating these films within the protected realm of the movie theater lessens our terror and contains our anxieties by inevitably arriving at a finite conclusion. Thus, the films release our repressed demons and desires, simultaneously overpowering them by restoring the social order.

Spielberg's Monster Movies

Most books about monster movies pay scant, if any, attention to Steven Spielberg's forays into the genre: *Duel* (1971), *Jaws* (1975), *Jurassic Park* (1993), *The Lost World* (1997), and *War of the Worlds* (2005). Yet each film falls within the norms of the genre and has clear antecedents in earlier classics: *Duel* in the motiveless-madman movies (*Psycho*); *Jaws* in the *Godzilla* series or *King Kong*; *Jurassic Park* and *The Lost World* in the *Frankenstein* films; and *War of the Worlds* in the mode of superintelligent creatures with extraordinary powers who seek to destroy us (such as *Dracula*). To further explore these basic connections, I will use an essay by David J. Russell and a book by Andrew Tudor to make some generalizations about these movies before looking at them in more depth. Russell's valuable contribution to the field is his taxonomy of monsters: real (abnormal human behavior), unreal (magical and supernatural creatures), and partially real (related to space but having no relation to nature as "normally" experienced) (241). Within these categories, the unseen driver of *Duel* falls into the first realm, the shark of *Jaws* and dinosaurs of *Jurassic Park* and *The Lost World* into the third, and the aliens of *War of the Worlds* into the second. *Jaws* and the *Jurassic Park* movies also fit neatly within the "revenge of nature" category so common within monster movies, what Russell identifies as "deviant nature" (247). Thus, Spielberg's monster films have clear connections to a tradition of movie creatures that stretches back to the earliest days of the cinema.

Andrew Tudor's book *Monsters and Mad Scientists* offers a sophisticated discussion of the cultural history of these movies. Like many other critics, he observes a crucial shift in post-1960s horror movies from exotic sites to everyday locations amidst contemporary landscapes. His notion that "the familiar invaders of the fifties and sixties are transmuted into the 'natural nasties' of the seventies" and that the 1970s and 1980s feature "eco-threat" movies that deal with "inexplicable attacks from nature . . . some revolving around encounters with evolutionary leftovers" (62) encompasses *Jaws* and the two *Jurassic Park* movies. Asserting that these types of monster movies descend directly from Hitchcock's *The Birds* (1963), and using the shark's fin speeding through the water in the seemingly safe lagoon as one clear example of the "eruption of abnormality into a mundane setting" (123), Tudor demonstrates how these films generate power by the "matter-of-fact way in which we are shown" the monster that fractures "a naturally represented physical order [and] simultaneously affirms both the precariousness and significance of that order" (124). Though Tudor dismisses *Jaws* as "barely meriting the genre designation" (175), the fact remains that it, along with *Duel, Jurassic Park, The Lost World,* and *War of the Worlds,* illustrates his main points, and his comments shed light on why these five films function as effective monster movies.

Concomitant with his historical progression, Tudor categorizes monster movies as an ongoing set of dichotomous alternatives, each pairing a "broad tendency within the genre, not an exclusive option": supernatural/secular, external/internal, and autonomous/dependent (8). All of Spielberg's monster films fall within this third category, in which, according to Tudor, "the threatening force is quite simply there, quite independent of humanity, though posing a threat to it," or, alternatively, the creatures remain "dependent on human volition, and the threat they pose stands in significant contrast to that presented by more autonomous monsters" (10). The shark in *Jaws* and the aliens in *War of the Worlds,* for example, would fall within the realm of the autonomous, the dinosaurs in *Jurassic Park* and *Lost World* into the dependent, and the truck driver in *Duel* somewhere along the continuum between them. The crucial question posed here is the assigning of personal and societal accountability: "Are we responsible for creating the threatening situation, or does it emerge quite independently of our intentions and actions?" (11). In *Jaws, War of the Worlds,* and *Duel,* the shark, the aliens, and the truck arrive mostly independent of human action, while in *Jurassic Park* and *The Lost World* human intervention is responsible for creating the dinosaurs.

Spielberg's genre movies usually appear traditional because he skillfully adheres to many of the external aspects of particular cinematic conventions, but a closer investigation reveals how often he deviates from traditional audience expectations in his science-fiction, fantasy, and action/adventure films. The same cannot be said for his monster movies. Though these pictures exhibit consummate technical craftsmanship, superb storytelling, and adroit pacing, they offer little intellectual or emotional complexity. Take, as an important and representative example, his monsters themselves. The most effective films in this genre slyly encourage audience involvement with their creatures, making their deaths somewhat bittersweet events: "Few horror films have totally unsympathetic Monsters; . . . in many . . . the Monster is clearly the emotional center, and much more human than the cardboard representatives of normality" (Wood 80). We may not condone the murders committed by Frankenstein's creature, the bloodsucking of Count Dracula, or the urban destruction of King Kong, but we understand their plights and, at least to some extent, sympathize with them. Like players in an ancient Greek tragedy, they are helplessly locked into their destinies. But no viewer will express ambivalent feelings or experience a moment of regret about the demise of Spielberg's monsters. Basically, his motiveless and mindless antagonists attack anything that strays into their paths, including the cutest of children, and represent brutally primitive instincts that must be crushed for human society to survive.

Spielberg constructs his films as integrally closed universes within which the forces of civilization defeat those of chaos and darkness: nothing here to keep us awake at night once we leave the theater. His movies are throwbacks to the pre-1960s "secure horror" pictures (as differentiated from the "paranoid horror" films that emerged in the 1970s), which Tudor characterizes as showing successful human intervention, effective expertise, legitimate authorities, sustainable order, external threats, center-periphery organization, defined boundaries, and closed narratives ("Paranoia" 108). Spielberg's monsters all represent external threats: the truck (a monster of technology), the shark (a monster of nature), the aliens (monsters from space), or the dinosaurs (monsters of science and industry). The director fits comfortably within Robin Wood's "reactionary wing," since Spielberg's monsters conform to the basic descriptions of movies in this category: "[T]he designation of the monster as simply evil" and "the presentation of the monster as totally nonhuman" (192).

Stephen King, who surely knows something about popular horror fiction, claims that the genre is essentially "as Republican as a banker in a three-piece suit" (Underwood and Miller 9). This observation applies to Spielberg's works, since they consistently present abnormality, in the form of his monsters, as something to be wholly and permanently obliterated. The destruction of the rampaging creature strongly reaffirms the ideological force of the status quo embodied within the makeshift families of *Jaws, War of the Worlds,* and the *Jurassic Park* films. If the essential struggle in the horror story occurs between the normal and the abnormal, then Spielberg's five films can be "conceptualized as a symbolic defense of a culture's standards of normality. . . . The abnormal is allowed center stage solely as a foil for the cultural order, which will ultimately be vindicated by the end of the fiction" (Carroll 199). We leave the theater after Spielberg's monster movies feeling confident that threats to our survival and our value system exist outside ourselves; we remain secure, reassured that humankind can defeat whatever evil forces seek to oppose or even dramatically alter it. The status quo seems more appealing, not to mention more powerful, after such dramatic confrontations because it has emerged triumphant over the lethal challenges posed by the forces of darkness, such as sea creatures, mechanical monsters, and mutant reptiles.

I have organized my discussion of Spielberg's monster movies out of strict chronological order, saving the most significant and widely written-about film in this category, *Jaws,* for an extended discussion at the end of the chapter. While this arrangement may be disconcerting to readers expecting a historical transition from *Duel* to *Jaws* to the *Jurassic Park* movies to *War of the Worlds,* such a pattern would not fully emphasize how Spielberg's filmmaking technique is more sophisticated and mature than virtually all the critics who assail him claim. To respond to them most effectively, it is necessary to leave ample space to elaborate the charges leveled against *Jaws* and to offer my counterarguments to these invectives.

Still on Land

Jaws did not spring fully grown from the head of twenty-six-year-old Steven Spielberg. This watershed film's enduring effect upon the director's subsequent career, its pervasive impact on the public's movie expectations, and its profound influence on the industry's marketing strategies followed two smaller films made before Spielberg cast off to sea: *Duel* (television debut, 1971; expanded theatrical release, 1972) and *The Sugarland Express* (1974). Making these pictures taught the fledgling filmmaker valuable technical lessons and thematic refinements he employed with far greater panache and to much wider acclaim in *Jaws,* ultimately transforming a conventional novel into one of the most popular movies in cinema history. But like almost everything else in its path, David Mann (*Duel*) and the Poplins (*Sugarland Express*) became chum for the shark. In the wake of *Jaws,* for better or worse, film directors, theater audiences, and Hollywood moviemaking would never be the same again.

Duel: Beyond the Screen

Before the shark, the dinosaurs, and the aliens, there was the truck. *Duel* tells the story of David Mann (Dennis Weaver), a typical suburban businessman on his way to a crucial meeting with an important client. Driving though the California desert, Mann unwittingly becomes the target of a monstrous truck and its maniacal driver, who unleash an escalating series of increasingly violent and potentially lethal attacks against him in the sparsely populated terrain. The relentless spiral of this onslaught forces the diffident Mann to defend himself and ultimately to destroy his brutal adversary. In the film's climactic showdown, Mann steers his car toward the truck, leaps out just before impact, and watches his automobile propel the murderous vehicle and its driver over a steep cliff. Throughout the movie, the audience never sees the trucker's face or learns what provokes him to torment the seemingly innocuous Mann.

Duel aired originally as ABC's "Movie of the Weekend" on November 13, 1971; Universal expanded the film from seventy-three to eighty-eight minutes, spending an additional hundred thousand dollars for three days of extra shooting and adding four additional scenes: Mann beginning his journey from his garage, through the city, and into the desert (written by Spielberg); Mann apologizing to his wife (Jacqueline Scott) on the phone in the laundromat (written by the producer, George Eckstein); the truck pushing Mann's car into a train (written by Spielberg); and the truck and the stalled school bus (written by Eckstein). Dennis Weaver recorded a narrative voiceover that continues throughout much of the movie, a running commentary not in Richard Matheson's original screenplay (adapted from his short story published in the April 1971 issue of *Playboy*). The studio released this expanded version, which won Best Picture prizes in French and Italian film festivals, to European and other theaters around the world almost exactly a year later. *Duel* made Spielberg an instant hit with international critics, such as the influential Dilys Powell of the *Sunday Times* in London: "Dylis Powell saw the picture and flipped out for it, and she gathered all the London critics together in one room and showed it to them one night, and the criticism got Universal and the CIC to release the picture in Europe" (Helpern 4–5). Shot in a mere sixteen days, mostly on Highway 14 just north of Los Angeles, and with an original production budget of only $750,000, *Duel* proved a pleasant box-office surprise by grossing $8 million (in overseas revenues) and even earning re-release in U.S. theaters in 1983, with little additional box-office profits.

THE TECHNIQUES OF TERROR

Spielberg initially envisioned *Duel* with very limited dialogue, and the original television edition had only fifty or so spoken lines. Putting his storyboard on clusters of IBM computer cards, Spielberg set out to pictorialize the entire movie:

> I had an artist paint an entire map, as if a helicopter camera had photographed the entire road where the chase was taking place. . . . And I was able to wrap this map around the motel room, and I just crossed things off. . . . The overview gave me a geographical sense, a lot of help in knowing where to spend the time, where to do the most coverage, where to make a scene really sing out. (Qtd. in McBride 202)

This basic visualization led many commentators to discuss *Duel* as close to a silent film, noting that it relies almost exclusively on visual images. While not downplaying the pictorial dexterity necessary to sustain tension in what is essentially one long extended chase sequence, such an analysis ignores Spielberg's imaginative use of sound other than dialogue throughout the picture. More importantly, the film's soundtrack demonstrates that, even at this early point, Spielberg experimented with sound (the film won an Emmy for Outstanding Achievement in Film Sound Editing) in a variety of creative ways that became more sophisticated in *Jaws* and have developed throughout his career. For example, the sound he blends to make the crashing truck cry out like a dying animal, a combination derived from *The Creature from the Black Lagoon* and a T-Rex growling in a B-level science-fiction film, he recycles as the shark sinks slowly into the ocean's depths at the end of *Jaws*.

Another good example of Spielberg's subtle yet expressive use of sound is how he employs the car radio in the film's early scenes. As Mann drives from his darkened garage though the crowded city streets and into the desert, the radio spews forth a litany of corny commercials for a car dealership, dog food, a grocery store, and hemorrhoid cream, along with weather reports, musical interludes, and scores from baseball games and golf matches. Spielberg heightens and lessens the volume as Mann's car plunges in and out of tunnels along the highway, providing a realistic accompaniment to his journey from home to the desert. The perpetual din of mundane advertisements alternately blends and competes with various traffic and city noises, the aural clamor of urban life making it difficult to distinguish one set of sounds from the next: words lose their meaning as they meld into the cacophony of blaring horns, squealing tires, and roaring engines. As we learn in retrospect, the perpetual dissonance of modern city life represents an objective correlative for Mann's disheveled state of mind, his anxiety about his cowardly behavior, and his bitter, still unresolved, quarrel with his wife.

Spielberg juxtaposes this urban chaos with the initial tranquility of the desert. In the longest radio sequence, Mann listens to an extended conversation between a talk-show host and a representative from the Census Bureau. Part comic routine and part psychodrama, the caller, who describes himself as a member of the "silent majority," remains uncertain how to fill out the government's form, particularly the question, "Are you the head of a family?": "I lost the position as the head of the family. I stay at home. She works, and I do the housework and take care of the babies . . . I'm really not the head of the family, and yet I'm the man of the family. . . . How should I answer that question?" During this exchange, the director reveals David Mann's face, for the first time, in the rearview mirror, his eyes screened by tinted glasses. We later learn that he and his wife argued heatedly the night before about his reluctance to protect her when a man "practically raped me in front of the whole party." David's imperiled manhood is reflected by the radio conversation, as it expands on the new and often uncomfortable roles men must occupy in a rapidly changing society.

MALE ANXIETY IN MODERN SOCIETY

Duel presents a similar ideology of masculinity as the much more violent, critically respected, and controversial *Straw Dogs,* a Sam Peckinpah movie released in December 1971 and no doubt still playing in theaters when Spielberg's film was released in early 1972. Like Peckinpah, Spielberg is preoccupied with how men ought to act in their culturally assigned positions and how they often fail to perform these roles adequately. This theme characterizes the director's career: it is evident in early films like *Duel* and *Jaws*, obsessively present in his war films *Empire of the Sun* and *Saving Private Ryan*, prominently featured in fantasy films such as *Hook* and *Always*, and it substantially undergirds his later movies such as *Minority Report* and *Catch Me If You Can*. As Mann pulls into the dusty gas station, Spielberg accentuates his emasculation with some heavy-handed dialogue. The attendant tells him, "You're the boss," and Mann responds, "Not in my house I'm not," echoing the uncertainty of the radio caller. The director reinforces Mann's predicament during an apologetic, almost humiliating, call home. Mann stands in a laundromat, the circular open door of a washing machine visually entrapping him within a feminine domestic space, as he unsuccessfully attempts to mollify his irate wife. She warns him that he'd better be home on time and abruptly hangs up. Broad changes in modern American life have altered traditional male roles, and David Mann has no idea how he should behave or, for that matter, what his responsibilities are in this brave new world. As *Duel*'s narrative unfolds, circumstances force him to redefine that role, as he increasingly abandons his refined ideals and responds to a deadly threat with primal passion.

Mann's battle with the unidentified trucker represents an assertion of his primitive masculinity in a desperate struggle against threats from a hostile outside force. As in many monster movies, Mann confronts two competing sides of himself, "one rational and civilized and the other uncontrolled and irrational" (Wells 8). As with Ferrier in *War of the Worlds*, the breakdown of the status quo, the way people are supposed to behave in civilized society, forces Mann to confront the darker forces within himself. Spielberg said that he "'wanted the film to be a grim awakening to the man who plays it safe . . . and this truck represents all the hidden dangers of life that can happen to a man who isn't aware of his own mortality'" (qtd. in Taylor 79).

But it is more than that. This theme of modern men facing contemporary challenges—whether great white sharks, aliens from outer space, rampaging dinosaurs, or wartime atrocities—stands at the center of Spielberg's best films: the way a man defends himself, his family, and his community against the onslaught of deadly evil and malignant power remains one of the most obsessive themes of his career.

Spielberg, like most filmmakers of his generation, was profoundly influenced by the themes and techniques of Alfred Hitchcock, despite the fact that the older director invariably posited evil as a reflection of social mechanisms

David Mann (Dennis Weaver) tries to assert his primitive masculinity to combat a contemporary world of mechanized threats and confusing domestic upheavals in *Duel* (1971).

rather than the external forces Spielberg envisions. Though a novice director could hardly be expected to match the polish and sophistication of the cinema's master of psychological darkness and dramatic suspense, *Duel*'s plot of the common man trapped in a dangerous situation over which he can exert little control mimics the essential formulations of Hitchcock's works. The sequence where Mann tries to calm himself in Chuck's Cafe after crashing his car into a fence and sustaining whiplash reflects Spielberg's early debt to his British predecessor. Though marred by a heavy-handed and pretentious voiceover ("We're right back in the jungle again"), the best moments in the cafe are silent, as a shaken and sweaty Mann struggles to identify the driver who almost killed him. Ultimately, he has only one clue: the boots worn by his attacker. But this proves a typical Hitchcockian ploy that promises much and provides little, as most of the men in the cafe wear similar boots, making identification impossible. Mann's mounting hysteria culminates in him accusing the wrong man, instigating a fight, and being ejected from the place. Throughout the sequence, Spielberg demonstrates his nascent ability to evoke powerful emotions visually within mundane settings, though at this point he had neither the confidence nor the clout to allow the images to speak for themselves.

CONCLUSION

Duel provides ample evidence of Spielberg's burgeoning technical expertise and persistent thematic obsessions. All are vital precursors of the style and point of view that pervade *Jaws,* which the director characterized in its DVD version as a "sequel to *Duel* but on the water." For example, the truck and the shark (and eventually the dinosaurs of *Jurassic Park* and *The Lost World* and the aliens of *War of the Worlds*) represent brutal forces that attack without remorse or logic. Their appearance demonstrates Spielberg's insistence that evil always lurks just beneath the calm veneer of our familiar existence (highways, beaches, amusement parks) and that civilized behavior inadequately shields us from its savage malevolence. Like Hitchcock, Spielberg persistently focuses on Everymen, characters like David Mann (as well as Chief Brody, Alan Grant, and Ray Ferrier) who are forced to confront extraordinary situations. Yet for all its delicious pleasures, *Duel* remains a piquant appetizer that titillates our taste for more substantial fare.

Jurassic Park: Beyond the Screen

Spielberg has described *Jurassic Park* as "'a sequel to *Jaws* on land'" (qtd. in McBride 418), though the film more accurately crossbreeds Michael Crichton's earlier movie *Westworld* (1973) with Spielberg's watery epic. It also remains a handbook of effective commercial filmmaking techniques. The film focuses on the deaths and disasters that occur when the unholy trinity of scientific hubris, capitalistic greed, and uncontrolled technology coalesces in an attempt to breed dinosaurs in the modern world and turn them into amusement-park attractions. The highlight is the director's seamless integration of highly sophisticated computer-generated images (CGI) within the flow of the onrushing narrative. The arriving party's first sighting of the grazing brachiosaurs on Isla Nublar, the rampaging T-Rex chasing the fleeing tour jeep, the running gallimimus herd, and the final battle between the T-Rex and the raptors in the visitor center amid crumbling skeletons all enhance audience identification with the main characters; we view these creatures through their reactions to them. Geoff King's visual analysis of key "on-screen spectacle" scenes demonstrates how skillfully Spielberg blends these special effects within the "narrative space of the action" (48). Strictly speaking, they cannot be separated from the narrative because they create its action, but Spielberg never segregates them merely into isolated curiosities for admiring audiences. The very fact that most viewers get drawn into the narrative, that they get emotionally involved with the fate of the characters rather than sitting back and marveling at the quality of the special effects, testifies to Spielberg's emphasis on narrative over spectacle and characterization over technical wizardry.

Jurassic Park offers a tempting array of technical (see Shay and Duncan), scientific (see Davies), and economic (see Balides) elements to consider beyond its thematic implications and positioning within Spielberg's career. In particular, Spielberg's embrace of the nascent technique of CGI, his ability to meld this emerging technology seamlessly with older forms of special effects (particularly animatronics), and then to integrate the various dinosaur creations within a compelling narrative marked a turning point in American filmmaking. It raised the bar for acceptable renditions of "reality" that audiences would ultimately require for their disbelief to be suspended. Pioneered by George Lucas's Industrial Light and Magic (ILM) company under the direction of Dennis Muren, CGI had been seen before, most conspicuously in James Cameron's *The Abyss* (1989) and his second *Terminator* film (1991). But Spielberg's inclusion of over fifty CGI shots (approximately six and a half minutes of screen time) in *Jurassic Park* marked the technology's first widescale usage and essentially consigned stop-motion miniature techniques to the bin of historical artifacts. The extended sequence of the ferocious T-Rex racing after the fleeing jeep, his image memorably trapped within the side mirror and underlined with the phrase "Objects in the mirror are closer than they appear," as well as the scene in which characters run inside a gallimimus stampede, dramatically demonstrate why Phil Tippett, Dennis Muren, Stan Winston, and Michael Lantieri won Academy Awards that year for Best Visual Effects.

If the Academy of Motion Picture Arts and Sciences handed out Oscars for merchandizing, *Jurassic Park* would have swept that category as well. A survey conducted a year after the film's release concluded that 98 percent of the population of the United States had heard of the film an astonishing 25.2 times (Balides 139). Opening on June 10, 1993, *Jurassic Park* became a financial juggernaut, taking only four months to surpass *E.T.*'s previous box-office record of $701 million and finishing its worldwide theatrical run by earning a staggering $913 ($357.1 million in the United States) in ticket sales. But that was only the beginning. Given Spielberg's extensive marketing strategy, which saw the licensing of some fifteen hundred products with the *Jurassic Park* logo, the film could hardly be avoided. As Balides astutely notes: "*Jurassic Park's* merchandising strategy is also a textual strategy in the film. The T-Rex logo appears on many objects . . . and the merchandized products themselves appear as product placements" (150). Thus when Spielberg pans across various *Jurassic Park* items for sale in the visitor center gift shop—including the requisite stuffed models, lunch boxes, mugs, and pajamas—one cannot be certain if he means this as an ironic comment on our commodified culture or a sly advertisement: is it a Marxian critique or a spot on the Home Shopping Network? In effect, the ubiquitous T-Rex logo visually represents a brand name inside and outside the diegesis of the movie, a "corporate product line" (Balides 144) launched by the film but filtered into innumerable aspects of American daily life.

Another fascinating beyond-the-screen aspect of *Jurassic Park* is its unlikely juxtaposition to Spielberg's next movie, *Schindler's List* (1993). While on location in Poland filming his Holocaust epic, Spielberg worked three nights a week, via satellite, on crucial postproduction tasks to complete his dinosaur drama, whose principal photography had wrapped three months before he left the United States. George Lucas (who received a special-thanks credit at the end of the film) graciously agreed to supervise many of the daily technical tasks, as Spielberg continued to oversee the development and integration of the CGI images, as well as to collaborate with John Williams on the movie's score. While laboring on two such dissimilar movies testifies to Spielberg's concentration, discipline, and ability to compartmentalize, it is also likely that focusing on the concrete tasks required to finalize a skillful but reasonably conventional monster movie allowed him vital respites from the perpetual strain of making the emotionally draining *Schindler's List*. This odd coupling seems part of Spielberg's perpetual highwire act, his attempt to balance himself between the competing claims of artist and showman. In another way, however, the two films have a fundamental similarity. They both explore the brutality that surrounds and threatens us: *Jurassic Park* the savagery in our natural surroundings, and *Schindler's List* that same cruelty within human nature.

HAMMOND AND FRANKENSTEIN

Though not strictly a researcher, John Hammond (Richard Attenborough) falls within a long tradition of literary and cinematic "mad scientists" who tamper with nature, such as Dr. Moreau and Dr. Jekyll. Most notably, he harkens back to the prototype for these figures, the infamous and tortured Victor Frankenstein who animated dead matter and created a monster that destroyed his life and murdered those he held most dear. On one level, *Jurassic*

Park replays some of the warnings commonly associated with Mary Shelley's celebrated novel and its seemingly endless series of film adaptations. Hammond tampers with the natural and spiritual order of things; he ventures into dangerous and forbidden realms far beyond the understanding of humankind, into areas of creation and destruction best left to natural selection, evolution, chance, or God. Hammond's reasons are complex and, at times, even contradictory. He is motivated by money and purchases the expert services of the paleontologist Dr. Grant (Sam Neill) and paleobotonist Dr. Sattler (Laura Dern) by funding their dig for the next three years. He constantly assures everyone that he "spared no expense" building the theme park, though such boasts ring hollow in light of subsequent disasters. Driven by obsession, pride, and greed (see Hawkins), Hammond hatches disaster by disrupting the natural order and attempting to transform the brutality of the wild into an entertaining amusement-park ride.

His influential wealth and capitalist mantra firmly established, Hammond still responds hostilely to the salivating greed of Gennero (Martin Ferrero), the "blood-sucking lawyer" who sees the dinosaurs simply as cash cows. Hammond rebukes Gennero's assertion that "we can charge anything we

John Hammond (Richard Attenborough), surrounded by Alan Grant (Sam Neill), Ellie Sattler (Laura Dern), and Ian Malcolm (Jeff Goldblum), hatches disaster by disrupting the natural order of evolution in *Jurassic Park* (1993).

want . . . and people will pay it" by responding, "This park was not built to cater only to the superrich. Everyone in the world has a right to enjoy these animals." Gennero's condescending suggestion to accomplish this is a coupon day. The lawyer's cowardice and greed results in his humiliating death when the T-Rex rips him off the toilet seat and devours him like a wriggling worm, a blackly comic demise for a man consumed by "filthy lucre." But like the far more vulgar Gennero, Hammond remains inextricably entwined with monetary concerns. Despite his avuncular appearance and grandfatherly concern about Lex (Ariana Richards) and Tim (Joseph Mazzello), his park's "target audience," the industrialist willingly lets the children venture forth on the tour to calm his nervous investors, even after the grisly death of an employee. The potential for danger is clearly evident and fully realized, yet for financial reasons Hammond risks turning his grandchildren into palate cleansers.

At crucial times, Hammond offers alternative reasons for his obsession with creating this vast and ingenious attraction. His first explanation comes during the lunchtime debate and undergirds defenses of scientific investigation stretching from Galileo to Darwin to the Human Genome Project. Countering Dr. Malcolm's (Jeff Goldblum) insistent charges of arrogance, lack of responsibility, and crass commercialism—of being so preoccupied with seeing if something *could* be done that no one bothered to ask if it *should* be done—an exasperated Hammond justifies his actions by citing the need for human progress: "How can we stand in the light of discovery and not act?" Not surprisingly, the cynical Malcolm rejects this reasoning, calling discovery a "violent, penetrative act . . . the rape of the natural world." Later, after the dinosaurs have broken loose, Hammond reveals a more personal reason to Sattler. The first attraction he built was a flea circus in Petticoat Lane, a deception based on persuading customers to see something that did not exist. In his prehistoric theme park, however, he "wanted to show them something that wasn't an illusion, something that was real, something they could see and touch." He wanted, in explicitly Frankensteinian terms, to bring something back to life that once was, to take the past and turn it into the present. Yet whereas Victor Frankenstein stands as an aberrational figure within his cultural surroundings, a solitary scientist trapped in an obsessive and lethal cycle, John Hammond represents a broader corporate perspective that values increased profits over communal safety and moral responsibilities.

Spielberg starts this Hammond/Sattler sequence by panning over the numerous dino-items for sale in the visitor center, ending with a shot of

Hammond eating melting ice cream, a perishable treat representing his crumbling theme park. With such a visual linking, he explicitly ties Hammond to the park's strident commercialism so that, while intimately sharing his past with Sattler, we never lose sight of his entrepreneurial motivations. Hammond started his career as a huckster, a fraud, and a creator of illusions. Yet as he sits in the ruins of his melting playground, this wealthy industrialist fails to comprehend what has transpired and why. He never takes responsibility for the catastrophes caused by his creation of Jurassic Park. When Hammond prattles on with almost maniacal desperation about how things will be flawless next time, how overdependance on automation was his major mistake, and how "creation is an act of sheer will," Sattler interrupts him and drives home what he should now understand: "You never have control; that's the illusion." Hammond never grasps that mankind must learn to live with nature, not struggle to dominate it. Ultimately, Sattler joins him in eating the ice cream; but she sits at the opposite end of the table, giving her employer little emotional or physical comfort. To her comment that the ice cream is good, Hammond can only add his once jaunty tag line and now barren capitalistic motto, "spared no expense."

Many critics note that Spielberg softens Hammond's character, turning Crichton's raging megalomaniac into a gentler and more charming figure. The director demonstrates his character's maternalistic side by showing Hammond midwifing the birth of a cuddly baby dinosaur, never realizing that the emerging valicoraptor contains the seeds of his destruction. Commentators also observe that his casting of Richard Attenborough, a prominent movie director who had not acted on the screen for fifteen years, into this pivotal role shows how much Spielberg identified with parts of Hammond's personality. "'No film could be more personal [to Spielberg] than this one,'" observed Richard Corliss in his *Time* magazine review, "'a movie about all the complexities of fabricating entertainment in the microchip age'" (qtd. in McBride 421). Like Hammond, Spielberg sees himself as a populist entertainer, a showman and creator of spectacles: the director who makes movies that feel like emotional roller coasters fabricates a theme-park adventure that becomes one of the most popular attractions at Universal Studios, a journey that takes customers through a dinosaur-filled jungle and down a steep waterfall. Unlike Hammond, perhaps Spielberg understands that, despite his wealth and power, he only exercises the illusion of control over the process and products of creation. Conversely, Hammond functions as another familiar Spielberg character—the unreliable father figure who abandons his familial responsibilities. By putting his grandchildren into danger for commercial expediency, Hammond—and the corporate mentality he embodies—becomes an irresponsible and ultimately dangerous figure, despite his considerable appealing qualities.

Hammond's dual nature finds an objective correlative in his cane. It highlights his frailty, his need to lean on something sturdy to progress from one place to another. Metaphorically, it represents his scientific endeavors: in Malcolm's words, he leaned "on the shoulders of geniuses to accomplish something as fast as you could." Most crucially, its head, a prehistoric mosquito sealed in tree sap and encased in glass, visually encapsulates his hubris: attempting to entrap nature and the awesome power of genetics into a seemingly innocuous commercial project designed exclusively for the pleasure and use of mankind. But objects meant to support can break, and those designed for beauty can be used as weapons—sometimes even against those who create and trademark them. Ultimately, the film does not hold Hammond personally responsible for the disasters that occur in Jurassic Park. But he remains guilty of severely underestimating the power he unleashes and, like his nineteenth-century forebear, of not considering the consequences of his actions. Through Victor Frankenstein, we understand how the scientific arrogance of one man can bring death and destruction to many innocent victims; through John Hammond, we contemplate how such presumptuousness, backed by huge corporate resources, can reach devastating proportions far beyond an immediate circle of family and friends to threaten all of us.

THE RECONSTITUTED FAMILY (THE FATHER)

If John Hammond functions as the unreliable father figure in *Jurassic Park*, Dr. Alan Grant evolves into the film's responsible parent. Grant's obvious distaste for children, none of which appears in Crichton's novel, brings a distinct tension between himself and Sattler, as well as revealing the palentologist's moral and emotional development. Early in the movie on a remote dig in the Badlands of Montana, Grant cruelly teases a disdainful teenager who claims that raptors "don't look very scary—more like a turkey." Drawing a "six-inch retractable claw like a razor" from his pocket, Grant graphically illustrates on the boy's body how these ancient predators killed their prey, "leaving them alive as they started to eat" them. Later, reconstituted raptors will reenact his gory description inside the theme park. "So, you know," he tells the chastened boy, "try to show a little respect"—the same message Malcolm gives Hammond during their lunchtime debate. As he and Sattler stroll away from the scene, Grant shakes his head, muttering, "Kids. You want to have one of those? . . . They're noisy, they're messy, they're expensive, they smell." This man who digs in the earth for a living responds to children simply as disruptive annoyances, acute distractions from the more important work of scientific research and discovery.

Grant's initial reaction to Tim and Lex resembles his response to the boy on his Montana excavation site, though Sattler unsuccessfully tries to maneuver them into the same vehicle for the tour. Tim's incessant questions irritate him, and Lex's computer skills leave him unimpressed. Yet Grant heroically becomes their guardian once Gennaro abandons them, transforming the aloof paleontologist into a protective parent. Following their too-close encounter of the T-Rex kind, Grant and the children take refuge in a giant tree for the night. Climbing astride a large tree branch jutting out between his legs, an apt if exaggerated symbol of his assumption of patriarchal control, Grant mimics the "singing" of the vegetarian brachiosaurs, as the soundtrack breaks into a gentle lullaby. "They're not monsters," he patiently explains to the frightened Lex. "Just animals. They do what they do." He climbs off the branch and sinks back into the trunk, exhausted. The children lean against him and, for a moment, Grant seems uneasy with their need for affection, reassurance, and protection. He expresses a bit of pain, uncomfortably shifts his weight, reaches into his back pocket, and extracts the raptor claw he used to scare the boy in Montana, silently contemplating the artifact. "What are you and Ellie going to do now if you don't have to pick up dinosaur bones anymore?" asks Lex. "I don't know," responds Grant. "Guess we'll just have to evolve too." He then patiently laughs at Tim's dinosaur riddles and assures Lex that he will safeguard them, even if it means "staying awake all night." Grant takes one last look at the claw, a symbol of his hostility toward children, and throws it to the ground, shifting his focus from past enmities to present obligations. Spielberg restates this exact father/children configuration in the last scene, when the characters flee from the island, as Sattler smiles approvingly, and Grant, also with a shy smile, accepts his evolution to fatherhood.

Geoff King observes that Grant's discovery of his dormant but instinctive parental role is brought about by his "engagement with nature, unmediated ... through their shared experience of hazards in the wilds" (63, 62) and that this metamorphosis results from a classic American bonding experience. Indeed, *Jurassic Park's* essential narrative structure resembles a western more than a conventional monster movie; it recapitulates the classic battle between civilization and savagery that unfolded in countless Hollywood movies set on the American frontier. The dinosaurs represent the forces of unrestrained nature, usually embodied by fierce and uncivilized Indians, who oppose the forces of progress; Sattler is the civilizing female presence, often the schoolmarm, who brings refined eastern values into the uncouth West; Grant becomes the unfettered cowboy who must subdue the forces hostile to civilization if social growth is to be achieved; Hammond and his laboratory workers function as the townsfolk who carve out their places in the wilderness, suppressing nature so that others may follow their path. By utilizing the basic narrative structure of the western, Spielberg endows *Jurassic Park* with a mythic scope, natural grandeur, and nationalistic imperative far beyond the typical monster movie.

THE RECONSTITUTED FAMILY (THE MOTHER)

Sattler's civilizing function, her culturally determined role, is to turn the maverick into a contented homesteader, the career-oriented loner into a family-minded father. Though a prominent scientist herself, she consistently displays her maternal tendencies and desire to have her own children despite Grant's objections. She volunteers to help nurse the sick triceratops, though her background in paleobiology seems less suited to this task than Grant's skills or those of the park's veterinarians. Surrounded by men of action, Sattler remains the only one willing to plunge into dinosaur poop to ascertain the cause of the animal's illness and restore its health—a practical mother's response to a ill child in contrast to a finicky father's hesitation to soil himself. She even stays with the sick animal as Grant and the others continue on the tour. But Spielberg's heroine functions in other significant ways throughout *Jurassic Park*. She has, for example, the most extended female action sequence in a Spielberg movie since Marion Ravenwood's barroom brawl in *Raiders of the Lost Ark*.

Over Hammond's lame sexist objections, Sattler bravely volunteers to turn the park's power system back on and, in this dangerous quest, is treated with respect by the film's most overtly masculine figure, the hunter Robert Muldoon (Bob Peck), who physically resembles a raptor himself. They emerge from the visitor center together, and Sattler's subsequent dash—vaulting over downed trees, swinging from hanging vines, leaping over obstructive branches, splashing through standing water, and bursting through steel fences—marks her daring and strength. Once inside the shed, she restores energy to the park, bringing light and hope back to her compatriots, though almost electrocuting Tim in the process. Feminist critics might rightly argue that, to accomplish this feat, she simply follows the orders of Hammond and Malcolm over the walkie-talkie, but neither man could accomplish this vital mission given the former's infirmity and the latter's wound. Despite her own injury, Sattler battles and escapes from the predatory raptor who killed Mr. Arnold (Samuel L. Jackson) inside the shed, though she crumbles into a crying heap once she is temporarily safe outside the building.

In fashioning the character of Dr. Ellie Sattler, Spielberg attempts to depict a woman who combines professionalism and maternalism; she has a successful career and wants a family. Unlike Marion Ravenwood, whose strength disintegrates as *Raiders* progresses, Ellie remains a relatively feisty and dynamic character throughout *Jurassic Park*. So, for example, when Malcolm ticks off his version of evolution—"God creates dinosaurs, God destroys dinosaurs, God creates man, man destroys God, man creates dinosaurs"—Ellie continues his progressive litany with wry wit: "Dinosaurs eat man, woman inherits the earth." Like the vast majority of female heroines in monster movies, Sattler spends much time screaming and crying in the best Faye Wray tradition. But she remains far more active than most of the frenzied women in these movies who serve mainly as helpless sacrifices needing masculine rescue, as frail victims (often in scanty underwear) perishing in the first act, or as raving hysterics shrieking their way through events. Ellie Sattler is a powerful and aggressive heroine who represents a distinct improvement over most female figures in horror movies and within Spielberg's other productions.

THE RECONSTITUTED FAMILY (IDEOLOGY)

Twelve-year-old Lex and nine-year-old Tim play vital roles in the emotional matrix of *Jurassic Park,* though they represent potential victims rather than Wordsworthian splendor. Their vulnerability brings out the best in Grant, allowing him to mature emotionally into their protector, but Spielberg never hints that this development necessitates discovering his "inner child," as he does with father figures in earlier films such as *Close Encounters* and *Hook*. Grant has far more in common with the good doctor in *Empire of the Sun* than he does with Peter Pan. As critics such as Peter Wollen have noted, "Spielberg both seeks to nurture children and at the same time often threatens to terrify them" (187). Children in emotional and physical danger permeate nearly all his films, a characteristic situation his detractors label as manipulative and his defenders justify as psychologically understandable; only *Duel, 1941, Always,* and *The Terminal* remain devoid of their structural and emotional presence.

For critics who conceptualize the nuclear family as symptomatic of capitalistic, heterosexual, and patriarchal oppression, its reconstitution embodied in the union of surrogate parents (newly sensitized man and spirited woman) with deserted children of divorce represents yet another blatant example of Spielberg's paleolithic ideology, an attempt to heal his childhood

Dr. Alan Grant (Sam Neill) evolves into a protective father, sheltering Tim (Joseph Mazzello) and Lex (Ariana Richards) Murphy while symbolically reconstituting the nuclear
family in *Jurassic Park* (1993).

wounds and simultaneously reinforce conventional social standards. They
claim that *Jurassic Park* once again reveals Spielberg's insistence on positioning traditionally formulated gender roles as normative absolutes within his
movies, of circulating conservative middle-class values as paradigms rather
than alternatives. The final shot of the flying birds, for example, not only
validates Grant's thesis about dinosaur evolution but also Sattler's about the
necessity of social groupings, of natural and extended families. It consecrates
community. Geoff King, for example, asserts that the film's "most sustained
work as a cultural product" is to propagate "the ideal of the nuclear family, a
social and historical construction constantly sold in terms of its supposedly
'natural' basis" (61). Such arguments have validity. No viewer scrutinizing
Spielberg's films could deny his obsession with rebuilding families, since this
narrative development occurs repeatedly throughout his career. But some
difficulties arise if this idea is pushed too far in *Jurassic Park*.

If heterosexual relations are posited as "natural" in the process of human
evolution, then events in the "constructed" world of nature within Hammond's theme park contradict this supposition. Much is made about how
the scientists "control the chromosomes" of the dinosaurs and consequently
"engineer" them all to be female. When Grant declares that "T-Rex doesn't

want to be fed, he wants to hunt," he employs the wrong pronoun. As Dr. Wu (B. D. Wong) condescendingly explains, this biosimilitude is "not too difficult" to achieve: "All vertebrate embryos are inherently female, anyway. They just require an extra hormone given at the right developmental stage to make them male. We simply deny them that." Wu confidently asserts that, because the dinosaurs cannot procreate on their own in the wild, his scientifically regulated population control is one of the park's security precautions: "There's no unauthorized breeding in Jurassic Park." Yet Grant's discovery of hatched eggs and baby dino footsteps outside the laboratory discredits Wu's pronouncement and validates Malcolm's earlier observation:

> The kind of control you're attempting is not possible. If there is one thing the history of evolution has taught us it is that life will not be contained. Life breaks free. It expands to new territories. It crashes through barriers, painfully, maybe even dangerously. . . . I am simply saying that life finds a way.

Much as Frankenstein created life without female participation, Hammond and Dr. Wu "find a way" to do so without males. Thus, the film juxtaposes the supposedly spontaneous formulation of the traditional human family against this "unnatural" asexual reproduction in the scientifically created animal realm.

NATURE VERSUS TECHNOLOGY

Jurassic Park can be seen as Spielberg's most overt and sustained "back to the future" narrative, a cautionary tale that pits the natural world, represented by the dinosaurs, against mankind's technological intrusions, symbolized by mechanized objects and computers. Yet such a stark dichotomy belies a significant but muddy interpretive problem: the dinosaurs do not result from any natural evolutionary process; they are brought back to life by cloning, a procedure made possible only through scientific research and advanced technology. So how can these reconstructed animals represent "nature" when they owe their existence to sophisticated machines and the men who operate them? One can wade through this dilemma by citing other examples of the birth process altered by technology whose "product" we accept as genuine. Race-horse owners, for example, carefully breed their stock with hopes that combining various bloodlines from past winners will produce future champions, and physicians now employ a wide range of reproductive technologies to help infertile couples have children. No one claims that the children who result from in vitro fertilization are any less human, or behave any less naturally, than those conceived in the traditional manner. More pointedly, human cloning offers the possibility of endlessly reiterating human beings. Such reasoning would seem to justify the use of the dinosaurs in *Jurassic Park* as symbols of the natural world, though hatched in climate-controlled laboratories and rotated by mechanical arms.

Understanding that science and technology combined to propagate the dinosaurs, no matter how they behave once they are born, leads to an even more complex issue that undermines the standard critical explication of nature versus technology: Jurassic Park itself is not a natural environment but an elaborate and illusory simulacrum, a gigantic flea circus. How natural is a setting in which immense wooden doors signal your entrance, all the inhabitants are designed to be female, predatory animals feed on sacrificial goats, mechanized roads cut into the jungle, jeeps traverse the landscape (which is encircled by high-voltage fences), and armed gamekeepers patrol the grounds? Jurassic Park is Disneyland writ large and represents a human projection of how things ought to be, not how they are: the Paris of Epcot Center rather than of France. What frightens us is nature's erratic inconsistency, exemplified by the freak storm that attacks the island. In Hammond's circumscribed view of "the wild," animals kill each other, but only in prescribed and systematic ways. *Jurassic Park* enacts a human attempt to impose mechanical predictability upon natural uncertainty via technological inventiveness. Hammond and his researchers develop an idealized reconfiguration of the natural world and its inhabitants. The dinosaurs ultimately display unruly instinctual behavior, but this results from the inevitable and lethal progression of unchecked scientific research: the T-Rex crushing the jeep or the raptor leaping atop the control-room computer exemplify better-engineered machines triumphing over their more limited predecessors.

The irony at the heart of *Jurassic Park* (and every other work inspired by *Frankenstein*) is that scientific advancement and technological development, which purport to be rational and orderly endeavors, repeatedly bring forth results as unpredictable and chaotic as the wildest natural environment. Spielberg presents differing views toward science and technology by juxtaposing conflicting characters. Dennis Nedry (Wayne Knight), the film's most blatantly negative and thoroughly corrupt character, is wedded to computer technology. Stamped as fat, messy, and greedy—sure signs of ravenous evil in Hollywood's pantheon of stereotypes—Nedry tapes Robert Oppenheimer's portrait to his computer screen, clearly demonstrating his reckless disregard for the power unleashed within the park. That he becomes food for the spitting dilophosaurus seems only his just dessert. (Dinosaur experts like Jose Luis Sanz [113] generally praised the accuracy of Spielberg's creations, though they noted that no evidence exists for the dilophosaurus's ability to project poison.) In contrast, Grant's first words in the film are "I hate computers," and his mere touch makes the computer on their digging site go haywire. Sattler laughingly comments that "Dr. Grant is not machine-compatible," to which he replies, "They've got it in for me." Little does the film's hero know how prophetic those words will be.

Though Spielberg is no Luddite, he has expressed his desire for "limiters on how far we allow ourselves to go—ethical, moral limiters" (Kennedy 109). The production and distribution of cinema on any level is impossible without technology, and he has embraced special-effects advances throughout his career. In particular, computer technology has always been entwined with his personal and professional life. The director's oft absent father, Arnold, was a pioneer in computer research at RCA and IBM with several patents to his credit, and Spielberg's long association with George Lucas (and ILM) allowed him access to cutting-edge technical advances that enhanced his pictures. But even with such intimate private and public connections, Spielberg's films, particularly *Jurassic Park, A.I.,* and *Minority Report,* disclose an ambivalent attitude toward technology. No doubt, he recognized the irony coiled around the heart of *Jurassic Park:* he was making a monster movie that warned about the dangers of technology that could only be made realistic by using the most advanced technology available. *Jurassic Park* ultimately celebrates and castigates technological progress. Though the park's human inhabitants become prey hunted by the products of science and technology, they can only be saved by Lex's knowledge of computer programming and a helicopter to whisk them off the island. The movie never posits scientific and technological developments as intrinsically evil but fears the motivations of those who employ them.

In an interview with *Wired* magazine in the summer of 2002, Spielberg talked with Lisa Kennedy about his ambivalent attitudes toward technology. It "can be our best friend," he begins, "but it interrupts our ability to have a thought or a daydream, to imagine something wonderful because we are too busy bridging the walk from the cafeteria back to the office on the cell phone" (109). He speculates that "technology may give us far better tools to communicate our stories" (113). But in the very next sentence, he bemoans the probable extinction of the photochemical process, the "magic of chemistry and film" (113). Acknowledging the advantages of digital filmmaking—particularly the steadiness and cleanness of the shot—he nonetheless argues that this sanitization robs the image of its texture: "The screen is always alive with chaos and excitement, and that will certainly be gone when we convert to a digital camera and digital projection" (113). Most surprising for the man who was among the first to employ extensive digital technology, Spielberg adamantly declares, "I am going to be the last person to use digital technology to shoot my movies" (113). Summing up his feelings about the connection between creativity and technology, he observes that "the dreamers give us technology, and I am not being cynical when I say that technology curbs our dreams" (146). Spielberg clearly recognizes the dual nature of the technology that he helped plug into mainstream American culture. The digital revolution giveth and taketh away.

VISUAL HALLMARKS OF JURASSIC PARK

Along with computer-generated images, Spielberg employs more traditional techniques to engage his audience, relying on devices long part of the monster-movie repertoire. He often registers human fear and foreboding in concrete items, objective correlatives that display internal states of emotions externally in physical objects. Such striking moments appear throughout *Jurassic Park,* most notably the rippling water in two plastic cups on the jeep's dashboard that measure the ominous approach of the T-Rex and the quivering green Jello on Lex's spoon as the raptors draw near. His use of parallel editing throughout the film, particularly evident as Grant and the children climb the fence and Sattler works to restore its high-voltage power, draws out the tension in crucial scenes. Visually, Spielberg stuffs the film with obvious and sly images of food, an ongoing motif that ties the humans to their fellow creatures and makes a clear point about their shifting status on the food chain from eater to eaten, as the deaths of Nedry and Gennaro graphically illustrate. Appropriately, the philosophical conversation between Malcolm and Hammond occurs over lunch—right after they watch the dinosaurs being fed—and the raptors hunt the children in the visitor center's kitchen.

THE PAST

Before exiting *Jurassic Park,* I'd like to proffer an alternative reading of the dinosaurs beyond their role as embodiments of potential technological disasters, the result of scientific research for the wrong reasons. Psychoanalytic critics have traditionally interpreted cinematic and literary monsters as incarnating repressed individual and generational fears, be they threats of atomic destruction, dread of outsiders, frightening sexual desires, or anxiety about bioengineering. *Jurassic Park* clearly demonstrates the latter, but it also reverberates with a deep concern about how the past can be appropriately incorporated into the present, a particular consideration for a director who often situates his films in earlier eras. Speaking more generally about horror films, Leo Braudy observes that "the revenge taken on the present by a forgotten and ignored past, and its energetic preoccupation with the clash of the normal and the abnormal, accords well with the theme of a nature run amok because it has been obliterated and repressed" (294–92). The very image of dinosaurs conjures up prehistoric ages far before the appearance of mankind on the planet; they ruled the earth for centuries and are the closest creatures we have to mythological beasts such as dragons. No wonder, as Peter Wollen notes, that they have become "fetishised attractions in the Society of the Spectacle" (183). These awesome creatures that mystify and terrorize us embody our fascination with the long-lost past and our fears for the distant future.

If this species of fierce and gigantic creatures perished, what hope do we have of surviving the chaos of existence? Are we to leave nothing but our bones buried deep in the earth to mark our passing? Grant's Montana dig site offers one approach to exploring this disquieting issue: the slow and cautious brushing away of the sands of time to reveal, bit by bit, skeletal outlines of things that preceded us, to learn prudently, to take lessons from the past to help illuminate the future. Hammond's elaborate theme park proposes a more radical and perilous alternative: bringing the past fully alive into the present, but primarily as entertainments and commodities. Such a dramatic rupture in humankind's actual and psychological history causes a trauma in the developmental scheme of things, a simultaneity of past and present that results in severe shock and, ultimately, death. Its most visible representation occurs in the climactic scene where first the humans take refuge, and then the T-Rex and raptors battle each other, among the skeletons of their own ancestors. As the scene dramatically illustrates, the past provides insight into our individual and communal history, but the dangers of disrupting the present with a too-full evocation of the past, shattering its fragile construction, loom over *Jurassic Park* like an ominous shadow. Like Hammond, Steven Spielberg often seeks to re-create past events lavishly as spectacles for our consumption.

In interviews given around its release date, Spielberg stressed his determination not to let *Jurassic Park,* with its ninety-five-millon-dollar budget, eighty-two-day shooting schedule, and complicated special effects, overwhelm him, as had *1941* and *Hook.* (Like the characters in the film surprised by the sudden storm, he never counted on being interrupted by Hurricane Iniki, which struck his Kauai location during the final days of the shoot.)

Before any of the script was written, as Michael Crichton reveals, Spielberg conceptualized the various dinosaurs as individual beings with particular visual traits and told the novelist that "'effects are only as good as the audiences's feeling for the characters'" (qtd. in McBride 419). His instincts proved correct, yet even with its spectacular economic success, Spielberg fully grasped that financial rewards never guarantee artistic approval and critical acceptance: "'Part of me is afraid I will be remembered for the money my films have made, rather than for the films themselves'" (qtd. in McBride 424). Though he ruled Hollywood as the T-Rex of commercial moviemaking, the director still feared extinction, leaving few cinematic bones to mark his passage.

The Lost World: Beyond the Screen

After completing the emotionally debilitating and physically taxing *Schindler's List,* Spielberg did not venture behind a camera for almost three years, his longest sojourn away from moviemaking. Critics who praised his Holocaust drama and lauded his newfound "maturity" were disconcerted when, instead of tackling an equally serious subject, he agreed to direct the sequel to *Jurassic Park,* a film that he candidly acknowledged was not among his five best movies (Biskind, "'World'" 198). Spielberg fully understood that such a project would not stretch him very far; indeed, that was part of its appeal: "I didn't want to jump into the deep end of the pool. I wanted to step into the shallow end and get used to the water. I wanted to do something familiar" (198). He also worried about letting the *Jurassic Park* franchise disintegrate, as happened with the disastrous *Jaws* sequels. Though Spielberg claimed that *Schindler's List* had little connection to his dinosaur movies, others, like his production designer Rick Carter, disagreed: "Here, there are darker intentions and darker problems to deal with. I think it's *Jurassic Park* post–*Schindler's List.* . . . I don't think it's the same Steven Spielberg now" (200). The director hungered for more substantial fare than could be provided by a return to the land time forgot:

> I found myself, in the middle of the sequel, growing more and more impatient with myself with respect to the kind of films I really like to make. And often feeling that I have stuck myself in Doc Brown's DeLorean and gone back in time four and a half years, and I was just serving the audience a banquet, but I wasn't serving myself anything challenging. I found myself saying . . . "It's not enough for me." (Biskind, "'World'" 206).

Disconnected emotionally from the film, Spielberg even allowed the scriptwriter, David Koepp, to direct two scenes for him, the first with Malcolm on the subway, and the second with his arrival on Isla Sorna.

The Lost World represents a shift into reverse for the director, a disappointing jaunt to the land of Spielberg light—very light. Only two sequences in this film deserve a place among the director's best visual work. One is the terrifying moments when the heroine finds herself dangling over the edge of a steep cliff, spared from certain death only by hugging the windshield of her vehicle that, slowly and excruciatingly, begins to crack. The second is when the velociraptors attack the fleeing humans in a field of tall grass, their frightening progress marked by a dark line that eventually merges with the path made by their unsuspecting victims. Otherwise, the film unfolds mechanically, a by-the-numbers commercial project from a director marking time until he could reengage with more personally satisfying material. Even the in-jokes and movie references seem stilted and listless: advertising posters with Arnold Schwarzenegger (starring in *King Lear*), Tom Hanks, and Robin Williams; calling the ship that brings the T-Rex to San Diego the S.S. *Venture,* the same as the one that brings King Kong to New York City. Spielberg teeters on the edge of self-parody by having the mommy and daddy dinosaur rescue and protect their endangered offspring, a situation replayed time and again by human characters throughout his movies.

MALCOLM IN THE MIDDLE

Spielberg imports recycled character types from *Jurassic Park* to inhabit *The Lost World:* Dr. Ian Malcolm (Jeff Goldblum) simply slips into the central persona of sexy scientist and reconstituted daddy vacated by Grant; Dr. Sarah Harding (Julianne Moore) develops into a braver, more maternal, and still hysterical Dr. Ellie Sattler, nursing a baby dinosaur, tranquilizing the rampaging Rex, and screaming in the face of danger; Roland Tembo (Pete Postelthwaite) assumes Robert Muldoon's great-white-hunter role and survives to search for new challenges; Nick Van Owen (Vince Vaughn) functions as a militant gadfly in the earlier Malcolm mode; Kelly Curtis (Vanessa Lee Chester) becomes a politically correct version of Tim and Lex, her gymnastic skills as vital as Lex's computer expertise; Peter Ludlow (Arliss Howard) emerges as a slicker edition of the greedy Nedry; Dieter Stark (Peter Stormare) is a more sadistic Gennero; and Eddie Carr (Richard Schiff) is a Dr. Wu–like sidekick and provider. John Hammond, of course, remains as John Hammond, though as the deposed chairman of the InGen Bioengineering Corporation he morphs from entrepreneurial showman into ardent conservationist. He wants to save the animals, to keep them beyond the reach of greedy exploiters, instead of trapping them behind electrified fences and turning them into commodified tourist attractions.

There are, however, some distinctive narrative shifts. Whereas *Jurassic Park* traces its lineage back to mad-scientist monster movies with their danger-of-scientific-research motif, *The Lost World* posits scientists as the film's moral figures who, along with their allies, protect the dinosaurs as an endangered species (see Freer 241–42). "The first movie was really about the failure of technology and the success of nature," said Spielberg. "This movie is much more about the failure of people to find restraints within themselves, and the failure of morality to protect these animals" (Biskind, "'World'" 200–1). In this sense, *The Lost World* stands as Spielberg's "green" movie. Hammond's last words, spoken in a CNN television interview aired before a sleeping Harding and Malcolm, succinctly sum up the thrust of the production. A lapsed capitalist, he now wants to "establish a set of rules for the preservation and isolation of that island. These creatures require our absence to survive, not our help. And if we can only step aside and trust in nature, life will find a way." On these final words, Spielberg cuts to the now peaceable kingdom on Isla Sorna: the reunited T-Rex family, the lumbering stegosaurus herd, and the majestic pteranodon (a species of pterodactyl) uttering a triumphant cry. If, as Spielberg claimed, *Jurassic Park* was a version of *Jaws* on land, then *The Lost World* is a copy of a copy, a pale imitation that bears only faint and momentary resemblances to the vibrant original.

War of the Worlds: Beyond the Screen

It initially seems logical to place Spielberg's *War of the Worlds* into the science fiction and fantasy chapter rather than among his monster movies. After all, the film is based on H. G. Wells's classic 1898 novel about space aliens invading the earth, takes its dramatic flair from Orson Welles's October 30, 1938, radio drama that caused frightened citizens to flee their homes, and draws some of its visual imagery directly from George Pal's 1953 adaptation of Wells's fiction. (The stars of that earlier film, Gene Barry and Ann Robinson, make cameo appearances as grandparents in Spielberg's update.) But the film's narrative arc, dark tone, and pernicious creatures fit more comfortably among the director's killer sharks and lethal dinosaurs than they do his kindly visitors from other galaxies in *Close Encounters of the Third Kind* and *E.T.* Morgan Freeman's voiceover preamble, taken almost directly from the opening of

Wells's story, reveals that the aliens have been studying earth for centuries with "envious eyes." But this explanation remains murky and unexplored. Furthermore, the aliens' relentless drive to "exterminate" rather than conquer earth's inhabitants transforms them into mindless killing machines driven by instinct rather than any discernible intelligence, however malevolent. As with his shark and dinosaurs, Spielberg's aliens become natural predators, though on a far larger scale than in *Jaws* and the *Jurassic Park* movies. Like those blockbusters, however, *War of the Worlds* racked up impressive box-office receipts: $76.3 million over the July 4 holiday weekend, reaching a cumulative $234.3 million since its release on June 29, 2005.

Acknowledging the change in geopolitical reality, Spielberg shifts the location for his *War of the Worlds* from Wells's Britain to contemporary New England, much as Orson Welles set his radio broadcast of Howard Koch's adaptation in Grovers Mill, New Jersey, and George Pal situated his production of the director Byron Haskin's movie in California. The story begins as Mary Ann (Miranda Otto) delivers her shuffling seventeen-year-old son, Robbie (Justin Chatwin), and precocious eleven-year-old daughter, Rachel (Dakota Fanning), to their reluctant, nearly absentee father, Ray Ferrier (Tom Cruise), and then drives off with her new husband, Tim (David Alan Basche), to visit her upper-crust parents in Boston. Soon after her departure, dark clouds smother the earth's skies, heavy winds shake buildings, and lightning sets off fires across the globe. Confused citizens gather around large sink holes, their curiosity turning to fear and then panic as gigantic machines atop tripod-like legs emerge from deep beneath the ground and commence firing deadly heat rays that incinerate humans on contact. The invasion of earth has begun. Rushing home, Ray gathers his frightened children and begins a desperate flight to reunite them with their mother. Their trip becomes a series of narrow escapes, not only from the killing machines and their ruthless operators but also from frenzied mobs, a deranged survivalist, Harlan Ogilvy (Tim Robbins), and their own dysfunctional family relations. Ultimately, the aliens are defeated, but not by America's military might. They fall prey to "the humblest things that God, in his wisdom, has put upon this earth" (Wells 243): germs to which human beings, over the centuries, have gained immunity destroy the far more scientifically advanced invaders. Ray delivers Rachel to her mother, and they are joined in Boston by her brother, who earlier left to fight the enemy. Like so many previous Spielberg films, the family is resurrected and revitalized by the trials its members, especially the fathers, have suffered.

While many of the plot's discrepancies can be traced back to Wells's novel, the screenplay by Josh Friedman and David Koepp fails to satisfy the most cursory requirements of narrative logic. Most glaringly, how could an advanced race capable of hiding complex machinery beneath the earth's surface for thousands of years not bother, during all that time watching and studying us "as a man with a microscope might scrutinise the transient creatures that swarm and multiply in a drop of water" (Wells 111), to take air, water, and food samples and ascertain whether they are compatible with their biological systems? How deeply were the tripods buried so that no one digging underground—placing sewer lines or drilling for oil—ever unearthed them? What is the goal of the invaders? If it is to harvest human beings as fertilizer for the red vines, then why kill so many of them? What do the aliens envy? Certainly not the human beings or edifices they indiscriminately destroy. The reason they attack at this particular historical moment remains unclear. (Wells's Martians carried "warfare sunward" (113) because their planet was rapidly cooling and could barely sustain life.) Smaller points also hinder the necessary suspension of disbelief. If electrical storms have shut down everyone's tools and instruments, even down to Ray's wristwatch, how is it that a man's camcorder still functions so effectively? And why is Ray the only civilian on earth who can figure out how to make a car run?

Finally, there is the consistent and often controversial issue of the Spielbergian happy ending. In earlier films, such as *Jaws* and *Empire of the Sun,* a reasonably joyful conclusion feels dramatically warranted and emotionally satisfying, since the narrative action naturally culminates in a reconciliation. However, in films such as *Minority Report* and *A.I.* the director's overriding need to conclude on a happy note feels like a flimsy veneer crudely plastered over traumas too complex to resolve so neatly. Though Spielberg clearly wants the seeds of Ray's emotional growth to bring forth fruit, *War of the Worlds* ends with a dry thud. And the questions continue. One cannot help but wonder why the aliens have not leveled Boston along with American's other major cities, though some indications of their presence are clearly evident. More importantly, it is too convenient that every member of this clean and tidy family is left unscathed from the chaos and destruction that surrounds the entire earth. I raise such questions not as niggling objections or continuity flaws. They become glaring intrusions that disrupt the rush of the narrative by ignoring internal logic and consistency within the world on the screen. Once such objections occur to the viewer, even Spielberg's considerable gifts as a visual artist are not sufficient to immerse him or her in the cinematic experience.

SPIELBERGIAN MOTIFS

While often drawn to literary works for inspiration, Spielberg habitually filters deeply personal elements into the source materials that undergird his narratives, obsessively incorporating a consistent series of themes that stretch from his earliest to his most recent productions. At the start of *War of the Worlds,* Ray Ferrier is a typical Spielberg man-boy. His souped-up car, near-empty refrigerator, and disheveled apartment—complete with a car motor spread across his kitchen table—resemble the lifestyle of a teenage boy rather than a man in his forties. Worst of all, he has failed as a parent, the primary sin in Spielberg's canon. For example, he doesn't know about his daughter's allergy to peanut butter and can't sing any lullabies to soothe her, resorting to "Little Deuce Coupe" as a weak substitute. His son may wear similar clothing, but his Red Sox cap marks a defiant slap at his father's love for the Yankees. Arriving late to pick them up, he can't even provide for their basic needs, telling Rachel and Robbie to order a takeout dinner and ambling off to take a nap. His son and daughter actively dislike visiting on the rare weekends they spend with him, displaying little respect or affection for their father. Ray, whose ex-wife has left him for a wealthier man and is now pregnant again, suffers from the anxiety so prevalent among Spielberg's central male figures. His ragged uncertainty about his conventional masculine roles and deep-seated feelings of inferiority as a husband and a father make it impossible for him to function as an effective parent.

Ray's reluctance to accept his parental responsibilities creates an emotional chasm that separates him from his children, as well a from his former wife. This situation changes drastically with the merciless attack of the tripod army. Like the preceding male protagonists in Spielberg's work, Ray totally loses control of his ordinary life and, as a consequence of external events, must assume the role of parental protector, an obligation that seemed totally incompatible with his previous state of perpetual adolescence. Extraordinary events force him to abandon the security of his familiar Newark neighborhood and venture into an precarious environment where the traditional rules of civilized behavior no longer apply; he must confront the deadly and unruly forces let loose upon the world—both global and individual. Surrounded by physical danger from the deadly alien invaders, along with intermittent threats from terrified citizens and the deranged ravings of Harlan Ogilvy, Ray is compelled to occupy a traditional masculine position that has previously eluded him: the assured and sympathetic father who must shield his children from harm and satisfy their emotional needs. The journey to safety becomes, as with

Ray Ferrier (Tom Cruise) must learn to accept parental obligations and protect his daughter Rachel (Dakota Fanning) in *War of the Worlds* (2005).

most of Spielberg's estranged fathers, as much about the man's acceptance of mature commitments as it is about his daring prowess.

As usual in Spielberg's films, Ray's metaphoric journey home—to the space occupied by his ex-wife and her parents from which he has been barred since the divorce—becomes a series of ethical and practical lessons that reshape his fundamental worldview, mature him emotionally and psychologically, correct his distorted values, and reveal his suitability as a parent. The director displays this inner passage from boyhood to manhood in various ways, notably the gradual change in Ray's clothing. As noted in the press kit, Spielberg strips Ray of his protective covering, literally layer by layer, as his emotional maturation progresses: "[H]e begins with a jacket, a hoodie, and two t-shirts. Then slowly peels them away until he's left with just a t-shirt and jeans" (13). Ray, the macho dockworker, must shed his insulation and make himself vulnerable before he can gain the inner strength to assume his role as a father. Yet, unlike men in Spielberg's previous movies, Ray harbors no fragile illusions about actually reconstituting his fragmented family. Instead, he must atone for his pervious failures as a husband and father while earning his right to be part of an extended family that also includes another respected—and perhaps even loved—male figure, his childrens's stepfather.

In the film's final moments, we see him standing alone, an image strongly reminiscent of Ethan Edwards (John Wayne) at the end of *The Searchers,* a man who brings the family back together but cannot join them.

War of the Worlds also features another Spielberg motif, one much criticized throughout his career: it lacks a powerful, or even substantially present, female figure. Mary Ann appears to be a strong and efficient woman from a background considerably different from Ray's roots. She still cares for her ex-husband, but his reluctance to grow up and accept the duties necessary to raise children dooms their marriage. In the film's production notes, the director says that he also envisioned the couple as permanently divided by their disparate economic classes:

> [T]wo people who married young and were never able to transcend their different social backgrounds. He's this blue-collar worker who unloads those big cargo containers and is a big kid at heart. He married a Connecticut aristocrat, someone who had horses growing up, and they fell in love and had a couple of kids. . . . There was such a great chasm between their upbringings that they never really could see eye-to-eye on many things. (7)

Ray's first impulse, according to screenwriter David Koepp, "is to get the kids to their mother because he knows she can take care of them and he believes he can't" (8). Despite this backstory and plot motivation, Mary Ann is barely in the film and operates, as do most of Spielberg's females, as a secondary figure, another woman who functions simply as a narrative device and disappears while the men face obstacles and achieve nobility.

NARRATIVE STRUCTURE

As is common in Spielberg's films, *War of the Worlds* particularizes large social and historical events by filtering them through the eyes of a few individuals, such as World War II through the platoon in *Saving Private Ryan,* extraterrestrial contact through Elliott in *E.T.* and Roy in *Close Encounters of the Third Kind,* and displaced persons through Viktor in *The Terminal.* In this manner, Spielberg conveys an epic story on a personal scale; by showing common people swept up in events beyond their control, he narrows the gap between viewer and protagonist. Those who could never identify with powerful figures like Eisenhower or Patton feel a kinship with Captain Miller and Private Ryan. They are just like us—or at least as we imagine ourselves at our best—ordinary people within our power to emulate, not grand figures to idolize from afar. Using the international star-power of Tom Cruise to sell *War of the Worlds,* Spielberg consciously works against his lead's screen persona: "I said to Tom when we first started working on this project that I really want to make a movie where your character isn't heroic—he's running away" (Press kit 5). Indeed, after being forced to surrender his car at gunpoint, Ray puts his head down on his arms and sobs, an emotionally vulnerable moment rather rare in Cruise's career.

Though Ray's specific agenda revolves around getting his children back to their mother, his actions are repeatedly dictated by the space invaders, the hordes of other displaced persons, and the progress of earth's destruction. In fact, one of the most frightening scenes takes place in a cramped cellar when he must kill Ogilvy because his mania threatens Rachel's safety. Spielberg shoots the scene with a unsettling juxtaposition of innocence and murder: Ray blindfolds Rachel, tells her to sing a lullaby, and then murders Ogilvy behind a closed door. The horror is reflected on his child's face as she slowly realizes what her father is doing and, simultaneously, continues to mouth the words to the child's song. While some critics may accuse Spielberg of once again shying away from the world's cruelty, such a scene attests to his skills and his subtle style as well. Rather than showing the violent physical deed itself, the director relies on a character's reaction and the viewer's imagination. How Ferrier kills Ogilvy is ultimately unimportant. The fact that he murders him, however, sets up a moral dilemma that pits the primal necessity of a precarious situation against the conventional rules of civilized behavior. It asks us to consider what we are capable of given the mandate to defend someone we love, a vulnerable person in need of our protection. At this moment, perhaps most of all, Ray assumes the physical and psychological obligations of fatherhood: safeguarding your child no matter what actions are required, and tending to their emotional needs despite your own.

TECHNICAL AND VISUAL ELEMENTS

Many of Spielberg's films incorporate innovative technical devices, such as CGI in *Jurassic Park* and the narrow degree shutters in *Schindler's List*. In *War of the Worlds*, the major technical novelty came before the shooting actually began with a process called "previsualization" (or "pre-viz"). In the film's production notes, Spielberg describes how this procedure, which George Lucas demonstrated for him, allowed him to take traditional storyboards and animate them into 3D digital sequences that "depict not only what a scene will look like, but reveal every aspect of a given location, including sets, actors, cameras, and crew" (12). As usual, Spielberg scouted locations while planning for the production phase, but he then had everything scanned into a computer and built the shooting sequences around the digitized locations generated on the monitors. The previsualization supervisor, Dan Gregoire, from Industrial Light and Magic, describes the effect of this process on the production:

> It starts as just a paragraph of text: "A Tripod rises out of the ground in Newark, New Jersey." Steven has it all in his mind, but it's tough to explain that to everybody involved. We came in and built that intersection in 3D. We built the Tripod; we cracked up the ground; we blew everything up. We developed the sequence from scratch so that we could actually play the movie on set in Newark and everybody who saw it could understand what Steven was talking about. (12)

Spielberg used these computer programs for the actors as well as the crew, allowing them to get a sense of the size of the Tripods and how their blocking would occur in relation to the machines. As a communication tool, previsualization allowed Spielberg to actualize his images before shooting them on film, making his storyboards into miniature movies for all to see.

Visually, Spielberg's stated goal was to "put the audience inside the events of the film . . . not a bird's eye view of what was happening, but a man's view, a child's view" (Press kit 14). To achieve that effect, Janusz Kaminski, the cinematographer, employed a great deal of handheld camera shots to simulate an individual's point of view, as well as naturalistic lighting, to create a spectacle that integrated supernatural events into a believable visual environment. Kaminski was also aware of color composition throughout the production: "It's got a really beautiful color palette where it starts a little bit with the blue and gradually becomes more colorful. It's stylized but stylized within the confinements of trying to make something real" (Press kit 14). When Ray first sees the expanse of red weed blanketing the landscape, "Steven's idea was that he wanted to go from basically black and white in the hallway, a long shot moving up the door, and when it opens it's like in *The Wizard of Oz* . . . the whole movie turns to color" (Press Kit 19). Pointing to the scene where Ray and his family join a swelling mob of refugees, Kaminski notes how the different kinds of lights "from Coleman lamps to oil lanterns to flashlight to Maglights to flashlights running out of juice . . . adds to the texture of the scene, creating a frenetic, chaotic, scary environment inside the car" (Press kit 15). For Spielberg, fantastic events work best when set within a context the audience can easily identify as commonplace. He creates fear and audience identification by injecting life-altering events into a seemingly stable, recognizable world.

Spielberg crams *War of the Worlds* with visual images and verbal references to eyes and seeing, not surprising in a post-9/11 America dominated by fearful citizens who increasingly exist under the gaze of the mechanized state. The preamble from Wells's novel and Spielberg's accompanying images place earth's inhabitants into the position of unsuspecting insects being intensely studied by superior beings. This motif continues throughout the film. At various times, Ray shields his daughter's eyes from some horrible sight, as when he tells her not to look at the crashed 747 and blindfolds her while he kills Ogilvy. Almost every scene contains some allusion to sight, be it the camcorder recording events, Robbie leaving his father and declaring, "I want to see this," or Ogilvy telling Ray that, from his experience as an ambulance driver, the patients who survive are those who "keep their eyes open." Most dramatically, the aliens dispatch snakelike electrical devices to seek out hiding citizens, their gliding necks and unblinking lenses casting light into the dark corners and dank cellars that temporarily shelter frightened refugees. Spielberg posits a similar future in *Minority Report,* where Anderton must outwit omnipresent detection devices, and in *The Terminal,* where Viktor Navorki's actions are habitually monitored. In *War of the Worlds,* no one is safe from prying eyes and the violence that inevitably follows.

A COUNTERNARRATIVE READING

In the swarm of interviews and stories that preceded the release of *War of the Worlds,* Spielberg consistently invoked the September 11, 2001, attack on the World Trade Center as the inspiration for the film. "It's certainly about Americans fleeing for their lives, being attacked for no reason, having no idea why they are being attacked and who is attacking them," he told Larry Fine (E1). "We live under a veil of fear that we didn't live under before 9/11," he reflected. "There has been a conscious emotional shift in this country" (Breznican 2A). Indeed, the film incorporates tropes from and direct references to that traumatic event, including Ray being covered in ashes, sleeper cells, posters of "the missing," crowds of panicked civilians fleeing, army units mobilizing, and Rachel's question, "Is it terrorists?" Spielberg fashions a powerful evocation of an urban apocalypse replete with mobs committing violent acts, corpses floating in a river, a speeding train with its coach cars aflame, and the charred remains of a crashed airplane. It even includes a striking image from the Vietnam era: as the last Hudson ferry hurriedly casts off, some of those left behind desperately jump onto it, clinging to the gate as it is lifted upward—a stark reminder of Vietnamese civilians vainly clutching onto the final American helicopters leaving Saigon.

But let me offer an alternative reading. From its inception, *The War of the Worlds* has proven an extraordinary vehicle for encapsulating first England's and then America's worst communal nightmare: invasion followed by annihilation. The readers of H. G. Wells's novel saw the aliens from outer space as tentacled allegories for a German sneak attack on their country. With a growing number of troops nestled just across the channel from their tiny island, British citizens were frightened that the Kaiser's expansionist dreams included their demise as a nation. Orson Welles's Halloween-eve listeners also feared Germany, but this time it was the relentless power of the Third Reich, which had already marched into Austria and invaded Czechoslovakia. George Pal's cold war viewers felt threatened by Soviet military buildup and the peril of a nuclear Armageddon. These potential foes were all standard fighting forces composed of powerful armies, vast navies, and sophisticated air forces. It was easy to envision the Germans or the Russians attacking England or America, to substitute their frightening war machines for the rampaging Martians.

In the post-9/11 world, however, the geopolitical map is vastly different than in 1898, 1938, or 1953. Most Americans don't fear an attack by a highly mechanized force commanded by a ruthless dictator. There is, in fact, no country that can offer a viable threat to the military might of the United States. The fearful specter that haunts us comes not from tanks and planes; it arises from individual acts of terrorism, men with explosives strapped to their chests, not armies goose-stepping into our cities. Who best fits the role of the invaders reigning down death and destruction from the skies? The answer, of course, depends on your point of view, but I would argue that, consciously or not, Spielberg provides dramatic examples of what it must have been like for Iraqi civilians during the American invasion/liberation of their country. The "shock and awe" created by the aliens in *War of the Worlds* resembles the panic generated by the American military more than it does the devastating, but as yet singular, attack on the World Trade Center. In essence, the film asks us to consider what it would feel like to be at war with a country stronger and technologically more advanced than the United States, one bent on our destruction. As Wells's novel transformed England into a nation whose people are subjugated or massacred, so Spielberg shows Americans as refugees in their own country, forced to abandon their homes and suffering under direct siege from a superior military force.

Support for this reading comes from literary history and internal elements within the film. Wells was a political activist, a member of the socialist Fabian Society, whose fiction often critiques a smug and complacent English society. Some critics interpret *The War of the Worlds* as an invective against British imperialism: the author transforms the world's foremost colonial power into a colonized nation whose citizens are treated as cruelly as the British had dealt with inhabitants of the various countries they conquered and pillaged. "Are we such apostles of mercy as to complain if the Martians warred in the same spirit?" (113), he asks pointedly. Lest we judge the invaders too harshly, his narrator continues:

> [W]e must remember what ruthless and utter destruction our own species has wrought, not only upon animals, such as the vanished bison and the dodo, but upon its inferior races. The Tasmanians, in spite of their human likeness, were entirely swept out of existence in a war of extermination by European immigrants, in the space of fifty years. (113)

For Wells, the Martians were doling out revenge on British civilians whose imperialist ambitions had resulted in untold brutal hardships for those who tried to defend themselves against the empire. This is not to say he wanted the earth destroyed by the aliens, or to see England overrun by its enemies. But he clearly recognized the irony inherent in the Martian onslaught and understood that they who are preyed upon sometimes use similar methods and share the same fate as their predators.

The dialogue contains two passing references to "occupation." Robbie is writing a paper on the French occupation of Algiers, a repressive and ultimately futile attempt by a colonial power, and Ogilvy tells Ray that the aliens "can't occupy this country because history tells us occupations always fail." Equally important, some of the visual imagery seems taken directly from nightly newscasts of the war with Iraq, but with Americans playing the roles inhabited by Arab civilians. In essence, we are put into the perspective of frightened citizens seeking shelter from a relentless military onslaught, of seeing our country without electricity, of becoming displaced persons wandering across barren landscapes, of viewing invaders searching our houses to stamp out insurgents, and of envisioning our sons running off to defend their homeland. By depicting the United States as vulnerable to large-scale military attack from beyond its borders, *War of the Worlds* forces viewers to understand the desperate plight of those trapped between two warring parties and consequently to empathize with those whose lives are reduced to a desperate struggle to save themselves and their families.

I am not arguing that most viewers watching *War of the Worlds* will necessarily think to themselves, "Ah. Now I know what it must have been like for Arab civilians during the Gulf Wars." On its most overt level, the movie taps into the growing sense of America as an accessible site for terrorist attacks. It derives its power from the gnawing belief that, despite our overwhelming military supremacy, we remain susceptible to an enemy willing to justify mass murder in the name of ideology and religion. As Wells says toward the end of his novel, "[W]hether we expect another invasion or not, our view of the human future must be greatly modified by these events" (252). I have no idea whether Spielberg has read Wells criticism or understood *The War of the Worlds* as a castigation of British imperialism before he started to work on this film. Nor do I much care. Whatever forces were at work in the making of *War of the Worlds*, and on whatever level he was conscious of them, the fact remains that Spielberg propels American viewers into a position of fear and trembling, of feeling what it must be like to have our country invaded, and of facing a technologically superior foe intent on destroying our country. It is an inversion few filmmakers would dare to attempt. By doing so, he raises uncomfortable questions about America's role in the world as the remaining superpower, questions about both its past actions and its future endeavors.

Jaws: Beyond the Screen

A magazine advertisement for Sun Microsystems in early 2000 showed a man dressed in a business suit, tie, and shoes swimming on the surface of the ocean, the waterline sharply separated from the stark, bleached horizon; just below him, a large dark globe speeds menacingly toward him. Between the unsuspecting man and the ominous globe, the tag line reads: "Just when your competition thought it was safe to do business." What other film made over thirty years ago (besides, perhaps, *The Godfather*) could evoke such immediate recognition, even among the dot-com generation who never saw the film in theaters? *Jaws* remains a powerful visual emblem for the dark forces that lie in wait, just beneath the surface, to devour us. The story of three vastly different men who join together to save their oceanside community from a marauding killer shark captured the nation's imagination and rang up record box-office figures. Opening in 409 theaters, the film grossed over seven million dollars in its first three days, over $458 million in the ensuing weeks, and took only seventy-eight days to replace *The Godfather* as the highest grossing movie of all time (until *Star Wars* eclipsed it two years later). *Jaws* became the first movie to crack the hundred-million-dollar mark and spawned the biggest merchandizing frenzy since the Davy Crockett fad of the mid 1950s. It inspired theme-park rides and political cartoons, its box-office success changed the way studios marketed and distributed their products, and it jump-started the summer-movie phenomenon.

Oceans of words have been written about the production events, particularly the litany of disasters, that afflicted the *Jaws* set (see Gottlieb, Blake, Griffin, and the anniversary collector's edition DVD): the nearly constant failure of the three mechanical sharks (collectively nicknamed Bruce, after Spielberg's lawyer, Bruce Ramer); the escalating and often cruel rivalry between Richard Dreyfuss and Robert Shaw; the editing of Verna Fields; the nightly script rewrites and daily rehearsals; the arduous ocean filming, which yielded only about six seconds of usable footage per day; the original fifty-five-day shooting schedule that swelled into 159 brutal days; the budget that ballooned from 3.5 to ten million dollars; the special equipment that the cinematographer, Bill Butler, invented to capture the underwater scenes; and the director's prolonged anxiety attack in a Boston hotel following the end of shooting. It was more than enough to shatter the confidence of a veteran director with a substantial record of hit movies to prop up his or her ego, let alone a virtual novice with only a handful of television programs, a movie of the week, and a single commercially feeble feature to sustain him. These widely reported facts and fables have become part of the Spielberg legend and the lore of Hollywood. With such a comprehensive record available, little more need be said here about either the film's production background or financial record. Instead, I will concentrate on the themes and techniques that account for the movie's continued appeal to audiences more than thirty years after it first swam into American life.

JAWS IN SPIELBERG'S CANON

Of all Spielberg's films, *Jaws, E.T.,* and *Schindler's List* have generated the most popular and scholarly writing, and each, in its own way, has seared itself into the American psyche and remained an abiding part of our national consciousness. On the surface, these three pictures appear remarkably different: *Jaws,* the flamboyant, broadly communal nightmare of a young director; *E.T.,* the emotional, poignantly innocent fable of an emerging filmmaker; and *Schindler's List,* the thoughtful, deeply personal reflection of a mature visual artist. They seem to emanate from distinctly different parts of Spielberg's sensibility and represent major turning points in his career. Perhaps the nearest analogy is John Ford, who veered between moderately budgeted genre pieces such as *Stagecoach* (1939), *My Darlin' Clementine* (1946), *The Searchers* (1956), and *The Man Who Shot Liberty Valance* (1962) and high-profile prestige works such as *The Informer* (1935), *The Grapes of Wrath* (1940), *How Green Was My Valley* (1941), and *The Quiet Man* (1952). While Ford was actively working in Hollywood, the industry rewarded him with Oscars only for his "serious" projects, and many wondered aloud why he wasted time and obvious talent on pedestrian westerns. Scholars now cite those once-maligned works as the most genuine representations of Ford's personal philosophy and visual aesthetics. So while most critics agree that *Schindler's List* ranks among the best American movies ever made, and many would argue that *E.T.* also deserves a place on that list, I maintain that *Jaws* is equally deserving of that honor.

THE INTERPRETATIONS

Because of its vast commercial success, critics have espoused a panoply of interpretations to explain the continuing hold of *Jaws* on the public's imagination:

Literary: A modern *Moby Dick,* with contemporary Ahab (Quint), Ismael (Brody), and Queequeg (Hooper).

Freudian: An ongoing battle between the id (Quint), the superego (Hooper), and the ego (Brody), which ultimately join together to destroy the repressed other (the shark).

Feminist: A reenactment of the myth in which the mother figure (shark) is slaughtered by violent men, reaffirming the patriarchal social order at the expense of the feminine and displacing fear of women onto the shark, which must be killed for the masculine world order to survive.

Marxist: An alliance between multinational corporations (Hooper) and the forces of the law (Brody) is cemented by the killing of the shark and the sacrifice of the individual capitalist, Quint.

Nationalistic: A communal tale in which three hunters subdue the savage forces of the natural world (the shark) and make it possible for civilization to advance and prosper.

Historical: An allegory of the Vietnam War in which Americans feel powerless against guerilla attacks (the shark), corrupt civic leaders govern, and decent, common men (Brody) must take personal responsibility for restoring order.

Ecological: A force of nature (the shark) takes revenge on those who invade his domain and pollute his world.

Generational: An old man (Quint) gives way to a young man (Hooper), and this transition is mediated by a middle-aged man (Brody).

Economic: A town filled with greedy people who exploit nature and sacrifice their children for monetary gain. The shark must be destroyed because it threatens the fiscal well-being of the community.

Moralistic: The shark is the figure of moral rectitude sent to punish Quint for his part in delivering the atomic bomb. Brody and Hooper struggle to save him, but he is doomed because of his sin against humanity.

Legalistic: Quint is our primal nature, Hooper scientific reason, and Brody law (moral code); only the latter can save humankind because it separates and protects us from destructive forces outside civilization.

Class: A film about socioeconomic issues that separate society, with Quint representing the working class, Brody the middle class, and Hooper the upper class.

Personal: As a director, Spielberg, like Brody, must mediate between his love of the past (particularly his interest in history) and his fascination with the future (his involvement with science fiction and fantasy).

Psychosocial: Three men comprise a dysfunctional family, with the harsh father (Quint) at odds with the rebellious son (Hooper), and the disinterested child (Brody) dragged into family disputes.

Sociological: The strong men in the tribe must protect their women and children from the threat of outside forces that seek to destroy their community and their culture.

Genre: A cross between horror and adventure films, with each man playing a traditional role: Quint (grizzled veteran), Brody (reluctant hero), and Hooper (technical wizard). There are even echoes of the western, as the sheriff rounds up a posse consisting of the old gunslinger and the new kid in town.

While most of these interpretations seem fundamentally incompatible, many share a common feature: Quint represents an older, more individualistic code of action and system of values, and Hooper a more technological and contemporary approach. Brody consistently mediates between these seemingly conflicting positions.

In the first extended shot on the *Orca*, for example, Chief Brody wears his life vest as he chums bait for the shark, suntan oil slathered over his nose and the scent of Old Spice ineffectively blotting out the smell of dead fish. Watching him with a bemused expression, Quint sits in the fishing chair, his pole at his side, as Hooper incessantly fiddles with his technological equipment. Throughout the voyage, both men teach the chief to manipulate components of their world. Quint shows him how to tie a basic sheep-shank knot (speaking to him as a father might to a child), and Hooper teaches him to use his fancy scientific equipment. In the *Indianapolis* scene, Brody wears glasses and a watch, elements associated with Hooper, while toying with his sailor knots, an activity related to Quint. Most tellingly, neither Quint nor Hooper can defeat the shark alone; the old man's harpoons and barrels are as ineffectual as the young man's shark cage and poisons. Even working together, they fail to kill the shark. Only the inexperienced outsider to life on the water can destroy the monster, and only then by combining weapons specifically identi-

Quint (Robert Shaw), the rugged individualist, Hooper (Richard Dreyfuss), the man of science, and Brody (Roy Scheider), the mediator, bond together against a common enemy in *Jaws* (1975).

fied with each of his absent companions: Brody uses Quint's old-fashioned M-1 rifle to explode Hooper's air tank lodged in the fish's mouth, melding facets of the traditional and the modern. As is often the case in Spielberg's films, the seemingly ordinary man who appears awkwardly out of place in the environment he is forced to inhabit defeats the threat to society, not those who initially seem better trained and more prepared for that heroic task.

MALE BONDING

Jaws remains one of the clearest expressions of male bonding in Spielberg's movies, and this connection between male characters forms a consistent leitmotif throughout the director's work. His prolific output contains scant instances of mature relationships between men and women, instead focusing on how men relate to each other. Similar to the works of Howard Hawks, many of Spielberg's films revolve around men who initially compete against each other but ultimately learn to understand and respect each other, to work together to defeat a common enemy. In *Jaws,* as in many other American films about male bonding, these connections often occur with alcohol as a catalyst for and symbol of changing feelings. When Hooper first visits Brody in his home, for example, he brings along bottles of red and white wine, uncertain which color the chief prefers. It takes but a few drinks for them to decide to go into town and investigate whether the shark caught by some drunken fishermen really is the killer terrorizing the town. In a parallel scene, Brody shares a drink with Quint when first visiting his home, but this time it is a homemade brew—not upper-class wine—and Hooper is pointedly excluded from this masculine ritual. Quint and Hooper represent polar opposites in almost every imaginable realm, and Spielberg uses alcohol to put comical exclamation points on their disparity at several points in the film. When, for instance, Quint finishes a beer, he nonchalantly crushes the can. Hooper looks at him, takes a final sip from his drink, and melodramatically crumples his styrofoam cup. Later, following Quint's riveting account of the *Indianapolis* tragedy, he and Hooper "drink to their legs," and all three men sing together to solidify their newfound common bonds.

It takes time for such bonds to form between these essentially different men. Early in the voyage, Quint and Hooper continually harangue each other and point out what each does wrong. In the first chase sequence, for example, they even disagree about whether or not they snagged a shark on the line. Quint calls Hooper an "idiot" and accuses him of being unable to admit his errors. Hooper responds with a series of obscene gestures and silly facial expressions, asserting his outrage but not proving that his high-priced education can match Quint's personal knowledge of the sea and its inhabitants. In their initial encounter with the shark, Quint almost misses a crucial shot because Hooper, setting up some fancy equipment, nearly fails to tie the rope onto a barrel in time. Later on, a disgruntled Quint must use Hooper's steel cage and scientific knowledge after his traditional methods prove ineffectual. In the final, climactic fight, Hooper's compressed air tank saves Brody by providing a weapon to kill the shark and destroys Quint by slamming into his hand, dislodging his grip, and precipitating his slide into the mouth of the beast—a final visual acknowledgment that he cannot adjust to the modern world of technological gadgets. Yet all the verbal snipping and internecine warfare changes dramatically in the justly famous *Indianapolis* scene.

This scene, which epitomizes male bonding and camaraderie, mimics the progression found in traditional love encounters between men and women: playful bantering, teasing foreplay, and eventual union. As it unfolds, more flesh is revealed and greater touching becomes conspicuous. It begins with

Brody gingerly feeling his forehead and moves to Quint and Hooper comparing scars with each other, the chief left only with a skimpy reminder of his appendix operation that scarcely equates with their nautical injuries. Quint and Hooper's bodies record their battle histories with men and beasts, from the old shark hunter's false tooth and lump on the head to the young ichthyologist's damaged forearm, a vivid reminder of the eel that bit through his wetsuit. Finally, they both exhibit scars on their calves from sharks—Quint's a thresher and Hooper's a bull—and throw their legs over each other to cement their deeper connection. The "scar" segment of the *Indianapolis* scene establishes emotional intimacy between these two distinctive men. In recognition of this shift, the veteran sea captain offers his youthful counterpart the drink he earlier denied him on land, showing new respect for his shipmate; at precisely that moment, Brody asks Quint about the scar on his arm, a concentration camp–like tattoo that initially seems like only another reminder of a bygone brawl.

Thus unfolds the celebrated soliloquy of the disaster aboard the ill-fated USS *Indianapolis,* the ship that transported the atomic bomb to be dropped on Hiroshima (see Stanton and Kurzman), and without which *Jaws* would "be like *Hamlet* without 'to be or not to be'" (Andrews 142). It begins with deadly silence, save for the ship's creaking planks, and ends with Quint's grisly statistics: "1,110 men went in, 316 came out, sharks took the rest, June 29, 1945. Anyway, we delivered the bomb." Hooper gasps in amazement. Brody's eyes bulge with astonishment. Now they understand, as does the audience, Quint's fanatical hatred of sharks, his quest to destroy the beast with "lifeless eyes, black eyes, like a doll's eyes," who doesn't "seem to be living [until] he rips you to pieces." Quint, similar to Coleridge's Ancient Mariner, watched as men died all around him, and he, like "a thousand slimy things / Lived on." To compensate for surviving the tragedy, he dedicates his life to destroying the creatures that killed his shipmates. As if to break Quint's incantation, the eerie sound of a distant whale slices through the silence and the three men slip out of their shared reverie. To seal their intimacy, Hooper launches into a jaunty version of "Show Me the Way to Go Home." He is immediately joined by Quint and then Brody, a show of masculine affection and longing abruptly halted by the shark's nocturnal attack.

Several people take credit for the *Indianapolis* speech. Spielberg says that the playwright Howard Sackler (*The Great White Hope*) conceived it, the director and writer John Milius fleshed it out, and the actor and playwright Robert Shaw rewrote Milius's draft. He concludes, in the DVD interview, that "it is Shaw's version of Milius's version of Sackler's version."

"Show me the way to go home." In a recurrent literal and metaphoric quest in Spielberg's movies, lost men like Quint (Robert Shaw) and Hooper (Richard Dreyfuss) in *Jaws* (1975) anxiously search for physical and emotional security in a changing social environment.

This sequence signals the major turning point in the relationship between these men. Previously, they had fundamentally different views of almost everything, including what to do with the shark: Quint wanted to kill it, Hooper wanted to study it, and Brody wanted to chase it away from Amity. Each represents a distinct response to evil. Quint, the man of action, simply wants to destroy it, to blow it off the surface of the earth. Hooper, the academic, opts to pinion it under a microscope or, if dead, to dissect it and learn how it functions. Brody, always somewhere between the two extremes, simply desires to send it elsewhere. Drawn neither to destruction nor study, he seeks to move the threat beyond his jurisdiction. The three usually occupy distinctly separate visual spaces aboard the *Orca*. Most often, Hooper stands atop the cabin steering the boat; Quint controls its center, sitting and then strapping himself into the deep-sea fishing seat as if it were a throne; Brody remains at the stern doing various menial tasks. At film's end, however, the chief ascends to the highest spot in the rapidly sinking ship, scrambling to the top of the mast to get one last shot before the shark devours him.

In the cramped cabin during the *Indianapolis* scene, however, Spielberg visually aligns Hooper and Quint by sitting them together at the rickety table, with Brody standing off to the side, a landlubber still separated from the sea lovers despite his hospital scar. Even as Quint spins out his horrible tale, Brody occupies space detached from Quint and Hooper. Finally, as they sing together, he joins his shipmates in a linked trio, side by side on the bench. Following the nighttime shark assault, Spielberg underlines this new emotional and psychological configuration visually: Quint and Hooper struggle to repair the moribund *Orca,* each thrusting one arm above deck; but, since they wear identical blue shirts, we cannot tell which arm is Hooper's and which is Quint's. What begins as a series of physical challenges and verbal taunts ends with these men working together as equals, literally depicted as two arms of the same man, to overcome a common threat.

VISUAL HIGHLIGHTS

The novelist Peter Benchley was not particularly enamored with Spielberg's adaptation of *Jaws,* saying that the director had "'no real knowledge of reality but the movies,'" that he inevitably "'reaches for movie cliches of the forties and fifties'" (qtd. in McBride 239), and that he will "'one day be known as the greatest second-unit director in Hollywood'" (qtd. in Andrews 21). History has proven Benchley a poor prophet and an ingrate, since the movie substantially increased book sales and kept his novel in the public consciousness far beyond its expected shelf life. Yet his charges, often couched in more theoretical jargon, remain part of the standard attack on Spielberg: his movies are trite, recycled pastiches from previous eras driven by action with little character development. His detractors often acknowledge his cleverness and craftsmanship, but they demean or ignore his visual expertise beyond creating light shows and spectacles. For example, much has been written about how Spielberg turned a potential disaster—the inability of the mechanical sharks to work consistently—into a triumph, not revealing the creature for the first eighty of the movie's 125 minutes, and then showing progressively more of the monster with each subsequent appearance to intensify the audience's dread and fear. Such a tactic transformed *Jaws* from "a Japanese Saturday-matinee horror flick to more of a Hitchcock thriller" (Biskind, "'World'" 199).

Much less analysis, however, has been devoted to the director's visual mastery born of an extremely arduous and complicated shoot that went a grueling 104 days beyond its original schedule. The gruesome death of Alex Kintner, for which Brody feels responsible and seeks vengeance, clearly demonstrates Spielberg's deft command of the complex elements of film construction: cinematography, mise-en-scène, editing, movement, sound, language, and acting. It displays his broad technical skills and, even more impressively, how he uses them to further the narrative flow and deepen the emotional power of the story, as he forces viewers to share the anxiety of Chief Brody. The transition onto crowded Amity Beach occurs directly after the town fathers, led by Mayor Vaughan (Murray Hamilton), convince Brody to leave the recreational area open for commercial reasons, despite a suspected shark attack on Chrissie Watkins (Susan Backlinie). Spielberg adroitly constructs the beach scene with particular attention to color combinations, musical cues, visual and auditory pacing, and ambient sounds, all fused into a symphony of sustained tension worthy of Hitchcock himself. This intricate blending takes innocuous elements from everyday life and transforms them into a progressively heightened maelstrom of actions that finally burst into full-blown tragedy, the death of a child. For Spielberg, no moral transgression is greater than for those charged with parental—or in this case, communal—responsibility to forsake their fundamental obligations and abandon those who rely upon their judgment for their safety.

Spielberg begins the scene with unnamed secondary characters who appear at various points to distract us from—and in one case, draw attention to—the shark's presence. In the first shot, for example, a heavyset woman wades into the water, followed by an unnamed boy in a red bathing suit, who comes out to ask his mother, wearing a paisley bathing suit and floppy yellow hat, if he can stay in the ocean a little longer. She reluctantly allows him "just ten minutes more," and he happily heads back to the water, the camera following him as he walks past a crowd of women, including Mrs. Brody, talking on a blanket. On screen right, the chief, seated in a low-slung beach chair, stares intently at the ocean. He seems oblivious to the conversations swirling around him and to anything else on land. With this initial structure, Spielberg immediately establishes a typical scene of people relaxing at the seaside; only the audience shares Brody's anxiety, obsessively watching the water with him for the lethal attack that will destroy the innocent pleasures of this island community. Throughout this scene, a cacophony of ambient noises bombards our ears, including news reports, pop and classical music from radios, beach conversations, and playful water games. Such dissonance further upsets audience expectations, adding to the overall tension in the scene.

Spielberg elongates the suspense in this four-minute scene by incorporating secondary characters and never clearly indicating who will be the shark's victim or when. The conventional moments on the beach continue, but they now seem permeated with dangerous possibilities. A teenager, dressed in a yellow shirt, throws a stick into the ocean for his dog to fetch. The heavy woman from the opening moments floats alone and contented in the ocean. All the while, Spielberg concentrates on Brody, cleverly using passersby as human camera wipes to draw us in and then back from the chief, whose position in relation to the camera changes with each frame alteration. While Brody tries inconspicuously to watch the ocean, Spielberg blocks his (and our) view, first with a businessman who has a parking problem and then with an old man ("Bad Hat" Harry) in a black bathing cap and with a yellow towel, who tells him all the islanders know he never goes into the water. Screams that others barely notice propel Brody off his chair, leaving him relieved to discover that these squeals of pleasure emanate from teenagers frolicking in the water.

Two things finally settle him down: first, he allows his own children to go into the water, signaling that he feels secure enough to risk it; second, his wife tells him that he is uptight and gives him a shoulder massage, introducing a sensual element into the taut sequence. To accentuate this change in attitude, Spielberg shifts his camera so that Brody and his wife dominate the foreground, the beach swarming with people is in the midground, and the calm ocean and clear sky in the background. The chief, shot in close-up, sits on the right side of the screen in profile, constantly distracted from surveying the water. Ellen Brody occupies the right center of the frame in a full shot, wearing a dark bathing suit, a floppy beige hat, a blue scarf, and oval sunglasses. Alternately looking at his wife and glancing back to the ocean, Brody tries to continue the conversation with her while maintaining his nervous vigil. To heighten our anxiety, Spielberg denies us the chief's panoramic view of the ocean, distancing the viewer from the water and making it impossible to see what Brody observes. In other words, we share Brody's frustration at the various interruptions but are unable to share his sight of the scene. Ellen slides a bit closer to Brody, takes his hand in hers, and tells him that it's fine if he doesn't want to allow his children into the water. "It's alright," he says, "let 'em go," and quickly kisses her hand.

Spielberg briskly cuts to the activities in front of Brody, but without actually including the chief in the composition: kids running excitedly into the surf and splashing each other, as Alex Kinter, in the center of the frame, floats on his raft. Following the comic intrusion of Bad Hat Harry, Ellen slowly works her way behind the chief and begins to rub his shoulders, accompanied by the syrupy strains of "I love you. I honestly love you." Brody, for the first time in the scene, starts to relax a bit, his body losing some of its rigid posture. But, as he slackens his guard, hints of danger mount, unknown to him but not to the viewer. We now grasp more than Brody because we see more than he is capable of at this crucial moment. While he becomes calmer and more secure, we get increasingly nervous anticipating a bloody catastrophe. The editing pace quickens. Spielberg sets up a series of rapid cuts of children playing in the water, his younger son building a sand castle and singing to himself near the water's edge, and most ominously, the yellow-shirted boy not being able to find Pippet, his dog. Only the abandoned stick bobs forebodingly among the waves. Then the pulsating music begins; we see underwater shots of Alex's arms and legs dangling off the rubber raft; the music gets louder and faster as the camera moves closer and closer to Alex's knees; cut to an above-the-water shot of the shark bisecting the raft and sending up a geyser of blood. "Did you see that?" exclaims a man sitting next to the oblivious Mrs. Kinter and rising to his feet. Cut back underwater as Alex is pulled downward, and the ocean turns red with his blood.

At that moment, Spielberg executes his now famous push/pull shot (much as he did in an equally decisive moment in *The Sugarland Express*), perhaps inspired by the last belltower scene in Hitchcock's 1958 classic *Vertigo* (see Freer 51). Roy Scheider describes how Spielberg constructed this shot by moving the camera toward his face while, at the same time, moving his body on the beach chair and Lorraine Gary kneeling behind him toward the camera (Andrews 161). For a moment, time stands still: the camera zoom freezes the frightening instant into an eerie tableau of the two characters with only sand and shrubbery as a backdrop. It is a technique meant to heighten the moment, to externalize Brody's internal emotions as he struggles to grasp what he witnesses and remains powerless to prevent. Panic ensues. The children who moments ago were frolicking in the water scream as a circle of Alex's blood envelops them. Brody rushes to the edge of the water and begins to yell, "Get everybody out! Get 'em out!" Quick cuts of parents dragging their children onto the beach, but the chief, still afraid to go into the ocean, lets his wife pull their son to safety. What's left is the tragic denouement: Mrs. Kintner's frightened voice searching for her son—"Alex! Alex!"—and finally the slashed yellow raft washing onto shore, accompanied only by sounds of the lapping waves and plaintive seagulls.

Among its many virtues, the bloody beach scene is a textbook example of splendid editing. In a 1980 interview, Verna Fields (who won an Oscar for the film) talked about the rhythm and pace of *Jaws* and this scene in particular. Spielberg initially designed it with people walking in front of the camera and blocking Brody's sight. Then Fields asked him if she could experiment with an editing pattern that, as far as she knew, had not been tried before:

"We kept the editing rhythm going at a very even pace and then broke it. You have a cut, cut, cut, no cut. You almost immediately felt that the person seen on the no cut was going to get taken, especially when we then went back to cut, cut" (Friedman, "Mother" 54). Adding this editing design to an already carefully constructed scene heightened the tension significantly; in fact, Fields used it other times in the film, particularly after Brody first sees the shark and says, "I think we're gonna need a bigger boat." Many commentators have awarded Fields a great deal of credit for the success of *Jaws*, some noting that Spielberg was galled when she received an Academy Award and he did not even get nominated. The producer Richard Zanuck, for one, claims that Fields "'came in and reconstructed some scenes'" (qtd. in McBride 252), making them far different than Spielberg originally intended. Whether because of bruised feelings, professional insecurities, or Fields's promotion to feature production vice president at Universal Studios, she and Spielberg never worked together on another project.

A young Steven Spielberg shares a laugh aboard the *Orca* with the stars of *Jaws* (1975), Robert Shaw, Roy Scheider, and Richard Dreyfuss, during the film's arduous shoot.

THE MUSIC

While Spielberg had worked effectively with the composer John Williams on *Sugarland Express,* their collaboration on *Jaws* cemented their relationship. For *Jaws,* Williams—who won an Oscar for his work—created an enduring theme that Spielberg used masterfully. His pulsating cello theme for the shark still sends shivers up the spine of the most jaded viewers brought up on far more grisly movie fare. As the director put it in 1995, on the twentieth anniversary of the film, "'the music became the soul of *Jaws.* John Williams rediscovered my vision though his *Jaws* theme. And gave *Jaws* an identity, a personality, a soul'" (qtd. in Griffin 100). Initially, however, he felt that the music was too simple and not particularly effective. But the composer convinced him otherwise, describing his own leitmotif as having "'the effect of grinding away at you, just as a shark would do, instinctual, relentless, unstoppable'" (qtd. in Andrews 60). Precisely so. Throughout *Jaws,* Spielberg uses Williams's theme to trigger apprehension in the viewers, to alert us to danger, and to replace our rational consciousness with an irrational fear.

Since we never see the shark itself until late in the film, Williams's music and the underwater point of view function as its surrogate. In the opening attack on Chrissie Watkins, for example, the theme appears as the shark approaches the girl, gets faster and faster until the attack is over, and then slowly subsides as it swims away. In the beach scene described above, twenty-five minutes later, the music appears for the second time, signaling the real danger and not a red herring. Juxtaposed with this broodingly foreboding theme, Williams includes what Spielberg calls triumphant "pirate music" to engage the audience during the shark chase, a slower version of which accompanies Brody and Hooper as they swim to shore once the shark is dead. Throughout *Jaws,* Spielberg demonstrates the importance of musical placement within scenes: its absence is as crucial as its presence, and sound can "establish a set of memory triggers throughout the sixteen reels" (Andrews 60).

Williams subsequently wrote the music for all of Spielberg's films except *The Color Purple,* which had Quincy Jones as producer and part of the music team. Unlike most of Spielberg's other collaborators, Williams had a very free hand to create the film's music:

> Johnny Williams I have very little control over, except we listen to music together and I'll show him my film and try to talk it through, to give him a sense of my taste in musical atmospheres. But once Johnny sits down at the piano, it's his movie, it's his score. It's his original overdraft, a super-imposition. (Tuchman 51)

While acknowledging this enduring relationship, I find that Williams's music works best in Spielberg's broader, more action-oriented pictures such as the *Indiana Jones* trilogy, *Hook,* and the *Jurassic Park* movies, whereas it sometimes becomes intrusive, even overpowering, in the most intimate moments of *Schindler's List, Always,* and *Amistad.* That said, Spielberg himself claims that "[t]he only person I've had a perfect association with is John Williams" (Royal, "Steven Spielberg" 92).

POPULARITY

Why did Spielberg's big fish story capture the imagination of the American public in 1975 and continue its grasp on audiences into the twenty-first century? Nigel Andrews makes a salient point by suggesting that, at the time of the film's release, feelings of vulnerability, fear, and frustration created an unstable national mood that found a convenient outlet for temporarily resolving these tensions. The United States was suffering through a crisis of confidence: it had been forced to exit ignominiously from Vietnam, its vaunted military might overcome by men in black pajamas who struck and then disappeared into the countryside. Given this shocking defeat, citizens had "begun to realize—the *message of Jaws*—that the strongest bulwarks of civilization are powerless against a guerrilla attack that is fast enough, fierce enough, unexpected enough" (Andrews 5). Of course, the ending of *Jaws* belies this harsh reality. Much like the World War II combat platoons discussed in chapter 4, Quint, Brody, and Hooper overcome their seemingly insurmountable differences to forge an alliance and defeat a common enemy that threatens their civilization and their lives. Such a conclusion offers momentary solace and resolution, though it does little to dispel the persistent fear that such lethal threats will periodically reoccur.

Jaws plunges us into deeper primal realms as well. Human beings are out of their natural element in the ocean. They become dangling legs and flailing arms, hardly a match for creatures who glide swiftly through the water toward their prey. In the blink of an eye, a playful moment can turn into a tragedy, as unseen predators lurking beneath a deceptively calm surface strike and kill. As in all of Spielberg's best movies, danger is omnipresent in *Jaws,* hiding just outside the frame and restively waiting to devour us. The most precarious times for Spielberg's characters occur when things seem most calm and pleasant, when they relax to enjoy an event or another person. Critics who assail the director as being too warm and cuddly fail to see that his films repeatedly demonstrate that apparent safety is the most dangerous illusion of all, since one can never be protected from disaster anywhere or at any time.

When men cannot safeguard their women, as in the movie's first scene, and their children, as in the bloody beach sequence, their fragility as defenders of the family—and by extension, their civilization—is called into question. It is a theme perhaps even more resonant in our time of terrorist attacks and suicide bombers than of Vietnam's distant rice paddies and firefights, a time when violence bloodies our native soil and children strap explosives onto their backs. *Jaws* is far more than a big fish story. Beneath its pop-culture appeal, the film challenges some of society's most cherished beliefs and defies its classification as simply an action-packed popcorn flick.

JAWS AND HOLLYWOOD'S BLOCKBUSTER MENTALITY

A consistent charge leveled against *Jaws* is that the film and its maker initiated the summer blockbuster mentality. In its wake, it set financial expectations so unreasonably high that jittery studios have refused to fund more experimental and individual moviemakers. The emphasis on action spectaculars, the so-called Big-Bang movies with bloated budgets, they argue, took films out of the hands of creative directors and returned the power to studio functionaries, effectively ending a fertile auteurist period of American filmmaking. Peter Biskind provides a good example of those who routinely fall into this type of *Jaws*/Spielberg bashing:

> *Jaws* changed the business forever . . . diminishing the importance of print reviews, making it virtually impossible for a film to build slowly, finding its audience by dint of mere quality. . . . . In a sense, Spielberg was the Trojan horse through which the studios began to reassert their power. . . . Such was Spielberg's (and Lucas's) influence that every studio movie became a B movie, and at least for the big action blockbusters that dominate the studios' slates, second unit has replaced first unit. (*Easy Riders* 278)

Such overstatements make for good polemics, but they rarely hold up under careful scrutiny. To avoid rehashing a complicated history of Hollywood economics, let me endorse the basic sentiments Thomas Schatz outlines in his discussion of the New Hollywood:

> If any single film marked the arrival of the New Hollywood, it was *Jaws,* the Spielberg-directed thriller that recalibrated the profit potential of the Hollywood hit, and redefined its status as a marketable commodity and cultural phenomenon as well. The film brought an emphatic end to Hollywood's five-year recession, while ushering in an era of high-cost, high-tech, high-speed thrillers. ("New Hollywood" 17)

He goes on to note that *Jaws* was not a particularly big-budget project in the age of lavish musicals and costly disaster epics, that the film was released in the summer rather than during the standard Christmas-holiday period studios reserved for their potentially biggest hits, that the producers Zanuck and Brown spent $2.5 million (most of it in a media blitz the week before the film opened) promoting the film, and that it debuted on 464 screens across the country (18).

The runaway success of *Jaws* ultimately did change how movies were sold to the public. Marketing strategies like "saturation booking" (getting the picture on as many screens as possible) and "front loading" (getting the picture as much publicity as possible before it actually opens) became common tactics. Summer became the time to release action movies, leaving winter for more cerebral, Oscar-worthy films. The "youth market" shifted from college students to high schoolers. Shopping malls with cineplexes became the major sites for viewing movies, replacing downtown theaters and drive-ins. Are *Jaws* and its director responsible for all these shifts in demographic patterns, sociological alterations, and advertising stratagems? To hold Spielberg responsible for these developments is akin to blaming the Wright brothers for delays at O'Hare Airport. Schatz makes two points that bear repeating: "only positive audience response and favorable word-of-mouth can propel a film to genuine hit status," and the release of *Jaws* coincided with events "both inside and outside the movie industry in the mid-1970s which . . . [had] little or nothing to do with that particular film" (17). *Jaws* appealed to a broad spectrum of moviegoers and appeared at a propitious moment—as do most films that evolve into cultural events—when what it offered corresponded with what people wanted.

Some of this was not even new with *Jaws*. As Biskind himself notes, massive television spots had already been used to plug less elevated fare, such as *The Golden Voyage of Sinbad* (1973) and *Breakout* (1975). *The Godfather* opened in approximately the same number of theaters as *Jaws*. Spielberg's film may have redefined the youth market, but it certainly did not create it. *Bonnie and Clyde* (1967), *The Graduate* (1967), and *Easy Rider* (1969), among others, had amply demonstrated the financial rewards available for films that could draw younger viewers into theaters for repeated viewings. To argue that Spielberg invented the blockbuster mentality is to ignore the decades of filmmaking that preceded it. More aptly, one might ask when blockbusters were not part of Hollywood life? *Gone with the Wind* (1939) was certainly such an event. Filmmaking, particularly mainstream Hollywood moviemaking, is always a struggle, a balancing act, between art and commerce. All filmmakers, even purists working outside the studio system, hope that their efforts find as widespread an audience and as much acceptance as possible. To censure Spielberg for making a successful film is hypocritical and disingenuous. Should he have wanted only moderate success, a slice of cinematic artistry shown only in art houses and museums with no thought of a wider audience?

If we acknowledge that the vast majority of artists want to have their works seen by as many people as possible, that Spielberg was not particularly responsible for the marketing strategies that worked so successfully with *Jaws,* and that he made a wonderful movie with a compelling narrative and fascinating characters, why has this enduring link been forged between *Jaws*/Spielberg and the death of "quality" filmmaking? Terrence Rafferty gets at part of the answer by noting that *Jaws* is essentially a horror movie and, as such, suffers the slings and arrows of "prejudiced" film historians and "higher-minded" audience members, although most horror-film scholars barely mention it. Even though the picture spawned a slew of appalling imitators, "*Jaws,* like *The Godfather* . . . deserves immunity from prosecution for the crimes of present-day Hollywood" (Rafferty 30). The creator cannot be held accountable for the illegitimate offspring of his original creation—not even for those dreadful *Jaws* sequels. Spielberg should also not be held liable for the way that studios choose to sell their products, even if they base some of their marketing decisions on the popularity of his film. On the simplest level, Spielberg's job was to generate terror. That he did so with a visual panache rarely matched in the American cinema, that he infused the film with thematic depth and poignant characterizations far beyond most monster movies, that he made a film that allows viewers to experience fear on a visceral level rarely equaled, and that in his twenties he demonstrated technical skills beyond the reach of most veteran moviemakers are not reasons to malign him. Indeed, it is time to celebrate *Jaws* and the considerable accomplishments of its creator.

* * *

Through they aptly demonstrate his technical proficiency and narrative skills, Spielberg's monster movies remain among the most conventional and, according to various interviews, least personal productions of his career. His trucks, sharks, dinosaurs, and aliens are murderous, savage, and barbaric threats to civilized communities that elicit screams but invite little understanding or compassion. They all emanate from the surrounding world, violent external threats that endanger humanity rather than deranged individuals from within our midst. We feel no conflicting emotions when confronting them on the screen; we simply want these killing machines, natural predators, and brutal invaders destroyed. Their demise strongly reaffirms the ideological force of the status quo embodied within the makeshift families of *Jaws, War of the Worlds,* and the *Jurassic Park* films. We may jump out of our seat while viewing Spielberg's monster movies, but we leave the theater comfortable that our survival has been assured and that the forces that imperil us have been permanently defeated. After witnessing battles with creatures of darkness on the land, in the sea, and from the air, we return home secure in the knowledge that humankind possess the physical, intellectual, and emotional skills to overcome the malevolent and destructive forces let loose upon our world. Traditional communal values emerge triumphant in Spielberg's horror movies.

4

"The World Has Taken a Turn for the Surreal": Spielberg's World War II Combat Films

The World War II Combat Film

The films discussed in this chapter—*1941* (1979), *Empire of the Sun* (1987), and *Saving Private Ryan* (1998)—all conform to Kathryn Kane's basic definition of the World War II combat film genre as encompassing movies set during the Second World War that focus on "uniformed American soldiers fighting uniformed enemy soldiers on foreign soil" (1). Because Spielberg's other films situated during this era, *Schindler's List* and the *Indiana Jones* trilogy, use combat between uniformed soldiers only as a backdrop, I have placed them in other chapters. The three films considered here all contain uniformed German or Japanese military personnel. *1941* confronts them humorously, with a mixture of servicemen and civilians; *Empire of the Sun* shows the awe and fear of noncombatant prisoners of war; and *Saving Private Ryan* tells its story with equally matched squads of servicemen. To grasp how Spielberg's combat movies incorporate conventional tropes and deviate from traditional World War II movies—those made during the conflict itself and those constructed over the subsequent decades—it is useful to establish the boundaries and borders of this genre, a important category of production, reception, and exhibition that has received relatively little scholarly attention.

As highlighted repeatedly in books by Kane, Jeanine Basinger, and Thomas Doherty, World War II marked a significant turning point in how the Hollywood film industry conceived of itself and, even more importantly, how the general public responded to the studios' products. As Doherty aptly notes, "The nature of the contract between Hollywood and American culture was rewritten during 1941–1945" (4). Prior to that time, sophisticated discussions of movies beyond their entertainment and commercial values surfaced only in limited ways, even though eruptions of moral outrage from various quarters regularly shook the industry. Moving pictures had been mostly consigned to the lower rungs of the arts ladder and championed by only a few lively intellectuals, such as Vachel Lindsay. This benign neglect disappeared once the Hollywood studios eagerly enlisted in the war effort. Manufacturing countless reels of stridently ideological footage, the well-oiled and prolific dream factories assembled fictional and documentary productions to inspire the troops abroad and hearten the folks waiting for them at home. As Gen. George Marshall astutely noted, "'The war had seen the development of two new weapons: the airplane and the motion picture'" (qtd. in Doherty 266). The war also permanently altered the status of the Hollywood cinema and, by extension, the role that the mass media played in American culture.

As a result of its activity from 1941 to 1945, "the motion picture industry became the preeminent transmitter of wartime policy and a lighting rod for public discourse" (Doherty 5). The significance of film's power to engage and motivate audiences became increasingly evident to the government, the American public, and moviemakers themselves during the turbulent and traumatic war years, causing a pronounced shift in the perceived social role of filmmaking. No longer conceptualized as merely innocent entertainment, films often became hotly contested sites of cultural confrontation between various political forces and pressure groups philosophically at odds with each other. For example, the emerging worldviews that first drove the youth rebellion of the 1960s and 1970s and the conservative counterreaction of the 1980s found their most memorable distillations in the imagery of American films. As Doherty insightfully observes about the war films of the 1940s, "American culture was more satisfyingly nourished by popular entertainment than state propaganda" (85), a statement that remains as true for wars today as it was during the years of fighting the Axis powers.

If World War II had not occurred, Hollywood would probably have invented it: "More than any other war—more than any other twentieth-century American experience—it was motion-picture friendly" (Doherty 271). The subject matter and the visual opportunities it offered were perfectly suited for the movies. As Basinger puts it, the fighting during this time "seems to be the combat that speaks to the American soul" (*World War II* 81). How could it not? The pictures of men from across the United States slogging their way through jungles on remote Pacific Islands and trudging through the war-torn cities of Europe, fighting enemies who threatened American security, could not help but mesmerize moviegoers. As one would naturally expect, the conventional World War II combat movies made between 1941 and 1945 graphically illustrate and enthusiastically support America's involvement in the war, despite its heavy cost in lost lives abroad and continual domestic sacrifices. In most of these films, victory is often "justified to some extent if one suffers sufficiently for it" (Kane 13). Little time is spent ruminating over complex geopolitical, ideological, or moral issues. Foxholes leave little room for practicing ethicists, and combat allows little time for pondering ambiguities.

Wartime settings generally provide numerous opportunities for ascertaining, distilling, reinforcing, and sustaining key American ideals of appropriate behavior, valiant action, and gratifying achievement. The war "had the consolation of closure and the serenity of moral certainty. For Hollywood and American culture, the Second World War would always be a safe berth" (Doherty 271). According to Kane, a set of "group values" emerges from these movies, an interconnected system of fundamental beliefs that differentiates us from the enemy and ultimately defines our way of life: freedom, the home, honor, cooperation, and duty. These group values transcend differences of race, ethnicity, geographical region, age, rank, and attitude that the men bring to the combat outfit, and the experience of fighting as a unit allows them to understand the values that join them together, rather than what separates them, as Americans. Thus, as Kane observes, these films visually reinforce the ideal of American unity in the face of the enemy with recurring images stressing conformity of physical appearance, military formations, and combat actions (91). The group, and each man's place and function within it, remains of primary importance, transcending personal problems and individual needs. The demands of the state during such times of crisis trump the wishes of the individual, and the specific person necessarily becomes a unit, a cog, in the military activity demanded for victory.

For all its military dangers and domestic disturbances, World War II ushered in a period of moral certitude for most Americans. The United States did not enter the conflict voluntarily; a sizable isolationist sentiment effectively lobbied to keep the country out of "Europe's War" until the Japanese attack on Pearl Harbor forced citizens to take up arms. Americans therefore felt secure about their military role, accepted the violence and sacrifices deemed necessary to win the war, and celebrated the Allied victory. No halfway measures (as in Korea) or ignominious retreats (as in Vietnam) clouded the triumph, and the films made during this period clearly reflect these attitudes: American servicemen demonstrate their moral authority and earn their ultimate victory by fighting bravely, honorably, and fairly. Unlike their German and Japanese counterparts, usually depicted as fanatical zealots who sanction sadistic cruelty and disregard human worth, America's reluctant fighters kill only when necessary and treat their prisoners with respect. The various soldiers embody the values of their respective societies: ethical values predicated on basic equality on the one side, and global ambition and blind obedience on the other side.

In retrospect, one can delineate instances of social injustice in these combat pictures, but these were downplayed by filmmakers pictorializing more immediate physical dangers; unresolved cultural fissures cracked open in subsequent decades featuring less popular and more distant wars. Defying bigotry and prejudice are peacetime activities more suited to courtrooms than trenches. The end result "is a body of films which relates an idealized world. . . . It is a world governed by a metaphysic of perfect order, of universal truth about men, and of absolutes of good and evil" (Kane 147). One paramount irony exists in all these movies: "[M]en fight for a society which protects their individualism but sacrifice this precious commodity to it, ostensibly temporarily, along with their right to think independently" (15). Orders must be obeyed. Such a situation inherently places absolute faith in the highest rungs of the command chain. Although soldiers in the field may not understand why they are told to do something, they trust in their superiors and believe that their lives would not be put at risk unless it were necessary to insure victory.

Such anti-individualism runs counter to the general narrative tendency of several significant genres in the American cinema. From the earliest one-reeler to the latest epic, the image of the rugged individualist has dominated Hollywood's "masculine" genres. The lone hero remains at the center of the western, as does the tough private eye or the ruthless gangster in their respective categories. Most science-fiction and horror films culminate in battles between the hero and the monster. But in the combat films made during World War II, rugged individualism is forsaken for communal efforts. Such a radical reconfiguration created a seismic shift in the "conceptions of heroic behavior for men and women" (Schatz, "World War II" 109), a transformation of romance as well as combat movies. In romance movies, couples elevate their communal duty to the war effort over their personal desires, much as the men of the combat unit put aside their individual differences to fight the enemy. *Casablanca* represents the most memorable example of what Dana Polan characterizes as the "conversion narrative" in which "an individual converts to a new and proper set of values and beliefs" (75): "I stick my neck out for nobody" becomes "this is the start of a beautiful friendship." As Rick would put it, the films from 1941 to 1945 preached that individual problems during wartime are not worth a hill of beans.

The motion pictures made during World War II deeply affected Steven Spielberg, and movies about the war remained fertile ground for numerous filmmakers during subsequent decades. One reason for the continued popularity of these sagas, and for movies about different wars as well, is the panoply of visual pleasures such conflicts offer. "The vicarious thrill of combat, the titillating horror of death and destruction—all enjoyed from the security of a theater seat—have lent war and cinema a tight kinship" (Doherty 2). From the beginnings of cinema in the late nineteenth century, filmmakers have tried to make their depictions of war increasingly realistic: "Sophisticated special effects and in particular the use of squibs, slow motion, and sound have played an important part in the drive to depict the physical impact of bullets, shrapnel, and explosions on the human body and thus in contemporary American cinema more generally" (Hammond 63). Such violent portraits reach their current apogee in the Omaha Beach sequence of Spielberg's *Saving Private Ryan,* which extends and critiques all previous cinematic attempts to make viewers share the fear, horror, and exultation of soldiers engaged in warfare.

The appeal of World War II combat movies is not solely visceral. Jeanine Basinger argues that the "enduring issues" of the World War II combat film sustain its continued relevance. These films were

> about living and dying. What makes a good life and what makes a good person? What should you be willing to die for—and how do you die right? If you had to die young, what would make you a noble sacrifice and what would make it all a waste? What about killing? If you had to do it, did it make you a killer? . . . How did you resolve group conflicts and differences of opinion, background, and attitude? . . . Was it wrong to be selfish, and not want to make sacrifices, or was it exhibiting sanity to reject wartime attitudes? (*World War II* 80)

The answers to these and other questions seemed reasonably clear to Americans faced with enemies dedicated to the country's destruction and stationed not too far off its shores. The questions became harder to resolve as young Americans died in the distant rice paddies of Vietnam and, more recently, the deserts of the Middle East. For the generation that came of age in the 1960s, war movies were filtered through a dark lens, making uncritical acceptance of the ethos pervading the World War II movies virtually impossible. Memories of World War II, often inscribed in a vast array of films, essentially shaped American foreign and domestic policy and "became a dominant frame of reference and persistent standard of measurement" (Doherty 265). But the moral certainty of that period was shattered, perhaps irrevocably, by the confused agony of the Vietnam War.

Spielberg's World War II films were necessarily influenced by America's bloody immersion in Southeast Asia, though he never directly confronts this conflict. The vast majority of the movies made during what Basinger labels the fifth wave (January 1, 1965, to December 31, 1975) conform to her notion of this era as a period of "inversion" characterized by "turning the former beliefs and trust inside out," by "mocking the beliefs on which the genre is based," and by "testing the genre" (*World War II* 201). One such method is to utilize the weapons of parody and satire on previously sacrosanct subjects, as Spielberg attempted in *1941*. Another is to malign the current situation by undermining the values held dear by previous generations. American combat movies during the 1960s and 1970s function as subversive reinforcements and politically driven polemics of the counterculture's hatred of the Vietnam War (201). Films like *The Deer Hunter* (1978) and *Apocalypse Now* (1979) struggled to exorcise the perceived sickness within the American soul and psyche by lacerating the values that had been celebrated during World War II. In essence, as Pogo immortally observed, "We have met the enemy, and they are us."

History and Collective Memory

George Lipsitz argues persuasively about the effects of electronic mass media on society's collective memory: "Rather than signaling the death knell for historical inquiry, electronic mass media makes collective memory a crucial constituent of individual and group identity in the modern world" (viii). By their ability to transcend the limitations of time and space, mass communications can "disconnect people from past traditions" (5). But this same capability can liberate individuals, allowing them to "experience a common heritage with people they have never seen [and] acquire memories of a past to which they have no geographic or biological connection" (5). Such ideas make "time, history, and memory qualitatively different concepts" (5) within a culture that can access a wide range of images with merely the click of a mouse. In this sense, films about World War II remain an integral and vibrant part of our culture, even more so after the broad success of *Saving Private Ryan*. Doherty reminds us that the "mythos" of World War II films has never been successfully "deconstructed" and predicts it will never be "as long as historical memory can conjure the Army Signal Corps footage of the Holocaust" (296). Instead, we will no doubt see more variations on the basic premise of these movies, though with more attention paid to those stories absent in the original narratives.

Writing about individual or communal past events, whether as a historian or creative artist, has always struck me as akin to being a disc jockey at an oldies station: authors select certain tunes to play repeatedly, while they leave others to languish in the dustbin of obscurity. As Isabel Allende concludes in the epilogue to her sprawling novel, *Portrait in Sepia:*

> Memory is fiction. We select the brightest and the darkest, ignoring what we are ashamed of, and so embroider the broad tapestry of our lives. . . . Reality is ephemeral and changing, pure longing. . . . I write to elucidate the ancient secrets of my childhood, to define my identity, to create my own legend. In the end, the only thing we have in abundance is the memory we have woven. (303–4)

Allende gives literary grace to what Freud earlier noted in his discussion of "Screen Memories": childhood memories "show us our earliest years not as they were but as they appeared at the later periods when the memories were aroused." As such, they do not "emerge" but rather are "formed" by a variety of "motives" with "no concern for historical accuracy" (Freud 322). In this sense, an individual's memories are always contextualized and reformulated in combination with his or her needs, desires, and circumstances in the present. As the sociologist Maurice Halbwachs reminds us, "'[A] remembrance is in very large measure a reconstruction of the past achieved with data borrowed from the present'" (qtd. in Storey 103). This process is substantially the same on a communal level, where members of particular cultural groups seek to create and sustain a national or broadly social identity.

In the age of mechanical reproduction, where images of the past can easily be recorded, re-created, and recirculated, remembrances are forged and reforged by the ideological needs of the present and the technological dispersal of images. Consequently, the cinema "has become central to the mediation of memory in modern cultural life. . . . Hollywood has functioned strategically in the articulation and codification of the cultural past" (Grainge 2, 4). The democratization of technology—allowing for widely disseminated and readily attainable images—means that anyone can summon up past events, both personal and communal. In light of these developments, Alison Landsberg's term "prosthetic memory" aptly denotes that "the kinds of memories one has 'intimate,' even experiential, access to would no longer be limited to the memories of events through which one actually lived" ("Prosthetic" 146). Cognitive scientists, for example, have coined the term "flashbulb memory" to designate instances when people claim to "remember" actually watching significant events (such as the Challenger explosion or the first plane hitting the World Trade Center) as they happened when, in reality, they saw them replayed numerous times in various media outlets; in essence, they come to believe they witnessed an event firsthand. Such "secondhand" memories, transmitted by an endlessly multiplying procession of technological innovations, permeate our culture and become "part of one's personal archive of experiences" (Landsberg, "America" 66). Historical events propagated in motion pictures—be they totally replicated visuals of incidents crafted some time after they occurred, edited constructions of images captured during the actual situations, or some intermingling of the two—make movies into communal photo albums commemorating shared national experiences: films become the historical texts read by the majority of the world's citizens.

In *The Ethics of Memory*, Avishai Margalit writes at length about two types of human relations that he labels "thick" and "thin": the former are "anchored in a shared past or moored in a shared memory," while the latter are simply "backed by the attribute of being human" (7). To further demarcate types of remembrances, he draws a distinction between "common memories," which he defines as the "aggregate memories of all the people who remember a certain episode which each of them experienced individually," and "shared memories," which "integrate and calibrate the different perspectives of those who remember the episode" (50–51). According to Margalit, a "community of memory" is based on thick relations to the living and the dead: "it is a community that deals with life and death, where the element of commemoration verging on revivification is stronger than in a community based merely on communication. It is a community that is concerned with the issue of survival through memory" (69). Collective memory is usually manipulated for particular purposes, while visual images "give us a sense of reliving an emotion in the imagination" (140).

Writing in a similar vein about "communities of memory," but with a concrete emphasis on how the Vietnam War and the AIDS epidemic evolved into significant roles within the national consciousness, Marita Sturken analyzes the various ways that present needs define particular uses of the past, and how "collective remembering" provides a coherent cultural identity formed by acts of forgetting and recollection:

> The process of cultural memory is bound up in complex political stakes and meanings. It both defines a culture and is the means by which its divisions and conflicting agendas are revealed.... Cultural memory is a field of cultural negotiation through which different stories vie for a place in history. (1)

Sturken persuasively argues that those representational images that decisively shape our cultural narratives are manufactured by "technologies of memory" (8). Not merely "vessels in which memory passively resides," these various apparatuses become "objects through which memories are shared, produced, and given meaning" (9). Not surprisingly, camera images "constitute a significant technology of memory in contemporary American culture," since "cinematic representations of the past have the capacity to entangle with personal and cultural memory" (11). The images that constitute our personal memories and the broader images that define our national consciousness are produced and enshrined in images that remain "the most compelling of memory objects" (11). Cultural memories are therefore never neutrally recorded by the camera; instead, they are actively produced by those who control it and become the manifestations of a particular ideological agenda. In essence, as the director Peter Greenaway observed, "There is no history, just historians."

Sturken argues that "the Hollywood docudrama is a central element in the construction of national meaning" (23). For her, World War II films demonstrate how the reenactment of historical events in "popular narratives supersede and overshadow documentary images and written texts" (23), particularly for generations who never experienced them firsthand. These movies develop broad national memories by "creating a sense of shared participation and experience in the nation" (24). By blending historical facts and dramatic narratives, docudramas not only become sources of information; even more importantly, they "afford a means through which uncomfortable histories of traumatic events can be smoothed over, retold, and ascribed new meanings" (85). They are not neutral representations but interpretations of past events from different viewpoints that coalesce to form our cultural memory. Equally crucial, "[P]opular films not only significantly shape historical narratives but also provide a catharsis for viewers and, ultimately, for the nation. Reenactment is a form of reexperiencing: within the codes of realism, viewers are allowed to feel that they, too, have undergone the trauma of the war by experiencing its cinematic representations" (Sturken 97). A film such as *Saving Private Ryan* reshapes the national consciousness about World War II by retelling historical events from a contemporary perspective, functioning as a commemoration of those events and a wider discourse about history.

Spielberg's World War II Combat Movies

"My father filled my head with war stories," Spielberg said in 1988, adding, "I collect documentaries, and I think I have every one made on that period" (Forsberg 128–29). Arnold Spielberg enlisted in the Army Signal Corps in 1942. Serving first in Pakistan, he eventually became part of the Burma Bridge Busters, a B-25 bomber squadron headquartered outside Calcutta that "destroyed Japanese railroad lines, shipping, and communications in Burma" (McBride 31). Though he flew a few missions, Arnold's ability to use and repair radios made him more valuable on the ground, and he spent most of his active duty keeping the unit's communication room in operation, despite his desire for the more adventurous role of airplane gunner. Young Steven listened with breathless reverence to his father's tales about World War II, particularly those about the fearless pilots whose bravery Arnold indelibly etched into his child's mind, along with vivid images of the planes they rode into the clouds. Turning over such tales in his own imagination, Arnold's son made models of these airplanes, reenacted battle scenes with his buddies, and constructed short amateur movies with combat sequences. In eighth grade, in 1960, he devised and shot an ambitious fifteen-minute black-and-white movie called *Fighter Squad,* which interspersed documentary footage of aerial combat with scenes shot in a local airport (employing vintage planes) and featuring his middle-school friends.

Two years later, Spielberg elaborated on these earlier ideas by directing the forty-minute-long *Escape to Nowhere,* a story of World War II combat between American and German soldiers set in North Africa but shot in the desert near Camelback Mountain outside Phoenix. It won first place among young Arizona amateurs at the 1962–63 Canyon Films Junior Film Festival; Spielberg took home a 16mm Kodak camera as his prize. Because the Kodak was too expensive to operate on a schoolboy's budget, Spielberg traded it for an 8mm Bolex-H8 Deluxe, which gave him the ability to produce special effects and make his films look more professional. To support and encourage his budding prodigy, Arnold purchased a Bolex projector and Sonerizer, the "first sound system out for consumer use" (McBride 103). These allowed Spielberg to post-sync sound (dialogue, music, and so on) and then record it directly onto his movies. (Using this equipment two years later, and bankrolled by his father's six hundred dollars, Spielberg made his first feature film, the two-hour, fifteen-minute *Firelight,* about UFOs. As the director says:

> I'm closer to the '40s personality than I am to the '80s. I love that period....
> I have identified with that period of innocence and tremendous jeopardy all

my life. It was the end of an era, the end of innocence, and I have been clinging to it for most of my adult life. (Forsberg 128–29)

Spielberg would continue to revisit the World War II era throughout his
career; he would play its characters and themes across the various genres he
employed, and its mythos would form the foundation for many of his most
deeply held beliefs.

Each of Spielberg's wartime movies represents a different approach to the
subject matter that reflects the prevailing attitude of the film industry and
the director's personal evolution at a particular time: *1941* satirizes homefront
hysteria in the spirit of anarchic seventies films; *Empire of the Sun* posits
admiration for soldiers, much like the respectful eighties movies; *Saving
Private Ryan* pays tribute in the nineties to wartime sacrifices depicted in
forties films. Using Basinger's time line for the genre's evolution, *1941* falls
in the fifth wave, the period of inversion in the 1960s and 1970s. *Empire of
the Sun* and *Saving Private Ryan*, both of which appeared after her book was
written, herald new waves, the first being a variation from a child's point of
view, and the second a nostalgic reaffirmation of the values that undergird
her second wave, films characterized by their "awareness" of previous works,
allowing filmmakers to employ visual shorthand that "demonstrates the
belief that an audience can look at a group, a hero, or an objective and supply dialogue and meaning it *knows* from prior films" (Basinger, *World War
II* 124). (Basinger wrote about *Saving Private Ryan* in 1998, focusing on how
it conformed to traditional aspects of the combat film genre and suggesting
why that genre had been "reactivated" at this particular cultural moment.)
As always, Spielberg adds his distinctive stamp to each of these projects.

1941: Beyond the Screen

And so, as it must come to all directors, Steven Spielberg made a flop. The
lavish praise heaped upon him for the cinematic virtuosity he demonstrated
first in *Jaws* and then *Close Encounters of the Third Kind* changed into an ava-
lanche of negative responses to *1941*, burying him in mounds of hyperbole
that matched the film's frenetic tone. Ranging from Charles Champlin's
(*Los Angeles Times*) comparison of the film to "'the last major oil spill,'" to
Bruce Williamson (*Playboy*) labeling it "'one of the most inept comedies
of the decade,'" to Gary Arnold's (*Washington Post*) summary of the film
as "'pointless, tasteless, an artistic disgrace'" (qtd. in Freer 89–90), critics
gleefully pitched Spielberg off the boy-wonder perch and into the murky

abyss of maybe-he-has-shot-his-wad. As inevitably befalls hugely expensive productions, commentators paid as much attention to the film's ballooning budget (which grew from an original estimate of six million dollars, to a production projection of twenty-six million, to a final figure of $31.5 million) as to what they characterized as its gaudy visuals, noisy soundtrack, and diffuse narrative. Aljean Harmetz even hypothesized that contemporary audiences who saw it "'in a time of deepening recession'" appeared "'quite obviously outraged at the waste and extravagance and wanton destruction'" (qtd. in Geng 59).

Despite this blizzard of negative press, Spielberg and his co-creators continue to point out that *1941* was judged a box-office "failure" simply because it never met the swollen expectations surrounding "a STEVEN SPIELBERG film." In fact, the movie ultimately garnered respectable worldwide grosses of ninety million dollars. It did better in European venues, perhaps because during a difficult national crisis foreign audiences were more inclined to accept ridicule of American military institutions than were domestic viewers: humiliated by the imprisonment of U.S. citizens in Iran and the Carter administration's feeble attempts to rescue them, Americans displayed little appetite for a comic film that, as Spielberg describes it on the collector's edition DVD, "sticks a pie in the face of the Statue of Liberty." Yet a handful of critics did seem to be on Spielberg's wavelength. Veronica Geng compares him to the great French comic director Jacques Tati and argues that "*1941* ranks with *Duck Soup* as a great slapstick comedy about war and even civil defense as self-obliterating" (59), while Ian Freer contends that "many films that don't have a fiftieth of its craftsmanship or imagination did not get as mercilessly vilified in the press" (92). However, such positive responses represent a distinct minority.

Listening to the quartet of Spielberg, John Milius (executive producer), Robert Zemeckis, and Bob Gale (scriptwriters) talking about *1941* on the bonus features segment of the collector's edition DVD, one hears defensive frustration about the film's early reception and smug satisfaction that (at least in some circles) it has become a "cult classic" and "the Europeans love it." Even so, their disparate characterizations of how they initially conceptualized the project provide valuable insight into why it never coalesced: a "dark satire" (Zemeckis); a "Three Stooges–like comedy" (Gale); a "screwball comedy" (Spielberg); a "socially irresponsible" movie (Milius). Interestingly, Spielberg's "innermost dream" was to mold *1941* into an old-fashioned Hollywood musical; he talked at length with John Williams about how they might use Big Band music from the 1940s as a model for their 1970s film.

Tantalizing remnants of this idea appear in one of the movie's most technically dazzling sequences, the elaborate canteen dance number highlighted by Williams's parodic use of Benny Goodman's classic "Sing, Sing, Sing" and a virtuoso shot that lasts seven minutes. Eventually, Spielberg decided that he "did not have the courage to tackle a musical." Yet, as evidenced by the ornate cabaret number he staged as the opening sequence of *Indiana Jones and the Temple of Doom* and the father/daughter reconciliation scene in *The Color Purple,* he retains the "mad chocolate craving to direct a conventional musical" (Biskind, "'World'" 206).

Hearing Spielberg's comments, one quickly senses his continued ambivalence about *1941*. "It wasn't a film from my heart," he said, distancing himself from the project during an interview in 1980, adding, "Rather than a bastard adoption, I like to think of it as if it were a project I was forced to take because of my own state of mind" (Hodenfield 76). Warming to the subject, he compared the "utter horror" of making *1941* "to getting x-ray treatments" and slowly realizing that "the cure is worse than the disease" (78): "Every day I'd go onto the set, it would just get worse and worse. The utter pressure of having to deliver funny material" (78). Yet what constituted his "state of mind" and why it "forced" him to direct *1941* remains unexplored in the interview; instead, he makes a statement that, in retrospect, indicates how little he knew about himself and the direction his career would travel: "Hopefully, *1941* is the last movie I make that celebrates the boy in me. And then hopefully I can go on from here and do something more adultlike" (76). This wish to leave his boyhood behind is particularly ironic on the eve of directing *Raiders of the Lost Ark,* hardly the complicated stuff of "adult" entertainment, and a scant few years before *E.T.,* one of the most evocative hymns to childhood in the history of the cinema.

Spielberg's interviews on the DVD point to the frantic pace he tried to achieve while making the movie. "It was written and directed as one would perform in a demolition derby, a no-holds-barred free-for-all in which anything goes." The director cites the rapid pace of the Looney Tunes cartoons as his model, and at one point in the production he even solicited ideas from the animator Chuck Jones, famed for the speedy slapstick in his Road Runner series. Today, Spielberg compares the movie to *Doom 2,* a kind of video game on the big screen that was "ahead of its time." Emblematic of his desire to rachet up the pace of the movie, Spielberg employed a technique he labeled "cut time": he used a stopwatch to clock how fast the actors spoke their lines, forcing them to say their words in half the time indicated on the script page: "If the script girl says that this scene will run sixty seconds, because it's one page long, I'll do it in about thirty" (Hodenfield 79). But nothing really compensated for "stretching the credibility of the story line beyond all recognizable shape for a simple yuk" (74), the continual reach for laughs that he described derisively as "panhandling for your supper" (74).

Ultimately, Spielberg decided that full-frontal comedy was not his strong suit. "I'm comically courageous when comedy isn't home plate," he said. "I'm much better when I'm playing shortstop and I can add comedy, for instance to *Jaws*" (Hodenfield 75). Clearly, he was not comfortable with the material and, as his anxiety increased, so did his intensity: "'It wasn't making me laugh, or any of us laugh, either in dailies or on set. So I shot that movie every way I knew how to try to save it from what it actually became, a demolition derby'" (qtd. in Freer 92). In retrospect, as he says on the DVD, "I really didn't know what I was doing. I really didn't have a vision." Zemekis and Gale conceived of their screenplay as a dark satire on American paranoia, not the screwball comedy that became Spielberg's finished production: their original conception was to end the film with Wally Stephans (Bobby Di Cicco) becoming the bombardier on the *Enola Gay* and releasing the atomic bomb on the citizens of Hiroshima. For Spielberg, the film was also a bitter lesson in curbing his own hubris. Describing this as his "little general period" (Hodenfield 79), he seemed to understand what had befallen him: "'Power can go right to the head. I felt immortal after a critical hit and two box-office hits, one being the biggest hit in history up to that moment'" (qtd. in Freer 92).

For all its flaws, *1941* contains some radiant special effects. Spielberg shot the entire movie on a Hollywood soundstage, including the submarine shots in an immense water tank and the reconstructed airplane needed for the seduction scene between Birkhead (Tim Matheson) and Donna Stratton (Nancy Allen). He also set himself a challenge by deciding to use only techniques that directors could have employed in the early 1940s—though in a far more costly and lavish manner, as Spielberg shot over a million feet of film. Nearly everything we see on screen, therefore, took place directly as the cameras rolled. The intricate miniature sets designed by Gregory Jein, particularly the Hollywood Boulevard and Ocean Pier Amusement Park segments, remain impressive for their attention to minute detail and visual appeal even in our world of sophisticated computer-generated images. Spielberg also hired A. D. Flowers—a longtime special effects expert whose career ranged from "The Untouchables" television series (1959) and *Tora! Tora! Tora!* (1970) to *The Godfather* (1972) and *Apocalypse Now* (1979)—to handle the large-scale sequences, such as the technically difficult scenes when Wild

Bill Kelso crash-lands his plane onto Hollywood Boulevard and the lighted ferris wheel rolls down the hillside, onto the pier, and into the sea.

The one major deviation for Spielberg's self-imposed restrictions was his extensive use of a new device, the Louma Crane, a "lightweight, remote-controlled camera perched at the end of an extendible fifteen-foot boom that made the trickiest camera moves achievable while the director watched the results on a monitor" (Freer 83). The device permitted him to move effortlessly from tight close-ups to medium shots to expansive long shots, and from one scene to another, with extraordinary ease. Spielberg wielded the intoxicating mobility of the Louma in numerous creative ways, most evidently in the frenzied jitterbug segment when Sitarski chases Wally as the dance contest unfolds. The virtuoso 360-degree pan of the dance hall remains "one of the greatest sequences within the Spielberg canon" (Freer 83): "'I'm very demanding when it comes to filling the frame . . . and found that, with the 15 foot arm on the Louma Crane, I could fish for the right shot by looking at the monitor and I could get just the shot I wanted'" (qtd. in Mott and Saunders 80). Yet for all the freedom the Louma gave to Spielberg, and for all his frantic inventiveness, seeing *1941* still feels like watching a beached whale struggling to get back into the ocean.

THE HISTORICAL/HYSTERICAL BACKGROUND

As unlikely as it may seem to contemporary viewers, the Zemekis/Gale screenplay is based upon actual events that occurred two months later than the movie's specified date of December 13, 1941: a Japanese submarine shelled some oil fields along the Southern California coast on February 22, 1942. Though one army officer was hurt disarming an unexploded shell's detonator, the "attack" on the mainland caused little actual damage beyond a few potholes and a wrecked oil derrick (McBride 301); it did, however, severely frighten the already jumpy residents of Los Angeles, making them acutely aware of their vulnerability to the forces of the Imperial Japanese navy and air corps. Two nights later, reports of enemy planes flying over the city provoked a full-scale panic punctuated by a citywide blackout and a forty-five-minute barrage (consisting of over fourteen hundred rounds of anti-aircraft shells) fired into the California skies. More people were injured in the ensuing chaos (a few even died of heart attacks) than in the initial bombardment, an irony not lost on the youthful scriptwriters of *1941*. Gen. Joseph W. Stilwell, who was in charge of California's costal defenses, was not in Los Angeles during February 1942.

As several commentators have noted, the film struggles to capture the momentary madness of this singular event but totally ignores the surrounding racism, particularly the internment of Japanese American citizens and the infamous zoot-suit riots that shook Los Angeles in 1943. The former has been well-documented and remains a dark stain in the fabric of American tolerance; the latter, which most historians now characterize as a blatant outbreak of bigotry, consisted of pitched battles between servicemen about to be shipped overseas and Hispanic youths costumed in brightly colored outfits. It seems likely that such "heavy" material found little time to breathe within Spielberg's hyperkinetic shooting and editing pace. *1941* appeared long before Spielberg felt competent to tackle such social problems, as he would do in *The Color Purple* (1985), *Schindler's List* (1993), and *Amistad* (1997). Nonetheless, his failure to incorporate at least passing mention of these well-known events robs the film of any deeper resonances. In the throes of pre-release anxiety, but with several disastrous previews already behind him, Spielberg told the critic Bill Davidson, "'I'll spend the rest of my life disowning this movie'" (qtd. in Brode 86). While that has not been strictly the case, he has spent lots of time trying to explain what he was trying to accomplish in *1941*.

CRASH AND BURN

In many ways, *1941* covers familiar Spielbergian territory. Henry Sheehan sees it as furthering his "Pan" themes and characterizes Wild Bill Kelso (John Belushi) as "the lostest of the lost boys ever" (58). James Clarke talks about how it foregrounds a "typical family and community under threat from outside forces" (59). Darren Slade and Nigel Watson emphasize that the movie shows, once again, how humans cannot control the technical paraphernalia that surrounds them (35). Doug Brode responds to the director's "love for old movies," particularly in the scene where the hypermasculine General Stilwell (Robert Stack) sheds tears while watching the sequence in *Dumbo* (1941) when the mother is separated from her child (84). Various critics note in-jokes and intertextual references: Susan Backlinie parodying her *Jaws* role, Kelso refueling his plane in the same desert gas station used in *Duel,* Sergeant Tree's (Dan Aykroyd) tank named Lulubelle after Bogart's vehicle in *Sahara* (1943), and Stevie Douglas (Christian Zika) wearing a Boy Ranger uniform right out of *Mr. Smith Goes to Washington* (1939). But even with these types of observations, *1941* seems like less of a Spielberg film than any of his other works.

Part of the problem has to do with Spielberg's failure to control his material. In retrospect, he admitted that "'we would have been better off with $10 million less, because we went from one plot to seven subplots'" (qtd. in McBride 306). More important than the sheer number of plots that never coalesce into an integrated whole and gallop by so quickly that it often remains hard to remember what exactly happened where, the director never provides any recognizable point of human identification. Who are these

The cartoonish *1941* became Spielberg's first big-budget flop, despite the wild and crazy presence of the comics John Belushi and Dan Aykroyd.

people who appear, start shouting or fighting, and then disappear for goodly periods of time? We are left "with a movie full of strangers" (Hodenfield 73), and we don't care what happens to any of them. The problem runs even deeper: at this point in his career, Spielberg's skills seem ill-matched with the black cynicism shrouding the heart of *1941*. It would take him another twenty years to approach such issues. In 1979, however, his tepid social satire becomes smutty frat jokes. On the DVD edition of the movie, he rightfully proposes that the pre-Gumpian Zemeckis, he of *Used Cars* (1980) and *Death Becomes Her* (1992), "would have been a better director for his own screenplay." McBride suggests that part of Spielberg's motivation was "to fit in with that era's 'wild and crazy' humor, typified by John Belushi, Dan Aykroyd, and the rest of the *Saturday Night Live* crowd" (300). Indeed, one does get the feeling that *1941* was made by the nerdy little kid in the front row, the one who always got good grades and sought the teacher's approval, and who, just this once, went out and got roaring drunk to prove that he could be one of the boys.

Empire of the Sun: Beyond the Screen

Empire of the Sun remains the least explored and most undervalued of Steven Spielberg's best films. Repeated viewings provide sustained pleasures in varied realms of thought and feeling. Each time I watch it, I discover something new and worthwhile, some subtle movement or startling moment or revelatory image. I inevitably shed tears at its conclusion, as Jim Graham (Christian Bale) enters his mother's embrace and, at long last, closes his eyes and rests—at least temporarily. These are honorably earned tears, for I have accompanied this hollow-eyed boy along a winding and treacherous path filled equally with despair, desperation, and triumph. I have watched him driven from his pampered existence in Shanghai's English enclave, seen him survive ragged years as a prisoner of war, borne witness with him to the atomic bomb's fearful light, and joined him in his mother's enfolding arms. We have been companions, he and I. While due credit must be given to the director's source material, the novelist J. G. Ballard's artfully written novel and the playwright Tom Stoppard's literate screenplay, Spielberg's visual sensibility endows the film with a series of indelible images that remain etched into my heart and mind long after they have faded from the screen.

Spielberg came to this project via the British director David Lean, who asked him to acquire the rights to Ballard's 1984 book and produce the work he hoped to direct. Spielberg could hardly refuse the request of a man whose films left a lasting impression on him: "I think *Lawrence of Arabia* is the film that inspired me to become a motion picture director. More than any single movie in my memory, that was the one that sort of decided my fate" (Royal, "*Always*" 136). Along with Martin Scorsese, Spielberg was instrumental in convincing Columbia Pictures to distribute a restored print of Lean's 1962 epic masterpiece. But after working for a year on preparing to film *Empire of the Sun*, the older director decided that Ballard's diary-like entries of traumatic boyhood experiences lacked sufficient dramatic structure for a film and dropped the project to adapt Joseph Conrad's *Nostromo*. Spielberg, who later admitted that he "'had secretly wanted to do it myself'" (qtd. in Brode 162), took over the directorial reins and brought *Empire of the Sun* to fruition. He would later repeat this process of finishing the work of another revered cinematic father figure when he completed Stanley Kubrick's *A.I.*

As the ghost of Kubrick hung over that later film, so Lean's presence naturally filtered into *Empire of the Sun*. Sometimes Spielberg acknowledges him directly via references to specific films, most significantly *The Bridge on the River Kwai* (1957), but also with homages to *Oliver Twist* (1948), *Dr. Zhivago* (1965), *Lawrence of Arabia* (1962), and *A Passage to India* (1984). For example, Jim's obsession with the road built by the prisoners ("our road") in the Soochow camp clearly resembles Captain Nicholson's (Alec Guinness) construction ("my bridge") in *Kwai*. Equally evident are the parallels between Jim as an urchin-like Oliver Twist and Basie (John Malkovich) as his Fagin, particularly when Jim begs for more food, overtly echoing *Twist*. On a more general level, *Empire* often displays the visual style of his British forbear. Freer rightly notes that Spielberg consciously appropriates Lean's "sense of scope, sweep, and camera stylings—in particular, Lean's signature crane shot moving from a lone figure to reveal a mass of swarming people" (159). As a zealous student of film history with a particular love of Lean's films, Spielberg internalized many of these tendencies long before making *Empire;* having used them earlier in films such as *Close Encounters,* he would continue to employ them in future works, particularly *Schindler's List* and *Saving Private Ryan*. More crucially, he incorporates aspects of Lean's visual techniques to embroider variations on themes that had haunted him since his earlier days as a commercial filmmaker and continue to preoccupy him today.

Empire of the Sun represents an important turning point in Spielberg's career, a conscious attempt to stretch himself creatively and emotionally: "I really had to come to terns with what I've been tenaciously clinging to, which was a celebration of a kind of naivete. . . . But I just reached a saturation point, and I thought *Empire* was a great way of performing an exorcism on that period" (Forsberg 129). Though detractors often categorize Spielberg as a sentimental romantic or a cynical merchandiser, he is acutely aware of the contradictions, the ying of popular acclaim and yang of artistic aspiration, that vie for his attention: "I have that real pull between being a showman and being a filmmaker and there is a tough netherworld between both titles. It's filled with contradictions and bad choices" (131). In choosing to direct Ballard's story, he was aware that it conformed to the patterns he had already established in his work, but he recognized its uniqueness as well: "I had never read anything with an adult setting . . . where a child saw things through a man's eyes as opposed to a man discovering things through the child in him" (128). The story showed precisely the opposite of his earlier films: the death of innocence rather than its rebirth. In *Empire of the Sun,* Jim's childhood is reduced, not expanded, as critics have always accused Spielberg of doing in his life and his work. The director noted, "This was the opposite of Peter Pan" (127). For most of the film, this lost boy loses his ability to fly when faced with the necessity to survive.

To turn Ballard's sprawling book into a viable script, Spielberg hired one of the best writers in the world: Tom Stoppard. Like Ballard, the playwright had spent his early years in Asia (Singapore, not Shanghai) and had experienced the Japanese invasion of China firsthand. Stoppard and Spielberg ultimately developed a mutually respectful relationship; the director taught the writer how to tell a story more visually, and the playwright instructed the moviemaker how to use dialogue more subtly (Freer 159). Stoppard classified the first hour of *Empire* as "'somewhere in the masterpiece class. . . . The balance there just seemed to me to be perfect'" (qtd. in McBride 395). He was less keen on the camp section, claiming that it lacked the "compression" and "density" of the opening portion. From a dramatic perspective, Stoppard's analysis is understandable. The crowded camp scenes are more diluted. By expanding the importance of Basie, Spielberg risks diffusing Jim's emotional power. Yet Jim's point of view remains dominant throughout this section, and the surrounding cast of characters emphasizes the various contradictions within his emerging personality as the external world puts increasing pressures upon him to choose between dignity and survival.

FATHER FIGURES

JOHN GRAHAM In typical Spielbergian fashion, *Empire of the Sun* offers conflicting variations on masculine roles by depicting alternative, ideologically antithetical father figures. Each represents a set of personal values and cultural beliefs, a certain approach to defining—or avoiding—male responsibilities.

Jim's biological father, John Graham (Rupert Frazer), represents the distant, emotionless stick figure of the English businessman abroad. Initially, Spielberg links him with golf clubs and silver dollars (used as golf tees): phallic and economic symbols of masculine privilege and power. The first time we see the elegant Mr. Graham, he seems to embody an idealized father right out of a movie: tall and slim, handsome and intelligent, impeccably groomed and tailored. Spielberg frames him full-figure in the foreground, with the large swimming pool in midground, and his sumptuous house dominating the background and dwarfing the human characters. Amidst this portrait of colonial opulence, Jamie (as his father calls him) furiously pedals his bike around the manicured grounds, carrying aloft a burning model airplane. His father's various responses—from telling his son to keep off the grass, to reminding him that the battle between China and Japan is not "our war," to directing him to get out of the way—demonstrate a man accustomed to giving orders and being obeyed. Yet, as is repeatedly the case with Spielberg's male characters, outward appearances conforming to pervasive masculine stereotypes often prove little more than hollow shells that crack under pressure, leaving those who depend upon them adrift and abandoned.

John Graham exemplifies Spielberg's habitual deconstruction of venerable icons of masculine and cultural authority, a reoccurring motif usually ignored by detractors who skim the surface of his work and ignore its complexity. Dressed as a jaunty pirate (shades of Captain Hook) for Mr. Lockwood's (Robert Stephens) costume party, Graham's false bravado becomes painfully evident when his son unexpectedly stumbles upon a troop of armed Japanese soldiers billeted in a gully, an event that dramatically shifts the tone from frivolity to fear. Seeing Jim's predicament, Graham panics, rushing toward the boy and putting both their lives in jeopardy. "Stand still, John," Mr. Maxon (Leslie Phillips) commands him in calm and measured tones, immediately halting Graham's headlong and foolish dash. Frozen in place, Graham listens like a child as the older and wiser Maxon takes control of the situation. "It's not their anger, it's their patience" that worries the astute Maxon about the waiting soldiers, and he sagely advises John to get his son and wife "somewhere safe, like Singapore." But Maxon's warning comes too late. John Graham procrastinates until the family can no longer flee Shanghai together. We never learn why he delays their departure, though a scene of him furiously burning papers hints at some secretive, and perhaps illegal, activities that he cannot easily abandon. Then again, he may just be greedy or unwilling to forsake his lavish life abroad.

Whatever the reasons, Graham fails to provide safety for his wife and child and thus to fulfill his responsibilities as a husband and father. In or out of costume, his seeming strength becomes a thin disguise for his irresponsibility and failure. Similarly, in one of the movie's most harrowing sequences, he loses his grip on his wife's hand in the terrified crowd swarming into Shanghai's streets, fearful of flying bullets and exploding bombs. Frantically, he yells at her to "stay together" and "to hang on to Jamie," but he can only watch helplessly, as at Lockwood's party, when they're torn apart: the distraught mother carried forward by the surging throng, and the hysterical son, still dressed in the red Cathedral school outfit that marks his privilege and foreign status, left behind, scrambling atop a cart and desperately screaming for his mother. No longer looking down on the crowd from his lofty hotel room or insulated from them by the windows of his family's limousine, Jamie finds himself suddenly vulnerable, the quiet peace of his sheltered life shattered by the pounding of marching feet and deadly street battles. Spielberg's mise-en-scène masterfully captures this stark realization: in the midground, Jamie stands screaming on the cart, fire and smoke billow behind him in the background, and fleeing Chinese civilians cram the foreground.

For Spielberg, this painful image of a father who cannot protect his family represents the most grievous of sins. These scenes become particularly telling reflections of Spielberg's personal anxiety when compared with their source material, Ballard's 1984 novel. At Dr. Lockwood's party, when Jim chances upon the Japanese soldiers billeted in trenches and waiting for their orders, Graham, not Maxon (called Maxted in the book), saves his son by coolly returning him to the festivities. As Ballard writes, Mr. Graham "forced himself to stand still, in the way that least unsettled the Japanese" (27). The boy immediately recognizes the danger and his father's courage, knowing full well that "[s]olitary Europeans who strayed into the path of the Japanese were usually left dead on the roadside" (Ballard 28). In this potentially lethal situation, Graham provides a rock-solid example for his son: he recognizes the imminent danger, acts intelligently to avoid a confrontation, and demonstrates his courage. Ballard's John Graham is thus a far different father than the one Spielberg fabricated in his version of *Empire of the Sun*. Viewers who compare the book to the film can readily see how the director altered this figure according to his own persistent pattern of weak or absent biological fathers.

Even more striking differences between book and movie occur in the Shanghai street scene. Instead of abandoning his son because of weakness, as in the film, Graham acts bravely and patriotically. Telling Jim to "look after your mother" and ignoring the machine-gun and rifle fire swirling around him, he takes off his overcoat, jumps into the muddy harbor, and saves a wounded British sailor from the sinking H.M.S. *Petrel:* "The tide had risen to his chest when he caught the injured petty officer drifting between the piers of the wharf. He pulled him into the shallow water, dragging him by one hand, and knelt exhausted beside him on the oily mud" (Ballard 41). Having lost his mother in the crush of the fleeing throng, Jim "wades through the damp soil toward his heroic father," and amidst "the flickering light along the quays like silent gunfire" lies down beside him for six hours until they are captured by invading soldiers and taken to St. Marie's Hospital (Ballard 44). From there, they transport Graham to the military prison in Hongkew, and Jim begins his adventures alone. These pivotal alterations in depicting Graham, appearing as they do within a generally faithful adaptation of Ballard's work, demonstrate Spielberg's personal intervention, his angry obsession with inadequate fathers equally demonstrated in the complex reunion sequence that ends the film.

Spielberg begins this final sequence with a sweeping shot above the roof of the building that houses the displaced children, a sprawling glass arboretum whose missing panes provide an apt emblem of the physical and psychological damage sustained by people during the war. He allows us to peek through these jagged holes in the disfigured exterior to glimpse the children below. Quickly, he cuts to a group of adults passing through the outer gate, hopeful of finding their missing children still alive. Mrs. Graham immediately recognizes her son and almost silently whispers his name; Mr. Graham, however, walks right past him. Even after identifying his boy, the father utters not a word to his long-lost child, offering him neither a greeting nor an embrace. As Jamie touches his mother's hand, then her lips and her hair, Graham soundlessly observes them; mother and son reconnect physically and emotionally while the father lingers behind them. Even when the weary Jamie draws his mother into an embrace, and she wraps her arms tenderly around him, Graham never touches either his wife or his son. Perhaps embarrassed by their public display of emotion or humiliated by his failure to safeguard them, he remains isolated from their intimate connection. As he did when the boy was threatened by the patient Japanese soldiers, and again when mother and son were torn apart in the streets of Shanghai, Graham can only watch—soundlessly, separately, helplessly.

This moment epitomizes a typical misconception on the part of Spielberg's most strident detractors, many of whom castigate him for such supposedly maudlin reconciliations at the conclusions of his films. Often these commentators fail to note the delicate complexity of the director's images.

Superficially, the ending of *Empire of the Sun* appears to be yet another example of Spielberg's tendency to oversentimentalize by tying up his narratives with brightly colored ribbons that blot out the harsh realities that preceded them. Closer examination, however, reveals a decidedly harder edge and a more sophisticated understanding of family dynamics, not merely a romanticized portrait of the loving nuclear family recuperated and renewed after traumatic events. Graham's physical exclusion and Jim's hollow eyes subtly counterbalance the mother's warm clasp and the son's apparent relief. It is a backhanded tribute to Spielberg's visual skill and the emotional power of his artistry that even critics hostile to his work are drawn into his cinematic embrace and, in struggling to escape, often miss the intricate subtleties they lavishly praise in the works of other directors.

Consider another more subtle way Spielberg unobtrusively layers our response to Graham and offers an implicit metacritique of his actions. He remains physically absent throughout most of the film, the missing or deficient father in so many Spielberg movies; even so, a displaced representational image remains as a constant reminder of his failures, though Jim may not consciously perceive this bitter contradiction. Early in the film, Jim's parents come to his bedroom to say goodnight. As James Clarke (67) and Susan Goldman Rubin (58) note, Spielberg fashions the scene into an unmistakable replica of one of his favorite paintings, Norman Rockwell's *Freedom from Fear, 1943,* a wartime image meant to provide comfort for frightened Americans and to raise the nation's spirits. Rockwell completed his Four Freedoms series after hearing Franklin D. Roosevelt's famous 1941 State of the Union address. The artist sought—by using everyday images of common people and employing his Arlington Vermont neighbors as models—to capture the freedoms enumerated by the president as basic rights due all human beings (freedom of speech, freedom to worship, freedom from fear, and freedom from want). The paintings first appeared as *Saturday Evening Post* covers, "Freedom from Fear" on the March 13, 1943, issue. Rockwell donated all four paintings to the federal government, which used them to galvanize war-bond purchases, ultimately raising $133 million dollars in sales from their reproductions.

But there are distinct differences between Rockwell's and Spielberg's images of parental protection. Graham wears a fancy bathrobe, clutches his newspaper (with "Japanese Occupy Shanghai" as its headline) and eyeglasses in his left hand, and stares down at his wide-awake son; he is superficially similar to his counterpart, who is dressed more plainly, with a newspaper headline reading "Bombings Kill. . . . Horrors Hit" as he regards his two sleeping children. Rockwell's father wears lighter-colored clothing and a prominent white shirt, while Spielberg's father sports a dark covering, with the collar and sleeves of his white pajama top barely visible. Also, the images of the two mothers present stark contrasts: Rockwell's plain country woman dresses in a dark top, a denim dress, and a matronly apron as she stands beside the bed to make sure her children are firmly covered; Spielberg's sexualized, almost voluptuous, maternal figure sits garbed all in white upon the bed, never pulling up the blanket to her son's chin. While Rockwell optimistically shows light in the corners of the frame illuminating the darkness, Spielberg's image appears far more somber, the windows shuttered, the ceiling crowded with wartime aircraft, and the shadows replacing the light evident in its original source.

Beyond these and other physical variations, however, rests an even greater and more unsettling emotional contrast between the two parental images, one that becomes more prominent as the film progresses. The Rockwell painting depicts children safely sleeping, tucked warmly beneath their covers and protected from harm by their parents. Although Jim literally carries a copy of this picture ripped from the *Saturday Evening Post* wherever he travels, his increasing difficulties make Rockwell's image function as more of an ironic comment than a scrap of nostalgia. His parents utterly fail to protect him. Never sure where he will be taken, what will happen to him, and whether he will survive, he must constantly find substitute father figures. So while the treasured Rockwell picture overtly sparks memories of the lavishly cloistered and deceptively innocent world Jim inhabited on Amherst Avenue before the Japanese invasion, it simultaneously reveals the growing distance between the essential requirement of the father to be protector and Graham's failure to discharge his primary obligation. Given that Ballard never specifically describes this painting, calling it only "the photograph of the unknown man and woman he had pinned to the wall of his cubicle" (222), Spielberg's selection of this particular Rockwell picture, one fused with historical significance and emotional implications, provides further evidence of his subtle emotional depth.

DR. RAWLINS If any figure would be capable of fulfilling the fatherly role vacated by Mr. Graham, it is Dr. Rawlins (Nigel Havers), the brave and kindly physician who runs the hospital at the Soochow Creek Internment Camp. We first see him as he elbows his way through the mob of civilians desperately trying to escape the overcrowded Shanghai detention center. Realizing his value as a doctor, Sergeant Uchida (Guts Ishimatsu) awards him a precious seat on the dusty transport truck where, along with Jim, Basie, and other lucky survivors, he makes the lumbering journey to Soochow. Once aboard, Rawlins quickly slides into conflict with Basie, who will become his competitor for Jim's soul in the internment camp. Basie, readily willing to abandon Jim and ingratiate himself with other children by doing magic tricks, confides that he was looking after Jim "for his daddy" and secretly working for the Kuomintang (the official government of China during the Pacific war, ultimately exiled to Nanking). "As a conjurer," replies the doctor sarcastically, and Basie's sly smile grudgingly acknowledges a skeptical equal. Immediately upon their arrival at Soochow, Japanese soldiers demand that the weary civilians haul rocks up a steep hill to build a runway for their planes to land. "No, no, no," responds Rawlins, whose refusal provokes a sharp rifle butt to his shoulder, a vicious blow that drops him to his knees clutching his wound in pain. Basie wordlessly picks up a rock and trudges up the hill. Jim does likewise, stooping to retrieve the rock dropped by the fallen doctor, totally ignoring his clenched murmur, "I'm alright," and scampering after the pragmatic Basie. The battle lines have been drawn.

Once the movie shifts to Jim's life at Soochow in 1945, Rawlins emerges as the camp's most humane leader, a man of science who compassionately oversees the cramped hospital, tends to the sick inmates, and comforts the dying. The first extended scene between Jim and Rawlins occurs when the boy bursts through the hospital doors hollering "I've got my homework," as if completing his Cathedral school assignment back on Amherst Avenue. Entering this medical space in the role of schoolboy, Jim must immediately assume a far more responsible position, as Rawlins orders him to do chest compressions on a woman he is trying to resuscitate. Unexpectedly, the woman shifts her eyes toward Jim, who momentarily believes he has brought her back to life, exalts in his triumph, and breathlessly offers "to do it again." But the exhausted Rawlins knows better. He forcibly rips the boy away from the lifeless body, tosses him onto a nearby cot, and tells him that he merely "pumped some blood into her brain, just for a moment." Spielberg quickly cuts to nurses carrying the hospital's only mosquito net from the dead woman's bed and placing it onto the cot of a shivering patient, panning past Jim and the doctor reviewing the homework at a small table. "Is that what you do," asks the stunned young boy, "give the mosquito net to whoever is dying next?"

The scene reveals the perpetually shifting roles Jim must occupy at Soochow. He remains a young boy eager to please his elders, while at times he assumes obligations that would normally be fulfilled by older men. A bit later, he will even usurp the protective, fatherly position from Rawlins, saving the physician from a severe beating for defying their captors. Jim slips between these roles with seemingly effortless ease, although he clearly suffers sustained psychological damage evident at several points in the movie. Here, however, Rawlins thoughtfully strokes his stubby mustache and looks over Jim's homework, as the boy covertly glances at the fancy pair of black and white golf shoes neatly set at the foot of the bed containing the man who received the mosquito netting. That footwear conjures up two references: his father, because of their association with golf, and Basie, because of his expressed desire to own those shoes. Rawlins, initially unaware of Jim's interest in them, asks him to conjugate the Latin verb "to love," both men oblivious to the irony that in this place love is as scarce as extra potatoes. As Jim inserts the doctor's stethoscope, symbol of his power, into his ears, he inquires, "Can I have those shoes when he's dead?" "God, you're a pragmatist, Jim," replies the distracted physician, continuing with the lesson in the foreground as the nurses in the background cover the shivering man with the net, a cocoon of death.

But the conversation soon turns to more pressing matters. The doctor talks about beating the Japanese by "refusing to die," while Jim wonders about postwar events and expresses unabashed admiration for the bravery of the Japanese soldiers. In the book, Ballard emphasizes Jim's ambivalent loyalties, with the boy actually wishing "he had flown with the Japanese pilots as they attacked Pearl Harbor" and destroyed the U.S. Pacific fleet (144). Rawlins desperately struggles to sustain the fiction that even amidst the deprivation and death of the camp, the hallmarks of an idealized England function as viable models of civilized behavior. "Remember, we're British," chastises the doctor. "Yes," answers a disconcerted Jim, "I've never been there." Then he rushes through a poem and explains why he has raided the camp vegetable garden to find tomatoes for Basie: "I have to give him something every day." Instead of reproach, Rawlins tell the boy, "That's alright. It's a good thing you're friends with Basie. He's a survivor." As Jim rushes breathlessly out the door, the doctor tells him to "rest. You'll wear yourself out looking after everyone"—a warning that applies to the fatigued doctor as well as to the young boy he tutors in Latin.

Again, a variety of elements collide to make the seemingly simple scene rife with meaning. Rawlins's conspicuous attempt to fill the role of Jim's absent and deficient father remains clear, but the strained attempt at some semblance of prewar normality in the foreground of the scene—the wooden effort to reenact a conventional scene of father and son reviewing homework—is totally undercut by Jim's expressed desire for the golf shoes and the prim nurses tending to the soon-to-be-dead man in the background. In a long take with a carefully fashioned mise-en-scène artfully shot in deep focus (an aesthetic decision that should bring joy to the heart of any Bazanian acolyte), Spielberg, far from manipulating his viewers with flashy techniques, allows us slowly to grasp the cruel paradoxes inherent within the scene's visual construction and conflicting dialogues. Ultimately, a nurse calls Rawlins back to his medical responsibilities, back to his culturally defined role as protective and knowledgeable father for the entire camp—not only for Jim. But those positions will be reversed shortly.

Following a destructive nighttime air raid by American pilots, Sergeant Nagata (Masato Ibu) directs his men to exact reprisals by destroying parts of the prisoners' buildings. Seething, he marches purposefully to the hospital and raises his bamboo stick to smash its windows. When the courageous Rawlins attempts to stop him by grabbing the staff, the enraged sergeant first stares in shocked disbelief and then turns his murderous wrath on the unfortunate doctor, severely beating him with sharp staccato blows to his shoulders, stomach, back, and neck. The camp's adults, paralyzed by fear, can only watch silently as Nagata brutalizes Rawlins. The only sounds breaking the dark stillness of the night are the dull whir of airplane engines and the physician's cries of pain—except for a furiously running Jim Graham. Speaking Japanese and hoisting a wooden stool over his head, the boy begins breaking the hospital windows as the startled Nagata, momentarily distracted from the supine doctor, pauses to watch the destruction. Jim acts out Nagata's rage. For a few brief moments, he becomes one of the Japanese soldiers he admires, unleashing his tightly contained fury. He also addresses the sergeant in a rush of his own language, sinking to his hands and knees in a bow of respect and an acknowledgment of Nagata's power.

Spielberg shoots the scene in deep focus: the prostrate doctor on his arms in the foreground, Nagata's polished boots and threatening stick (figuratively placed atop Jim's neck like an executioner's sword) dominating the midground, and Jim's supplicating pose in the background—the three directly tied to each other in an intricate dance of cause and effect. Suddenly aware of being surrounded by the stunned prisoners and sensing the breakdown in his military discipline and demeanor, Nagata looks down at Jim, throws away his stick, buttons his disheveled uniform, and marches off into the dark, passing an untouched Basie in the American barracks. Bent over in agony with blood dripping from his ear, Rawlins hobbles into the hospital and returns with the one prize he knows Jim wants most: he awards the kneeling boy the coveted golf shoes. Rubbing them like a magic lamp, the child whose actions just made him father of the man accepts the shoes, a crucial link to his former life as well as a bribe to purchase Basie's loyalty, at least temporarily.

Finally, a scene occurs between Jim and Rawlins that reasserts the more traditional child/adult power relationship before the doctor basically disappears from the film. As American P-51s drop bombs and strafe the camp, Jim climbs the rickety steps to the roof of the camp's tallest building, dressed in combat pants with dogtags dangling around his neck. There he cycles through a range of emotions and across a spectrum of responses as the planes that will help liberate him simultaneously destroy the only home he has known for the last four years. Spielberg presents the boy's jumbled state of mind via a subjective, slow-motion pan shot; cutting out all the ambient sound and replacing it with a chorus of celestial voices, he depicts the open-mouthed Jim watching a lone plane fly past him, the cockpit encasement open and the pilot—goggles on his forehead—waving to him. "Wow!" screams the excited boy laughing dementedly. "Go! P-51! Cadillac of the sky!"

The angelic revery abruptly ends when the plane blows up the Japanese

Bombs and Rapture. Jim Graham (Christian Bale) thrills to the attack of American P-51s ("the Cadillacs of the sky!") as they strife the Soochow Prison Camp in *Empire of the Sun* (1987).

hangar, plunging Jim back into the harsh realities of his present situation. Seeing Jim dancing madly atop the exposed roof of the building with bombs exploding all around him, Dr. Rawlins races up the stairs, grabs the raving boy, and tries to drag him to safety. "I can taste them in my mouth. Iron and cordite," raves Jim, still gyrating dementedly on the rooftop. "Try not to think so much," Rawlins commands him, shaking him back to actuality. "Try not to think so much."

His words slap Jim into recognizing what he has tried desperately to repress: "I can't remember what my parents look like," he sobs, and collapses into Rawlins's embrace, numbly conjugating the Latin verb for "to love" that first drew the man and the boy together. Lifting his weary eyes to the sky in a visual foreshadowing of the reconciliation with his mother at the conclusion, Jim watches a pilot gracefully parachute to earth, returning to the hard ground as he must as well. Rawlins scoops up the boy and carries him to safety. To seal his restoration to semichildhood, Jim returns to the British compound, banished from the manly American barracks and silently crying as Mrs. Victor unpacks his tattered suitcase and pins up his Rockwell magazine cover. The American raid on Soochow marks the end of the camp and signals the sure defeat of the Japanese army. Soldiers line up the prisoners, Sergeant Nagata departs, and the camp inmates march off toward the Olympic stadium and the dockyards of Nantao. Amid the crowd, Rawlins stands in the back of a truck, surrounded by nurses and sick prisoners; later during the arduous trek, he helps exhausted captives climb aboard his mobile hospital. Our last glimpse of him occurs right before Jim chooses to stay with the dying Mrs. Victor. Ever the dedicated physician, he is protecting others and arguing with his Japanese captors, the always righteous if at times ineffectual embodiment of personal morality and professional ethics: "We are civilians. I am a British doctor. These people are my responsibility."

BASIE If Mr. Graham offers the external image of how a father should look, and Dr. Rawlins an idealized personification of how he ought to behave, then Basie embodies the distasteful reality of family life under dire conditions. Here the harsh flames of necessity and survival burn away the bonds of parental responsibility. Basie, as his name implies, represents humankind's baser instincts, though Spielberg mutes the pedophilic insinuations more evident in Ballard's book. According to the novelist, "Jim's entire upbringing could have been designed to prevent him from meeting people like Basie, but the war had changed everything" (96). Spielberg discloses essential elements in Basie's character by showing the objects that surround him before fully revealing his face: a table strewn with bottles of wine and books, a radio (playing "South of the Border"), an ashtray filled with cigarette butts, and some scrambled playing cards. Gently interspersed with the music, the sound of sizzling food wafts through the frame, as a wooden spoon in a man's hand carefully turns over rice in a large skillet. "Come on in, boy," are the first words that ooze out of Basie's mouth. "You look like you need to lie down." Spielberg allows Basie to dominate the foreground, his hands constantly stirring the rice, while a frightened Jim in his schoolboy outfit shivers behind him, breathlessly torn between fear of this ominous figure and hunger for his food.

"My father will be ingratiated to you," says the boy, barely able to lift his eyes from the simmering rice. "Ingratiated," replies Basie, "that's a fine word." As Jim moves almost hypnotically toward the saucepan, Basie picks him up and unceremoniously plunks him in a wooden chair, roughly probing his mouth with his fingers. "Now that's a well-kept set of teeth," he tells his partner, Frank (Joe Pantoliano). "Someone has paid a lot of bills for that sweet little mouth." (Basie sells gold teeth in the Hongkew market, but the sexual threat also lingers.) Still, Spielberg hides Basie's face; he is nothing but clenched teeth, peaked hat, dangling cigarette, wispy smoke, and stubbly beard. Recognizing the Cathedral school badge as he rifles through Jim's pockets, Basie removes a number of objects (a *Wings* comic book, a model airplane, a book, and a coin), immediately covering his eyes with the boy's aviator sunglasses. Jim freely hands over a miniature chocolate bottle of curacao, which the former cabin steward on the Cathay-American Line quickly devours. "What did you say your name was, boy?" he asks. "Jamie," comes the tired response. Basie thinks a moment and then rechristens this stranger in an ever stranger land: "Jim. A new name for a new life."

Spooning some rice onto a plate, Basie ignores the hungry Frank and passes the steaming food over to Jim, who shovels it into his mouth with greedy fingers. "Jim, chew your food. Chew every mouthful six times to get the benefit," admonishes Basie, appropriating the fatherly role vacated by Graham and not yet challenged by Rawlins. Exhausted, Jim falls asleep in the chair, the tin plate sliding from his hands. "You're a tired boy, Jim," says Basie, scooping him up and carrying him to a dingy cot. Above him, pictures of posing bodybuilders and preening movie-magazine pinups dot the cabin's gray walls; beneath his feet lay crushed glossy magazines. Earlier in the film, Jamie's mother sat on the bed and his father stood comfortingly above it, though this image of security proved more illusion than reality. Now, Basie sits menacingly on the cot, and Frank, even more frighteningly, bends forward above the sleeping child: Fagin and the Dodger eyeing their Oliver Twist. "It's all buying and selling," Basie tells Frank with a sly chuckle. "You know, life."

The next scene accentuates this mercenary attitude, as Basie attempts to sell Jim to skeptical Chinese merchants. But no one wants to buy the scrawny boy. As Frank cruelly explains, "You're worth nothing. You're skin and bones. Pretty soon you'll be sick all the time." In an extended tracking shot through the congested Shanghai market—the foreground jammed with merchants, rusty objects, and refugees—the trio returns to the dilapidated truck. Basie flips Jim the coin he stole from his tattered pockets and, with a callous tilt of his head that delights the jealous Frank, motions for the boy to leave, to return to the savage streets. Desperate to remain, his hat literally in his hands, Jim begs him to relent but to no avail. Finally, he appeals to Basie's greed, claiming that he can lead them to "some rich pickins. Hundreds of houses left empty. They were luxurious. There was opulence." "Opulence," chuckles Basie, savoring the word like a juicy grape and finally succumbing to its tantalizing promise. Signaling Jim to return the coin, he agrees to "go and take a look at some of these houses," much to the annoyance of Frank. As the scene aptly demonstrates, Basie measures Jim's relevance only in yen. It is a cash-and-carry relationship that never allows for extenuating circumstances. And no credit—ever.

Returning home through deserted streets proves a serious mistake. Jim hears the strains of piano music, glimpses flowing white robes through the billowing drapes, and, sure his mother has returned, eagerly rushes to the open front door. A smile plays on his lips as, from his point of view, we see a figure from the waist down clothed in a diaphanous white outfit, the outline of arms and legs clearly visible through the almost transparent material. Yet like most things in *Empire of the Sun,* the flesh only barely resembles the dream: the comforting fantasy swiftly turns into brutal reality. The figure proves to be an angry Japanese officer dressed in his military kimono, whose men severely beat Basie with their bamboo staves. At last we finally see his eyes, filled with pain, when he throws off Jim's sunglasses and absorbs the soldiers' punches and kicks. Jim awakes to find himself in the Shanghai detention center, where life lessons in survival from Professor Basie continue. He refuses to let Jim drink the infected camp water and substitutes boiled water instead. He instructs Jim how to get additional rations by using the dinner pail of a dead prisoner, adding, "Keep the ball in play. Light on your toes. First in line. I think your father would agree with me." Jim's response betrays a disconnection between his prewar and wartime lives. "Actually, Basie," he replies, "he would agree with you. After the war, you two should have a game of tennis sometime. He's really good." As Ballard puts it, "Parts of his mind and body frequently separated themselves from each other" (113).

Once in Soochow, Basie and Rawlins alternate as Jim's father figures, though each possesses a wary respect for the other. Basie, who humorously refers to Rawlins as "Dr. Schweitzer," runs the raucous American men's barracks, filled with spirited inhabitants Ballard describes as "far superior to the morose and complicated British" (228). His room, dominated by a large circular window looking out over the entire camp, resembles a mock version of a ship captain's quarters, with Jim filling the role of clever cabin boy who does his master's bidding. Like Rawlins, Basie instructs Jim in what he calls "the university of life," encouraging him to increase his word power. Not surprisingly, he responds favorably when Jim reveals his new word for the day, "pragmatist." To illustrate his understanding of the term, Jim negotiates a bargain with Basie: if the boy will set the trap and catch a pheasant outside the camp fence, a dangerous feat because of the riflemen stationed in the guard towers, then he can move into the American men's dorm. Basie just smiles, and we realize that Jim has neither learned the true meaning of his new vocabulary term nor how fully Basie embodies it.

Nothing illustrates Basie's well-developed pragmatism better than his allowing Jim to risk his life and betting on whether or not he will survive. While his ostensible reason is to secure a bird for a Thanksgiving celebration, Basie callously employs Jim's daring with a more practical purpose in mind: to see if the Japanese have hidden mines around the camp's perimeter. In one of the film's most tense sequences, Jim slips beneath the wire, wades into the swampy water, and emerges into the muddy fields beyond. A watchful Sergeant Nagata finds his fancy golf shoes and sets out to find their owner, rifle in hand. Suddenly, Jim, not the pheasant, has become the prey. In the barracks, Nagata's presence incites a betting frenzy and increases the odds against Jim's survival. No one expresses fear or sympathy for the boy's plight, as Basie covers all the wagers.

Using his weapon to part the tall weeds near the cowering Jim, Nagata suddenly halts his search, called away by a young Kamikaze pilot-in-training (Takatoria Kataoka) who asks the sergeant to fetch his model plane and leaves with him. Befriended earlier by Jim, this youth looks back, smiles conspiratorially, and gently salutes his muddy British counterpart. To the soundtrack's bracing flutes and drums, and with mud still caked on his face and clothing, Jim marches to his new home in the American barracks, where the impressed soldiers line up and salute him. Jim immediately pins

Jim Graham (Christian Bale) crawls outside the Soochow Prison Camp believing that his mission is to trap a wild pheasant, but he is actually being used to test for deadly landmines, in *Empire of the Sun* (1987).

the Rockwell picture onto his cubicle wall, covering a scantily clad model. "Don't let me down, kid," Basie says. "You're an American now."

Although Basie initially abandons Jim, it is Jim who ultimately rejects Basie. Recognizing that the increasingly frequent appearances of American planes signal that Tokyo is now within bombing range and that the war will soon end, Basie tells Jim, "It's time to think about going home." For Basie, timing is everything: "First one side feeds you and the other side tries to get you killed, then it's all turned around," he says, playing with a homemade trap meant to capture a pheasant, though at the moment Jim, not the bird, is his prey. The adoring boy falls right into the snare. Kneeling like a supplicant in prayer, Jim wrings a promise from Basie to "tell me when its time" and, implicitly, to take him along. The very act of putting faith in anything Basie promises establishes that Jim still clings to the social conventions of his former life, a time when gentlemen kept their word as a point of honor. In Soochow, promises and honor count for less than a cigarette or a potato. As the guards gather the prisoners for the brutal march up-country, Jim hurriedly packs his Rockwell picture and book of *Shorter Latin Poems* and rushes to Basie's quarters, only to find a crestfallen Frank guarding an empty cubicle and muttering sadly, "He's gone." Crying, Jim first expresses his pain, "He can't have, he promised me," and then his understanding. "He knew it was time," he mumbles as he leaves the barracks. "He knew it was time."

Following the death of Mrs. Victor, Jim returns to Soochow, dragging a canister filled with food behind him. There he finds his Japanese counterpart, the distraught young pilot whose kamikaze mission was aborted before he could perform his suicidal, patriotic duty. As they are about to share a mango, a car bursts through the wall of a burning building and from it emerges Basie and his new gang, one of whom shoots the Japanese boy. "He gave me a mango!" screams Jim. "He was my friend. The war is over." Ever the pragmatist, Basie says, "I'll give you a whole goddamn fruit salad. There are Frigidaires falling from the sky. He was a Jap." Telling Basie about his experience in the Nantao stadium, Jim hypnotically describes the dazzling white light he witnessed as being "like God taking a photograph," not knowing it was caused by the exploding atomic bomb forty miles away. He then tries to bring his friend back to life. As he did to the woman in the camp hospital, he rhythmically pumps his chest endlessly repeating, "I can bring everyone back. Everyone." For a brief moment, Spielberg substitutes the body of the young Jim, dressed neatly in his Cathedral school outfit, for the dead pilot, an apt image of Jim urgently trying to resurrect his old life, his former innocence. But, as in the hospital, his efforts are doomed.

Basie forcibly drags him away from the body. "Jim!" he shouts, "Didn't I teach you anything?" "Yeah," Jim responds, nodding his head. "You taught me that people will do anything for a potato." Stunned at this fitting summation of his worldview, Basie actually hugs Jim, unctuously crooning a siren call meant to recapture him: "Come on. I'll take you back to your dad. You can retire. We'll fill up the pool. We'll eat three meals a day." But Jim has heard Basie's promises before; he now understands how easily the words slide off his tongue and how little they mean. Wresting himself out of this lethal embrace, Jim springs to his feet. For the first time in the film, Spielberg shoots over Jim's shoulder, as he looks down at his former mentor sitting sprawled in the dirty water. Jim dominates the visual space as the new man and the old boy stare at each other for a brief moment, the frame silent but for some muted bird sounds in the background. Then Basie casts his eyes downward and looks away. His wry, somewhat embarrassed smile contains understanding; he knows the spell he once cast over Jim has been forever shattered. Exiting in a speeding car, Basie tosses Jim a Hershey bar as the boy rips off the dog tags clinking round his neck, symbols of his familial allegiance, his emotional dependence, and his physical servitude to Basie.

Without pushing Freudian correspondences too far, I read Graham, Rawlins, and Basie as roughly embodying elements within Jim's own psychological makeup, coarse personifications of his superego, ego, and id. Graham (superego) functions best in clearly defined, socially ordered, and not particularly fluid situations. He remains perfectly suited for the Shanghai world prior to the Japanese invasion, a fixed environment with explicitly delineated social strata and rules of conduct. Within these seemingly secure and immutable perimeters, he conforms to the image of the perfect father. Rawlins (ego) must negotiate his path within two dramatically different worlds: the one before the war that conformed to his sense of British moral behavior, and the one in the camp, where moral codes often prove inimical to survival. He mediates between the harsh realities of the latter and the refined rules of the former, seeking a respectable course between diametrically opposed systems of behavior. While Rawlins overtly recognizes the value of Jim's friendship with Basie, he consciously subverts the American's pragmatic cynicism by incarnating a nobler worldview and behaving as honorably as possible. Basie (id) slides comfortably between the cracks in society. He operates most successfully when the traditional codes break down under the strain of extraordinary events, as is always the case in wartime. When peace reestablishes conventional order and solidifies customary behavior, Basie must slip back into the night, a figure banished to the tattered, dark fringes of society.

MOTHER FIGURES

Mothers figure less prominently in *Empire of the Sun* than do fathers. We first see Mrs. Graham (Emily Richard) seated at the piano playing Chopin's *Mazurka,* opus 17, no. 4, a musical piece associated with her throughout the film and one that reappears at various points to remind us of Jim's past, cloistered life in prewar Shanghai. Her image reflected on the shiny wood of the instrument, a lit cigarette burning in an ornate crystal ashtray, Spielberg's camera first captures her in a medium shot and then slowly moves toward her with a graceful sweeping motion, shifting from her image to the carefully positioned collection of pictures housed in gilded frames on the piano top. They are mostly of her son and husband posing awkwardly for the camera, frozen images of the picture-perfect life that will soon be destroyed. She next appears in Jim's bedroom with her husband and son, a scene that starts with the light from her match illuminating the model Japanese plane hanging from Jamie's ceiling. "Hello, ace," she says in a low voice. Perched on the corner of his bed, she appears as a distant but seductive figure swathed in a white silk nightgown and robe. Hearing her son's dream about God playing tennis and musings about why He is invisible, she can only respond to his probing questions with, "I don't know about God," kiss him goodnight, and tell him to dream of flying.

After she loses Jim in the Shanghai streets, the boy returns to his house on Amherst Street, now the property of the Japanese emperor, and anxiously calls for his mother. The house sits silent, food rotting in the refrigerator. In one of the film's best visual moments, Jim enters his mother's bedroom and finds it in disarray. The rumpled bed remains unmade, expensive clothes strewn around, delicate lamps smashed, fragile perfume bottles shattered, and costly furniture broken. An exposed drawer in her dressing table attracts his eye, talcum powder still dropping onto some lacy silk undergarments and then downward onto the polished parquet floor. Jim's eyes trace the white trail, and he smiles as his mother's delicate bare foot appears outlined in the snowy residue. But the smile quickly fades as he notices other footprints, heavy boots and the marks of someone having been dragged along the floor and handprints and fingers scraping against the boards. He flings open the window to drive these images from his mind, and wind from the outside world sweeps across the floor, blowing away the powder and along with it the last vestiges of his former life and innocence. He rushes out of the room and breathlessly runs down the stairs. The mother he knew forever disappears and will return as a different woman in the reconciliation scene that ends the movie.

During most of the movie, Mrs. Victor (Miranda Richardson) substitutes for Jim's mother in the Soochow camp. Spielberg depicts her as a more overtly sexualized figure than Mrs. Graham, an appropriate portrait given that the film is shot through Jim's point of view and that he moves into adolescence during his imprisonment. Glimpsed fleetingly at the Shanghai detention center, she first becomes prominent as she and her husband (Peter Gale) wait among the jostling crowd to board the truck bound for the prison camp. "I want you to say something. I want you to tell him who we are so we can get out," she urges her reluctant husband, who counsels a less strident tactic. Dressed smartly in a light gray woolen coat, a dark gray blouse set off by a black and white string tie, and a floppy brown hat, she appears confident and attractive, her wavy hair perfectly combed and makeup neatly applied. She appears, in other words, just as Jamie's mother would under these circumstances. Over the three years in Soochow, Mrs. Victor slowly deteriorates. When the prisoners rush forward to fight for the scraps of food allotted them, she must rest on a nearby cart, coughing weakly into her handkerchief. Here, again, the boy must assume the role of provider and protector vacated by an ineffectual older man, in this case Mr. Victor, by sharing his extra rations with her.

Jim also shares a room with the Victors, living, as Ballard puts it, "within inches of each other for two and a half years" (179). Inside this cramped, dirty, and not well-lighted space, Jim watches Mrs. Victor examining her loosening teeth in a dingy mirror, peering at the attractive woman through a gauzy haze of undergarments that serve as a makeshift curtain. Once more, the boy appropriates the parental role, lecturing the Victors about the "university of life" and admonishing them to eat weevils for their protein. "Perhaps it's time you moved out of here and into the single man's dormitory," she responds. "You're not twelve anymore." The next scene supports her observation. Spielberg begins with a high-angle ceiling shot, moving smoothly from the foot of the Victors' bed to Jim's small adjacent space. The couple lay uncovered in the hot China night, Mrs. Victor coughing quietly and wearing a silk nightgown reminiscent of one Jim's mother donned earlier in the movie. This movement ends with a static and overtly sexual shot over the tops of Jim's feet and looking directly between his legs—almost up his undershorts—as he reads a magazine in bed. He spreads apart the pages, one with a colorful coke advertisement featuring an attractive young couple and the other with pilots and their planes, to reveal the object of his rapt attention: Mrs. Victor's face bathed in the eerie moonlight. Snapping the pages together, Jim tries to divert himself from these sexual longings by shoving open his shutters and watching the American air raids over Nantao.

Searchlights bisect the night sky to provide light for Japanese anti-aircraft gunners, but for once planes don't monopolize Jim's attention. Slowly, with equal measures of lust, curiosity, and guilt, he turns back to watch the Victors—likely not the first time he has done so. The husband's hand reaches across to gently cup his wife's breast. At that moment, Jim blows out the candle dimly illuminating his space and, turning his back on the air raid, watches as the man slides atop the woman and covers her mouth with his. Her hands caress the back of his neck, as Jim breathlessly watches. Her head lolls to one side with pleasure. Reminding us of the disturbing scene in his mother's deserted bedroom, the wind blowing in the window ruffles the pages pinned to Jim's wall, most conspicuously the *Saturday Evening Post* cover with the Rockwell painting. Suddenly, in close-up, Mr. Victor looks up, his eye trapping Jim, who screams out, "They're bombing the Shanghai docks!" The boy runs outside just in time to see a B-29 dropping its payload on the camp and infuriating Sergeant Nagata. The explosion is Spielberg's displacement of sexual culmination, either of the Victors or perhaps even of Jim ejaculating as he watches them. We can speculate that this is not the first time that he has spied on the couple and that he is quite aware of what they are doing. Another part of his childhood has ended.

During the march to the Olympic stadium, Jim chooses to stay with the dying Mrs. Victor. Her final moments begin with an image of his cupped hands bringing water to her parched lips, the child sustaining the woman who licks his palms in thanks for providing the last droplets of precious liquid. "Don't go. It's better here," she whispers, begging Jim not to join Mr. Maxton and the other prisoners in their trek up-country. "Pretend you're dead, Mrs. Victor," says the boy, assuming the parental role for the last time in their relationship. He drops onto the grass, and she slips from her ornate chair to the ground beside him, resting her weary head on his shoulder. Spielberg's camera pans up over the Xanadu-like collection of objects spread throughout the stadium as the Soochow inmates march off into the watery blueness of the director's day-for-night lens. Morning arrives, with sunlight reflecting off the gleaming objects stored in the abandoned stadium, shiny expensive cars, lustrous marble statues of horses and birds, shimmering crystal chandeliers, and gilt-framed paintings. Spielberg pauses on a graceful marble statue of a woman sleeping in bed, her flowing nightgown calling to mind images of both Mrs. Graham and Mrs. Victor. He then superimposes Mrs. Victor, lying on the ground with Jim staring at her inert figure. She is dead. Among these objects of luxury, she has become another image of Jim's past life, now gone.

But it is not only Jim's past that vanishes. As he stares down at Mrs. Victor's body, the living and the dead are suddenly bathed in a harsh, bright light. Jim looks upward to see a band of light slicing horizontally across the sky, a ball of light at its center point. Sparks seem to shoot into the sky, as he whispers, "Mrs. Victor." The light intensifies, ultimately washing the entire frame in white and bleaching out the image of the boy. In a few seconds, Jim emerges from the light, staggering and hungry. We hear a radio announcer proclaiming the surrender of Japanese forces and the destruction of Hiroshima and Nagasaki via "two single bomb explosions which effectively brought the war to an end. . . . Her ambitions to create and dominate a new empire in the Pacific incinerated in a flash of light and a fireball hotter than the sun . . . a ghastly white light—the atomic bomb." Suddenly, Jim realizes what he beheld. It was not, as he imagined, "Mrs. Victor's soul going up to heaven" but rather the end of the world's childhood: "[T]he sight of his small soul joining the larger soul of the dying world" (Ballard 286). Spielberg, echoing Ballard, understands that Jim's individual movement, because of its speci-fied time and place, had much larger resonances. He witnesses the birth of the atomic age and, with it, the destruction of an old order. As Spielberg explains, "I wanted to draw a parallel story between the death of the boy's innocence and the death of innocence of the entire world. When that white light goes off in Nagasaki . . . two innocences have come to an end and a saddened world has begun" (Forsberg 129).

MUSIC

Music plays a crucial role in *Empire of the Sun,* especially John Williams's use of the haunting Welsh melody "Suo Gan," which appears at three crucial points: as background to the opening image of coffins containing the bodies of Chinese whose families are too poor to pay for their burial floating among wreaths of paper flowers in the river, the camera moving to Jim singing it as a solo in his school choir; when Jim vocalizes the song to express his admi-ration for, and salute to, the brave kamikaze pilots flying off to their deaths; and finally in the reconciliation scene between Jim and his parents that ends the movie. Critics such as Ian Freer properly identify this song as a lullaby. Its lyrics talk of children swathed in their parents' protection: "Round thee mother's arms are folding / In her heart a mother's love / There shall be no one come to harm thee / Naught shall ever break thy rest." As such, it func-tions as a lyrical equivalent to Spielberg's ironic use of the Rockwell painting, more striations of doubt and uncertainty that he paints into his portrait of family responsibility and security. As well as a secular lullaby, however, "Suo Gan" is a traditional religious hymn. The lyrics herald the birth of baby Jesus: "Born to suffer for us all; / Blessed Mary watches o'er you / Singing sweetly lullaby." Again, the director seems to juxtapose the protection inherent in the lyrics, this time for all of humankind in the birth of a benevolent sav-ior, with the images of wartime horrors, the specter of omnipresent death encapsulated in the bright light of the exploding A-bomb.

A TECHNICAL NOTE

As had been the case with the Louma crane in *1941* and would be equally evident with CGI imagery in the *Jurassic Park* movies, Spielberg harnessed emerging technology to shoot highly complicated scenes in *Empire of the Sun.* In this case, he wanted to pull back slowly from the rioting in the streets of Shanghai to reveal the soldiers perched high above the crowd and firing into their midst. To accomplish this difficult maneuver, he installed the newly developed Multicrane atop a ten-story building. As Doug Brode describes the technology, "It consisted of a standard camera car with an arm, though this arm could come off and move onto a pipe track dolly, allowing for remarkable flexibility" (166). Such a harnessing of technical expertise in the service of emotional impact and thematic elaboration highlights Spielberg's consistent drive for an organic blending of form and content. Despite his obvious enthusiasm for state-of-the-art technological advancements, he remains, at heart, a traditional narrative storyteller wedded to the time-honored concepts of dramatic structure, characterization, and imagery. Rarely in his best work does he indulge in technique for the sake of technique or spectacle devoid of human emotions. In direct opposition to his detractors' claims, I would argue that it is the human beings who endow Spielberg's spectacles with meaning beyond the obvious visceral delights provided by his visual imagination and technical proficiency.

CONCLUSION

I started this section by noting that *Empire of the Sun* is the least explored and most undervalued of Spielberg's finest productions. It is also his least commercially successful film, costing thirty-eight million dollars to make and grossing around $66.7 million worldwide. In looking over his career, it seems clear that Spielberg's experience making *Empire* proved the necessary transition, along with *The Color Purple,* that allowed him to become a more mature filmmaker, though one could argue that he regressed (perhaps because of the film's weak financial performance) with disappointing productions such as *Always* and *Hook.* The film deserves a place among his best works, and I hope that my discussion will encourage readers to rent the movie. It stands as an extraordinary accomplishment of artistry and substance, a striking example of Spielberg's ability to blend form and content organically into a emotionally and intellectually satisfying whole.

Saving Private Ryan: Beyond the Screen

In Spielberg's case, one can never be sure if his work actually creates a cultural moment, if it acts as a focal point that brings together various strands of thought, if it shines a spotlight on already existing materials, or if it simply rides atop the waves of the social zeitgeist. As with other blockbusters like *Jaws, E.T.,* the *Indiana Jones* trilogy, and *Schindler's List, Saving Private Ryan* shows that it remains impossible to separate the dancer from the dance as the cultural ripples expanded beyond the screen. Newspaper stories cited the film, along with Tom Brokaw's *The Greatest Generation* and Steven Ambrose's *Citizen Soldiers,* as inspiring renewed national interest in World War II. America Online reported that its "Saving Private Ryan Area" was visited in record numbers by those who wanted to exchange stories, talk about their experiences, and answer questions from younger cybernauts about the war. Tourism shot sharply upward at the Omaha Beach memorial in France, with tour guides having to tell disappointed visitors that no grave existed for Captain John Miller. The *New Yorker* carried an article, with photos by Helmut Lang, about military chic as the new "in style." And, as *It's a Wonderful Life* (1946) has become the traditional film shown at Christmastime, *Saving Private Ryan* has emerged as the movie to accompany Memorial Day (despite recent fears that the FCC would punish stations that show it uncut, complete with graphic violence and uncensored language, as Spielberg demanded).

Political appropriations were inevitable and immediate. Conservatives like Condoleezza Rice—at the Republican convention no less—thanked "all those Private Ryans who served over the decades so that tyranny would not stand," and George F. Will opined that the overwhelming popular response to the film was a "measure of the depth of the nation's yearning for honor as it tastes the bitter dregs of Clinton's presidency" (70). Such interpretive revelations no doubt startled Spielberg, a generous supporter of liberal causes who publicly proclaimed himself an ardent FOB (Friend of Bill's). Predictably, some groups were not happy. Black veterans, for example, complained that Spielberg's platoon contained only white men, ignoring the fact that until the Korean War racially integrated platoons existed on the screen but not on battlefields and the fact that blacks were not members of the units highlighted in the movie: the Second Ranger Battalion, the Twenty-ninth Infantry Division, and the 101st Airborne (Kodat 90). Wartime allies of the United States, particularly the British and the French, complained about the director's Americentric view of events that ignored the contributions of their soldiers.

Throughout all the hubbub, Spielberg maintained a divided attitude regarding his historical predecessors. He saw himself as a card-carrying member of the Baby Boomer generation, a bulging demographic fundamentally shaped by the harsh legacy of the Vietnam War and the vast protest movement it spawned. "'Without Vietnam,'" he said, "'I never could have made *Ryan* as honestly as I did because it . . . prepared audiences to accept war for what it was, not war as an excuse to romanticise an event'" (qtd. in Hammond 70). Amplifying this point, he told *Newsweek* that "'Southeast Asia . . . shattered every Hollywood stereotype when the casualties from Vietnam stormed into our living rooms seven nights a week for nearly a decade'" (qtd. in Meacham 50). Such a point of view never stopped Spielberg from enjoying a previous generation's war movies, but the visible scars that Vietnam left on the American national consciousness meant that he could not simply emulate those earlier, less morally ambiguous works: "I love those movies, but I think Vietnam pushed people from my generation to tell the truth about war without glorifying it. As a result, I've taken a much harder approach to telling this particular story" (Pizzello 209). Yet, for his critics, Spielberg's "harder approach" was not sufficiently rigorous.

Despite his invocation of a post-Vietnam skepticism, commentators such as Neal Gabler saw *Saving Private Ryan* as part of the "renewal of patriotic fervor tinged with nostalgia" that replaced the "bitter cynicism" engulfing the country after the humiliating military defeat in Southeast Asia (4). Casting war movies as "metaphors for America's attitude toward authority," Gabler concludes that the film makes "war seem again purposeful, and those in charge again respectable" (4). Other critics were even harsher, arguing that the film employed the "most tried-and-true dramatic plot known to man" (Menand 251), restored German dignity for "having accepted their destiny and faced battle as worthy foes" (Jaehne 41), reunified "white masculine identity . . . [and] longing for ideological consensus" (Owens 259, 274), exalted "American arms" (Auster 1), and assured viewers that "[white] Americans are a good people who have *earned* their considerable perquisites in the current global economic order" (Kodat 91). These critiques are best summed up in two comments, the first by Stephen Hunter, who proclaimed that "'*Saving Private Ryan* is probably the most conservative film of the decade'" (qtd. in Calwell 50), and the other by the screenwriter William Goldman, who described the post–Omaha Beach portions of the film as a "'detestable piece of shit'" (qtd. in Nathan 120). While Spielberg sidesteps the sanitized violence and uncritical patriotism characteristic of conventional war movies, he claims that "World War II was the most significant event of the last 100 years, that the fate of the Baby Boomers and even Generation X was linked to that outcome" (Pizzello 208), and that he purposely sought to "'memorialize what they did for us'" (qtd. in Hammond 74).

ON THE BEACH

In a rare case of critical and popular unanimity, nearly everyone who writes about *Saving Private Ryan* agrees that Spielberg's masterful depiction of American troops landing on Omaha Beach on D-Day (June 6, 1944), where some twenty-five hundred soldiers lost their lives, stands as one of the most powerful and influential re-creations of combat ever put on film. When, for example, the critic Stephen Holden reviewed *Cold Mountain* (2003) five years later, he remarked that the "new explicitness in the depiction of combat" remains one of *Ryan's* significant legacies and that Spielberg raised "the bar on realism in the screen portrayal of bloodshed" (B1). This lacerating twenty-five minutes, with its harrowing melange of indelible images and deafening sounds, of technical brilliance and grisly replication, calls to mind the novelist Tim O'Brien's passages about the inherently paradoxical nature of warfare:

> The truths are contradictory. It can be argued, for instance, that war is grotesque. But in truth, war is also beauty. For all its horror, you can't help but gape at the awful majesty of combat. . . . It's not pretty, exactly. It's astonishing. It fills the eye. It commands you. You hate it, yes, but your eyes do not. Like a killer forest fire, like cancer under a microscope, any battle or bombing raid or artillery barrage has the aesthetic purity of absolute moral indifference—a powerful implacable beauty—and the true war story will tell the truth about this, though the truth is ugly. (80–81)

Like O'Brien's invocation of a "powerful implacable beauty" that "commands you," Spielberg's Omaha Beach landing "fills the eye" and partakes in what Constance Balides characterizes as a "'cinema of immersion'" that invites viewers "'to experience ephemeral effects as if they were inside diegetic events'" (qtd. in Hammond 69).

Commentators part ways while analyzing the remaining portions of the film. Some argue that it degenerates into a stereotypical B war movie, while others claim that it becomes a unique hybrid by filtering a World War II plot through a Vietnam-era sensibility, but the D-Day landing sequence remains a critical DMZ where traditionally warring parties share a small patch of common ground.

To understand how Spielberg assembles this memorable facsimile of combat, it will be useful to break the D-Day sequence into five segments to grasp its structural logic and linear composition: 1) on the boat and in the water; 2) the initial landing; 3) moving up the beach; 4) trapped by enemy fire; and 5) overrunning the German machine-gun pillbox. I will then examine the various techniques he manipulates to deliver a visceral punch felt by even the most jaded, violence-saturated filmgoers. Spielberg ushers in the Omaha Beach sequence with sound rather than pictures, the extreme close-up into the old man's (Harrison Young) eyes accompanied by the ever louder noise of crashing waves. This transition from present to past events creates an illu-

The cinema of immersion: Spielberg raises the bar on depicting combat realism with his re-creation of American troops landing on Omaha Beach in *Saving Private Ryan* (1998).

sionary point of view, a sleight-of-hand trick that ultimately confounds the audience's narrative expectations. Because the first individual most viewers immediately recognize is Tom Hanks, we naturally surmise that he and the man back among the graves are the same person at different points in his life, even though we're not sure of the character's name at this early point. Retrospectively, one realizes that Ryan was not present on the beach that day in June 1944, so what initially seemed like a first-person remembrance becomes a third-person account, a conjectural narrative pieced together long after most of the events depicted in the story actually transpired.

ON THE BOATS AND IN THE WATER The first images shown are rows of metal hedgehogs set up as barriers along the shoreline, with waves lapping and curling against them. "June 6, 1944," establishes the date, followed by "Dog Green Sector, Omaha Beach," to set the place and provide a documentary feel to the sequence. Next, a quick series of long shots shows a squadron of Higgins boats fighting against the waves and straining toward the dropoff point. Men vomit over the sides of the boat. Spielberg cuts to a man's hands shaking as he twists open his canteen and raises the metal cup to his lips. The bars on his helmet are the only bright spot in a darkly foreboding frame. We come to learn that this is Captain Miller (Tom Hanks). A shaky, handheld camera moves back to reveal him surrounded by men, one of whom we later learn is Sergeant Horvath (Tom Sizemore). Horvath plops a wad of tobacco into his mouth. More vomiting. "Clear the ramp! Thirty seconds! God be with you!" screams the boat's captain, followed by a volley of orders issued alternately by Miller and Horvath: "Move fast and clear those murder holes. Keep the sand out of your weapons. Keep those actions clear. I'll see you on the beach." A series of close-ups of men waiting anxiously to disembark from the boat catches the fear lurking in their eyes and creeping around the corners of their mouths; some pray, and one kisses his crucifix. But other than Miller and Horvath, we have no inkling as to who will be part of the continuing narrative and who will be left dead on the beach. The sound of a whistle slices through the air, a wheel turns and spins open, the front of the boat slaps down, bullets clank against the its metal hull and mow down the first row of soldiers. The horror has begun.

For the first time in the sequence, Spielberg shifts the point of view from the disembarking American soldiers to their enemies firing down on them. Shot now with a jerky horizontal pan from behind the backs of the Germans, and glimpsed between spewing machine guns being fed bands of ammunition, the running Americans seem small and helpless on a darkling plain, "Swept with confused alarms of struggle and flight" (Arnold, "Dover Beach" ll. 36–37). Maintaining this point of view for only a few furious seconds, the director cuts back to the men desperately seeking a relatively safe patch on the beach. He then shifts back to the Higgins boats, more men tumbling over their sides and into the sea, the camera slipping underwater with them. The blue sea and the bubbles of breath that surround the wriggling bodies momentarily muffle the sound of combat, like a wet blanket wrapped tightly around them. Rifles and helmets slide into the darkness beneath their dangling feet. As they struggle to untangle themselves from the heavy gear dragging them downward, some of the men drown; bullets slice through the water, first missing then finding their targets and mixing red into the blue waters.

Following some men swimming upward, Spielberg's camera breaks above the waves, the sounds of battle resuming its loud and disjointed cacophony, then bobs beneath the surface again, then into the air, then below again, and finally stays above the depths for a few moments. We catch glimpses of men helping their comrades ashore, of others clinging to the hedgehogs or lying dead in their metal arms; we hear bullets clinking dully against the steel. A man Miller drags toward shore is shot and sinks beneath the water. Slowly, the Americans move forward, their feet eventually finding the momentary security of dry land. Quick cut back to the enemy pillbox to remind us who holds the high ground and who remains vulnerable. A few bullets whiz past Miller, who sinks to his knees in the shallow water, blood swirling around his legs. For an instant, we fear that Spielberg has out-Hitchcocked Hitchcock, daring to kill off his most recognizable actor even earlier than the old master disposed of Janet Leigh in *Psycho* (1960). He maintains this uncertainty by leaving Miller outside the frame, instead showing a man stepping on a landmine, flying into the air, and having his left leg ripped from his body. Behind him, Miller slowly crawling toward land finally clings to a hedgehog for a momentary respite.

THE INITIAL LANDING At this point, Spielberg abruptly shifts from his third-person perspective and drags us into Miller's subjective point of view. The concussions from exploding munitions render him temporarily unable to hear properly. Sounding as if Miller is standing directly under a waterfall, filtered through an echo chamber that softens some of its pounding monotony, a steady roar dominates his hearing and ours. Other sounds don't totally disappear, but they seem distant, less pronounced, unable to be clearly discerned. His numb gaze takes in the scene. He watches frightened soldiers huddling beneath the hedgehogs. A man gathers up his right arm from the ground and runs off with it. Miller gingerly picks up his helmet, now filled with red seawater, and places it on his head. The rivulets of blood crisscrossing on his face give him a weird, kabuki-like appearance. A soldier hollers into his face, but Miller cannot hear him. Finally, the whining explosion of a bomb restores his hearing: "What the hell do we do now, sir?" shouts the enlisted man. Turning to Horvath, he commands, "Move your men up the beach." "What's the rallying point?" inquires one of the men. "Anywhere but here!" answers Miller.

MOVING UP THE BEACH Ripping us away from Miller's first-person perspective, Spielberg returns to the third person, plunging us back into the confusion of the men working their way up the beach. But Miller remains his central point of contact, the focal point around which the action shifts and circles, dips and dives. "If you stay here, you're dead men," the captain tells a group of troopers too scared to edge forward. The camera tracks along parallel to Miller's progress as he pushes his way past dead and mangled bodies while German machine-gun fire indiscriminately selects targets for death. In one of the film's most gruesome moments, a soldier lies dying on the sand, his guts literally spilling out from his body as he calls out plaintively, "Mama, mama." Spielberg relentlessly continues his assault on our senses. Miller stumbles upon a platoon of medics clustered behind a hedgehog and, as he speaks with their leader, a man right in front of them gets shot repeatedly. They never miss a beat in their conversation or even take notice of the dead man's bullet-riddled body. At one point in his progression, Miller drags a wounded soldier toward safety when a bomb explodes, severing the man's body. Miller finds himself lugging the dead soldier's upper torso, now sheared off from his lower half. Eventually, Miller sprints forward, joined by a make-shift group of those who survived the brutal assault. They fling themselves down on a sandbar beneath the German gun emplacement, survivors more by chance than by skill.

TRAPPED BY ENEMY FIRE "Who's in command here?" demands Miller of the radio operator, telling him to relay back to headquarters that "Dog One is not open"—the objective has not been achieved. "You are, sir," comes the reply. According to Horvath, they are "right where they are supposed to be, but no one else is." Some other survivors arrive, slamming themselves down on the sand. Spielberg cuts back to a close-up of the T/4 medic Wade (Giovanni Ribisi) struggling to stem the bleeding of a fatally wounded soldier. "They're killing us," screams an enlisted man. "We don't have a fucking chance, and that ain't fair!" Spielberg never relents on the overlapping noise during this sequence: the sounds of bullets and explosions unrelentingly blend with the voices of screaming men. Stripping rifles and ammunition from dead and dying soldiers, the improvised group readies for an assault on the German stronghold. A bullet ricochets harmlessly off one man's helmet. "Lucky bas-tard," says his comrade, as the man hastily removes the steel pot to check his head for wounds. The next second a bullet splats into the same spot, killing him. Luck is a temporary commodity on Omaha Beach. While Wade tends to the wounded, the rest of the men ready themselves to attack the German pillbox, crawling their way behind a stone structure.

OVERRUNNING THE MACHINE-GUN PILLBOX Demonstrating his ingenuity, Miller uses chewing gum to paste a mirror onto a knife blade, slides it around the corner, and gets a bead on the German position. "Let's get into the war!" he yells to his men, directing them with the calm skill of a natural-born leader. Inch by inch, they move closer to the deadly pillbox but remain pinned down by the German fire. Miller calls for Private Jackson (Barry Pepper), the south-ern sharpshooter. We recognize him as the man kissing his crucifix on the Higgins boat prior to the landing, and he repeats that religious gesture here. Spielberg moves in for a close-up of Jackson's squinting eye as he mouths a prayer and squeezes off a round that kills a German soldier. The frame is suddenly filled with praying men, common soldiers and chaplains giving fallen warriors the last rites. Again, Spielberg closes in, this time on Jackson's lips as he asks for God's help to steady his aim. The prayer is answered, as more Germans flop forward. Now the Americans move more quickly upward toward the pillbox, as Horvath screams out, "We're in business!"

Next, Spielberg delivers a long shot of the beach, the first one that furnishes spectators with any real sense of geographical perspective and which, in most films, would have served as the opening establishing shot. Having denied his viewers this conventional shot earlier, instead plunging us directly into the lethal chaos alongside the advancing soldiers, Spielberg finally looks back to the oncoming waves of Americans landing on the beach. But this is only a temporary respite. The camera immediately swings around and rejoins the small platoon in its ongoing assault. Higher and higher the men climb, killing the fleeing Germans who, seeing that their cause is lost, are abandoning their posts and quickly meeting their deaths. Once they reach the pillbox, the Americans shoot the Nazis as they emerge into the daylight. Finally, a flamethrower ignites the entire structure, and the remaining Germans pour from its bowels. When they raise themselves up holding their hands above their heads, the angry GIs take no prisoners. Having seen so many of their friends maimed and killed on the beach, they mow the Germans down like frightened cattle. Mercy is not an option on this day. Dog One is open at last, but at a terrible cost.

To celebrate the moment of victory, Capazo (Vin Deisel) gives Mellish (Adam Goldberg) a Hitler Youth knife, which he jocularly rechristens "a shabbat challah cutter." Totally exhausted, severely shaken by what he has just witnessed, and finally unable to contain his emotions any longer, Mellish breaks down into sobs, externalizing the emotional state of the entire squad. Meanwhile, Horvath scoops sand into a tin canister, which he shoves into his knapsack alongside samples from Italy and Africa. As he had in the Higgins boat, Spielberg again zeroes in on Miller's shaking hands lifting the canteen to his lips for a long, slow drink. For the moment, they can all rest. "That's quite a view," says Horvath to Miller. "Yes it is," comes the weary reply, as Spielberg moves the camera back from a close-up of Miller's face and eyes (reminiscent of the similar shot of the old men in the cemetery) to the blood-soaked waves slapping rhythmically against the beach and the lifeless bodies strewn along the shoreline. Finally, a long traveling crane shot comes to rest on the backpack of one dead soldier lying face-down in the wet sand. His name, stamped upon it in black letters: Ryan S.

TECHNICAL ELEMENTS

The D-Day sequence in *Saving Private Ryan* has become the model against which all subsequent combat scenes are judged. As a "spectacle of authenticity" (King 118) that set new standards for battlefield realism, it demands a detailed focus on the technical aspects of Spielberg's cinematic artistry. The director's re-creation of Americans troops landing in Normandy represents one of the foremost examples of his ability to employ highly sophisticated technology in innovative ways to further his narrative and engage his audience. As Doherty remarks, "Spielberg's watchmaker's skill with every unit of cinematic grammar is always breathtaking: seeing the gears turning and the bells chiming on cue never diminishes astonishment in the precision of the instrumentation" (309). In the beach sequence, Spielberg sutures together a variety of modern technical devices to construct an accurate cinematic replication of events that occurred in 1944, resulting in "the first major World War Two combat film fashioned in the modern age" (Doherty 305).

A tireless student of cinema history, Spielberg cites several artistic forebears as his thematic and stylistic inspirations for this sequence: the D-Day photographs of Robert Capa; the combat fiction films of the directors Lewis Milestone (*All Quiet on the Western Front* [1930], *A Walk in the Sun* [1945], and *Pork Chop Hill* [1959]), Sam Fuller (*The Steel Helmet* [1951]), Don Siegel (*Hell Is for Heroes* [1962]), and William Wellman (*Battleground* [1949]); wartime documentaries such as *The Memphis Belle* (1944), the *Why We Fight* series (1942–45), *The Battle of Midway* (1942), and *The Battle of San Pietro* (1945); and the color 16mm Signal Corps footage shot by George Stevens (see Pizzello 209). Of these wartime documents, the eight surviving stills Robert Capa took during the assault on Omaha Beach most significantly determined the overall look of the sequence. Spielberg also understood the limitations of these precursors: those working during the war had little time for moral reflection, their job being to inspire the boys on the front lines and support those engaged in the war effort on the home front; those working in subsequent years were hamstrung by rigid Hollywood censorship codes that constrained depictions of violence and what might be construed as anti-American sentiments.

To capture the confused horror and intense claustrophobia of the D-Day landing, Spielberg departed from many of his standard practices, jettisoning his tradition of meticulous and comprehensive storyboarding and improvising the combat sequences (Pizzello 210). In addition, he staged all the battles in strict chronological continuity, forcing the actors to experience a progressive sense of fatigue, discomfort, tension, and fear. Although the scenes were extensively blocked and the director watched the unfolding action on video-playback monitors and could repeat sections, Spielberg's cameramen were told to follow the action as it occurred, were never sure what might happen during the actual shooting, and had to react to unexpected events as did combat photographers during a World War II battle. Another crucial decision was to shoot 90 percent of *Saving Private Ryan*—and all of the battle scenes—with handheld cameras, incorporating many unconventionally long takes. Because he wanted "the cameras to be a real participant in the film" (Probst 37), Spielberg also insisted on placing them almost at ground level, not the more common shoulder level, to mimic the point of view of disoriented soldiers running low to the terrain.

Later in the film, when the exhausted platoon gets a temporary respite from combat, Spielberg establishes a different visual and emotional effect by incorporating more typical dolly shots. To generate this alternative feeling of temporary calm, the cinematographer Janusz Kaminski sometimes used a special "switcher track" that allowed the camera to move in one direction, arrive at a particular junction, and then move smoothly ninety degrees in another direction (Probst 38–39). Employing anywhere from two to five film cameras running simultaneously, and averaging only a 4:1 shooting ratio, the director "didn't want to telegraph anything and also wanted viewers to be just as surprised as the combat G.I.s when the enemy threw something new at them" (Pizzello 213). He also shot the film in the 1.85:1 format, rather than in a more expansive widescreen format (such as CinemaScope's 2.55:1), feeling that this aspect ratio was more lifelike in that it more "closely approximates the way the human eye really sees things in everyday life" (212).

Spielberg's goal throughout the D-Day sequence was to present combat as accurately as possible "from the frightened viewpoint of a 'dogface' who's hugging the sand and trying to avoid having his head blown off" (Pizzello 212). To accomplish this, he consciously sought a "deconstruction of the slickness that you usually get with modern lenses" and felt he needed to "deglamorize the technology we were using" (212). So, for example, to get modern lenses to function like those used during the 1940s, Kaminski instructed Panavision to strip the protective coating off a set of older Ultra-speeds, and he found that without this veneer "'the light enters the lens and then bounces all around, so the image becomes kind of foggy but still sharp'" (qtd. in Probst 33). He also mismatched the lenses on cameras filming the same scene, resulting in a "'lack of continuity in picture quality which suggested the feeling of things being disjointed'" (qtd. in Probst 33). All these maneuvers were "intended to make you feel as if you were right in the middle of combat, as opposed to watching it like an armchair civilian" (Pizzello 212). Some effects, however, could be fashioned only in the editing room. Turning to the postproduction experts at ILM, Spielberg had them add digital wounds "to intensify the graphic nature of the scene without ever putting the actors at risk from explosive squibs" (Freer 269). The indelible image and sound of bullets traveling underwater to strike the desperately thrashing soldiers trapped beneath the waves was also generated far from the actual film site, digitally added in ILM's Northern California studios.

One much-discussed method Spielberg employed to highlight the gruesome action was the extensive use of narrow degree shutters on the camera instead of the usual 180 degree configuration, a technique later emulated in *Three Kings* (1999), *The Patriot* (2000), and *Gladiator* (2000). Since the shutter of a camera allows light to pass through the gate and onto the film by opening and closing for specific periods of time, the narrowing of the shutter, as detailed in Stacey Peebles's in-depth discussion, "renders the resulting images more staccato, intermittent, and yet sharper" (Peebles 1). The result closely resembles stop-motion animation, "where the film frames do not blur together and instead the eye detects a kind of jerkiness" (3). Kaminski notes that this technique was especially effective in capturing explosions: "'When the sand is blasted into the air, you can see every particle, almost every grain, coming down. . . . It created a definite sense of reality and urgency'" (qtd. in Probst 34). Psychologically, "the use of the narrow degree shutter speed creates a sense of gritty realism in the context of war and signifies the character's emotional engagement with the action," as well as the presence of an "outside force that bears down on the characters and is seemingly out of their control" (Peebles 7). At times, Kaminski threw the shutter out of sync to create a streaking effect from the top to the bottom of the frame: "'It looked great when there were highlights on the soldiers' helmets or epaulets because they streaked just a little bit. The streaking also looked fantastic with fire'" (qtd. in Probst 34).

To heighten the sequence's realism and to simulate the type of authentic footage that cameramen working during the war might have produced, Spielberg desaturated the film's color through a Technicolor process; the resulting sharpness brought out the texture and pattern of the soldiers' clothing and made "metallic surfaces and water reflections become like mercury" (Probst 33). Kaminski also "flashed" the film stock to give it an overexposed, garish look and allowed blood and dirt to smudge the lens at various times during the Allied invasion. "'Our camera was affected in the same way a combat cameraman's would be when an explosion or bullet hit happened,'" claimed Spielberg (qtd. in Freer 267), striving to create "the illusion that there were several combat cameramen landing with the troops at Normandy" (Probst 33). Finally, to simulate the disorienting nausea felt by the troopers, Kaminski utilized Clairmont Camera's Image Shaker, a device that allows technicians to dial in the degree of vibration needed with vertical and horizontal setting; the device was mounted on the handheld cameras, giving the wobbling effect that simulated how "the camera itself felt the impact of the explosion" (Probst 34).

In his highly technical interview with *American Cinematographer*, Kaminski also talks about the heavy use of smoke as an "'essential ingredient in his photography'" (qtd. in Probst 38), particularly since the D-Day sequence was shot almost totally in overcast natural light. To achieve the desired effect, drums of diesel fuel were burned to create huge clouds of black smoke. White smoke was incorporated into the action by affixing two-hundred-gallon tanks of diesel fuel onto the back of pickup trucks that would drive up and down the beach as needed. Interestingly, observes Kaminski, "'the lighting for the whole sequence was more about taking light *away* and when they turned those smoke machines on, it would cut down three or four stops of exposure'" (qtd. in Probst 38). "'You don't always have to have beautiful lighting,'" he told Christopher Probst. "'I often think ugly lighting and ugly composition tells the story much better than perfect lighting. . . . We've all got the ability to do groundbreaking work, and nothing is stopping us from using very experimental techniques in a major Hollywood movie if the subject matter allows and the director is willing to go there'" (42). Ironically, one of the directors most willing to "go there" is the man often derided by critics for his conventional filmmaking.

If, as Pauline Kael famously claimed, *Bonnie and Clyde* put "the sting back into death" (157), the D-Day sequence in *Saving Private Ryan* hit audiences with the force of a howitzer shell. Unlike Peckinpah's balletic violence that renders spurting blood and writhing figures somehow beautiful, or Tarantino's relentlessly wry violence that ultimately numbs us, Spielberg's use of technical devices to restage the Omaha Beach landing never filters the horror; instead, he personalizes it, forcing us to share the agony of characters whose names we never know. Enduring the American onslaught along with Spielberg's battered and bewildered soldiers, most filmgoers feel like they have slogged though the bloody assault beside the grunts on the beach, a particularly effective form of cinematic basic training. For the rest of the movie, viewers carry a sense of dreadful uncertainty in their mental backpacks, a frightful premonition that behind the next wall lurks an enemy soldier, his gun pointed directly at our heads. Not even the beauty of the French countryside can allay the anxiety, confusion, and fear that wrap themselves around our throats pressing insistently inward. Moral issues are never separated from physical dangers. They remain intimately entwined throughout *Saving Private Ryan:* the physical dangers make ethical decisions that are obvious in peacetime—saving a desperate child or sparing the life of an unarmed man—less certain amidst the murky swamp of combat.

SAVING PRIVATE RYAN AS MORALITY TALE

In a number of the interviews given around its release, Spielberg stressed that he saw *Saving Private Ryan* basically as a morality play. Many of the dilemmas that most concern him radiate outward from one essential question: is it ethical to dispatch eight soldiers, all with loved ones of their own back home, to rescue one man (no matter the circumstances) and return him to safety? Under what conditions (if any) is it appropriate and acceptable to sacrifice the many for the one? In exploring the implications of that question, it remains important to realize that the film's central narrative structure runs counter to a well-established and recurring motif of conventional Hollywood cinema history. American films traditionally glorify the rugged individualist. Many mainstream films, particularly within certain genres, center on a lone figure's willingness to face danger, and even risk death, to insure the survival and reinforce the values of the group: the single gunman battling outlaws or Indians to defend the settlers or townsfolk, the space explorer sacrificing him- or herself to save the rest of the crew, the private eye facing danger to restore order to the populace.

These types of selfless acts remain the surest method for characters to demonstrate bravery, gain redemption, and garner audience identification. In the combat film, this sacrifice-of-the-individual-for-the-group mentality is mandatory: communal objectives must inevitably replace private goals. *Saving Private Ryan* fits this conventional pattern in its first and last sections, as the platoon participates in the landing at Omaha Beach and the defending of Remelle, but the whole middle section, where they search for Ryan, has no military target and consequently no direct bearing on the outcome on the war. This is not a case of brave men risking their lives to liberate Midway or Guadalcanal; Spielberg's soldiers are not patrolling at dawn, seeing action in the North Atlantic, or booking passage to Marseilles. Men engaged in those deadly missions rarely consider the implications of their actions; they simply try to survive as best they can. But the members of Spielberg's platoon have the luxury to question the wisdom of their superiors, challenge the logic of their mission, and contemplate their fate as they hike across the French countryside. Each situation they encounter generates a new series of ethical questions, a deeper and more insistent inquiry into what constitutes moral behavior within a wartime environment dominated by violence, brutality, and death.

The objective of saving Ryan shifts the narrative dynamic from defeating the enemy to coming home alive. "This time," Horvath tells Miller, "the man is the mission." Private Reiben (Edward Burns) overtly, and quite reasonably, protests that Gen. George Marshall's (Harve Presnell) order to rescue Ryan is illogical, since it puts an entire platoon in jeopardy to find and protect one individual: "You want to explain the math of this to me? I mean, where's the sense in risking the lives of eight of us to save one guy?" By the end of the movie, five of these eight men will be dead, and Reiben's question will still hang in the air. But even this most skeptical of soldiers unhesitatingly joins his comrades in fighting for the greater common good and defending Remelle, despite the fact that Miller's platoon accidentally ends up in this town simply because they locate Ryan there. Reiben neither doubts the overall necessity of fighting the war nor behaves like a coward; he fights bravely when the military objective is clear and meaningful. Although he never accepts the need to gamble his life to save Private Ryan, Reiben, like the other members of the platoon, continually moves forward to complete a mission he never fully understands, justifies, or embraces.

By conflating Ryan's deliverance with returning home, Spielberg transforms individual patriotism from a collection of abstract concepts and jingoistic expressions into a shifting constellation of concrete objects and particular people, the sepia-tinted portrait of hearth and home encapsulated within Ryan's idealized Iowa farmhouse. Miller, for example, rejects patriotic platitudes as the motivation for fulfilling his responsibilities. He worries that "every man I kill, the farther away from home I feel." This fear of escalating alienation forces his thoughts backward, and his actions drive him forward:

> Sometimes I wonder if I've changed so much that my wife is not even going to recognize me whenever it is I get back to her. How will I ever be able to tell her about days like today? Ryan. I don't know anything about Ryan, and I don't care. He means nothing to me. It's just a name. But if going to Remelle and finding him so he can go home—if that earns me the right to go back to my wife—well then, that's my mission.

Like Jim Graham (*Empire of the Sun*), who can no longer recollect his parents' faces, Ryan tells Miller that he can no longer remember the faces of his dead brothers. To soothe him, the captain spins out his vision of home, which is tangible and accessible: "When I think of home, I think about my hammock in the backyard, my wife pruning the rose bushes in a pair of my old work gloves." For Miller, these concrete images of ordinary daily life function as visual synecdoches, small snapshots that represent the whole portrait of his existence back in Pennsylvania.

Miller "embodies the Frank Capra vision of the American soldier . . . a schoolteacher who becomes a warrior of necessity not bloodlust, who wants only to finish the job and get back home to his wife" (Doherty 308–9). As such, he also represents the Spielbergian ideal of the common man called upon to perform uncommon deeds. But he also stands in a long line of Spielberg protagonists who experience acute anxiety as they struggle to bridge the gap between their personal feelings and the cultural expectations inherent in the roles they come to occupy. Even an unsympathetic critic like Robert Kolker admits that the "heroic male is under interrogation through *Saving Private Ryan*" (307). Miller is no hypermasculinized John Wayne storming the sands of Iwo Jima or heading back to Bataan. Neither is he a vengeful Rambo. Instead, "He is at once afraid, burdened, fatigued—he weeps from sheer exhaustion and grief. Yet, he is disciplined, resourceful, responsible. He is both courageous and compassionate, a warrior dedicated to his duty, and yet disdainful of romantic idealizations of war" (Owens 266–67). Miller's shaking hand, the initial image Spielberg presents to viewers and one stilled only by death, becomes the objective correlative of his internal state, and his ability to lead in spite of his psychological demons reaffirms his strength of character as well as his frailties. Resting in a bombed-out building, he tells Horvath how he justifies sending men to their deaths:

> When you end up killing one of your men, you tell yourself it happened so that you can save the lives of two or three or ten others. Maybe a hundred. You know how many men I've lost out of my command? Ninety-four. But then I've saved the lives of ten times that many. Maybe twenty. And that's how simple it is. That's how you rationalize making the choice between the mission and the men.

Yet Miller's sobbing breakdown following the battle for the radar station betrays how excruciatingly less than "simple" it is for him to make these decisions.

The Everyman as reluctant warrior: Capt. John Miller (Tom Hanks) in *Saving Private Ryan* (1998) as Spielberg's "Mr. Everyday Fella" who remains dedicated to his duty without romanticizing the war.

The fallible, brave, and cerebral Captain Miller, a man who recognizes when "the world has taken a turn for the surreal," may be the only version of the idealized American soldier possible in the post-Vietnam era, but one of the film's most striking moral conflicts occurs within the evolving character of Corporal Upham (Jeremy Davies), the bookish interpreter pressed into military action to rescue Ryan. Spielberg claims that the character with whom he most identifies is Upham, though he never elaborates which facets of that figure's personality most closely resemble his own (Calwell 49). The other members of the ethnically mixed platoon change little over the course of the film: the bellicose veteran Horvath, the tender Italian Capazo, the combative Jew Mellish, the religious southerner Jackson, the compassionate medic Wade, and the skeptical Reiben (from Brooklyn, of course).

These figures arrive on Omaha Beach fully formed, but Upham's moral code changes radically because of his experiences. Early in the movie, he tells Miller that "all this is good for me," though his exalted concept of war is gleaned secondhand through the words of writers such as Emerson: "War educates the senses. Causes and actions affect the physical constitution. It

Captain Miller's platoon in *Saving Private Ryan* (1998): Private Reiben (Edward Burns), T/4 medic Wade (Giovanni Ribisi), Private Mellish (Adam Goldberg), Sergeant Horvath (Tom Sizemore), and Private Jackson (Barry Pepper). Already dead is Private Capazo (Vin Deisel). Corporal Upham (Jeremy Davies) is not yet present.

brings men into such swift and close collusion at critical moments that man measures man." True to these sentiments, Upham convinces Miller to stop the men from shooting a defenseless Steamboat Willie (Joerg Stadler), despite the fact that the assault on the German radar station results in Wade's grisly death and that the captain's decision sparks a near mutiny. "Sir, sir," pleads the frantic Upham. "This is not right. He surrendered, sir." Upham, however, will eventually abandon this ethical high ground, the stuff of literature about war and not its harsh reality.

Later, in one of the film's most disturbing, bitter, and honest scenes, Upham fails to perform his duty, and his cowardice results in Mellish's agonizingly slow death at the hands of an anonymous Nazi infantryman (not Steamboat Willie, as some commentators insist). Given the responsibility of delivering a bandolier of bullets, Upham freezes in terror and fails to bring Mellish desperately needed ammunition. His speculations about brotherhood and bonding cannot be translated into action, leaving him cowering in a stairwell as Mellish is killed. His hands hold a fully loaded rife, but his brain cannot summon the courage to fire a single shot. Instead, Upham remains so paralyzed by fear that the German who stabs Mellish disdainfully ignores him, knowing he has nothing to fear from the man shrivelled in terror and shame. At Remelle, Upham hides from the advancing Germans, then watches in horror as Steamboat Willie, the man he convinced Miller to free, fires the fatal shot that fells the captain. Finally bursting into action as the American planes bomb the Germans into submission, Upham again faces a captured Willie. This time he calmly shoots him, despite that fact that the smiling German stands before him unarmed, hands raised above his head in surrender. Upham has become a man of action, not words, a man whose guilt and anger leave little room for compassion and grace; he now understands that mercy toward your enemies can result in the deaths of your friends. His trajectory veers away from a romanticized notion of warfare toward a sense of moral indifference or, at the very least, pragmatic actions rather than abstract principles of conduct.

As quiet descends following the furious battles scene, the central question returns to haunt the survivors—and the viewers: is the rescue of Ryan worth the lives of five men? One way to contemplate an answer is to consider whether he has "earned it." Ryan, himself, seems uncertain that his seemingly ordinary life has been enough to justify their early deaths. Years later, he searches the face of his wife (Kathleen Byron, one of England's most famous actresses during the 1940s) for verification, and asks her to "tell me I have led a good life. Tell me that I'm a good man." "You are," she firmly replies, confirming what he wants to hear. But is this enough? Several times throughout the film, Miller says that Ryan ought to be worth the price paid by the men of his platoon: "He'd better go home and cure some disease or invent a longer-lasting lightbulb, or something." Yet the image of Ryan, as a young soldier and as an older man, reveals little beyond the average and mundane. He is brave. When Miller offers him an easy chance to escape to safety, he chooses to "stay with the only brothers I have left," the men in his squad. Even so, he doesn't know the meaning of the word "context," and the most vivid memory of his siblings revolves around a crude adolescent sexual encounter. As an adult standing beside Miller's headstone, Ryan does not seem particularly impressive: a paunchy man dressed in nondescript clothing. "I tried to live my life the best that I could," he says at the gravestone. "I hope that was enough. I hope that I've earned, at least in your eyes, what all of you have done for me." Does "earning it" mean performing extraordinary feats, or does the valor of living a good and ordinary life with dignity suffice?

Thinking about Miller's last words every day of his life, Ryan has "tried to live my life the best that I could." We can only take his word for this, since Spielberg affords no glimpses into his life following Remelle and after the war, other than that he has a seemingly loving family. Even his terse summation is qualified, the tentativeness of "I tried to live" rather than the assertion that "I did live." We can never know if the world would have been a better place if Jackson, Mellish, Capazo, Wade, or Miller had lived instead of Ryan. Who could predict if these men, having survived this mission, would have encountered death elsewhere in Europe? Would any one of them have gone home and cured a disease or invented a longer-lasting lightbulb? The life of one man cannot be substituted for the possible lives of those who rescued him. Ultimately, the question of whether it was morally acceptable to risk the many to save the one cannot be answered by how well that one man led his life, other than the most obvious of choices: he didn't molest children, kill people, or beat his wife. Beyond those broad strokes, the gradations of "earning it" are hard to judge and, since we have no way to measure this character's postwar life, it remains impossible to balance the scale with any confidence. On a broader plane, of course, one can never do enough to "earn it." To provide recompense for lives lost by judging lives lived remains an inherently flawed and ultimately futile task.

Spielberg's film called out for post–World War II generations to acknowledge the debt they owed to the men and women who fought to defend America during the 1940s. In Doherty's words, *Saving Private Ryan* becomes a "sacramental rite, the baby boomer sons kneeling before their World War II fathers in a final act of generational genuflection. . . . It flickered less as a motion picture than as a ceremonial flame before which Americans might look back to the linchpin event of a vanishing century and contemplate the cost paid by the men who had won the Good War" (301). Certainly Spielberg, who was fifty-one when he made the film, felt the tug of a personal debt to his father, who was eighty-one at the time of *Ryan's* release—a debt he often admitted publicly in a series of interviews. As Jeanine Basinger puts it, the film was "an eloquent call for Americans to take a good look at themselves. Have we as a nation earned the sacrifices that were made for our freedom and way of life by the combat soldiers of World War II?" ("Translating" 46). But Spielberg's film is not an unambiguous celebration of American bravery during a time of acute national crisis. Within its frames, heroic men behave immorally, good men are sacrificed needlessly, cowardly men survive, and honorable men die because they acted ethically.

THE CRITICAL ATTACK

Before taking leave of *Saving Private Ryan,* I want to offer yet another example of how nothing Spielberg directs can please the cadre of critics who despise his work. They remain adamant in their castigation of him as a simplistic and conservative filmmaker, never noting the evolution in his art or the counterbalancing striations of genre subversion that appear consistently throughout even his most popular movies. Frank P. Tomasulo's article "Empire of the Gun" provides a representative example of this consistent vilification. Within the first paragraph, he labels the director as "the American Kipling" and cites him as "one of the chief purveyors" of the "America First . . . ethos of the Ronald Reagan–George Bush era" (115), a refrain common among Spielberg's detractors. Tomasulo, who earlier mounted attacks on *E.T.* and *Raiders of the Lost Ark,* continues his assault by arguing that even Spielberg's "flops contain the seeds of a chauvinistic and possible racist worldview" (116), that the director strives to "renew and revivify America's mythic rightness as a nation" (127), and that *Saving Private Ryan* "provides the self-perpetuating jingoistic justifications for future unilateral military invasions, incursions, and interventions" (127). Let me take only two points to demonstrate how Tomasulo arrives at these conclusions and to demonstrate the crucial elements he ignores.

Tomasulo argues that Miller's death scene goes beyond "legitimate human sentiment" and submerges itself in "bathetic sentimentality" (126). He criticizes *Saving Private Ryan* for its "oodles of melodrama, particularly in its tear-jerker climax" (126). But one can only imagine the howls of indignation that would have erupted if Spielberg had allowed Miller to live. Renewed charges of Spielberg's inability to confront harsh realities and his obsession with happy endings would have filled the pages of newspaper reviews and academic journals. Here, however, he actually kills off the film's hero, a realistic counterpoint to the mythic John Wayneism that permeates American combat movies, and simultaneously recognizes that brave men die in wars. Yet he goes further. Spielberg pinpoints that Miller's kindness and humanity (the freeing of Steamboat Willie) actually results in his demise. It is as cynical and brooding a statement as anything found in the films of Kubrick or Scorsese, directors accorded critical hosannas for their realism and depth. Yet because Spielberg invites us to mourn the death of Miller, because he encourages us to shed tears at the passing of this good and decent man, Tomasulo accuses him of crossing "the line into bathos" (126).

In direct opposition, I would assert that making audiences intensely feel the death of Miller, while at the same time understanding what has caused it, provides a complex and challenging experience: feeling does not necessarily eliminate thinking. In an e-mail exchange, Tomasulo wrote to me that "most American spectators mourn Miller's death as simplistically as they do E.T.'s departure. We care about him because he's an American; no one mourns the German POWs who are killed in cold blood." Since neither of us can climb inside the psyche of the typical filmgoer, I can only respond that the film explicitly foregrounds the bitterly ironic aspect of Miller's death. The fact that we care about Miller deepens the moral questions inherent in his death. In his e-mail, Tomasulo contends that by making this sympathetic face that of an American, Spielberg "makes OUR concern the universal human condition . . . another example of how the American cinema depicts American dilemmas and deaths as more important than the suffering of others." This is often the case in American films, but one could make a similar claim about virtually all national cinemas. Yet audiences seem to have few problems drawing general conclusions about love and life from movies made in other countries. The important point remains that Spielberg will not allow viewers to retreat into abstract logic, alternately weighing one carefully reasoned set of options against another. Instead, he puts human faces on universal ethical dilemmas and forces us to acknowledge the individual consequences intrinsic within every moral decision.

Tomasulo inevitably casts the movie's strongest elements in the worst imaginable light. For example, when Spielberg depicts American troops violating the most sacred tenets of the Geneva Convention by killing unarmed and surrendering Germans, an honest and brave directorial decision, Tomasulo concentrates instead on how he manipulates audiences to "identify with these acts of barbarity" (120). In his e-mail, Tomasulo writes that he does respect Spielberg for showing such scenes but adds, "What I don't admire is that the film appears to want us to APPROVE of this behavior, especially since it's shown after 25 minutes of German soldiers mowing down American troops." Because some of these killings directly follow the bloody slaughter on Omaha Beach, audiences viscerally grasp the soldiers' motivations: watching our buddies being blown to shreds would inspire most of us to seek revenge. Yet I would contend that the film never encourages us to "approve" of this behavior but only to contextualize it within a battlefield mentality; in fact, Miller's later release of Steamboat Willie specifically critiques these actions, if rather ironically, in light of subsequent events.

In addition, I would argue that understanding why a person behaves as he or she does remains in a distinctly different category than "identifying" with him or her, and that Spielberg provides the former without resorting to the latter. Forced to admit that within the film "the niceties of the Good (and moral) war are soon forgotten; bloodlust and vengeance trump honor and *esprit de combat*" (Tomasulo, "Empire" 123), an accomplishment that should endear Spielberg to commentators who decry the deification of militarism, Tomasulo never understands that such a thematic position subverts the uncritical thrust of most World War II films, placing *Ryan* closer in spirit to the bitter Vietnam movies of the 1980s and 1990s than those made during the patriotic fervor of the 1940s. How much of a "sentimental flag-waver" can a film be that shows clean-cut American boys shooting unarmed enemy soldiers? Like most of the critics who attack Spielberg, Tomasulo ignores the unconventional and subversive aspects of Spielberg's films, seeing his work through an ideologically narrow lens that demands adherence to certain political positions and displays little tolerance for the competing elements that demarcate and enrich his best movies.

CONCLUSION

Looking back on *Saving Private Ryan*, one can measure the distance Spielberg has traveled, thematically and technically, from the beaches of Amity Island to the blood-drenched sands in Normandy. In one sense, the film is a deliberate reflection on wartime combat and the previous films that attempted to depict it. While it never debates the moral and political demands to fight this particular war, it questions the grave toll such necessities take on the bodies, spirits, and souls of American soldiers. It stints on neither the physical brutality nor the moral quandaries of combat but focuses on how ordinary men struggle to maintain their balance and simply survive in the midst of the confusion and cruelty of war. Equally important, Spielberg refuses to "create a buffer zone protecting us from violence and uncertainty" (Maslin 9). Like any film, or any "nonfictional" account, *Saving Private Ryan* demonstrates a selective historical memory, a subjective squint at past events rather than a full account. It is as much about forgetting as remembering. We can therefore analyze it as a contested site "where matters of national identity, morality, and historical representation are negotiated" (Owen 273). Artistic creations never simply hold up a mirror to the past; they offer alternatives to previous interpretations and add further layers of meaning. More crucially, they provide valuable keys to understanding present events and guidance for future actions. In a rich and textured way, *Saving Private Ryan* has become a significant communal landmark, one of the "things we carry" in our nation's cultural memory, and a celluloid memorial etched into our national consciousness.

* * *

Spielberg's father ignited his young son's imagination with thrilling tales of World War II escapades, and, inspired by these exciting stories, the director sought to visualize them in his adolescent movies, fledgling attempts at feature filmmaking, and throughout his professional career. For Spielberg, the 1940s era remains a complex combination of "innocence" and "tremendous jeopardy" (Forsberg 128–29), a time of heightened fear, communal sacrifice, and national triumph. He has faithfully revisited this era, inserting its characters and incorporating its mythos into various genres from action/adventure movies (the *Indiana Jones* series) to fantasy films (*Always*), to social problem/ ethnic minority pictures (*Schindler's List*). Each World War II combat film represents a different approach to its subject matter that generally reveals conditions in the Hollywood film industry and the country at large: *1941* reflects the rebellious spirit of seventies filmmaking; *Empire of the Sun* demonstrates a deferential admiration for soldiers evident in the more conservative eighties; and *Saving Private Ryan* pays homage to military sacrifices mirrored in the America of the nineties. These movies also mark the artistic evolution of Spielberg as a visual artist: *1941* was the disjointed work of a relatively young filmmaker, *Empire of the Sun* is a vision of war from a child's perspective, and *Saving Private Ryan* offers an appreciation of the parental sacrifices made by a filmmaker who was now, himself, a father.

5

"Whoever Tells the Best Story Wins": Spielberg's Social Problem/Ethnic Minority Films

The Social Problem Film

This chapter will explore Spielberg's films that deal explicitly with racial and ethnic issues—*The Color Purple* (1985), *Amistad* (1997), and *The Terminal* (2004)—under the rubric of the social problem film, a recognized category with a long and respectful lineage. American movies, as Kevin Brownlow observes, were "born in the era of reform" (xvi), and while the Hollywood studios were more adept at entertainment than social enlightenment, they often transformed stories culled from the nation's headlines into dramatic vehicles distributed to a mass audience. This tradition of "issue-oriented movies" stretches from silent films such as D. W. Griffith's *A Corner in Wheat* (1909), through movies made from muckraking books by Upton Sinclair, Frank Norris, Lincoln Steffens, and Ida Tarbel, to American classics such as *I Am a Fugitive from a Chain Gang* (1932) and *Our Daily Bread* (1934), and into modern times with films like *The China Syndrome* (1979), *Silkwood* (1983), *Philadelphia* (1993), and *Erin Brockovitch* (2000). Legitimate heirs to this tradition can also be found in made-for-television movies that confront various societal problems such as *The Day After* (1983), *The Burning Bed* (1984), and *Something about Amelia* (1984).

According to Charles J. Maland, the social problem film can be defined as a movie "with a contemporary setting whose central narrative concern focuses on a negative condition in society that is perceived as a problem and whose portrayal of the victims or of crusaders against the social problems is empathetic" (308). As with most commentators who write about social problem films, Maland notes that these works never indict the American capitalist system as a whole but rather conceptualize isolated problems as "aberrations within a fundamentally sound society" (309). Similarly, Russell Campbell concludes that Hollywood's social problem films offer only "solutions that may be entertained without contemplating a decisive shift in existing power relationships" (60), and John Hill asserts that "the definition of a social problem presumes the ability to resolve it within the parameters of the social system; it does not imply structural change or social transformation" (35). Even during the more politically volatile historical period surrounding silent productions, these types of films "raised social issues while at the same time containing them in satisfactory bourgeois resolutions" (Sloan 54). The social problem film draws attention to particular social concerns without providing solutions that might threaten the core of American societal beliefs or its political organization.

The overwhelming number of mainstream social problem films maintain the basic narrative structure common in Hollywood movies, focusing on an individual's attempt to overcome obstacles instead of the larger political dimensions of the situation. When impediments emerge as social problems, the films emphasize personal, rather than more broadly activist, solutions. The assumption is that the protagonist's educative process—usually moving from an initial ignorance about the social problem to a concluding commitment to fight against it—offers the audience a potentially effective and socially acceptable method to confront and alleviate whatever ill is depicted. The formulaic happy ending implies the necessity for "limited social change" (Roffman and Purdy viii) that "paradoxically celebrates the system for being flexible and susceptible for amelioration" (Campbell 60). Such a narrative construction provides a means of "sugaring the didactic pill" and allows the "maintenance of social order by either assimilation or containment" (Hill 36). While social problem films challenge Hollywood's escapist fantasies and highlight the fissures in American society, they do so by using the same techniques that create those illusions, turning "social dilemmas into fairy tales of the day" (Sloan 43).

Two of Spielberg's social problem films—*The Color Purple* and *Amistad*—fail to meet the requirement of "contemporary settings" imposed by Maland and other commentators, instead using historical settings to explore contemporary problems of racism. They otherwise fit within the generally accepted generic conventions and narrative parameters of the social problem film. Even so, the historical scope of *The Color Purple* and *Amistad* compared to most movies within this genre makes me uncomfortable classifying them solely as illustrative examples of this category—it seems callous to equate problems with meat packing, governmental corruption, or the tyranny of railroad tycoons with the brutal horrors of institutional slavery. Even admittedly important topics such as abortion, labor-capital conflicts, and gun control seem less fundamentally evil and historically pervasive than the systematic imprisonment, exploitation, and mass murder of countless human beings simply because of their color. Along with understanding these movies as part of the social problem genre, therefore, it is equally crucial to situate them within the tradition of films about African Americans and other minority groups in the American cinema.

Because many comprehensive and scholarly books explore the ways in which Black people have been depicted in mainstream cinema, I need not recount the evolution of films about race or outline the key moments of their celluloid history from one decade to the next. A fair summation would be to note that Hollywood has a long, unsavory, and ultimately disgraceful history of depicting most minority groups, including African Americans. A small number of films directly confronted racial prejudice (such as *Pinky* [1949] and *Imitation of Life* [1959]), but for the most part, distasteful racial and ethnic stereotypes have dominated America's movie screens from the earliest days of cinema until the present time. One need look no farther than the nearest theater to see American prejudices of one sort or another on parade. Even movies that attempted to move beyond character cliches and narrative conventions were circumscribed by the ideological limitations of the social problem film. Although viewers were meant to generalize from specific instances of prejudice into thinking more broadly about bigotry, those earlier productions remain confined within carefully delineated borders designed to address individual problems, not the foundational assumptions of American culture and society.

Spielberg's Social Problem and Ethnic Minority Films

In discussing some of the issues surrounding social problem films with Charles J. Maland via e-mail, we talked about Spielberg's movies. Maland maintains that by setting two of his social problem films in the past, Spielberg "makes them a little more palatable to audiences because they can engage with the issues without feeling so personally implicated as they might with a contemporary setting." Even so, he can "hardly imagine an unflinching film like *Amistad* getting made without the involvement of someone as powerful in Hollywood as Spielberg." Since all three social problem films focus on exploring the dynamics of "an oppressed group within society," Maland sees them as a blend of various genres, including those depicting minority cultures. More to the point, he concludes that

> Spielberg's films have courageously grappled with these monumental social issues. It's not just the social problems he has explored; it's the large, distressing social problems that raise big questions about the nature of human beings and the difficulties we have in making social arrangements that make life livable for all people that raise them to a more significant level.

This statement articulately captures the director's attempts to move beyond mere entertainment and delve into subjects of universal importance.

The Color Purple: Beyond the Screen

Before looking specifically at this movie, let me throw at least one more ingredient into the overflowing pot of genre considerations. *The Color Purple*, though situated here within the social problem/ethnic minority category, would fit equally well within chapter 2's discussion of Spielberg's melodramas. I have noted that almost all of his movies could be classified as family-based narratives that center on tensions, fissures, and breakdowns within domestic relationships. Traditionally, such melodramas focus on either an individual (usually a woman) or a couple "victimized by repressive and inequitable social situations, particularly those involving marriage, occupation, and the nuclear family" (Schatz, *Genres* 222). Placing the movie squarely within this melodramatic tradition, Jane Shattuc chides feminist criticism's "refusal to own up to the political power of affect in melodrama . . . and, in particular, the racial implications of such a denial for the reception of *The Color Purple*" (148). Analyzing why Blacks and women have often chosen melodrama as the "form of their narratives of victimisation" (149), she makes a case for the "affective and political power of the film" (150), arguing that it belongs within the "long and powerful traditional of political tracts in black and feminine fiction that base their strength in the power of sentimentality" (153). "In the end," she concludes, "tears are not a sign of feminine weakness, as the patriarchy would have it, but they are more the manifestation of physical pleasure of Barthes's *jouissance*. Having a good cry represents the potential for the disempowered to negotiate the difficult terrain between resistance and involvement" (154). It is valuable to keep Shattuc's comments about melodrama in mind as I discuss the emotional and thematic significance of *The Color Purple*.

STEVEN SPIELBERG AND ALICE WALKER

Though he had previously converted an immensely popular novel into a blockbuster film (Peter Benchley's *Jaws*) and would subsequently make films based on the works of critically acclaimed writers (J. G. Ballard's *Empire of the Sun,* Thomas Kenneally's *Schindler's List,* and Philip K. Dick's *Minority Report*), Spielberg's relationship with the novelist Alice Walker represents a creative collaboration with a literary figure never duplicated at any other point in his career. Both participants, as well as those who closely observed their interactions, attest to the affection, warmth, and mutual respect that grew between the Black feminist writer and the white Jewish filmmaker. Initially, Walker knew little of Spielberg's works and, before they met, had only seen *The Sugarland Express.* Spielberg understood that his first visit with Walker in her San Francisco home was an audition, since she controlled the film rights to her book: "Basically, I was going to be interviewed, as I hadn't been since 11 years before when I was up for jobs, starting out as a director" (Collins 123). That the world's most successful director would willingly submit himself to this rudimentary process documents his passion for bringing Walker's novel to the screen, as does his willingness to draw no salary beyond the Director's Guild minimum of forty thousand dollars, most of which was ultimately spent on overages not covered by the film's budget.

Unfamiliar with his work, Walker immediately sensed that "for all his worldly success," Spielberg "remained a minority person. . . . She recognized that his sensitivity enabled him to share the feelings of characters of another race and another gender" (McBride 368). She was also "worldly" enough to retain a large amount of influence over the filmmaking. In an unusual pre-production agreement, Walker's contract stipulated that at least "half the crew members would be women or Blacks or Third World people" (McBride 369). She also brought Whoopie Goldberg, a relatively unknown young comedian who had never made a movie, to Spielberg's attention; ultimately, she was cast in the film's lead role of Celie. Walker further suggested Tina Turner to play Shug, a part the singer eventually turned down, as it was too close to her own experiences with spousal abuse. The novelist even tried her hand at writing a screenplay for the film (reprinted in her book *The Same River Twice*) which she and the director ultimately agreed not to use. Nonetheless, Alice Walker was on the set for about half of the shooting schedule, adding lines of dialogue when requested, helping the actors get the proper southern speech patterns, working with Menno Meyjes on the screenplay and with Quincy Jones on the musical selections, showing photographs of her grandparents' home to the production designer, J. Michael Riva, and, as Spielberg describes it, functioning as "a spiritual presence" (Collins 123). Most important, Spielberg understood Walker as an interpreter who helped him cross over from his culture to her own experiences: "Alice could take my hand and take me into a world that, at first, I didn't know anything about" (Spielberg interview, DVD special edition).

In her recounting of this time over a decade later, Walker reveals the physical and psychological traumas that afflicted her during the making of *The Color Purple*, including her mother's incapacitation from a major stroke and her own painful bout with Lyme disease. Suffering from what she characterizes as "the hidden trauma I endured during its creation" (Walker, *Same* 23), she recounts feeling "exactly as if I were being attacked from the inside at the same time I was being attacked from the outside" (27). As the filming progressed, she

> sat under a tree and offered speech lessons and tarot readings, painfully conscious of my fuzzy thinking and blotchy skin, my soul-deep exhaustion and almost ever-present nausea. I was unequal to the task of pointing out to Steven every "error" I saw about to be made, as my critics later assumed I should have, or even of praising the exquisite things he constantly thought up, which moved me to tears each evening as we watched "dailies." (30)

Even though she was on the set as much as possible, the novelist felt "more like a spirit than a person" (30). Spielberg never knew the extent of Walker's physical and emotional pain, but she firmly believes that "Steven intuited that I was extremely fragile as our film was being made, walking some days as if in a dream" (30).

Spielberg's film follows the general outline of Walker's novel. The narrative, set in rural Georgia, begins in 1909 and follows the life of Celie (Whoopie Goldberg), a poor Black woman suffering under the crippling yoke of sexism and racism. After being raped by the man she believes is her father (Leonard Jackson) and giving birth to Adam (Peto Kinsaka) and Olivia (Lelo Masamba), Celie's children are handed over to the Reverend Samuel (Carl Anderson), and she is forced into a marriage with the brutal Albert Johnson (Danny Glover), known to her only as Mister. Even worse, she is separated from the person she loves most in the world, her sister Nettie (Akosua Busia). Mister, who loves the flamboyant singer Shug Avery (Margaret Avery), treats Celie like a domestic servant, beating her mercilessly and making her rear his unruly son, Harpo (Willard Pugh), who eventually marries the domineering Sofia (Oprah Winfrey). When Shug comes to Celie's and Mister's home to recuperate from an illness, the two women form a strong emotional and sexual bond with each other. Sofia is sent to jail for hitting the mayor's wife, a sentence that breaks her physically and emotionally, Shug leaves and then returns with a new husband (Bennet Guillory), and Celie finds that Mister has been hiding Nettie's letters from Africa. Tearing them open, she discovers that her sister has joined the Reverend Samuel's missionary work and that Celie's children are thriving in their new home. Finally, Celie summons up the courage to confront Mister and leave him. She returns home after her father's death—learning he was actually her stepfather—and establishes a successful clothing store. The film ends with Celie's tearful reunion with Adam, Olivia, and, of course, Nettie.

Walker's first reaction after seeing the finished product in a nearly empty theater was overwhelmingly negative. "Everything seemed wrong, especially the opening musical score, which sounded like it belonged in *Oklahoma*" (Walker, *Same* 21), and she "noticed only the flaws" (161). She articulated concerns about the following points, most of which are echoed by the film's critics: 1) the deemphasis of Shug's bisexuality; 2) the lack of fullness in Harpo's character and his constant falls through various roofs; 3) the "bluntness" of Celie's erroneous statement about being raped and impregnated by the man she supposes is her father; 4) the falseness of Shug pretending not to understand why Celie can't speak up when left alone with Mister; 5) the absurdity of Mister not knowing where the butter is kept or how to start a fire; 6) the lack of forgiveness for Mister; 7) the avoidance of an erotic, sensuous relationship between Shug and Celie; 8) the overly well-dressed characters; 9) the distortion, at times, of the folk speech; 10) the sentimentality of the carved heart in the tree and the imposition of *Oliver Twist* into the story; and 11) the misinformation present in the African scenes about the location of the village, the sanctification ceremony, and the placement of the rubber plantation.

After that disastrous first screening, and as part of a far larger audience, Walker warmed to the film as an adaptation not a transcription, seeing "its virtues rather than its flaws" (Walker, *Same* 21). Even with some significant reservations, she feels generally positive about the movie and consistently maintains her admiration and affection for Spielberg: "When I think of Steven Spielberg's 'version' of my book, my first thought is of Steven himself. His love and enthusiasm for my characters. His ability to find himself in them" (30). The song "Sister," written by Quincy Jones, Rod Temperton, and Lionel Ritchie, remains, for Walker, particularly powerful, "a signal of affirmation that women could hum to each other coast to coast, an immeasurable gift to the bonding of women" (31). The scenes she particularly admires include the emotional parting between Celie and Nettie, the kissing scene with Celie and Shug, the section where Shug and Celie find the hidden letters (especially when she smells the dried flower petal), Shug's first song in the juke joint, and the moving ending (though she reaffirms her wish that "Mister had been up on the porch, too" [161]). Years later, on the DVD interview, Walker sums up her feelings by declaring, "I love it as a gift given to our people. A kind of medicine."

In an insightful and sympathetic summation of her personal connection to Spielberg, Walker hits upon a crucial element that directly and viscerally links the director with a wide range of viewers: "In more modern times, people say you think with your brain. Only there are a few of us who still actually think with our hearts, and after talking to Steven, I had a lot of confidence that he was one" (Walker, *Same* 176). That Spielberg "thinks with his heart" does not deny his brain nor his technical skills; it does, however, reveal one significant reason for his unparalleled success: the ability to transform his deepest emotions and obsessions into powerful visual images that strike broadly responsive chords in audiences. The ability to connect emotionally with audiences remains a primary reason for Spielberg's popularity, but it also accounts for the wariness expressed by some critics:

> Everybody loves the movie for the first few months, and then when it starts breaking records, some'll say, "Well, wait a second. I'm being tricked. There's some kind of evil seduction afoot. I don't trust that Spielberg. I know, I enjoyed it. I saw it four times, but that little bastard manipulated me! (Spielberg 16)

Walker also recognizes that, at the time the film was made, Spielberg was trying to move beyond his self-imposed limitations as a filmmaker. "Perhaps Harpo is Steven," she speculates, "falling down the stairs of his life at the time, breaking his bones against his parrot's cage, needing to rattle his own" (Walker, *Same* 35).

Spielberg and Walker instinctively knew that making *The Color Purple* represented a turning point in their lives. Looking back with some historical perspective, the novelist observes that "oddly, the experience of making a film of my work, as bewildering and strange as any labyrinth, and as unpredictable as any river, was an initiation into the next, more mature, phase of my life" (32). Similarly, Spielberg recognizes the inherent hazards in adapting this particular book to the screen. "I've been playing in the sandbox for years," he said on the eve of the film's release. "Something in me would say go for the easy challenge and not the hard task. So I went for the fast-paced, energetic entertainments" (Collins 121). Becoming a father during the making of the movie—his son Max was born as he was shooting Celie's childbirth sequence on June 12—Spielberg must have realized that his new role as an adult would ultimately be mirrored in his art, just as his childhood had played such a major role in his previous work. "It's as if I've been swimming in water up to my waist all my life . . . but now I'm going into the deep section of the pool" (121). Spielberg was clearly aware of the dangers involved in venturing beyond the shallow water: "[T]he biggest risk, for me, is doing a movie about *people* for the first time in my career—and failing. . . . It's the risk of being judged—and accused of not having the sensibility to do character studies" (120). Looking back over his career, *The Color Purple* can be seen as his first conscious attempt to create a mature film, the project that launched him into the rougher, more challenging currents of *Empire of the Sun, Amistad, A.I., Minority Report,* and *Schindler's List.*

THE CONTROVERSIES

Of the many controversies that swirled around *The Color Purple,* two dominate much of the discourse: the charge that the film fundamentally maligns Black men, and that Spielberg's alterations distort Walker's literary vision. Walker's feminist work, which won the National Book Award and the Pulitzer Prize for Fiction in 1983, sparked heated disputes because of its frank presentation of incest, spousal abuse, female sexuality, and lesbianism within African American society. The movie ignited a larger firestorm by bringing these incendiary issues to a wider audience. Outside the Black community, critics castigated Spielberg for candy-coating Walker's graphic narrative: typical of the hostile responses were David Ansen in *Newsweek,* who described "'the disorienting sensation that I was watching the first Disney movie about incest'" (qtd. in McBride 365); John Powers in the *L.A. Weekly,* who wrote that "'Spielberg's suburban background shows all over the place'" (qtd. in McBride 373); and Rita Kempley in the *Washington Post,* who called the director's version of rural Georgia "'a pastoral paradise that makes Dorothy Gale's Kansas farm look like a slum'" (qtd. in McBride 373). But these objections were tame compared to those arising from inside the Black community and typified by Donald Bogle's accusation that the film ignores "the broader context in which any of the characters must live: the larger dominant white culture that envelops—and certainly enslaves—them all" (292). Spielberg's "sensibility informs almost every frame, turning an intimate tale into a large-scale, overblown Disneyesque Victorian melodrama, full of 'big' moments and simplified characters" (293). The controversies spilled from the page into the streets, starting with boycotts from the Coalition against Black Exploitation and the Hollywood branch of the NAACP, as well as protest meetings in Black churches across the country.

CONTROVERSY 1: THE COLOR PURPLE MALIGNS BLACK MEN This movie "'depicts all blacks in an extremely negative light,'" claimed Kwazi Geiggar of the Coalition against Black Exploitation. "'It degrades the black man, it degrades black children, it degrades the black family'" (qtd. in McBride 274). Three pieces from within the Black community—one in the popular press by Tony Brown, the second by Gerald Early in the scholarly literature, and the third a sophisticated critique and audience analysis by Jacqueline Bobo in her book *Black Women as Cultural Readers*—represent the general charges against Walker, Spielberg, and the movie. Brown begins by bemoaning the "'growing inability of black men and women to love one another'" (qtd. in Walker, *Same* 223). The brutality of slavery forced humiliated Black men to deflect their hostility from whites toward those with even less power than themselves, "'women being the most vulnerable'" (qtd. in Walker, *Same* 223). Brown credits Walker for brilliantly capturing this "self-hatred," but he refuses to see the movie (which does not stop him from criticizing it) and contends that "'lesbian affairs will never replace the passion and beauty of a free black man and a free black woman'" (qtd. in Walker, *Same* 224). He asserts that because so few films are produced with Black themes, *The Color Purple* will become a definitive statement about Black men and broadly attacks the white-dominated publishing industry for only publishing "'books by black women or homosexual men with degrading themes or passive attitudes—and then mak[ing] them into movies of 'the black experience'" (qtd. in Walker, *Same* 225).

Walker admits that the accusation she found hardest to tolerate was that she hates Black men: not only does she admire many contemporary and historical Black male figures (from Langston Hughes to Bob Marley to Nelson Mandela), including those within her own family, she asserts that she "felt close to, and always affirmed by, the black male spirit within myself. This spirit's indomitable quality is fierceness of emotion, tenderness of heart, and a love of freedom" (Walker, *Same* 23). Even more importantly, she has "always considered men of color brave and daring beyond compare; it is from them I have learned much of what I know of gracefulness, of how to love and how to fight" (42). But she has also been irrevocably saddened by seeing and experiencing "that which destroys beauty in anyone: oppression of those over whom one has power" (42). Anita Jones, writing in the same journal as Tony Brown, responds directly to his article, contending that

> The Color Purple is not a story against black men: it is a story about black women. The fact that the men in the story are not all good guys needs no justification, for it is not the obligation of any work of fiction to present every possible angle or every possible situation. Walker chose a particular feminist theme and dealt with it, which resulted in many black men protesting and licking their egos. (226)

Even with such spirited defenses, Walker, and by extension Spielberg, never fully escapes the allegation that The Color Purple slanders Black men, spotlighting the violent deeds of a few to the detriment of the many. As such, argued many critics, the book and the film reinforce the worst white stereotypes about Black families.

Gerald Early's blistering rebuke makes Tony Brown's objections seem calm and circumspect. He savages The Color Purple (Walker's book as well as Spielberg's film) from a variety of aesthetic, sociological, historical, ideological, and racial perspectives. Early dismisses the literary work "because it fails the ideology it purports to serve . . . only *appears* to be subversive [and] . . . is far from being a radically feminist novel" (94, 102), while the film is "so undeniably bad that one wonders how Steven Spielberg ever acquired any sort of reputation as a competent artist" (94). He sarcastically surmises that Spielberg "was really directing a parody or a comedy and was not succeeding" (95). The blatant artistic failure of The Color Purple seems inevitable to Early, who characterizes the director's works as very expensive B movies that "combine hokum and splendor. . . . Spielberg's films essentially have the same moral and artistic visions as a professional wrestling match: the experience of an exaggerated morality in an excessive spectacle that is, I think, not an experience of art, but an experience of the negation of art" (95). He goes on to list the film's historical flaws, arguing that it reaffirms the "bourgeois pretensions and moral integrity" (96) of the "chronically insecure American audience" (96) and alienates Blacks from their own history (98), and censuring Black viewers who enjoyed the movie and participated in its creation.

Castigating the film as "narcotic art" that "moves an audience without disturbing it" (101), Early rejects any notion that it contains radical impulses. The Color Purple is "the ideal American protest art, freeing Americans from any criticism of their social or political order by denying that the film presents a problem open to any implication of a social or political solution" (100). Lumping Walker and Spielberg into culpable representatives of a stridently bourgeois orthodoxy (which certainly must have surprised Walker, if not Spielberg), he contends that *The Color Purple* simply recycles the Victorian cliche that "the individual still has the power to change and that power supersedes all others" (103). Walker's book "lacks any real intellectual or theological rigor or coherence, and the fusing of social protest and utopia is really nothing more than confounding and blundering" (104). The novel (and by extension, the film) endorses a "dimwitted" pantheism that resembles a "cross between the New Age movement and Dale Carnegie" (103). Early concludes by charging that the success of the book and the movie graphically illustrates American society's unwillingness to face the pervasive evil within its midst. Both works confirm the desperate and perilous middle-class illusion that "there are no devils in the end, no evil that cannot be repented and, indeed, no final rendering up of things because there will be no sin" (106).

Jacqueline Bobo's discussion of *The Color Purple* is the most fascinating of these three documents, in that she offers a critical feminist reading of the film and an enlightening dialogue with representative Black female cultural consumers who responded far less negatively to it than did Black males, mainstream reviewers, or radical commentators. Unlike Early, Bobo believes that Walker's novel incorporates "subversive form and content," and she situates it "within the continuum of black female creativity and activism" (64). In particular, she argues that Walker "continues the task of revising images of black women by taking the familiar and negatively constructed sexual images and imbuing them with power" (65). The fact that Celie, Shug, Sofia, and Squeak (Rae Dawn Chong) fashion a mutually beneficial, fundamentally supportive, and ultimately liberating female community as a counterbalance to the male brutality that surrounds them endows the book with a power that allows these women to move beyond "being dependent on men for emotional and economic support" (68). She makes a stark distinction between Walker's words and Spielberg's images.

For Bobo, Spielberg's most unforgivable transgression is to dilute these robust literary figures, replacing them with cliches and negative stereotypes, recycled caricatures from the mainstream media: Sofia becomes "the overbearing matriarchal figure . . . the castrating Amazon," Shug "the licentious cabaret singer . . . a victim of her insatiable sexual appetite [who] . . . longs for her preacher father's approval [and] regrets her life," and Celie simply "a victim of racism, sexism, and patriarchal privilege . . . an Orphan Annie" (68, 69, 73).

Although Spielberg, in his DVD interview, contends that the movie is "Celie's story, a woman's story, not Mister's," Bobo maintains that he turned

Critics attacked Spielberg for recycling Hollywood racial stereotypes in *The Color Purple* (1985), such as Sofia (Oprah Winfrey) as an overbearing maternal figure and castrating Amazon.

Walker's novel into "a chronicle of an abusive black man's journey toward self-understanding" (69). Resorting to these conventional formulations of character and plot, Spielberg harkens back to Hollywood's shameful history, and his film becomes a "revision to past racist works" (86). Although she admits that only "Spielberg could have obtained the financing to mount the kind of production that he did" (87), Bobo bemoans the fact that no Black woman has been "allowed to develop the track record" (87) of white male directors like Spielberg, and thus none could command the industry confidence and monetary clout to make *The Color Purple.*

Given her pejorative reading of the film, Bobo is astounded by the mostly favorable responses it has garnered from Black female viewers. How to account for such accolades for a film that "did not aid the cause of black women" (87)? She first attempts to explain this puzzling phenomenon by adopting the premise of the Marxist philosopher Louis Althusser, contending that the positive reactions were "another instance of certain audiences having been manipulated by the mechanisms of mainstream media into accepting its repressive ideology without question" (87). Somehow, these women "read against the grain of the film and reconstructed more satisfactory meanings" (90) than should have been expected in a movie that "portrayed black people disparagingly" (91). Bobo situates these "oppositional readings" within a history of Black women's resistance: "[I]t is a challenge to the mandate, given dominant media coverage, that black people should not have positive responses to the film" (92). In essence, the Black women who "clung tightly to their positive feelings about *The Color Purple*" (93) resisted the authoritative, sanctioned readings of the dominant media, not to mention of Bobo herself. Finally, she offers the possibility that "the pervasive absence of black people in the mainstream media" motivates Black audience members "to enjoy" rather than to "critically evaluate" works, thereby failing to "distinguish a harmful image from just the pleasure of seeing black women in roles other than comics or domestic workers" (128).

So which is it? Has Spielberg "manipulated" Black women into responding positively to a movie that belittles them, or is their enjoyment a radical act of "oppositional" reading? To my mind, the former implies being controlled and duped: a compliant viewer falls under the sway of powerful visual images and cannot dispute (or perhaps even distinguish) the negative ideas carried within them. Contention is not part of this process, nor is disputation or resistance. The latter response, however, explicitly incorporates a rejection of dominant readings and a conscious estrangement from the Black community and the white mainstream press. In this sense, the two ways of readings appear mutually exclusive, one grounded in acquiescent passivity, and the other in rebellious opposition. Bobo's third option—that these viewers derive pleasure merely from seeing a variety of Black women on the screen—suggests that Black women are so starved for representational images that they willingly and uncritically accept negative stereotypes and harmful cliches because these are the only things available to them. Again, this assumption sits far from a vigorous, consciously oppositional interpretation with implications for a radical reading of the text. In essence, Bobo insists that anyone who responds positively to *The Color Purple* must have been overpowered, deluded, or lacking in critical judgment.

Bobo ignores the most obvious possibility. Though her subjects consistently find "moments in the film that resonated with elements in their lives" (102), she never considers the possibility that—even with all the sins he commits against Walker's vision—Spielberg actually manages to make her book into an emotionally moving film, one that "resonated" with a broad range of Black women. Given their responses, one could easily conclude that these women fully recognized many of the negative issues raised by the film's critics, including Bobo herself, but that they found "Celie's urgency to fulfill her own destiny [and] to discover the things that belong to her self" (Collins 122) so touching that it counterbalanced their reservations and allowed them to negotiate a space within which they could enjoy the movie.

Although the film met with severe criticism, many viewers were deeply moved by Celie's (Whoopie Goldberg) struggle to overcome racism, a brutal husband, and the disruption of her family in *The Color Purple* (1985).

Such basic motivations never occur to Bobo. Given her own negative response to the film, she cannot understand why her subjects do not feel the same way. Joseph McBride gets closer to the truth when he observes that the director's "full-throated romantic mode of visual storytelling is not fashionable by the postmodernist standards of contemporary film criticism," a fact that often accounts for the gap between the "mass audience's often tearful enjoyment of a film such as *The Color Purple* and the distaste of critics who view any evocation of strong emotion as a form of directorial manipulation" (736).

"Steven has made a fantastic movie about the human experience," claims Whoopie Goldberg, defending *The Color Purple*. "There is not a 'mammy' or a 'nigger' in this film. I resent the fact that people think we actors would be involved in something that shows stereoptyed behavior. Do people think that neither I am capable of judging what's exploitative, nor Danny Glover nor Oprah Winfrey?" (Collins 124). Apparently, critics such as Brown, Early, and Bobo believe that the actors in the film, the people who enjoyed watching it, the woman who wrote the book upon which it was based, and the man who directed it are incapable of making such judgments. That said, I don't want to leave this portion of the conversation without stating that I agree with some of the criticisms leveled at this film, particularly those stated by Bobo at her most incisive. Though she consistently undervalues the emotional appeal of the film—as do many other critics who attack Spielberg throughout his career for being a simplistic manipulator of feelings—as well as its more positive feminist aspects, her comments offer perceptive insights about a variety of important issues that need further exploration and discussion, particularly how the director toned down Shug's brassy sexuality and eliminated Mister from the joyous reconciliation scene at the film's conclusion.

CONTROVERSY 2: SPIELBERG DISTORTS WALKER'S BOOK—SHUG'S DOMESTICATION In responding to challenges about his film's historical authenticity, Spielberg often cites Walker as his factual authority, thereby deflecting some of the slings and arrows back against those who originally launched them. When accused, for example, of transforming rural Georgia into an idealized pastoral setting and sprucing up the lives of Black people living there in the early years of the twentieth century, the director responds that his sets accurately re-created photographs supplied by the novelist and that some southern Blacks, including Walker's grandparents, had not resided in miserable poverty during this period. He argues that Walker's ancestors were financially successful, even considered wealthy, by the standards of the day.

Given this fact, Spielberg wryly notes that his detractors "had a kind of *Uncle Tom's Cabin* view . . . their own inclination for racial stereotyping, which is what some of the same people said we were guilty of" (Spielberg 14). Walker pointed out to the film's set and costume designers that "these particular black landowners did not dress in rags and could afford wallpaper," but she ultimately feels that everyone in the film was "too well-dressed" (Walker, *Same* 161). Similarly, although Spielberg incorporates the basic design of her grandparents' house into his design for Mister's home, his addition of columns, which Walker "lobbied against," turns that edifice into "the big house" (161). So while Spielberg based many of his creations on Walker's artifacts and remembrances, he embellished them beyond her expectations and recollections.

More substantial than these charges about set design and historical authenticity, Spielberg's detractors indict him for drastically attenuating Walker's sexually liberated stance by eliminating the overt and loving lesbian scenes between Celie and Shug. Given his acute discomfort with depicting any type of sexuality on the screen, Spielberg's decision to eliminate the more physically explicit scenes from the novel, such as when Shug convinces Celie to hold a mirror between her legs and examine herself, or when the women passionately kiss and caress each other, is unsurprising. Walker claims that it took her gentle insistence "'in talks with Menno, Steven, and Quincy, simply to include "the kiss," chaste as it was'" (qtd. in McBride 375–76). Instead of overt sexual scenes, Spielberg takes a more "poetic route" by substituting Shug's insistence that Celie take her hands away from her mouth and, for the first time in the film, smile openly. Shug's attentions enable her to accept herself as a woman, much as does her sexual awakening in the novel, and the women seal this scene of personal emancipation with a kiss that clearly indicates a sexual relationship, though with a discreet 1950s obliqueness rather than a 1980s frankness.

"I don't think a full-out love scene would say it any better," Spielberg contends on the DVD interview. In her interview on the DVD, Kathleen Kennedy, one of the film's producers and the person who first brought Walker's book to Spielberg's attention, says she believes that "the whole notion of anything that alludes to a same-sex relationship would have been considered borderline taboo at the time that we were making the movie." While Walker was initially "annoyed that there was not more cuddling and kissing and making love," she looks back (on the DVD interview) and concludes that this scene "was very, very well done because it captures the sweetness of their relationship." One does not need to be cynical to see that it also allowed Spielberg to keep the film's PG-13 rating, thus providing access to a wider audience than would have been possible with an R rating. Ultimately, Spielberg made an artistic, psychological, and marketing decision in depicting the physical connection between Shug and Celie obliquely. He conceptualizes the powerful bond between them as "a love relationship of great need. No one had ever loved Celie other than God and her sister. And here Celie is being introduced to the human race by a person full of love" (Collins 124). Yet his downplaying of their physical relationship elicits criticism from those who claim he showed too much and those who assert that he did not go far enough.

Along with constraining the love scenes between Celie and Shug, Spielberg made two significant alterations to the spirit of Walker's novel that overtly demonstrate his persistent psychological drives and tie *The Color Purple* securely to his other works: the inclusion of Shug's father (John Patton Jr.), and the refusal to reconcile Mister with Celie. Shug's intense desire to be loved and accepted by her minister father does, as many critics contend, domesticate the sexy jazz singer; her desperate need to gain his approval reinforces the practice and power of patriarchal privilege that the book, and sometimes the movie, seeks to expose and undermine. In the novel, Walker emphasizes Shug's "completely unapologetic self-acceptance as an outlaw, renegade, rebel, and pagan; her zest in loving both women and men, younger and older" (Walker, *Same* 35). In the movie, distinctly opposite to this rebellious exuberance, "Shug is seen as someone who regrets the life she has lived and who assents to others' perception of her as a loose woman. Her constant quest for absolution from her preacher father takes away her central source of power in the novel—that she does what she wants and has the economic means to do so" (Bobo 68). This "disempowerment" becomes evident early in the movie.

During the sequence entitled "Shug's bath," a time when the singer must recover from physical illness and spiritual depravation, she reveals the emotional frailness lurking beneath her bravado. It opens with jazz music from a Victrola filling the room as Celie obsequiously attends Shug, adding hot water and bubble oil as the singer belittles her. We view Shug from behind the metal tub, her hands holding a bottle of whiskey and a cigarette, her voice heard before we see her face: "What you staring at?" she barks at Celie. "Never seen a naked woman before?" Almost immediately, the singer turns the talk toward children, interrogating Celie about where hers might be. "You got kids?" asks Celie tentatively responding. "Yeah," says Shug. "They with my ma and pa. Never knowed a child to come out right unless there's a man around. Children gots to have a pa. Your pa love you? My pa loves me. My pa still loves me. 'Cept he don't know it. He don't know it." Shug entwines childhood and motherhood with the yearning for a masculine presence and recognizes the lack of such a figure in her life; slowly, she sinks back into the water, convulsed in tears of pain and sobs of regret. Celie, mesmerized but sensing Shug's need for warmth and human contact, begins gently to brush her hair. Lingering in her past for a moment longer, Shug melts into the rhythms of the brush strokes and begins to hum snatches of a melody that will eventually become "Miss Celie's Blues."

This poignant moment of contact between Celie and Shug—two women whose children have been taken away from them, whose fathers have either abandoned or raped them (as we believe at this point), and who have suffered irreparable emotional trauma inflicted by their fathers—sets the tone for the rest of the movie. It indelibly defines Shug's character. From this point on, even when we see her provocatively gyrating in her shimmering red dress and belting out lusty lyrics in Harpo's juke joint, we understand that a fundamental sadness pervades her life, a grief that no music can drown out and a thirst that no whiskey can quench. This moment also plants the seeds for Celie's eventual liberation. For the first time since Mister brutally separated her from Nettie, Celie feels something for someone else. She has seen pictures of Shug before, since Mister keeps one prominently displayed in their bedroom. But as she stares into this woman's face, a moment of quiet reverence steals over her, a calm that blossoms into love despite the awkward situation. Shug's appreciation of Celie's kindness and warmth will evolve into a deeply reciprocal love. Only by seeing herself through Shug's eyes will Celie come to recognize herself as a person of worth and substance and, as a result, attain the inner strength to escape the physical and psychological oppression represented by Mister.

As the film progresses, Shug becomes more and more traditional in her dress and actions. Recovering from her illness—clothed conservatively in a light purple outfit, her hair pulled back and tucked neatly under a large hat with a prominent bow, and carrying a pink parasol—she attempts to visit her father in his empty church. "What life like for her?" wonders Celie as she shyly follows Shug down the country road. "And why she sometime gets so sad? So sad just like me." Greeting her father tentatively, Shug tells him that she has been sick, that she is better now, and that she is staying down the road with Albert and Celie. He continues sweeping the church, never looking at her or acknowledging her presence. Finally, he sits down, his broad back to his daughter. "This place brings back memories," she tells him, revealing how she watched him in church, "the best preacher in the world." She continues to inch tentatively forward, the camera sometimes capturing them in a tense two shot and other times alternating between her face and his back. As she offers him some snatches from the gospel songs she once sang in his choir, her father slowly gets up and heads toward the back door. "It's alright," says Shug, retreating in the opposite direction. "I know you can't say nothing to me anymore 'cause things so different. Just thought I would stop and say hello." They leave through separate exits, shutting doors and closing themselves off from each other.

After her marriage, Shug and her husband Grady pay a surprise visit to Celie and Mister, both of whom are disappointed and somewhat bewildered by her new status as a wife. No longer does she resemble the raucous singer who shimmied in sparkling red sequins and outlandish headdresses, packed Harpo's juke joint, and nearly caused men to faint with lust and mutter how they would "drink her bathwater." She looks like a conservative, middle-class lady, her mid-calf blue dress and straightened hair evidence of a newly acquired sense of respectability and modest comportment. She even smokes cigarettes through a fancy holder, though her desperation for fatherly acceptance remains unfiltered. Unexpectedly, her father drives his horse and buggy past Mister's house, his outmoded vehicle and dark suit in stark contrast to Grady's snazzy yellow convertible and vivid clothes. Shug breaks into a smile, then trots hopefully out to the road to greet him. "I's married now," she yells out, holding up her hand and pointing to the ring on her finger. Silence. "I said I's married now," she calls after him, as he whips his horse and drives past her without a word or a glance in her direction. The smile fades from her face. Dejected, she lowers her hand, stares forlornly at the gold band encircling her finger, and softly begins to hum "Sister" as she approaches the mailbox and retrieves the letter that will lead to Celie's liberation.

Shug's reconciliation with her father comes, not surprisingly, through music. But it follows an important scene taken almost verbatim from Walker's novel, though with less pantheistic emphasis and without her character's bitterness about "Man corrupting everything" (Walker, *Color* 168). Celie and Shug casually stroll amidst a frame filled with exuberant purple flowers. "More than anything," Shug tells Celie, who trails after her holding a umbrella to shade herself from the sun, "God loves admiration. . . . I think it pisses God off if you walk by the color purple in a field somewhere and you don't notice it." Celie responds hesitantly, "Are you saying it just want to be loved like it say in the Bible?" "Yeah," responds Shug. "Everything want to be loved. Us sing and dance and holler just trying to be loved. . . . Oh, Miss Celie, I feels like singin'!" Interestingly, Spielberg keeps his distance from the characters in this crucial scene. We see them only from the waist up in the midground of the frame, the fore- and backgrounds filled with flowers. Instead of concentrating on their faces as they utter these words, he lingers on their surroundings, creating a moment in which the words seem more like voiceovers than dialogue. Here, as elsewhere, the director focuses on the visual and emotional import of the language as mediated through the images, on the visceral connection between sights and sounds.

The reconciliation scene between Shug and her father begins with ostracism: Mister sits rocking alone on the front porch, banished for his litany of sins. He never utters a word in the film again. He has lost his voice. As so often happens in this film, we hear characters before we see them: the sound of Shug singing "Sister" wafts over the forlorn and isolated figure of Mister before Spielberg brings us to the crowded site of her musical performance. This time, however, the joint and Shug have noticeably changed. No longer is she solely the focus of heated masculine gazes. In fact, the scene begins with well-dressed men and (conspicuously absent earlier) women swaying to her voice, as Harpo lowers the drawbridge between his place and the mainland. Dressed conservatively in a long, pale yellow dress with matching earrings and holding a bouquet of purple flowers in one hand and a blue handkerchief in the other, Shug continues to croon as Spielberg crosscuts between the juke joint and her father's Sunday church service. "All of us been prodigal children at one time or another," booms the preacher from his pulpit. "And I tell you, children, it's possible for the Lord to drive you home. To drive you home to truth. And he can fix things for you if you trust him." But his flock is already distracted. Hearing the sweet sounds of Shug's music, they fidget on the hard wooden benches, craning their necks toward the music flowing from Harpo's.

Sensing their dwindling attention, the preacher turns to the choir standing behind him who, dressed in white robes with collars nearly replicating the color of Shug's dress, rise to his call and harmoniously answer "yessss." Cut back to Shug, who hears the faint music emanating from her father's church, as his congregation just heard hers. She pauses for a moment, the past calling out to her, the prodigal child of her father's sermon. The jazz music slides to a halt, and the choir's blended voices fill Harpo's now-silent building. Cut back to the church. "If I were you I would say yes," belts out the lead singer, a young Black woman who holds the place no doubt once occupied by Shug. Cut back to Shug. "Speak, Lord," she sings, as we hear the choir singer echo the same phrase from across the river. "Speak to me," she continues. Quick cut to Mister, a smile playing across his lips. Again, her words are echoed by the church choir: "I was so lost until He spoke to me." Now the people pour out of Harpo's, cross the drawbridge, and head toward the church with Shug leading them. "Oh speak, Lord, speak to me," belts out Shug, as she guides the crowd through the dark woods and toward the plain white church. Spielberg continues to crosscut between the choir, who slowly become aware of another voice, and Shug; they occupy different frames but now seem to be singing together. Finally, her father recognizes the voice from outside, struck dumb by hearing it enter his sanctuary. "Oh, you can't sleep at night," sings both Shug and the choir leader. Finally, Shug throws open the doors to the church she had so sadly closed earlier in the film. "Maybe God is trying to tell you something," she sings out, as she and her father finally face each other across a painful divide.

As the patrons of the juke joint stream into the church, clapping and singing joyously along with Shug, she looks directly into her father's eyes and continues to implore him through her lyrics: "Maybe God is trying to tell you something," she repeats again and again. "Save me." The preacher gingerly removes his glasses to see his daughter more clearly, the woman standing before him, not the girl who defied him. "I praise your name," sings Shug, the choir responding, "God's trying to tell you something." Slowly, the preacher slips from behind the pulpit. As father and child stare at each other in a shot/countershot structure, Shug at last falls silent. As earlier, we see the preacher's back, but this time his daughter stands fully present in the same frame, momentarily caught in his gaze and her need. She rushes forward to hug him, tears streaming down her cheeks. "See, Daddy," she whispers into his ear, "sinners have soul, too." The preacher slowly raises his arms, still a bit uncertain about how to respond to the woman clinging tightly to him. Then he returns her embrace, Shug's face breaking into a broad smile of happiness and relief. The church erupts into even louder song, the patrons of the juke joint freely mixing with those in the congregation. Only Celie, in a close-up, remains silent. Though a small smile forms on the edge of her mouth, she remains apart from the celebration, perhaps remembering the cruelties of her own father, her pain at the hands of Mister, and her still-absent family.

This scene provides a good example of why some viewers feel emotionally moved by Spielberg's films, while others harshly reject his overt sentimentality and conservatism. Remember, first, that the preacher as a character is wholly Spielberg's invention and not found in the Walker novel. Depicting a daughter singing a gospel song about God the Father, while at the same time imploring her biological father to forgive her, surely provides ammunition for those who label Spielberg a reactionary filmmaker who merges religious obedience and patriarchal submission into a single moment. Yet the archetypal union of a child with a parent, here depicted as a spectacle witnessed and shared by the surrounding community (which is simultaneously joined together as well) possesses an almost irresistible visual power heightened even further by the mixture of Black musical traditions that permeates the scene. The action resembles a Vincente Minnelli musical number more than it does any other part of the film's narrative, but it simultaneously demonstrates Spielberg's sustained thematic obsessions, proficiency at finding unique ways to express them, and mastery of engaging audiences in them.

CONTROVERSY 3: SPIELBERG DISTORTS WALKER'S BOOK—MISTER'S OSTRACISM As the music continues on the soundtrack in the reconciliation scene between Shug and the preacher, Spielberg cuts back to a close-up of Mister's hand as he opens the mailbox and reads the return address on the letter it contains: U.S. Naturalization and Immigration Service / Washington, D.C., / Important Official Mail. To the sounds of the gospel hymn he turns, digs up his hidden strong box, retrieves his money, journeys to the office from whence the letter came, and pays the funds necessary to bring Celie's children and sister back to America. This is Mister's act of contrition, his attempt to earn Celie's forgiveness and perhaps even his own redemption. But it will prove to no avail. In the final scene, all the film's major characters gather on the porch or in the front yard of Celie's house: Squeak and Shug, Harpo and Sofia. Across a field of purple flowers, Celie spots a group of Black men and women standing beside their overloaded car. Their brightly colored pink and purple scarves billow upward in the breeze. Slowly, and then more rapidly, she realizes who it is: "Nettieeeeeee!" she screams, dragging out the last vowel and running through the field toward her long-lost sister and, as she is soon to discover, her children as well.

Mister, who makes this touching reunion possible, is never allowed back into the family fold dominated by women. Following Shug's glance into the field, we catch a glimpse of him, standing beside his horse, as Celie's joyful reunion continues. He watches the events, breathes a sigh, drops his head slightly downward, and smiles to himself. Spielberg situates Mister in long shot beyond the field of purple flowers, not in it. The film's final image shows Celie and Nettie replaying their childhood clapping game as the lengthening shadows of the setting sun grow deeper behind them. Mister, silently leading his horse, slips by them in the foreground, never glancing at them and receiving no hint of recognition in return. In *The Same River Twice* (and repeated again in her DVD interview), Walker regrets "that Mister was not 'forgiven' by Steven as he was by me" (41) and proclaims that "the ending was moving. But I wanted Mister up on the porch too!" (161). At the end of Walker's novel, Celie and Mister sit together "seeing and talking and smoking our pipes" (230). In his DVD interview, Spielberg claims that he saw Mister not as "a villain but as a victim. A victim of his father. A victim of his era." He contends that the film contains a moment of silent forgiveness as Mister stands in the darkened street outside Celie's pants shop, but this moment barely registers a glimmer of forgiveness.

In a very real sense, Spielberg's film is both more conservative and less compassionate than Walker's novel. His inclusion of a strong patriarchal presence in Shug's life undercuts her rebellion and, at times, tames her outlandish spirit. Bobo correctly concludes that "instead of a woman who lives her life according to the dictates of her value system . . . the film version of Shug is obsessed with winning her father's approval" (69). The film thus "casts a moral judgment on Shug," and in the reconciliation scene her song is one "of repentance" (72). Spielberg's refusal to incorporate a contrite Mister into the final family reunion speaks of his deep anger, perhaps touching upon his own psychological relationship with his often absent father. Here Bobo misses the point entirely when she claims that "the black female characters . . . are displaced as the center of the story. The film is a chronicle of an abusive black man's journey toward self-understanding. . . . The film grants the male protagonist salvation because he has arranged for a happy ending for the woman he misused throughout the film" (69). Quite the opposite, Celie's journey from abuse to independence remains Spielberg's clear and consistent focus, and no hint of "salvation" filters into his portrayal of Mister, who is less accepted than in Walker's book.

CONCLUSION

I have purposely conjoined Spielberg's version of *The Color Purple* with the novel upon which it is based and the woman who wrote it because at no other point in his career did he approach a literary work with such reverence or collaborate so closely with an author he respected. Yet despite these facts, Spielberg still infuses the work with his overriding personal concerns. Along with a number of other critics, Bobo ultimately castigates him for creating a production "in line with Steven Spielberg's experiences, cultural background, and social and political worldview. . . . He tapped into his consciousness and experiences and produced a work that was in keeping with his philosophy and knowledge of Hollywood films about black people" (76). But what kind of artist would he be if he didn't make a Steven Spielberg film?

Bobo condemns him for incorporating his persistent thematic preoccupations into his interpretation of Walker's text; I would contend that such acts are inevitable for creative directors who base films on novels. Unlike Bobo, I believe that Spielberg's characters in *The Color Purple* often transcend racial stereotypes, but her statements offer a congruent articulation of my fundamental approach to the director's work.

The best film adaptations seek the spirit rather than the letter of their source. Transferring that spirit to the screen often demands violating the letter of the work. This is one reason for the standard critical assumption that the better the novel the worse the film. As the director Lewis Milestone observes: "If you want to produce a rose, you will not take the flower and put it into the earth. This would not result in another rose. Instead, you will take the seed and stick it into the soil. From it will grow a rose. It's the same with film adaptation" (qtd. in Friedman, "Blasted" 60). Take, for example, a classic example of this process. If Akira Kurosawa's *Throne of Blood* (1957) were judged by how well it reproduces the events in Shakespeare's *Macbeth,* it might be deemed a rather poor attempt. But once we examine the themes and moods of Shakespeare's drama and then analyze how Kurosawa uses cinematic devices to re-create those ideas and feelings visually, we can easily see that, far from being a weak adaption, *Throne of Blood* remains faithful to the spirit and meaning of the play. The best directors become not illustrators of the written text but artists who draw inspiration from original sources, as Shakespeare himself drew from the *Holinshed Chronicles.* All adaptations offer subjective responses to their primary sources. In this sense, artists can never fully duplicate the Black experience in the early twentieth-century South but simply mediate it through their own eyes. If one wants Walker's vision of that time, then he or she should read the novel. If one wants Steven Spielberg's interpretation of Walker, then he or she should see the film.

Few would contend that *The Color Purple* stands as one of Spielberg's best films; but in light of his subsequent career, it was necessary for him to attempt such a challenging project to move forward as an artist. Ultimately, the ambitious movie fails because the director does not seem to trust himself or, at times, to allow his images to carry the narrative. The frames are too loaded, the music too intrusive, the action too overblown, the comedy too broad, and the film simply too long. Yet some scenes are undeniably powerful, particularly the ripping apart of Celie and Nettie, the sadness of Sofia's first homecoming and her ultimate resurrection, the frightening brutality of Mister, and the joyful reunion of Celie with her family. And Spielberg elicits marvelous performances from two first-time actors, Whoopie Goldberg and

Oprah Winfrey. The reception to *The Color Purple* left Spielberg with some deep scars. The film received eleven Academy Award nominations, though Spielberg was not selected to compete in the Best Director category. It won no Oscars, while an intrinsically more racist film, *Out of Africa,* captured the statuette for Best Picture. Spielberg did obtain some consolation by winning the Director's Guild of America Award. Most importantly, however, the film's reception and controversies neither deterred him from making another predominately Black film nor prevented him from tackling more complex and demanding subjects.

Amistad: Beyond the Screen

Given the withering criticisms and hostile responses that greeted his first attempt to deal with the Black experience in America, Spielberg easily might have resolved to swim clear of such projects: "'I got such a bollocking for *The Color Purple* I thought, I'll never do that again'" (qtd. in Phillips 42). Yet, twelve years later, he plunged into these turbulent waters once again. When the producer and choreographer Debbie Allen approached him with the idea to make a film about the 1839 revolt of fifty-three slaves aboard the Spanish ship *La Amistad* off the Cuban coast and their subsequent trial, Spielberg listened intently, impressed with her passion for the project. Allen had become fascinated with the story after chancing upon two volumes of essays on the incident. Consequently, she bought the film rights to William Owens's definitive history, *Black Mutiny: The Revolt on the Schooner Amistad,* although her attempts to secure funding over the next ten years sparked little interest in Hollywood. As Allen tells the story on the special features section of the *Amistad* DVD, "I saw *Schindler's List* and thought Steven Spielberg would understand the story and help me get this done." More to the point, she believes that "'nobody else could have gotten any studio to say yes to this project. Nobody else would touch it'" (qtd. in Phillips 42). What she didn't know was that she approached Spielberg at a moment in his personal and professional life that made him very receptive to her pitch.

The director had just finished *The Lost World,* a by-the-numbers project that held little personal interest and made few artistic demands upon him, but which fulfilled his contractual obligation to Universal for a *Jurassic Park* sequel. He was not yet ready to begin shooting *Saving Private Ryan.* Emotionally fortified by the overwhelming critical and popular success of *Schindler's List,* Spielberg could finally ignore the frightening voices that "whispered in my ear telling me to let Francis [Ford Coppola] or Marty [Scorsese] do the personal film. I was the circus master. I should just stay in the ring, in my space" (qtd. in Phillips 42). At home, his son Theo, an African American foster child originally adopted by Kate Capshaw and then by Spielberg after their marriage (the couple later adopted another African American child, Mikaela George), was starting to ask questions about his heritage: "So when I heard the story, I immediately thought that this was something that I would be pretty proud to make, simply to say to my son, 'Look, this is about you'" (Dubner 231). Perhaps Spielberg still smarted from the critical drubbing that followed the release of *The Color Purple* and wanted to show his detractors that he could make a powerful movie about Black people in American society. Finally, such a prestigious project seemed the perfect vehicle for his first film under the banner of the newly created DreamWorks SKG, a Hollywood studio he founded along with the former Disney executive Jeffrey Katzenberg and the recording mogul David Geffen.

Amistad proved even less popular with the moviegoing public than *The Color Purple:* the earlier film earned ninety-four million dollars in the United States and $142 million worldwide; *Amistad* grossed only forty-four million dollars in American box offices, earning an additional $16.2 million beyond its shores (Freer 152, 258). *Amistad* holds the dubious distinction of being Spielberg's worst financial failure, falling below worldwide figures for *Empire of the Sun* ($66.7 million), *Always* ($77.1 million), and *1941* ($90 million). Nominated for Oscars in four categories—Best Supporting Actor (Anthony Hopkins), Costume Design (Ruth Carter), Musical Score (John Williams), and Cinematography (Janusz Kaminski)—the film won no awards. *Amistad* struck no responsive chord in the Black community, and Julie Roy Jeffrey cites evidence that "black audiences were intensely negative—though not always in public" (12). Warrington Hudlin, the president of the Black Filmmakers foundation, offers one explanation for the film's failure in his community: "'It's no wonder black people don't want to go to this movie. Only a masochist would want to spend two hours watching themselves be degraded and dehumanized'" (qtd. in Jeffrey 12). As far as white audiences were concerned, a writer in the *New York Times* claimed that they were "'just tired of the whole subject'" (qtd. in Jeffrey 13). Spielberg, often the best critic of his own work, suggested this succinct reason for the film's failure to ignite much enthusiasm: "'I kind of dried it out and it became too much of a history lesson'" (qtd. in Freer 258).

THE REVOLT

If Spielberg thought the impressive roster of African American academics he assembled as advisors to the movie would function as a protective firewall, securing *Amistad* from the controversies that short-circuited *The Color Purple,* he was sadly mistaken. The rising chorus of negative responses was even more intense and widespread, and the stakes were even higher. This time, Spielberg was not adapting a beloved work of fiction but pictorializing a cherished—perhaps even sacred—moment in Black history: the only time that enslaved Africans in the United States were set free via the legal system and returned home. Historians attacked the film's authenticity from almost every imaginable angle. Many of their objections focused on seemingly inconsequential issues: men did not wear beards and mustaches in the United States during the early 1840s; snow was not falling on Long Island when *La Amistad* was seized; the ages of some characters (particularly Roger Baldwin) were altered significantly; the Capital Dome appears, even though it was built during the Civil War; only seven of the nine Supreme Court judges were present during the case; the position of President Martin Van Buren was distorted; Cinque and John Quincy Adams met not in the ex-president's home but in Westville (Connecticut) Prison in November 1840; Cinque was not in Washington for the hearings; Cinque spoke better English than is depicted in the film; and Adams's speech before the justices lasted far longer than in the film.

Other critics, such as Gary Rosen, assail Spielberg for the "denigration of Christianity, especially of the white, Protestant variety" (242). Because the director ignores the militant evangelical abolitionist organizations that raised funds, marshaled public awareness, and arranged legal counsel for the Africans, Rosen finds him guilty of reverse racism, an indulgence of political correctness that gives "blacks a prominence and importance they did not have while distorting or denying the role of whites" (247). Ultimately, argues Rosen, Spielberg "misrepresented, in a way that can only be intentional, the racial relations that form the very heart of the events he depicts. . . . [The film] will long contribute to making it harder and harder for us to tell the truth, either about our history or ourselves" (242, 248). Similarly, Warren Goldstein reproaches Spielberg for downplaying the role of religious faith in this story. Noting that "abolitionism was a brave, dangerous calling," he bemoans that "in its place, we find only Lewis Tappan . . . who is shown (falsely and shamefully) as willing to see the Africans sacrificed as martyrs to his cause—along with a wholly fictional black abolitionist . . . who says little but appears profound" (A64). Such comments dominate the discourse surrounding *Amistad* in the popular press and scholarly publications.

According to their various interviews and comments, Spielberg, Allen, and the scriptwriter David Franzoni consciously chose to downplay the role of the white abolitionists and to concentrate on the Africans, particularly the charismatic Cinque. "'Most movies that deal with slavery are unintentionally racist,'" said Franzoni, "'because inevitably the whites waged the good fight to liberate the black man'" (qtd. in Jeffrey 5). Those involved in creating *Amistad* tried to reverse this well-meaning but ultimately infantilizing Hollywood narrative structure so common in films such as *Cry Freedom* (1987), *Glory* (1989), and *Mississippi Burning* (1988). Franzoni claims that *Amistad* should not be viewed as a movie about a group of Blacks saved by two white lawyers:

> "My take, and the take that was followed, was that Cinque . . . saves John Quincy Adams, just as Adams saves him. . . . Cinque freed Adams by getting him to the Supreme Court where he could finally rage against slavery and so carry on the work of his father." (Qtd. in Jeffrey 14)

Cinque (Djimon Hounsou) and his fellow captives are charged with piracy and murder after their shipboard rebellion in *Amistad* (1997).

Similarly, Allen maintains that "'the Africans uplift everyone. They uplift the Supreme Court, who were just about all pro-slavers, to make that decision. And they uplift the abolitionists, a disenfranchised group who then have an image to come together with'" (qtd. in Jeffrey 14).

Despite these intentions, many commentators saw *Amistad* in a far less benevolent light. Catherine Kodat, for example, initially places the film "on the cinematic and ideological continuum that began with *The Birth of a Nation*" (80). Like Rosen and Goldstein, she chastises Spielberg for discrediting the abolitionist movement and ignoring evangelical Protestantism, though she recognizes that he probably did so "in a well-intentioned effort to keep the focus on Cinque and his fellow captives" (83). That attempt fails, she contends, because "*Amistad* shifts all its emotional and dramatic ballast onto John Quincy Adams" (83). Adams's appeal to America's Founding Fathers (including his own) and "the primacy of the lofty idealism of the Declaration of Independence" (84) elides the fact that "slavery *was* integral to the founding of this country" (85). Therefore, *Amistad* provides a striking example of how modern ideologies shape our interpretation of historical events, "constructing renewed credibility for (and shoring up ideological justification of) continued American global dominance" (79). Arriving at such a conclusion, Kodat's article provides an illustrative example of how scholarly indictments of Spielberg's supposedly conservative ideology continued unabated from the 1980s into the 1990s.

Kodat's positing of *The Birth of a Nation* as *Amistad*'s cinematic ancestor remains more hyperbolic rhetoric than realistic appraisal. If anything, Spielberg's most overt fabrications "come from a wish to make patterns of alliance and friendship in New England in 1839–40 resemble egalitarian hopes in late twentieth-century America" (Davis 128). Spielberg consciously threads a careful path between respecting the broad outlines of historical events and avoiding the dismal portrayals of Black people in American cinema. By illustrating how Cinque plants the seeds for his own defense in a visit with Adams, the filmmaker provides a cogent example of how the Africans assume responsibility for their own destiny, thereby demonstrating their intelligence. Cinque's bitter condemnation of the American legal system goes further. Rising up in indignant fury when told that the case must be retried before the Supreme Court, he roars out his anger: "What kind of land is this where you *almost* mean what you say? Where laws *almost* work?" An equally disparaging moment occurs earlier when an opulent pleasure craft, brimming with well-dressed passengers enjoying a sumptuous candlelight dinner serenaded by a trio of classical musicians, glides past the desperate Africans aboard *La*

Amistad. Words are not needed to reinforce the cruel differentials between the "passengers" on these vessels. Surely, such scenes remove *Amistad* from any continuum with D. W. Griffith's romanticized depiction of the Ku Klux Klan and his uncritical endorsement of southern white privilege.

In the most lenient appraisal of the movie's factual inaccuracies, Robert Brent Toplin cites Spielberg's involvement with DreamWorks and his on-location filming of *Saving Private Ryan,* the former during the development of *Amistad* and the latter during its editing, concluding that "under the circumstances Spielberg could not deliver his best" (75). Nonetheless, he praises Spielberg for creating "some impressive dramatic moments" (70), displaying the Middle Passage more realistically than any Hollywood film before it (70), demonstrating "great appreciation of the Africans' cultural diversity" (76), adding authenticity by having "African-born actors speak in native dialect" (76), and illuminating complex issues of slavery law (76). Finally, however, Toplin concludes that Spielberg manipulated "so many elements for dramatic effect that they undermined the overall truthfulness of their historical interpretations. . . . It was the accumulation of many objections to the film's historical details that wrecked confidence in the movie's storytelling" (69, 75). He insists that the most significant problems with *Amistad* lay in its lack of a dramatic structure, its failure to provide a principle villain, and its attempt "to cover too many facets of history briefly" (78) rather than in any corruption of the facts. For Toplin, Spielberg's failure was as an artist rather than as a historian.

Most significantly, historians rebuked Spielberg for overemphasizing the importance of the *Amistad* case in American history; they accused him of distorting the Supreme Court's extremely limited decision, thereby twisting the 1841 ruling into a broad antislavery triumph with little basis in reality. As noted by many commentators, the Court freed the Africans based on technicalities within the context of the slave trade, not on universal principles of liberty and justice. The judgment never rested upon the lofty foundation that the Africans were free men or guaranteed liberty by virtue of simply being human beings, but rather that "they had not become property legally" (Kodat 82). In many ways, the Supreme Court actually reaffirmed slavery as a legally recognized institution. Thus, in the opinion of most historians, the *Amistad* case was not a precedent-setting victory for abolitionism and had no direct connection to the Civil War, as implied in the film. Though the artist presenting a historical event is never free from the constraints of authenticity, his or her attention to detail is usually not the highest priority, as it is for the historian. Such fundamental distinctions become evident when professional historians judge popular movies.

AMISTAD AND E.T.

On a structural level, the film that *Amistad* most resembles is *E.T.* The majority of citizens in Spielberg's nineteenth-century America regard the captured Africans with the same mixture of astonishment, fear, and fascination as his twentieth-century Americans do the diminutive being from outer space; conversely, Cinque (Djimon Hounsou) and E.T. each find the culture they are forced to inhabit a confusing and often dangerous environment. Other similarities abound: both figures are distinctly different colors than most of those who surround them; both have trouble communicating and struggle to make themselves understood; both learn valuable cultural lessons from mass-produced narratives (books in *Amistad* and televised movies in *E.T.*); both adopt new customs to survive; both are surrounded by an overwhelmingly male world; both find sympathetic liberators who aid them; both are incarcerated by governmental representatives; both share essential values with those who seem initially dissimilar; and both are driven by an intense desire to return to their homeland. Spielberg invariably conceptualizes those who personify "otherness" as possessing identical core values as those understood to represent "us": they are socially acceptable minorities. E.T. and Cinque ultimately display the same compelling love of family, wish to "go home," and desire to be free as those characters who initially perceive them as strange and alien beings. While Kodat (repeating Andrew Britton's earlier charge) sees this aspect of Spielberg's work as fundamentally racist, it belongs more appropriately in the realm of humanistic idealism, a sincere belief that sentient beings share common desires and aspirations that, once recognized beneath surface differences, draw seemingly disparate figures together by virtue of mutual respect and understanding.

There does, however, remain one startling narrative difference between *E.T.* and *Amistad:* their endings. *E.T.* concludes with the tearful parting of Elliott and his alien friend, a bittersweet moment that nonetheless feels more happy than sad. E.T. achieves his ultimate objective and returns home. In *Amistad,* historical events end positively: the freeing of the Africans, the British destroying the Lomboko slave fortress and liberating its inmates, Harrison defeating Van Buren for the presidency, the Africans sailing homeward, and the Confederate army losing the battle of Atlanta. But, as the titles tell us, the dark "alien" at the center of this film will face misery upon his arrival home:

"Cinque returned to Sierra Leone to find his own people engaged in civil war. His village was destroyed and his family gone. It is believed they were sold into slavery." It would have been easy for Spielberg to close the film on a less ambiguous and less ironic note, and Cinque's loss is read rather than shown. But the filmmaker chooses to leaven the gratifying moment aboard ship with intimations of personal tragedy. Spielberg has clearly learned that victories always entail losses and that gaining one's objective does not ensure happiness.

THE FATHERS

The surface narratives of action and adventure that engage Spielberg's characters inevitably intersect with equally threatening internal quests, particularly the need to reconcile familial disruptions. This recurrent psychological drive manifests itself in an urgent compulsion to reconstitute broken families by repairing shattered relationships, as in *Hook, Minority Report, Indiana Jones and the Last Crusade,* and *E.T.* Alternatively, it results in the formulation of substitute, ad hoc combinations of adults and children designed to combat external threats, such as those in *Jurassic Park, Close Encounters of the Third Kind, Empire of the Sun, Schindler's List,* and *The Color Purple.* In *Amistad,* this obsessional thematic and structural pattern functions on multiple levels, ranging from the individual to the national. In essence, the film conceptualizes the United States of 1839 as a dysfunctional family ripped apart by bitter disputes about slavery. Not surprisingly, given his earlier works, Spielberg seeks guidance in the words of the Founding Fathers, who conceived of America as a radically different place than the Europe of their forebears.

Early in the film, John Quincy Adams (Anthony Hopkins) rejects Theodore Joadson's (Morgan Freeman) ardent plea that he join their cause. Joadson, a composite figure fashioned on emancipated African Americans such as James Pennington, Henry Highland Garnat, and David Walker who dedicated their time, money, and energy to liberate their less fortunate brethren, calls upon the frail ex-president to finish the work begun by his father(s):

> Sir, I know you and your presidency as well as any man. And your father's. You were a child at his side when he helped invent America. And you in turn have devoted your life to refining that noble invention. There remains but one task undone. One vital task the Founding Fathers left to their sons before their thirteen colonies could precisely be called United States. And that task, sir, as you well know, is crushing slavery.

Later, Cinque invokes his own familial tradition for strength and guidance. "We have my ancestors on our side," he tells Adams. "I will call into the past, far back to the beginning of time, and beg them to come and help me at the judgment. I will reach back and draw them into me. For at this moment, I am the whole reason they have existed at all." Inspired by Cinque's reach backwards into his history and heritage, Adams points around the Supreme Court chambers to the busts of Franklin, Madison, Jefferson, Hamilton, Washington, and his own father, and declares:

> We understand now, we have been made to understand, and to embrace that understanding, that who we are *is* who we were. We desperately need your strength and wisdom to triumph over our fears, our prejudices, ourselves. Give us the courage to do what is right. And if it means Civil War, then let it come. And when it does, may it be finally the last battle of the American Revolution.

This invocation of America's Founding Fathers prompted by Cinque's summoning of his forebears, at least as far as the film is concerned, moves the Supreme Court to free the other African prisoners and send them home.

"We have our ancestors on our side," Cinque (Djimon Hounsou) tells former President John Quincy Adams (Anthony Hopkins) with the help of his Mende translator, James Covey (Chiwetel Ejiofor), before his trial in *Amistad* (1997).

Critics attacked Spielberg for emphasizing this particular portion of Adams's original speech, particularly for focusing on a relatively minor aspect of the former president's lengthy argument (seven hours, spread over two days): "[W]hat in the original speech were little more than passing glances at the Declaration of Independence are made in the film to bear the entire philosophical burden of the defense" (Kodat 81). In addition, as many noted, several of the Founding Fathers to whom Adams defers owned slaves themselves. Adams's speech paints an idealized portrait of American history, one more indebted to the spirit of Frank Capra's *Mr. Smith Goes to Washington* (1939) than to historical documents. Both movies acknowledge the underbelly of American politics, Capra's with the corruption of Senator Joe Paine (Claude Rains) by Boss Jim Taylor (Edward Arnold), and Spielberg's with the venal racism of John C. Calhoun (Arliss Howard) and pandering cowardice of President Martin Van Buren (Nigel Hawthorne). Yet in each case, the vision of America at its best triumphs over the grinding denigration of its most cherished ideals. When reminded of the underlying principles muddied by standard governmental practice—in Capra by the naive Jefferson Smith (James Stewart), and in Spielberg by the noble Cinque and the eloquent John Quincy Adams—those who have fallen from grace are inspired to act in accordance with the highest morality: to admit their guilt (Capra), and to set free the Africans (Spielberg). Spielberg's goal is not to present a subtle or totally accurate documentary of historical events (as does Howard Jones) but rather to dramatize a moment in the past when the dream became flesh and to kindle a desire in the present to live up to the loftiest promises of this "noble invention."

VISUAL ELEMENTS

With its bleak exteriors and murky prison sequences, *Amistad* resembles little else in Spielberg's canon. Ian Freer observes that the director purposely restricts his camera movements, noting that "there are only three dolly moves in the whole movie—two moves toward Adams, one into Cinque" (255). To capture the violent and frenzied scenes aboard *La Amistad*, Spielberg utilizes flashing montages, but the rest of the film—particularly the courtroom scenes—remains far more static, as if one is watching a play rather than a movie. Kaminski relates how this shooting strategy emerged from Spielberg's desire to "challenge himself" and to avoid the distractions of conspicuous camera movements that call attention to themselves and often draw viewers out of the scene: "'When you're in a courtroom, you're watching and not moving. People move toward you and away from you, and it's very dramatic.

We wanted the audience to feel as if they were observers in the courtroom'"
(qtd. in Freer 255). Spielberg also had a classic model in mind when he began
thinking about the film, as he reveals on the DVD of *Amistad*: "It might be a
little sacrilegious, since some of what the Africans went through was at the
hands of the Spanish and the Portuguese, but I thought Goya had a look
where things were darker and more brooding . . . that was a tremendous
inspiration." To replicate Goya's "dark and brooding" mood and "reduce
the warmth of the images" (Freer 256), Kaminski and Spielberg highlighted
the frame's darker areas and washed out its color.

Spielberg also makes substantial use of botanical imagery to reveal character throughout the film. One striking example occurs in his consistent
linking of John Quincy Adams to various flowers. When he first meets with
Joadson and Tappan (Stellan Skarsgard) in Washington, Adams pays more
attention to clipping a small budding flower than to the men's pleas for legal
assistance. Later, when the case must be retried, Baldwin writes Adams pleading that he join them; Adams, repotting plants in his conservatory, refuses,
crumpling up the letter. When Joadson visits with him at home, asking for
his help before the Supreme Court, Spielberg again situates the ex-president
in his conservatory, now conscientiously watering his flowers. Placing one
faltering plant into the sunlight pouring through his window, Adams cynically informs Joadson that, in the courtroom, "Whoever tells the best story
wins." As a disappointed Joadson turns to leave, Adams asks him, "What is
their story, by the way?" "They're from West Africa," replies Joadson. "No,"
says Adams, sitting gingerly in a chair that places him next to the potted
plant he just positioned in the light. "You and this young so-called lawyer
have proven you know what they are: they are Africans. Congratulations. But
what you don't know, and as far as I can tell haven't bothered in the least
to discover, is *who* they are." He picks up the plant, which now rests in the
shadows, and slides it back into the sunlight.

Cinque is finally brought to meet Adams at the old man's house, his feet
and hands manacled in heavy chains like a dangerous animal. Adams orders
the jailers to "unshackle him" and then shows the startled African around his
conservatory, telling him a brief history of his cherished plants: an orchid he
brought over from China, a primrose from an English garden, a lily from the
south of France, a rose from Washington, D.C. (the bud he clipped earlier in
the scene with Tappan and Joadson). Finally, the two stand before a beautiful
purple flower sitting beneath a protective glass jar. As Cinque removes the
barrier and gently strokes the flower, his fingers join in a close-up with those
of Adams also caressing the leaves. "An African violet," the former presi-

dent says. "I can't tell you how difficult that was to come by." Cinque lowers his face, closes his eyes, and breathes in the scent of the flower, obviously reminded of his native ground. Adams watches and then, delicately, averts his eyes, understanding the pain felt by this proud man forcibly uprooted from the earth that nurtured him. Ultimately, Adams defends the Africans by calling upon the Supreme Court to recognize the wishes of the Founding Fathers, as Cinque has called upon his own ancestors for strength. Like the plants that surround him, Adams has blossomed by accepting moral responsibility for these men, and like a good gardener, he will help return these flowers to their native soil.

Another example of Spielberg's subdued visual style in *Amistad* occurs when Martin Van Buren interviews Judge Coglin (Jeremy Northam), a man chosen to decide the case against the Africans and, therefore, guarantee his reelection by insuring the votes of the pro-slavery southern states. Previously warned by Secretary of State Forsyth (David Paymer) that a decision for the Africans would take the country "one long step closer to Civil War," Van Buren dismisses the original jury and "prevails" upon the judge to recuse himself. His young replacement is "monumentally insecure" about his Catholic heritage, which he has "striven all his days to keep quiet" for fear it would hinder his advancement. Coglin meets Van Buren as the president poses for an official photograph, seated at a large desk, his neck held stiffly in place by a mechanical device. While we hear the dialogue between the president and his hand-picked judge, Spielberg allows only the part of the frame shot through the lens of the camera taking the portrait to remain in focus, that image first of the seated president and then of the two men upside-down and miniaturized—an apt visual correlative for Van Buren's inverted position on this racial matter. Ironically, Coglin (an outsider in Protestant society) later seeks guidance in the faith of his fathers (like Cinque and Adams), praying in a Catholic church before rendering a decision to send the prisoners "back to their homes in Africa."

Two sequences in *Amistad* are most typical of Spielberg: the opening scene, which propels viewers into the insurrection, and the central section, which depicts the horrors of the Middle Passage. Perhaps because he had just finished the second of his dinosaur films, these sequences seem more indebted to the visual constructions in those movies than to their more powerful evocation in *Schindler's List* or even *Jaws*. For example, when Spielberg launches the film with a close-up of Cinque's eyes, it recalls a similar shot in the first segment of *Jurassic Park,* an unfortunate connection between a human being and a raging beast. Because we have no idea who this man is, or anything about him beyond his desperate fight for freedom, we remain initially confused during the ensuing battle between whites and Blacks, uncertain if these are captured slaves or dangerous criminals. Neither group speaks English, so we cannot understand their words, and the furious thunderstorm makes it difficult to discern what is happening—and more importantly, why. Mainly, we hear anguished grunts and see the outlines of clashing figures. The horrendous death of one sailor, apparently the boat's captain, followed by a low-angle, distorted shot of his murderer bellowing incoherently into the slashing rain, does little to clarify anything.

Clearly, Spielberg wanted to start the film with an arresting dramatic moment. He plunges viewers into an alarming confusion of violent images that can be fully comprehended only later in the narrative. It is a strategy, as my colleague Delia Temes observed, that is strikingly reminiscent of how Toni Morrison begins her novel, *Beloved*. As the writer explains in an interview for the 1987 PBS program "Toni Morrison: Profile of a Writer": "The reader is snatched, yanked, thrown into an environment completely foreign, and I want it as the first stroke of the shared experience that might be possible between the reader and the novel's population. Snatched just as the slaves were from one place to another, from any place to another, without preparation or defense." Morrison goes on to describe *Beloved* as a story about discovering and then using "rememory" as a creative reconstruction of the past to better understand and ultimately reconfigure the present. Spielberg's opening, like Morrison's, rips his audience from the comfort of familiar cinematic conventions and thrusts them into a jumble of violent events. His camera forges a bond between the captive Africans and visually approximates their disorientation and revolt. Later, he allows us to share Cinque's "rememory" of his life in Africa, his capture, and his life aboard the slave ship in order to better understand his actions and future events.

The harrowing Middle Passage sequence begins with Cinque's wistful remembrance of his wife and child, a scene quickly followed by his brutal abduction by Black slave traders, his imprisonment in the Lomboko Slave Fortress, his sale to white slavers, and his transport to the infamous slave ship *Tecora*. Once the kidnapped men and women are dragged on board, gun-wielding sailors strip them naked, chain them together, indiscriminately whip them, and douse them with cold water—all while they are being blessed by a Spanish priest. A few are killed to teach the others to obey. Forced down onto their bellies in the dark hold, piled upon each other, the captives wail in pain and terror. Their sea journey becomes a floating concentration camp. Some die, and their bodies are unceremoniously dumped overboard. The women are continuously raped. One mother, a baby clutched in her arms, slips quietly over the side to drown. Cinque watches the sailors lash a man to death, his blood splattered across the faces and bodies of his comrades. The food is barely edible, but the prisoners gulp it down, fighting each other for the few scraps allotted them and licking their fingers to swallow each speck. When necessary to conserve supplies, the captain orders a group of captives to be shackled together and to a bag of rocks and simply cast into the ocean. After arriving in Havana, the remaining Africans are cleaned up and sold on the auction block. Cinque is transported to *La Amistad* under the ruthless eyes of Ruiz (Geno Silva) and Montes (John Ortiz). Here Spielberg cuts to Cinque standing above the body of the dead captain and then to the courtroom, where the African finishes the tale he began telling in his prison cell. Now we understand the first scene. Now we know how it is that a man treated like an animal will behave like one to seize his freedom.

CONCLUSION

Whatever *Amistad's* faults, Spielberg deserves credit for confronting topics usually avoided by mainstream American filmmakers and detailing "events that have not been central in the abundant literature of African-American memoirs, stories, and songs" (Davis 70). His attempt to bring forth a simmering bouillabaisse of presidential politics, racial prejudice, judicial procedures, international pressures, and personal motivations shows Spielberg trying to use his considerable technical skills in the service of sophisticated issues. Toplin, among others, suggests that the film "raises important questions about past injustices . . . and delivers some powerful and memorable performances . . . [that] ought to inspire more reflective consideration of the movie's achievements" (78). Yet it is not difficult to feel a certain degree of discomfort with the story he chose to tell: one of the few documented narratives with a "happy" ending, one of the rare islands of uplifting sentiment in a sea brimming with misery and horror. As in so many of his other movies, the story stresses the formation of a community of disparate people who join together to support a common cause or to defend themselves against a mutual enemy. This time, however, the threat arises not from nature or outer space but from the monster inside the human psyche that sanctions the savage treatment of other human beings, ultimately creating a system of inequality, brutality, and death.

The Terminal: Beyond the Screen

Like *Amistad, The Terminal* deals with the plight of strangers in a strange land, though its central figure finds himself in the reverse of Cinque's position: he is not able to enter America, while the African is not allowed to leave. The film is loosely based on the predicament of Merhan Karimi Nasseri, an Iranian refugee stranded in Charles de Gaulle Airport in 1988 when thieves stole his passport. Spielberg's plot revolves around the adventures of Viktor Navorski (Tom Hanks), an Eastern European traveler stranded at John F. Kennedy International Airport after his country explodes into a bloody civil war that renders his passport useless. Critics focused almost exclusively on the improbable love story between the stateless Viktor and the beautiful, if self-destructive, airline attendant Amelia Warren (Catherine Zeta-Jones), a romance that distracts viewers from the terror of Viktor's helplessness in the face of an inhumane American homeland-security apparatus. Trapped within the airport, a gigantic Skinner box of glass and steel, this modern man without a country must improvise a new life in limbo, learning how to earn money, feed himself, and make friends. Most crucially, he must fend off the escalating attempts of Frank Dixon (Stanley Tucci), the grimly obdurate associate director of airport security, to remove Viktor from his jurisdiction and make him someone else's bureaucratic nightmare.

The Terminal contains many recurrent Spielbergian themes and motifs. First, the intimate connection with flight, so evident in previous films such as *Close Encounters of the Third Kind, 1941, Empire of the Sun, Always,* and *Catch Me If You Can,* appears here as well, even though the protagonist remains firmly grounded in the airport; ominously, Viktor mistakes the bright lights from a landing plane as a threat rather than as a promise of escape to freedom, the metaphor so common in the director's earlier works. Second, the powerful father remains a controlling emotional influence on his son, despite his physical absence: a dogged Viktor has come to America in an anxious struggle to fulfill his father's dying wish and thus to perform his proper role as a dutiful child. In the face of mounting psychological pressure and increasing physical danger, Viktor refuses to leave America without completing his filial responsibilities and, like Indiana Jones in the *Last Crusade,* ultimately substitutes for his father in completing an anointed task. Third, the main character is a common figure in Spielberg's films—another dislocated and vulnerable alien, the innocent stranger who dispenses lessons in wisdom, compassion, and love before returning home. Concomitantly, as in the director's earlier movies featuring a confused outsider, Viktor's inability to communicate becomes a major issue: circumstances beyond his control force him to discover methods to make himself understood and to comprehend those whose world he now inhabits. Spielberg depicts Viktor's inability to converse most poignantly when the increasingly distraught traveler from Krakozhia watches television images of the fighting in his homeland but cannot decipher enough English to grasp why his countrymen are dying.

POLITICAL IMPLICATIONS

In *The Terminal's* publicity material, Spielberg says: "This is a time when we need to smile more, and Hollywood movies are supposed to do that for people in difficult times" (*Terminal,* Press kit 4). Yet his seemingly innocuous grin conceals some sharp teeth. Given the broad outlines of his previous productions, one would scarcely expect Spielberg to fire howitzer shells into the heart of the American body politic; he would never stage a frontal assault or lob grenades directly at the Bush administration, as Michael Moore does in *Fahrenheit 9/11* (2004). But distinctly political viewpoints emerge in his recent work, particularly *Minority Report* and *The Terminal.* These films, featuring two of the most popular actors in the world (Tom Cruise and Tom Hanks), initially seem quite conventional. Yet within the traditional genre formats of the science-fiction film and the romantic comedy, Spielberg embeds explicit warnings about specific governmental procedures. *Minority Report* overtly critiques the federal government's expanding power to monitor our personal lives and its self-declared right to thwart "future crimes" before they are committed; the film demonstrates the inherent dangers in exchanging personal liberties for governmental assurances of security, a barter embodied in legislation like the Patriot Act. *The Terminal* comments on repressive governmental actions, in this case the restrictive practices and pervasive xenophobia sanctioned under the Department of Homeland Security and ostensibly meant to protect American citizens.

Although Viktor travels to New York to complete a specific task and evinces no desire to settle there permanently, Spielberg conceptualizes *The Terminal* as an "immigrant's tale" that "goes back to what made this country so great and so strong—immigrants coming here from around the globe to ... a place where they are allowed to dream of a better life for themselves. In some ways, we have lost sight of the immigrant's plight because security is more intense than ever before" (*Terminal,* Press kit 10). Viktor, snared in a web of bureaucratic red tape, encounters a microcosm of American society at JFK, a virtual rainbow coalition of blue-collar workers: the African American baggage handler Joe Mulroy (Chi McBride), the Indian janitor Gupta (Kumar

Pallana), the Hispanic food-service worker Enrique Cruz (Diego Luna), and the U.S. Customs and Immigration Officer Dolores Torres (Zoe Saldana). The film mirrors America's prevailing economic structure: On the bottom of the financial ladder, a group of multicultural manual laborers perform the physical work necessary to keep the airport functioning smoothly. Above them (at times literally standing right over the sign to Borders books), a small contingent of white-collar Caucasians oversees them, and a platoon of mostly Black security guards, led by Ray Thurman (Barry Shabaka Henley), enforces their supervisor's directives and maintains order. Such a racially constructed, fundamentally segregated hierarchy of labor will clearly be perpetuated, as power passes from the retiring white male head of security, Karl Iverson (Jude Ciccolella), to Frank Dixon, his white male protegee. *The Terminal* depicts immigrants as remaining at the bottom of America's melting pot, providing the menial labor necessary for wealthier citizens to keep flying.

But a deeper reading reveals an even harder edge. Spielberg's movies consistently revolve around the formation of makeshift or ad hoc surrogate families banding together to defeat some common enemy—be it sharks, Nazis, Japanese soldiers, dinosaurs, or Captain Hook. A similar structure evolves in *The Terminal,* as the multiracial workers rally to support Viktor against Dixon. However, in contrast to earlier Spielberg movies, the threat comes neither from nature nor from beyond our shores: the adversary is the local representative of the American government, the man in the office run by the Department of Homeland Security. Dixon, who embodies the white establishment and the power of governmental policies, persistently attempts to thwart Viktor. For example, when the clever immigrant discovers that he can place abandoned luggage carriers back into their holders and receive a quarter for each returned cart, Dixon assigns one of his men to perform this task and deprives Viktor of his revenue. The inventive outsider perseveres, however, eventually landing a job on a construction crew repairing an unused part of the terminal. Dixon also attempts to monitor every aspect of Viktor's life through a chain of strategically placed television cameras. This Big Brother tactic replicates governmental agencies assuming surveillance authority in the name of national security and snooping into the personal lives of ordinary citizens who may disagree with their policies or legitimately protest their actions.

In the progressively cruel confrontations between Navorski and Dixon, *The Terminal* reveals the dangers of government functionaries viewing people not as individuals but rather as obstructions to the implementation of their policies. As early as *Close Encounters* and *E.T.,* Spielberg warned against this dehumanizing tendency in the figures of Lacombe and Keys, though these essentially gentle admonitions become broadly tragic in *Empire of the Sun* and *Schindler's List* and absolutely strident in *Minority Report*. Many of Spielberg's central figures can aptly be characterized as isolated and obsessive men, and throughout most of his career the notoriously obsessive filmmaker has consistently voiced his affection for and identification with such driven loners. *The Terminal* displays a darker side to this consuming preoccupation, particularly when these figures possess power. Viktor, as obsessively committed to his responsibilities as Dixon, risks his sanity and even his life to fulfill his father's wishes; but in his case, personal commitment springs from love and respect rather than a drive to exert power and gain control over others. By contrast, Dixon, unlike the haunted characters in Spielberg's previous movies, becomes not the film's primary point of identification but its central villain, a prototypical example of those who simply "follow orders" and blindly obey governmental authority.

The differences between the two men becomes starkly evident when Dixon calls upon Viktor to translate for Milodragovich (Valera Nikolaev), a desperate Russian passenger caught transporting medicine for his seriously ill father. For Dixon, this act simply represents another attempt to break the rules; he will not allow the drugs to leave the United States, essentially condemning the man's father to death. Viktor readily grasps that Milodragovich is not a hardened drug smuggler but rather, like himself, a dutiful son performing a required filial task. He quickly invents a story that the medicine will aid a sick goat and therefore is not bound under the regulations that govern the transit of drugs for human beings. No one really believes this ruse, but Viktor's clever solution defuses a potentially dangerous situation—Milodragovich has threatened to kill himself if he is not allowed to leave with the medicine. Victor's innate understanding of human nature and fundamental sensitivity makes the displaced Krakozhian a hero in the eyes of the airport's blue-collar workers. This further infuriates Dixon, who sees Viktor as flaunting his authority instead of sympathetically interpreting the rules to alleviate human suffering.

STYLISTICS

The Terminal visually resembles *Amistad* more than Spielberg's more relentlessly kinetic features in that it lacks his characteristic reliance on special effects. Three specific shots demand elaboration. In the first, Spielberg consciously references one of the most famous images in American western movies, the high-angle shot away from Marshall Will Kane (Gary Cooper) in *High Noon* (1952) as he realizes that he must face the deadly and sadistic Miller gang alone. Fred Zinnemann's stunning crane shot, showing the deserted streets of the archetypal American town, underscores Kane's isolation, fear, and vulnerability. He realizes that he has been abandoned by those he considered his friends and who symbolically represent American justice, commerce, and religion. Spielberg emphasizes these same feelings as Viktor stands alone, helpless and disenfranchised among the streaming crowds in the airport, finally perceiving the severity of his plight. Instead of placing his protagonist in the midst of an empty street, as did Zinnemann in *High Noon,* Spielberg surrounds Viktor with a swirling crush of bustling humanity: hordes of arriving and departing travelers rush to and from their airplanes, while Viktor remains stationary, trapped in limbo and forced to face a determined opponent who wants to eliminate him. Yet, unlike Will Kane, Viktor Navorksi will discover a group who will nurture and help protect him.

Two other sequences work in counterpoint. In the first, Viktor gazes longingly into the glass window of the airport's Hugo Boss store, where the reflection shows how he will look dressed in one of those handsomely tailored and expensive suits. However improbably, Spielberg's world of compassionate capitalism—not to mention extensive product placements—allows for this dreamy image to become flesh. Viktor accumulates enough money to buy the suit, marked down to a level rarely reached by Boss products off the screen, and meets Amelia for a romantic dinner looking like a "real American."

In the other shot, the dyspeptic Gupta, armed only with his mop, resolutely marches onto the tarmac and obstructs an oncoming plane. His act forces the police to arrest him and thwarts Dixon's plan to blackmail Viktor by threatening to fire his friends. This image of a tiny man standing in the path of an advancing Boeing 747 evokes the emblematic shot of a lone Chinese student bravely facing an oncoming tank in Tiananmen Square. But even without this specific historical overlay, the image of this aged, Indian immigrant halting the mammoth and foreboding symbol of corporate America—even temporarily—resembles nothing else in Spielberg's canon.

CONCLUSION

A few weeks before the national release of *The Terminal,* Spielberg eliminated two scenes he probably would not have removed earlier in his career. In the first, the fountain Viktor has been secretly building—with purloined construction materials—to impress Amelia bursts forth in a spectacular shower accompanied by a crescendo in John Williams's lush score. In the second, after visiting a Manhattan jazz club and obtaining the final signature necessary to fulfill his father's dying wish, Viktor returns to his taxi and finds Amelia waiting for him in the back seat. Both scenes would most likely have pushed an already improbable love story into bathos. The petals of romance shared by Viktor and Amelia conceal thorny political issues in the year 2004. "Viktor experiences an immersion in the American culture by way of the condensed world of the terminal," says Tom Hanks. "Racial diversity and racial divisions can be readily sampled at the airport" (*Terminal*, Press kit 3–4). Jeff Nathanson, who wrote the screenplay for *Catch Me If You Can* and for this film with Sacha Gervasi, added the script changes that ultimately convinced Spielberg to direct the project himself. "This story," Nathanson remarks, "allows us, in a very entertaining way, to explore some issues that I think are paramount to everything that's going on in our country right now" (4). Clearly, more was occupying the minds of those creating this movie than telling a love story, no matter how offbeat and charming that tale might have been. "America is closed," says Frank Dixon early in *The Terminal*. Such a statement runs counter to Spielberg's consistent liberal humanism that envisions this country's greatest virtues in terms articulated by Frank's soon-to-be-retired boss: "Compassion is what America is all about."

"America is closed!" In *The Terminal* (2004), an alliance of multiethnic, blue-collar workers—Joe Mulroy (Chi McBride), Enrique Cruz (Diego Luna), and Dolores Torres (Zoe Saldana)—help the stranded Viktor Navorski (Tom Hanks) gain entrance to New York City.

No doubt, Spielberg's detractors will once again charge that he remains incapable of depicting true difference, that all his "aliens" share conventional middle-class values. Some truth resides in this observation. Yet Spielberg rarely ignores external differences, obviously sees the dark side of life, and increasingly seems less naive about the evil nesting within the human psyche. Even armed with this knowledge, however, he consistently illustrates that most people across the spectrums of racial, ethnic, economic, and religious variations share fundamentally common needs: for love, for freedom, for their homeland, and for emotional security. While such bland shibboleths may sound more like political slogans than deeply held convictions, Spielberg's films strive to strip away the prohibitions and transcend the differences between us.

*   *   *

Spielberg's social problem/ethnic minority films explore the dynamics of oppressed groups within mainstream society. At their heart lie issues of prejudice, racism, persecution, and ultimately genocide. Though Spielberg demonstrates courage in tackling such disturbing and painful topics, many of his most vociferous critics cite precisely these movies as evidence that, while he may be a technical wizard, he will always remain a superficial thinker: "[N]o figure in American culture has worked harder to stupefy it, to stuff it with illusion, to deny the reality of evil, to blur the distinctions between fantasy and fact" (Wieseltier 42). They grant that he can generate thrills and screams but maintain that his techniques denigrate societal problems. For them, Spielberg's films inevitably convert true tragedies into soap-opera polemics. Slavery, they maintain, is far different from a rampaging shark or cuddly aliens, but the director treats them as fundamentally similar. Such comments overstate the situation and ignore the demands of narrative film-making. What ties *The Color Purple, Amistad,* and *The Terminal* together is Spielberg's determination to get beneath the skin of polite society and examine the dark underside of cultural attitudes toward the marginalized other, the people denied the status of humanity by those in power.

6

"Control Is Power": Imagining the Holocaust

The Holocaust in American Culture: The History

Before I wrote the first word of this book, I instinctively knew that my discussion of *Schindler's List* would constitute its final chapter, for personal and professional reasons. This film remains the single most important work in Steven Spielberg's long career, the one that advocates claim catapults him across the perceptual canyon separating gifted entertainer from serious artist; it also remains his most critically praised and persistently attacked creative endeavor. More than any of Spielberg's movies, *Schindler's List* sits within an intricate web of intersecting historical, cultural, theoretical, and aesthetic issues that range far beyond the borders of any movie screens. My personal responses can best be summed up with the oxymoronic concept of passionate ambivalence. As a Jew who lost grandparents in the Holocaust, I am deeply moved each time I watch *Schindler's List*, sincerely admire Spielberg's courage in making the film, and applaud his willingness to challenge himself technically, thematically, and emotionally. Yet as a film scholar trained to analyze moving images and the reasons those images affect audiences, I find it difficult to embrace the film uncritically. To understand the pivotal role of *Schindler's List* in Spielberg's career, therefore, I needed to have his other works laid out before me, to see the spread of the forest before intently fixing my gaze on one of its tallest trees. So let me begin this final chapter with some personal history.

I grew up in Port Jervis, a town located at the point where New York, New Jersey, and Pennsylvania converge, as a thoroughly assimilated, second-generation American Jew. With a population of about ten thousand and a Jewish community of roughly a hundred families composed mostly of the town's merchants, my high school graduating class contained only two other Jews. I had a Bar Mitzvah and regularly attended Sunday school classes at the Conservative Temple Beth El, but my sense of religious obligation never came close to my intense commitment to playing sports during those years. I had barely heard of the Holocaust. It was probably mentioned somewhere during my religious classes, but no days were set aside to commemorate its victims, and no survivors were invited to speak at my school or even at my synagogue. Years later, my father revealed what happened to his parents: in the waning days of War World II, returning Nazi soldiers and sympathizers marched his mother, father, and sister across the snowy fields outside their small Czechoslovakian village of Rachov until they died. Growing up, however, we never spoke about this.

I arrived at Alfred University, a small liberal arts college in upstate New York, in September 1963. Soon I heard rumors about Dr. Melvin Bernstein. "Whatever you do," my peer advisor told me with a slight roll of his eyes, "don't miss his Six Million Dead lecture. He cries during it. He actually cries." Bernstein, one of the university's few Jewish professors, taught in the English department and ran the local Hillel. On the day of his scheduled lecture, I trudged through knee-deep snow drifts, sat down in one of the classroom's unforgiving wooden chairs, and waited for the show to begin. I can't recall exactly what he told us about the Holocaust that chilly morning, but I clearly remember that my reaction was neither sympathetic nor compassionate. It was embarrassment—deep shame liberally sprinkled with anger. Who were these people he was telling us about? How could these gutless sheep be herded into lines and walk passively to their deaths without defending themselves, their wives, or their children? Better to die at the point of a bayonet or from a bullet to the brain, I thought indignantly, than to be shoved into ovens like loaves of bread. I looked nervously around at my classmates, wondering if they associated me with these cowards.

I recount this biographical sliver because my upbringing during this time was not aberrational; Spielberg reports never hearing the word "Holocaust" until he was in college in 1965 (Ansen 114). Nor, I suspect, were my initial responses upon first hearing about the European Jews who perished in the death camps uncommon. My narrative also marks the changing role of the Holocaust in American life since the 1960s. According to the historian Tim Cole, "the Holocaust has emerged in the Western World as the most talked about and oft represented event of the twentieth century" (3) and has now become "a ruling symbol in our culture" (18). The establishment of the United States Memorial Holocaust Museum in Washington, D.C., in 1993—legislated by President Carter and dedicated by President Clinton, it attracts over two million visitors each year—dramatically attests to this tragedy's significance in American culture. (Ironically, a Washington Mall museum to Native Americans was not dedicated until 2004.) Yet the very existence of this institution, along with its physical location among our nation's most enduring monuments, raises some intriguing and uncomfortable questions. How did atrocities that occurred in Europe come to loom so large in the mosaic of American life? Why does a memorial to events that directly affected a small portion of the American public stand within walking distance of edifices commemorating the American Revolution and the Civil War in our nation's capital?

It was not always so. Historians generally agree that the Holocaust played little part in our communal sensibilities until the early 1960s and 1970s. Its emergence resulted from the coalescence of several historical events: 1) the release of Anne Frank's *Diary of a Young Girl* (English translation, 1952) along with subsequent movie and television adaptations (eight English-language versions from 1959 to 1999); 2) the Eichmann trial in Israel in 1961; 3) the 1967 Israeli-Arab War; 4) the rise of the civil rights movement and identity politics in the United States during the 1960s and 1970s; 5) the social upheavals caused by the Vietnam War; 6) the popularity of the NBC's miniseries "Holocaust," watched by 120 million Americans over four days, April 16–19, 1978; and 7) the rise of academic Jewish studies programs and Holocaust classes. These milestones in the evolution of a sustained Holocaust consciousness allowed its events to become deeply woven into the tapestry of American communal memory. More universally, in the words of the French philosopher Emmanuel Levinas, the Holocaust unfolded as "the paradigm of gratuitous human suffering in which evil appears in its diabolical horror" (97). To understand this evolution, one needs to remember that like all the components of a nation's collective memory and a people's assembled identity, the Holocaust has been refracted through a series of narrative constructs and serves vital ideological purposes (for Jews and non-Jews alike) in the present cultural environment. To "read" it in light of these cultural dimensions does not diminish its profound significance, demean the memory of its victims, ignore the suffering of its survivors, or dismiss the insights of its scholars. It does, however, relate its current prominence as much to contemporary concerns as to past afflictions.

The Holocaust in American Culture: Jewish Identity

Prior to the heightened ethnic identification that began in the 1960s, U.S. Jews demonstrated little desire to emphasize their differences from the rest of society, and consequently the Holocaust was not an integral part of American Jewish identity. But as identity politics took over center stage in the 1960s and 1970s, coupled with the rise of what some leaders called "the new anti-Semitism," American Jews felt the need to define themselves internally and to the outside world. Within an increasingly rancorous climate of ethnic debate, the Holocaust emerged as the single most important event connecting diverse, sometimes overtly hostile, portions of the American Jewish community. For example, in the American Jewish Committee's opinion survey for 2000, 81 percent of the respondents rated "remembering the Holocaust" as either "extremely important" or "very important" in terms of defining their Jewish identity, compared with 68 percent who ranked "celebrations of Jewish holidays," and only 37 percent who cited "participating in Jewish services" (Wallerstein 3). The Holocaust has become "virtually the only common denominator of American Jewish identity in the late twentieth century and filled a need for a consensual symbol" (Novick 7). In Peter Novick's cynical observation, the Holocaust allows Jews to retain "permanent possession of the gold medal of the Victimization Olympics" (195), yielding a wide variety of sometimes contradictory meanings and interpretations that can be harnessed to advance particular ideological agendas.

The Holocaust in American Culture: National Identity

The essential role of the Holocaust in the group definition of American Jewish identity seems a natural and perhaps even necessary occurrence. But in what meaningful ways has the "Americanization" of the Holocaust come to reflect and refract the nation's conception of itself and its citizens? The memorialization of the Holocaust reconfirms America's "role as the world's savior" (Junker 6) and simultaneously allows the country to maintain moral superiority over its European counterparts: we are the liberators, and they are the persecutors. Such a wide interpretation intimately entangles the identity needs of the relatively small American Jewish population with the psychological drives of the larger American community. At the most elemental level, the Holocaust has emerged as a vital component of American culture because that culture draws positive reinforcement and universal lessons from its gruesome events. Holocaust memorials and remembrances, for example, offer opportunities for a communal moral catharsis. The Holocaust has become, among other things, an effective teaching tool used to dramatize broad lessons about the evils of bigotry and the necessity for tolerance. Far from being conceived as a specifically Jewish tragedy, the Holocaust has become a universalized symbol—the prototype, the benchmark, and the ultimate warning against mass atrocities wherever they may occur in the modern world.

THE ROLE OF THE MEDIA

Though the Holocaust may have been "up to the very moment it began unimaginable" (Habermas 167), artists have struggled to re-create it in almost every possible medium. "'The past becomes the present only through representation,'" observes the Holocaust scholar Jonathan Webber, "'we cannot know the past in any other way'" (qtd. in Zelizer 238–39). Even those narratives commonly designated as "histories" or "memoirs" are reconstructions: highly edited and subjectively mediated versions of events. Inevitably, fictional attempts to represent the Holocaust raise thorny issues about historical accuracy, narrative authenticity, and artistic motivation. Elie Wiesel's denunciation of "Auschwitz kitsch" (*Kingdom* 114) and the "desanctification of the Holocaust" (169), along with Alvin H. Rosenfeld's charge that most mass-media representations are inevitably a "vulgarization and trivialization" of historical events (58), represent typical arguments against television and film productions. Lawrence L. Langer offers the most sustained attack, denouncing the "Americanization of the Holocaust" with its emphasis on the "discourse of consolation" (7), its "moral oversimplification" (166), and its persistent attempt to find a "redeeming truth" (158) amidst the horror. For Langer and others, American narratives inevitably fail to confront the nihilistic horror of the Holocaust, a set of events from which no moral redemption is possible.

The mass media played a major role in making American society conscious of the Holocaust. Most of those without firsthand experience of the death camps received their primary knowledge of the Holocaust from productions that "created a bridge of empathic connection, even identification, between the fate of European Jewry and ordinary Americans who had no ethnic or religious link to the victims" (Mintz 17). Television presentations such as "Holocaust" and "Playing for Time" (1980) and films like *The Pawnbroker* (1964) and *Schindler's List* forged a common bond of suffering between Americans and Hitler's victims. By packaging Holocaust events within conventional formats, television programs and films affected a wide range of

American citizens who might otherwise not be engaged with a European or simply Jewish tragedy. Such productions spotlight victims who closely resemble middle-class Americans, those who could conceivably live next door, which raises the issue of social-class consciousness: "In so many books and movies about the Holocaust, I sense that I am being asked to feel a particular pathos in the rounding up of gentle, scholarly middle-class, *civilized* people who are then packed into cattle cars, as though the liquidation of illiterate peasants would not be as poignant" (Lopat 58). This implicit connection between the victims depicted in these movies and television programs and viewers sitting in theaters and living rooms across the United States did much to eradicate the sense of difference, of foreignness, that initially characterized the response to the Holocaust in America.

In the third edition of *Indelible Shadows: Film and the Holocaust* (2003), Annette Insdorf remarks how in researching her first edition in 1979 she found only a "few dozen films to warrant attention" (245). Since the second edition in 1989, she has screened some 170 new productions, enough to convince her that "films about the Nazi era and its Jewish victims [are] so numerous as to constitute a veritable genre" and that these movies have become "part of a wider cultural embracing of the Shoah" (245). She is right. Before *Schindler's List*, four American films dealing with the Holocaust (*The Diary of Anne Frank* [1959], *Judgment at Nuremberg* [1961], *Ship of Fools* [1965], and *Cabaret* [1972]) had been nominated for the Best Picture Oscar (none of them won), and seven European features (*The Shop on Main Street* [1965], *The Garden of the Finzi-Continis* [1971], *The Tin Drum* [1979], *The Boat Is Full* [1981], *The Assault* [1986], *Au Revoir les Enfants* [1987], and *The Nasty Girl* [1990]) received nominations (four won). Fueled by the phenomenal success of the miniseries "Holocaust" and then kicked into overdrive by the popular, critical, and financial achievements of *Schindler's List,* films and television programs about the Holocaust have become a virtual cottage industry.

Epitomizing the cynical and oft cited phrase, "there's no business like Shoah business," the 2001 TV season featured three big-budget, highly publicized miniseries during the sweeps period—NBC's "Uprising," CBS's "Haven," and ABC's "Anne Frank"—along with HBO and Showtime original features on cable during the same year. *Schindler's List* and *Life Is Beautiful* (1999) both garnered Oscars for Best Picture, *The Pianist* (2002) lost in the Best Picture category but won for Best Actor and Best Director, while Holocaust-related projects often swept the Academy Awards in the documentary (feature and short subject) categories: *One Survivor Remembers* (1995), *Anne Frank Remembered* (1995), *The Long Way Home* (1997), *Visas and Virtues*

(1998), *The Last Days* (1998), and *Into the Arms of Strangers: Stories of the Kindertransport* (2000). On the most significant level, argues Insdorf, "films about the Holocaust have provided images—of smoke, of barbed wire, of sealed train cars, of skeletal bodies—that now function as synecdoches, the visual part representing the unimaginable whole" (248). They have permanently hot-wired the Holocaust into the American collective memory.

THE ROLE OF SCHINDLER'S LIST

Of the many films about the Holocaust, *Schindler's List* remains the most influential within Hollywood and as part of the national—and global—communal consciousness. Viewing the film has become "a symbolic rite of passage introducing the Holocaust into mainstream American culture" (Loshitzky 2), a fact satirized in a famous "Seinfeld" episode where Jerry's uncle catches him necking during a screening of the film and the comedian's shocked family reacts with consternation and condemnation. The willingness of the most successful director in movie history to confront the Holocaust "'gives permission to other filmmakers, particularly Jewish filmmakers who maybe have been a little bit afraid of appearing parochial, to touch this area,'" observes Michael Berenbaum (qtd. in Wallerstein 3), the former deputy director of the President's Commission on the Holocaust, director of the Research Institute at the U.S. Holocaust Memorial Museum, and director of Spielberg's own Shoah Visual History Foundation. Clutching his long-denied Oscars before millions of viewers across the globe, Spielberg embodied the mainstream acceptance of the Holocaust into American culture.

Equally crucial, *Schindler's List* was the culmination of an evolving shift of focus from those who had perished in the Holocaust, to those who had valiantly fought against the Nazis, to those who had suffered but managed to survive, to those righteous Gentiles who risked their lives to assist Jews: "*Schindler's List* symbolically passes the torch from one generation to the next, reaffirming the role of generational identity in the symbolic memory culture of the Holocaust" (Loshitzky 4). In so doing, it dramatically capped the evolving "Americanization" of the Holocaust by concentrating on endurance beyond destruction, celebration amidst mourning, and hope over despair. Historically, Spielberg's film brings into sharp relief the inevitable migration from first-person accounts by rapidly dwindling numbers of survivors to the transmission of these events through the outlets of popular culture. It also firmly established a viable role—at times complementary, and at others adversarial—between past events as depicted fictionally or nonfictionally by the media and those same events presented by historians. Given its popularity and prominence, one can safely assert that *Schindler's List* remains the most important production about the Holocaust ever made. For good or ill, it has emerged as the master narrative of this event for a majority of American society.

Spielberg as a Jewish Filmmaker

When David Desser and I completed the first edition of *American Jewish Filmmakers,* written before *Schindler's List* was released, we discussed Spielberg's oblique incorporation of Jewish elements up to that point in his career. Although the characters played by Richard Dreyfuss, who Spielberg describes as his alter ego in *Jaws, Close Encounters of the Third Kind,* and *Always,* are never specifically designated ethnically, that actor brings a decidedly nontraditional leading-man look and feel to his roles. Spielberg cites his experiences with anti-Semitism as a reason he felt comfortable adapting Alice Walker's *The Color Purple,* and *E.T.* could be read as a parable of the immigrant experience in America. Prior to *Schindler's List,* Spielberg dealt with issues like prejudice, being the outsider, and the loss of religiosity through the Black experience or genre conventions—a strategy similar to the first generation of Jewish directors in America, European emigres who rarely tackled Jewish issues overtly. The best Spielberg could muster about the mass murderers who carried out Hitler's genocidal policies, before *Schindler's List,* was Indiana Jones's understated muttering, "I hate these guys."

An American Tail (1986) primarily belongs to its writer and director Don Bluth, but Spielberg had a sustained involvement with this animated feature, which stands as his single involvement with an overtly Jewish-themed film before *Schindler's List.* His official credit lists him as coexecutive producer. According to John Baxter, "Spielberg's executive productions were aggressively hands-on," and he often literally loomed over the shoulder of his directors (300). *An American Tail* focuses on Fieval (named after Spielberg's beloved grandfather, Philip Posner) Mousekawitz and his family, who fear for their lives because, when the Cossacks assault a Jewish household, the Katsacks simultaneously attack the Jewish mice within it. The Mousekawitzes dream of freedom and safety, best expressed in their song "There Are No Cats in America," but once they emigrate to the United States they discover cats prowling there as well. The movie conflates Jewish immigration from Eastern Europe with Italian and Irish immigration in the form of fleeing mice from all these lands, linking Jews to other persecuted ethnic groups. Its climax depicts the various ethnic mice banding together and banishing the cats. Although referencing the historical specificity of Russian anti-Semitism and the mass migration of Russian Jews to American, *An American Tail* denies the uniqueness of the Jewish experience in favor of universalizing it. All the ethnic groups are essentially alike in terms of their past experiences and willingness to be dipped into the American melting pot.

Representational Issues

Spielberg's explicit treatment of Jews in *Schindler's List* attracted as much criticism as it did sympathy. In this he was not alone. No mainstream American film or television production about the Holocaust has ever escaped condemnation by a shifting coterie of scholars and survivors for misrepresenting these horrible events by being (in some combination) too sentimental, too universal, too optimistic, too trivializing, or too uncomplicated. Summed up under the pejorative rubric "Hollywood," academic critics attack mainstream films and television productions for their fundamental economic tenets and ideological ethos:

> [I]ts unquestioned and supreme values of entertainment and spectacle; its fetishism of style and glamor; its penchant for superlatives and historicist grasp at any and all experience ("the greatest Holocaust film ever made"); and its reifying, leveling, and trivializing effect on everything it touches. (Hansen 80)

The inherently limited principles of traditional visual narratives, combined with the basic philosophy and fiscal demands of Hollywood productions, render filmmakers working within that system incapable of appropriately unfolding the events of the Holocaust. The very process of artistic re-creation in this stifling atmosphere demands a superficial, deceptive, and ultimately fraudulent sense of redemption and triumph that substitutes soothing platitudes for bitter realities. To appeal to a mass audience, some commentators acknowledge, "concessions are necessary . . . and you have to use a language it can understand" (Wiesel, *Kingdom* 114), However, most critics of mainstream Holocaust dramas echo Anton Kaes's claim that this particular subject matter cannot be appropriately represented by the "narrowly circumscribed Hollywood conventions of storytelling" ("Holocaust" 208). They bemoan how directors squeeze these sprawling and complicated events into trite, conventional, and melodramatic plotlines. For these critics, *Schindler's List* was doomed to fail before Spielberg shot his first scene.

These contentions derive from writers such as Theodor Adorno and George Steiner, who placed the Holocaust outside of history and beyond the reach of artistic re-creation. They argued that the inherent aesthetic pleasures derived from artistic works are inappropriate to the subject matter of the Holocaust, a belief summed up in Adorno's famous dictum that "[t]o write poetry after Auschwitz is barbaric" (112). While survivors such as Elie Wiesel and Primo Levi accept that their survival imposed a duty upon them to "combat forgetting" (Wiesel, *Memoirs* 80), including the sacred obligation to recount "the things we have witnessed and endured" (Levi, *Reawakening* 230), their preferred form of communication is the memoir or autobiography, the first-person journalistic account. They draw strict distinctions between fictional and nonfictional narratives, arguing that the human imagination cannot conjure anything that approaches the horrors of the Holocaust: "[T]here is no such thing as a literature of the Holocaust, nor can there be. . . . A novel about Auschwitz is not a novel or else is not about Auschwitz. The very attempt to write such a novel is blasphemy" (Wiesel, "Some" 314). For these writers, only survivors can bear witness to these horrible truths with an appropriate sense of pain, guilt, and authenticity.

The scholarly challenge to visual re-creations of the Holocaust springs not only from a demand for authenticity but also from a profound anxiety that the profusion of mass-media Holocaust dramas becomes "a strategy for undoing, in fantasy, the need for mourning by simulating a condition of intactness" (Santner 144). This "intactness" undergirds the structural premise of traditional visual narratives that inherently reduces events to a starting point, a series of complications, and an emotionally satisfactory conclusion: a conventional three-act construction. This classic structure fails to capture the essential components of chance, enormity, desperation, despair, and brutality that characterized the actual Holocaust: "The incomparable horrors of the concentration camp universe cannot serve as a context for dramatic action that involves narrative plotting in terms of causal development, neat story closure, and realistic, psychological characterization" (Avisar 50–51). Such contentions leave scholars and artists marooned within a perplexing aesthetic dilemma: to appropriate Jean-Francois Lyotard's metaphor, they are desperately trying to measure the profound effects of a catastrophic earthquake while lacking the necessary instruments to do so (56).

In his essay "The Book of Destruction," Geoffrey H. Hartman postulates that most audiences lack the ability to accept authentic images of the Holocaust. Conceding that technological progress has made it possible to "provide a mimesis of everything, no matter how extreme" (327)—including the most horrible images of the Holocaust—Hartman questions whether it is possible to believe what we see on the screen before us, if "the truth can offend probability" (328). "The infinity of evil," he continues, compels us "to demonize it, to divest the monster of human aspect and motivation, to create the stereotype of the evil empire" (329). Hartman sees the challenge of visual re-creation coming from the limitations of conceptualization, not the inherent deficiencies of representation: "[P]rincipally from a doubt about the ethics of a certain kind of mimesis . . . by grotesquing what it touches, or surfeiting our need for clear and distinct identities" (331). Such a view raises unsettling questions that move beyond the basic concerns of those who object to Holocaust productions solely because they are fictional or a combination of factual and imaginative re-creation.

Omer Bartov extends Hartman's concerns by exploring "inherent tensions" between the depiction of brutal events on screen and their trivialization, particularly when related to the Holocaust. He asks readers to consider the alternatives along a spectrum that runs "between the abhorrence evoked by human degradation and suffering, and a perverse, pornographic curiosity about the limits of human depravity" (52). Such questions have been raised about the depiction of violence from Hollywood's silent days through the contemporary era: What are the moral responsibilities of artists who depict violence on the screen? Does showing graphic violence intrinsically encompass shards of exploitation, voyeurism, and aesthetic pleasure? Regarding these questions, *Schindler's List* was attacked from two directions. Some critics accused Spielberg of failing to confront the true horror of the Holocaust, particularly in the shower sequence, where water and not gas cascades onto the naked women; others complained that he numbed viewers with unnecessary images of violence, such as Goeth (Ralph Fiennes) arbitrarily shooting prisoners from his balcony. In other words, Spielberg was simultaneously accused of being too realistic and not realistic enough. Such considerations lead to a broader and more fundamental question: what constitutes an "authentic" portrayal of the Holocaust?

The most consistently invoked counterposition to all these assumptions asserts that popular television programs and films make the events of the Holocaust accessible and its victims palpable to vast groups who might otherwise never know, or care, much about it or them. Those intensely engaged in studying the Holocaust willingly sit through all nine hours and forty-three minutes of Claude Lanzmann's *Shoah* (1985) and listen intently to the moving stories of survivors. They will read erudite treatises by such writers as Raul Hillberg (*The Destruction of the European Jews*), David G. Roskies (*Against the Apocalypse*), Emil Fackenheim (*The Jewish Return into History*), and Arthur A. Cohen (*The Tremendum*). Others, more tangentially interested, will buy popular books such as Wiesel's *Night* and Frank's *Diary of a Young Girl*. Yet their numbers are dwarfed by viewers who saw the miniseries "Holocaust" (120 million), watched *Schindler's List* during its American theatrical release (twenty-five million), or tuned into its broadcast on NBC television (sixty-five million) in 1997. Defenders of such re-creations readily admit that they have condensed events, added fictional characters, and rearranged historical events, but they argue that they do so to invoke strongly empathetic responses, to encourage further investigation, to learn from the past, and to warn current generations that such atrocities can occur again.

In addition to citing the sheer numbers of viewers drawn to television programs and movies, those who champion popular representations of the Holocaust extol their heartrending appeal as the primary method to insure a continuation of broad general interest by stimulating emotional identification and personalizing historical events. They claim that such docudramas allow viewers "to enter imaginatively into historical events in a way more revealing and intimate than may have been possible at the time they happened" (Mintz 132). Commentators such as Andreas Huyssen contend that this emotional connection can best be generated by utilizing the narrative conventions familiar to most viewers. Television and film presentations play a crucial role in sustaining widespread public involvement with the victims and survivors of the Holocaust, as well as helping to maintain the prominent position it now holds in the collective imagination. Far from robbing the dead of "whatever sanctity and protection historical memory properly bestows upon them" (Rosenfeld 58), such fictional re-creations cement an emotional bond between them and the current generation of viewers. More than historical treatises, authentic memoirs, or fictional literature, popular movies and television programs have the capacity to link the past vividly to the present and the future.

Schindler's List: Beyond the Screen

Given the significant role *Schindler's List* came to play in the American public's consciousness, as well as in Spielberg's personal life and professional career, I will briefly summarize several key elements that characterize the preparation, creation, and reception of this movie. In particular, I want to emphasize four intersecting elements during the film's lengthy gestation period, its formidable production schedule, and its subsequent appearance in theaters across the world: 1) Spielberg's concerns before starting it, 2) how making the film influenced his Jewish identity, 3) some specifics about the shoot itself, and 4) the honors it received.

SPIELBERG'S APPREHENSIONS

Schindler's List almost carried the credit "A Film by Martin Scorsese." Spielberg actually offered to produce the movie for his friend in 1988, only to regret his decision and to trade his fellow director *Cape Fear* (1991) in order to retrieve artistic control for himself. There were other suitors as well. After reading a rave review in the *New York Times* of Thomas Keneally's book (which won the Booker Prize for fiction), Sid Sheinberg (president of Universal Studios) secured the movie rights to *Schindler's List* in 1983, with Spielberg in mind as its director. But the man known at the time primarily for his giddy adventure films and childlike innocence was not yet ready to embark on such an emotionally arduous project. Not sure he ever would be, Spielberg considered several other directors for the project. Early on, he offered the assignment to Roman Polanski, who had escaped as a child from the Krakow ghetto just before its liquidation in 1943, had hidden from the Nazis until the war ended, and later discovered that his mother was killed in Auschwitz. Polanski, an obvious choice, had two uncles actually named on Schindler's about-to-be-famous list, but he choose not to relive those terrible memories by making the film. It was not until 2003 that he was ready to do so, eventually winning the Best Director Oscar for his highly praised Holocaust drama *The Pianist.* At another point, Spielberg considered Sydney Pollack (*Out of Africa* [1985] and *Tootsie* [1982]) and the Australian director Fred Schepisi (who filmed an earlier Keneally book, *The Chant of Jimmie Blacksmith* [1978]), but he never felt totally comfortable surrendering the property to either man—or ultimately to anyone else.

Then came the most intriguing option of all. The veteran director Billy Wilder, an Austrian Jew who had lost almost all his relatives in the Holocaust, petitioned Spielberg for the property. He passionately wanted to film Keneally's book as a memorial to his family, to punctuate a storied career by making his last movie the story of Oskar Schindler and the Jews he saved. Wilder's enthusiasm made Spielberg "look very deeply inside" himself and "tested his resolve" (McBride 427) to direct the movie himself. Spurred on by world events (particularly the "ethnic cleansing" in Bosnia and the growing prominence of Holocaust deniers), he finally felt prepared to tackle the complicated and disturbing subject matter and to weather the inevitable criticism directed at any film about the Holocaust with Steven Spielberg's name attached to it. In his own words, he needed "to grow into it" (Schiff 172), and he waited ten years until he felt mature enough personally and artistically to undertake its production with confidence. One wonders if the negative attacks on *Schindler's List* would have been less intense if Polanski's or Scorsese's name followed its last images, although both men would have made decidedly different pictures.

SPIELBERG'S JEWISH IDENTITY

Making *Schindler's List* forced Spielberg to relive the various anti-Semitic slights and outright attacks he suffered growing up as part of a Jewish family surrounded by an overwhelmingly Gentile community, a situation that continually reinforced his image of himself as an outsider. Several incidents of anti-Semitism reported during the shooting brought back those childhood memories, as well as making the cast and crew aware that anti-Semitism was alive and well in the world: finding graffiti with a Star of David hanging from the gallows in the Old Square of Krakow; the actor Ralph Fiennes, mistaken for the real Nazi he was playing, being congratulated by a local resident for killing so many Jews during the war; and a German businessman telling some of the Israeli actors that "Hitler should have finished the job" and drawing his finger across his throat (see Freer 228). At times, Spielberg became so depressed while making the movie—feeling sick, frightened, and breaking into tears as he filmed some of the heartrending scenes—that he implored his friend, the comedian Robin Williams, with a long-distance telephone request to make him laugh before he could go back to the set.

Simultaneously, the voyage into the bitter heart of darkness strengthened the director's commitment to the Jewish faith: "'I was hit in the face with my personal life. My upbringing. My Jewishness. The stories my grandparents told me about the Shoah. And Jewish life came pouring back into my heart'" (qtd. in McBride 414). He conducted a Seder for the cast and crew to celebrate Passover and was deeply moved when the young Germans playing Nazis sat down with the Israeli actors to celebrate the Jewish Exodus from Egypt. "I was so ashamed of being a Jew, and now I'm filled with pride. I don't even know when that transition happened" (Richardson 165), he admitted in several interviews. Spielberg's biographer, Joseph McBride, concludes: "*Schindler's List* became the transforming experience of Spielberg's lifetime. Making the film ... was the catharsis that finally liberated him to be himself, both as a man and as an artist" (414). Spielberg did not accept a salary for directing *Schindler's List* and did not take his usual percentage of the gross revenues until after Universal made back its production expenses. He donated the vast majority of the money he ultimately earned to Jewish organizations, such as the Holocaust Museum in Washington. Most significantly, Spielberg used this money to establish the Survivors of the Shoah Visual History Foundation, an organization he created to videotape and preserve testimonies of Holocaust survivors.

THE SHOOT

Beyond being an emotional ordeal for Spielberg, *Schindler's List* was a physical and economic burden as well. Budgeted for twenty-two million dollars and lasting seventy-two days, the shoot entailed 359 scenes and averaged thirty-five to forty shots per day, meaning that most scenes were done in two or three takes. It incorporated 148 sets, thirty-five locations, 240 crew members, 126 speaking parts, and thirty thousand extras (Richardson 182). Much of the footage was shot on the locations where the events actually took place (including Schindler's residence and enamel factory), though when the World Jewish Congress denied Spielberg's request to film on the grounds of Auschwitz itself, he was forced to build the train tracks and replicate the camp's buildings just outside its gates. All of this provided an emotional experience for cast and crew as well as the director himself. "'To touch history, to put my hand on 600–year old masonry, and to step back from it and look down at my feet and know that I was standing where, as a Jew, I couldn't have stood fifty years ago, was a profound moment for me in my life'" (qtd. in McBride 431). Most indicative of Spielberg's ability to compartmentalize, and a paradigmatic example of the different sides of his artistic sensibilities, he rented (at a cost of $1.5 million per week) two satellite channels from a local television station to communicate with the special-effects mavens at Industrial Light and Magic and finish editing *Jurassic Park* while filming *Schindler's List* in Poland. "Taking respites to play with fantasy dinosaurs," McBride speculates, "may have helped keep him from becoming immobilized by despair while going about the task of re-creating the Holocaust in places where it actually occurred" (416).

THE AFTERMATH

Nominated in twelve categories, *Schindler's List* won Oscars for Best Direction, Picture, Screenplay Based on Materials from Another Medium, Cinematography, Film Editing, Music–Original Score, and Art Direction/Set Direction. Liam Neeson lost in the Best Actor category (to Tom Hanks in *Philadelphia*), as did Ralph Fiennes for Best Supporting Actor (to Tommy

Lee Jones in *The Fugitive*). The film also won the Best Picture Award given by the Los Angeles and New York Film Critics, though both groups voted not to honor Spielberg for Best Director, instead turning to Jane Campion for *The Piano*. *Schindler's List* grossed $45.9 million in the U.S. market and an additional $225.1 million beyond American shores. Eventually, worldwide sales reach $321.2 million (see Freer 233), an amazing figure for a film shot in black and white and running 197 minutes. In theaters, *Schindler's List* was often screened without the standard prelude of movie trailers; when shown on national television (NBC; February 23, 1997), it was preceded by eight minutes of advertisements and then aired with no commercial interruptions (though intermissions featured the Ford logo), the longest TV broadcast without breaks since the funeral of John F. Kennedy (Freer 233). Ironically, its major sponsor was the Ford Motor Company, whose virulent anti-Semitic founder, Henry Ford, must have been rolling over in his grave as his descendants bankrolled the screening of a movie about the Holocaust from the world's most prominent Jewish director.

Jews in Schindler's List

At the conclusion of the war, as Oskar Schindler (Liam Neeson) prepares to flee, his grateful workers melt gold extracted from their teeth into a ring and emotionally present it to him with all the prisoners looking on. According to the screenwriter Steven Zallian, who notes that Keneally spends little time on this moment, Spielberg broadened the ceremonial impact of this scene to remind viewers that "although Schindler saved some 1,200 people, 6 million more died during the Holocaust" (Manchel 99). Despite such attempts, the most persistent charge against *Schindler's List* castigates Spielberg for depicting an essentially Jewish catastrophe from the point of view of a non-Jewish protagonist, thereby reducing Jews to bit players in their own tragedy. Dwarfed by the towering presence of yet one more of Spielberg's surrogate father figures, the film's infantalized Jews come to "represent the child in us" (White 5). Bill Nichols, for example, sees the film as one in a trilogy of patriarchal rescue movies: Saving the Jews (*Schindler's List*); Saving the Slaves (*Amistad*); and Saving the World (*Saving Private Ryan*). In all three films, the protectors of "those less fortunate or far-sighted than themselves are white male heroes of gentle character, empathetic nature, and altruistic impulse" (Nichols 9). Karen Jaehne even maintains that *Schindler's List* was so popular in Germany because it "relieved some of their postwar guilt . . . Spielberg brought relief by focusing on the hero among them and creating a masterpiece dedicated to their past" (39). Since the solitary example of Oskar Schindler hardly counterbalances the preponderance of sadists and greedy industrialists who populate the film, I suspect that this particular evocation of "their past" would bring little "relief" to contemporary Germans, particularly because it demonstrates that common citizens could choose not to participate in, and in fact could actively subvert, the Nazis' destruction of the Jews.

There is obvious validity to the claim that *Schindler's List* focuses on the handsome, charismatic Schindler more than on any other single figure; we often view events from his point of view. Spielberg introduces him in a style reminiscent of Michael Curtiz's coy unveiling of Rick in *Casablanca,* refusing to show his face until we desperately desire for it to be revealed, a titillating strategy he also employs in depicting the shark (*Jaws*), the aliens (*E.T.* and *Close Encounters*), the dinosaurs (*Jurassic Park*), and Indiana Jones (*Raiders of the Lost Ark*). In addition, the notion that compassionate capitalism, as epitomized by Schindler, is somehow an antidote to virulent Nazism strikes many as a cruel fable that absolves those corrupt industrialists who collaborated with the Nazis and willingly employed Jews as slave laborers. The prevailing critical sentiment claims that the film's Jews are "not distinguished in their individuality" (Mintz 138), that Spielberg depicts them merely as "pawns . . . with little power or subjectivity" (Gelley 233), and that he reduces them "to pasteboard figures, to generic types incapable of eliciting identification and empathy" (Hansen 83). Yet this view ignores some crucial elements in Spielberg's narrative design: the advantages of not concentrating on one or two specific families; the skillful braiding of Jewish characters throughout the film; and, most importantly, the central roles played by Itzhak Stern (Ben Kingsley) and Helen Hirsch (Embeth Davidtz).

Spielberg was well aware of the criticism leveled against the miniseries "Holocaust" for concentrating on the Jewish Weiss and the German Dorf families, thus turning history into a domestic saga tending toward sentimental melodrama. Clashing repeatedly with the screenwriter, Steven Zaillian, Spielberg insisted that the original script was too "vertical," too much a "character story of Oskar Schindler"; instead, he demanded a "horizontal approach . . . to invoke more of the actual stories of the victims—the Dresners, the Nussbaums, the Rosners" (Schiff 181). His requirements expanded Zaillian's original 190–page script into a robust 350 pages containing multiple stories (Freer 224). Like Robert Altman in his best ensemble works, Spielberg offers few highly refined characters, opting instead for a profusion of activities distributed among an array of families continually forced to interact within highly constricted social spaces. By forfeiting a more conventional strategy of following one or two families in depth, Spielberg provides viewers with a sense of the shared communal existence of his Jewish characters; simultaneously, he endows *Schindler's List* with a narrative breadth that allows his figures to represent a wide stratum of Jewish society and a broad range of emotional responses to their communal and personal tragedies.

Some of the film's detractors remind me of surly undergraduates complaining about foreign films being too hard to follow because they contain so many subplots and so few recognizable faces. Close and repeated viewings reveal a sustained interconnection of recurring Jewish characters that makes them far more than simply marginalized bystanders. Critics who read the film closely provide worthwhile insights into Spielberg's structural, visual, and thematic sophistication, even if they find the production lacking in some categories. Insdorf, for example, makes a compelling case for Spielberg's masterful pattern of intersecting Jewish characters, of introducing such figures early in the film, following them through the picture, seeing them in juxtaposition to each other, and then discovering their fate at its conclusion. We meet and follow the Nussbaums (Michael Gordon and Aldona Grochal), the Pfefferbergs (Jonathan Sagalle and Adi Nitzan), Mordecai Wulkan (Albert Misak), Marcel Goldberg (Mark Ivanir), Chaja and Danka Dresner (Miri Fabian and Anna Muchar), the Rosners (Jacek Wojcicki, Piotr Polk, and Beata Paluch), Rabbi Menasha Levartov (Ezra Dagan), Adam Levy (Adam Siemion), and Itzhak Stern and Helen Hirsch. Except for the last two, none of these figures has much psychological depth, but they reappear throughout the film in developing circumstances. It is probably impossible to follow all of them during a first viewing when the narrative rushes by, the violence horrifies, the emotions overwhelm, and the major characters demand our attention. But subsequent viewing uncovers Spielberg's artistry, particularly his ability to personalize history and create intense viewer identification.

Each of these figures represents a segment of Jewish society and/or a particular dilemma: the Nussbaums the wealthy upper class, the Pfefferbergs the struggling young couple in love, Goldberg the compromised young man, the Dresners a mother and daughter, the Rosners a typical family, Rabbi Levartov the man of God unable to practice his religion, and Adam the corruption of the young. As one quick example, take Rabbi Levartov's narrative arc. He first appears during the roundup of the Polish Jews and their forced internment in the ghetto; then he becomes part of the ghetto life (offering up prayers) before the Jews are transported. During the ghetto liquidation scene, he is initially shown saying his morning prayers and then being roughed up as he vainly tries to show the Nazis his papers. Next, he surfaces as a hinge maker who fails to complete enough products to satisfy Goeth. Taken out to be shot, the commandant's gun jams and Levartov escapes with a nasty blow to the back of his neck. He reemerges (thanks to Stern) in Schindler's factory and, along with the other workers, travels to Brinnlitz (Czechoslovakia) when they leave Poland; finally, Herr Direktor asks him to reinstitute the Sabbath service, and he performs this restorative ritual for the community. A similar course could be traced for all these characters. Slowly, but repeatedly, Spielberg distinguishes them as individuals whose faces emerge from the mass, a process that mimics how Schindler himself comes to view them and, ultimately, how this recognition becomes a crucial part of his moral conversion.

ITZHAK STERN

Steven Zaillian fused three people to form the character of Itzhak Stern: Abraham Bankier, Schindler's plant manager; Mietek Pember, Goeth's stenographer; and Raimund Titsch, the Austrian (Catholic) factory supervisor who oversaw the making of uniforms inside the Plaszow Forced Labor Camp and helped Schindler formulate the list (Freer 225). Stern represents the compassionate counterpart to SS Unterstrumfuhrer Goeth's inhumanity, the self-effacing bookkeeper who wrestles with the devil for Schindler's soul. While Schindler's perspective clearly dominates much of the movie, Spielberg strategically employs Stern's point of view to display the Jewish side of the story, effectively conveying their plight to Schindler and the viewer. As skeptical a reader as Miram Hansen notes how most critics overlook his crucial functions in the film: "Throughout the film, Stern is the focus of point-of-view-edits and reaction shots, just as he repeatedly motivates camera movements and shot changes" (85). Stern must find methods to exert influence even when physically powerless, as his near deportation to Auschwitz demonstrates. He resists the Nazis by maneuvering Schindler first to see, literally and metaphorically, and then to understand the condition of the Jews. For example, Schindler's first bartering of goods (a watch) for Jewish lives occurs after Stern recounts—and Spielberg depicts in horrifying flashback—Goeth's murder of twenty-five men as punishment for one prisoner's escape: "Stern can narrate the past and pass on testimony, hoping to produce action in the listener/viewer" (Hansen 86). His ability to make Schindler see the surrounding world through his eyes, which entails recognizing the depravity of Goeth and the individuality of the Jews, becomes a major part in Schindler's moral conversion.

In addition to making Schindler assume his perspective, Stern functions as the viewer's eyes in several important scenes, chief among them Spielberg's brilliantly horrifying fifteen-minute re-creation of the Aktion, the liquidation of the ghetto on March 13, 1943, during which the Nazis slaughtered some four thousand Jews. To summarize adequately the visual, aural, performative, and editing elements in the destruction of the Krakow ghetto sequence would probably demand a monograph of its own. Joseph McBride classifies this sequence as "the greatest *tour de force* of Spielberg's career to date" (432). Most commentators write that this pivotal milestone takes place from Schindler's point of view as he sits on horseback atop the hillside overlooking the city. Dressed in riding habit and joined by his elegant mistress, Oskar watches Goeth's troops attempt to wipe out the six-hundred-year-old history of Jews in Krakow: "By this evening those six centuries are a rumor," Goeth tells his assembled storm troopers. "They never happened. Today is history." From his aloof vantage point, Oskar is unable to see the individual events taking place below, or even the little girl in the red coat (the color added by computer); what we gain from that height, along with Oskar, is an overview, perhaps akin to a historical account, of the death and destruction.

Rather than maintaining Schindler's detached location, Spielberg uses Stern's ground-level perspective to thrust the audience into the brutal maelstrom swirling beneath Schindler and charts the destruction of the ghetto through specific personal responses: "[N]ested into this sequence is a pronounced point-of-view pattern that centers on Stern and makes him the first to witness the ominous preparations . . . emphasized by a close-up of him putting on his glasses and turning to the window" (Hansen 93). Spielberg takes viewers inside this event by foregrounding the response of particular human beings. "No one can watch this killing, with the SS, again with clipboards and the lists, barking orders, see the wanton destruction of property, hear the sound of the gunfire, and the men, women, and children screaming, and ever again be able to think about the Holocaust as an abstract term" (Gellately 480–81). Throughout this sequence, Spielberg follows every character we have met so far. Through them, he shows not the banality of evil but its vicious savagery. In doing so, he effectively dramatizes the emotional truth of a historical event by skillfully interweaving the personal experiences of individual characters and moving viewers to consider human consequences beyond mere facts and numbing statistics.

Commentators who describe Schindler and Stern as a decidedly unequal odd couple, claiming that the latter functions only through his connection to the former, misread the dynamics of their relationship. Such pronouncements ignore an essential reality: that resistance to persecution and subjugation, particularly for those with scant means for retaliation or revolt, comes in many forms, such as Schindler's large acts of daring as well as Stern's small moments of defiance. For example, Stern consistently maintains a modest but overt sense of independence by politely declining Schindler's offer of a drink. While this refusal may seem insignificant, it establishes Itzhak's refusal to admit Oskar into his personal life and, simultaneously, denies him any respect beyond that demanded by the situation. Schindler can force Stern to do his bidding, but he cannot buy his respect: that, Oskar must earn. More importantly, Stern skillfully manipulates Schindler for the greater good. He feeds the dull flame of Schindler's humanity until it bursts into an uncontrollable blaze that ultimately saves eleven hundred people. Another of Spielberg's common men forced by circumstances beyond their control to behave with uncommon bravery, Stern consciously places Schindler into situations that display the Jews as individuals, not simply as statistics or faceless workers. In many ways Stern, not Schindler, is the true hero and moral center of the film, for he finds the mechanisms necessary to save his people.

Denied the sword of a warrior king, he wields the only weapon available,

Itzhak Stern (Ben Kingsley), the real hero and moral center of *Schindler's List* (1993), motivates the transformation of Oskar Schindler (Liam Neeson) from hedonist to humanitarian.

his intellect, to battle for the survival of his fellow Jews; it is no accident, therefore, that Stern uses the creation of a list to save his people from the orderly Germans who compulsively manufacture lists and keep records, as we see numerous times in the movie. Stern's stubborn intelligence wedges its way through the small cracks in the Nazi killing machine, scraping out spaces with just enough air to breathe until the monsters are slain.

HELEN HIRSCH

If Stern is the intellect of the Jews, then Helen Hirsch is their body—an unbidden site of dangerous temptations and forbidden desires. For Goeth (whose last name is but one letter short of the most revered writer in German history), to see Helen as a sexual being involves admitting her personhood, a conceptualization that remains anathema to him because his entire belief system rests on certifying Jews as nonhumans. Several critics take Spielberg to task for the harrowing scene in which Goeth almost rapes and then viciously beats Helen. Ora Gelley, for example, rebukes him for "the camera's attraction to Goeth's bodily poses . . . and an anesthetization pervaded by violence and perverse pleasure" (221–22). She further argues that Spielberg "engages in a mode of spectacularization which at best neutralizes the horrors of Nazism and at worst exploits a continuing fascination with the power and glamour of fascism" (222). I would argue exactly the opposite: Gelley's reading misrepresents Spielberg's design and ignores the scene's emotional impact. The camera shares not Goeth's but Helen's point of view, allowing viewers to recognize the "power" he wields but finding it neither attractive nor glamorous. Instead, it is fearful and potentially deadly. Far from anesthetizing Goeth's violence, neutralizing its horror, or finding it fascinating, the director forces viewers into the position of his victims by juxtaposing intersecting scenes that make Goeth's frenzied sadism even more odious.

Pushing further, Gelley berates the director for losing "the context of the power relations between couples" (220) when that is precisely what Spielberg illustrates most forcefully. Gelley correctly draws attention to the parallel editing rhythm of four interconnected scenes—Goeth's attack on Hirsch, Joseph Blau (Rami Hauberger) and Rebecca Tannenbaum's (Beata Nowak) marriage ceremony, Schindler's flirtation with a nightclub singer, and his birthday party.

But she overlooks the fact that this montage directly follows Schindler's lecture to Goeth on the nature of true power ("Control is power. Power is when we have every justification to kill and we don't.") and the commandant's murder of the innocent Lisiek. It begins with a clear demonstration

"Control is power." Oskar Schindler (Liam Neeson) lectures the sadistic commandant Amon Goeth (Ralph Fiennes) on the true nature of power in *Schindler's List* (1993).

of that power: Goeth staring intently at Helen as she subserviently buffs his fingernails, peering down her blouse and moving ever closer to her. Immediately, Spielberg cuts to the wedding ceremony, conducted by women in their barracks. A pan of the camp brings us to Goeth's balcony, where he pours himself a glass of wine, still thinking (as we soon see) of Helen. Next, Spielberg transports us to a smoky nightclub, situating us behind the female singer and staring directly at Schindler sitting at a ringside table. Still faintly hearing her song (which will continue to play throughout much of the scene), he cuts to Amon's cellar (where Helen sleeps), as Goeth's ominous footsteps precede his appearance on the stairs. Helen waits in her slip, sweating profusely, breathing nervously, and standing at attention as he enters. "So," he says, "this is where you come to hide from me." Ostensibly talking about giving her a reference after the war, Goeth circles ever closer to his prey, the camera finally framing them in a steady two-shot.

A reverse-angle shot maintains this distance, though Goeth now stands fully frontal in the light and Hirsch, sideways, is in the darker portion of the frame. When she fails to respond to his questions, he informs her that "the truth is always the right answer," a statement dripping with irony, given the situation. He retreats, then moves forward again, bending his face slightly as if to kiss her. "I would like so much to reach out to you," he continues, "to touch you in your loneliness. What would be wrong with that? I realize you are not a person in the strictest sense of the word. They compare you to vermin, to rodents, to lice." Now he stands behind her, his face almost brushing against her tangled hair. Moving around to her front and tentatively curling a strand of her hair around his fingers, he asks, "Is this the face of a rat? Are these the eyes of a rat? Hath not a Jew eyes?" Spielberg quickly cuts back to the nightclub singer standing next to Schindler's table and directing her song at him. Her fingers slowly arc forward, as Spielberg match-cuts back to Goeth making the same movement toward Hirsch's hair, sliding his hand down from her head to cup her breast. Spielberg rapidly cuts back to the singer caressing Schindler's face in the same manner, finally taking it in both her hands, sitting on his lap, and leaning forward to kiss him—as Goeth bends forward to do with Helen.

But here Goeth stops himself. "I don't think so," he says, drawing back from her face. "You Jewish bitch," he spits out, "you almost talked me into it," though the shivering Helen has not uttered a word. Now the director shifts to Joseph and Rebecca's marriage ceremony, a lightbulb being wrapped and crushed beneath Joseph's foot, the sound blending into Goeth viciously slapping Helen across the mouth and Schindler enthusiastically applauding in the nightclub. Next, a kiss between the newlyweds and Schindler blowing a kiss at the singer. Kisses and hugs are being exchanged at the wedding, as Goeth continues brutally beating Helen, knocking her across the room and crashing down a cabinet filled with glass bottles on top of her. Cut to Schindler kissing women at his birthday party in the factory office. Goeth, dressed in his military best, and Stern, wearing a suit and his Jewish star, are toasting Oskar, so we realize that time has elapsed since the beating in the cellar. Enter two girls, a teenager and a younger one, with a birthday cake from the workers. "Thank you very much for the lovely cake," says Oskar, kneeling to give the young girl a kiss on both her cheeks; then rising, he places his hands on the face of the older girl (just as the nightclub singer did to him earlier) and gives her a lingering kiss on the lips—much to the shocked astonishment of the gathered Nazis and the stunned girls who run out of the room.

While Gelley argues that Spielberg's swift intercuts subvert power relationships, I contend that his shot selection and editing structure highlight these discrepancies. Who cannot feel Helen's lack of power as the scene's dominant emotion during Goeth's vicious sexual advances and her cruel beating? Who cannot share the joy of the married couple, the lure of the nightclub singer, and the uncomfortable silence of the stunned guests when Oskar kisses the adolescent Nuisa Horowitz (Magdalena Dandourian), an act forbidden under Nazi law? Spielberg visually reinforces the connections between these mostly simultaneous events by repetitive gestures (hugs, kisses, arm and bodily movements, and so on), camera shots, and character placements. These repetitions allow us to assess the differences between similar acts occurring in different circumstances. So, for example, Goeth's kissing of Helen and Schindler's of Nuisa both occur because the men wield almost total power over the women, but the former is unchallenged, while the latter lands Schindler in jail. Similarly, the kiss that the nightclub singer bestows on Schindler and that he gives to the women at his party are both performative gestures, far different from the kisses and hugs delivered and received by Joseph and Rebecca upon completion of the wedding ceremony.

Such an editing structure allows viewers to compare and contrast these repeated actions and the ways Spielberg visually displays them, allowing for a deeper understanding of their symbolic value as an overt index of the complex power relationships that dominate this sequence—and most of the film as well. Bartov rightly concludes that "by stressing the sheer brutality and sadism of the Holocaust as it was experienced by the victims, Spielberg has filmed some of the most haunting moments in any cinematic representation of the Holocaust" (44). Certainly the cellar scene between Goeth and Hirsch attests to that observation. In particular, the episodes containing violence against women, sometimes exposing their naked bodies, are not "an appeal to the audience's voyeurism" (Horowitz 127) like those in *The Night Porter* (1974) and *Seven Beauties* (1975), principally because Spielberg's visual artistry makes us stand alongside the bare feet of the victims and not in the boots of the Nazis. Far from allowing "aesthetic pleasure to undermine its attempts at representing traumatic events" (Gelley 214), *Schindler's List* remains a powerful achievement in part because Spielberg confronts the immense horrors of those events with an aesthetic that draws in viewers and encourages us to respond emotionally rather than distancing us by incorporating unfamiliar presentational techniques.

SEX AND VIOLENCE

Goeth's treatment of Helen Hirsch represents the most dramatic example of how Spielberg utilizes sexuality as an integral part of his character development throughout *Schindler's List*. Many critics take offense when he shows "bare chested Aryan women dallying with their Nazi paramours" (Gourevitch 49). Even a reasonably balanced reader like Bartov accuses Spielberg of exploiting women by catering "to Hollywood's tradition of providing sexual distraction to the viewers" and concludes that his depiction of naked Jewish prisoners in the shower scene "would be more appropriate to a soft-porn sadomasochistic film" (49). Such comments raise interesting philosophical questions as to whether a filmmaker can employ female nudity without being sexist, titillating the audience, or exploiting a prurient voyeurism. But they totally ignore Spielberg's history as one of the most chaste (some would say repressed) filmmakers in the American cinema and misread his restrained use of nudity in this movie to meet the demands of authenticity. One can easily imagine the howls of protest if he ignored these humiliating instances of degradation, the cries of critical indignation that would have accused Spielberg of shielding himself—and the viewers—from the true horror of the Holocaust. Spielberg incorporates the Nazis' decadent licentiousness—along with their bouts of gluttonous eating and drinking—as physical manifestations of their promiscuous evil; their desire and appetite for indiscriminate killing have no limitations and are never sated. It does not, as Sara Horowitz claims, "make genocide and fornication into moral equivalents" (132) but uses the latter as one index of the former.

Schindler initially partakes of these carnal pleasures, hopping from one mistress to another and literally stuffing his benefactors with expensive food and fine wines. As his moral conversion occurs, he rejects this libertine lifestyle for a monogamous relationship with his wife Emilie (Caroline Goodall). (The real-life Schindler fled Brinnlitz with his wife and mistress in the same car.) This is not, as some critics contend, "a renunciation of any sensual interests" (Bernstein 429), since we earlier see Oskar and Emilie enjoying a conversation following an apparently satisfying sexual coupling. It is, however, evidence of his commitment to a cause greater than his momentary pleasure, as well as a statement that he now sees his wife (as he has come to see the Jews) as a person rather than an object from whom he can gain what he wants and whom he can abandon when he no longer needs her. The fact that Oskar's declaration of fidelity to Emilie—"No doorman or maitre d' will ever mistake you"—takes place in a church as she is praying underscores his growing morality and perhaps even spirituality. In the opening pages of his book, Keneally observes, "Fatal human malice is the staple of narrators, original sin the mother-fluid of historians. But it is a risky enterprise to have to write of virtue" (14). The reaction of commentators to the conversion of Oskar Schindler, in terms of his sexuality, certainly justifies such fears.

THE CONVERSION OF OSKAR SCHINDLER

"I have been searching for a decade the way the characters in *Citizen Kane* searched for the meaning of Rosebud," Spielberg told Susan Royal soon after the film's release. "And I am no closer today, having made the movie, to discovering what motivated his character to do this than I was when I first read the book" (Royal, "Interview" 5). Spielberg is not alone. Neither Keneally nor any of the Schindlerjuden the director interviewed had any explanation for what turned an avaricious opportunist into a compassionate humanitarian. For some of those directly affected, such as the survivor Stanley Orzech, it didn't matter: "Whether Schindler was good or bad was beside the point. No other Germans wanted to get involved. Ninety percent of the German and Austrian people didn't give a damn what was going on in the camps—and they knew. Schindler wasn't a hero—just a human being. They were in short supply" (Salisbury 84). For these people, why Schindler acted as he did is not particularly relevant. Yet some critics remain bothered by the lack of simple psychological explanations for his alteration, while others, like Lawrence L. Langer, see no need for definitive answers: "*Schindler's List,* like all serious art, invites us to join in the creative process by speculating about the riddle of human nature without expecting simple answers, or perhaps, any answers at all" (10). But I think the movie does provide some clues to this transformation.

Although the real-life Oskar Schindler's motivations may remain a mystery, his celluloid counterpart's metamorphosis is motivated by one specific and many smaller events: his observing Goeth's carnage as he ravages the Krakow ghetto, and Stern's subtle maneuvering that allows Oskar to see the Jews as individuals. In subsequent interviews, Spielberg himself came around to the latter point of view: "'I think he decided to save his workers not because of any one precise event, but more because he got to know who they were as human beings'" (qtd. in Grayson 4). One might also suppose that being thrown into jail after innocently kissing Nusia Horowitz gave Schindler a glimpse of how vulnerable he really was and, in this small sense, established a greater kinship with his Jewish workers. While none of these explanations provides a full or even deep psychological motivation, they do make Schindler's conversion dramatically convincing by providing fragments that explain his behavior. Even so, his story remains an exception rather than a representative case during the Holocaust, a fact that caused many critics to question why Spielberg chose this particular story to bring to the screen.

The negative responses to *Schindler's List* begin with the assumption that

Spielberg selected the wrong story to tell. Typical are the remarks of Omer Bartov about how the director picked an extraordinary rather than a typical story to tell, thus "obliterating, or at least neglecting the fact that in the 'real' Holocaust, most of the Jews died, most of the Germans collaborated with the perpetrators, or remained passive bystanders, most of the victims sent to the showers were gassed, and most of the survivors did not walk across green meadows to Palestine" (46). While the inherent paradoxes in Schindler's character presented dramatic possibilities that immediately attracted Spielberg's attention, this industrialist-turned-savior really was an exceptional figure during this period; if his actions had been commonplace, his story would not have been chosen. Spielberg never presumed that his film would define the narrative of the Holocaust. But, as has often been the case in his career, he became a victim of his own success.

By virtue of the film's worldwide fame, it became (and will likely remain for some time) the preeminent account of the Holocaust, the one must-see film for those who may only see one film about the subject. As *Jaws* became the focal point for those who decried the arrival of the summer blockbuster, and the *Indiana Jones* series for those who lamented the infantalization of the American cinema, *Schindler's List* emerged as a lightning rod of contention

"What do we do now?" Speaking for his newly liberated fellow Jews, Itzhak Stern (Ben Kingsley) seeks directions from a Soviet cavalryman in *Schindler's List* (1993).

for those who inveighed against the "Americanization" of the Holocaust and its commodification into products of popular culture.

Bartov, for all his negative comments about the film, makes an important point about Schindler's conversion and its significance beyond the Jewish lives he saved. Schindler's actions prove that options were available:

> [A]t any given point during the Holocaust both bystanders and perpetrators were always faced with the choice to collaborate in, passively observe, or actively resist mass murder. . . . Hence the film qualifies the impression created by numerous historical, literary, and cinematic accounts of the Holocaust as an inherently inevitable, fateful, unstoppable event, one over which human agency had no control. (43)

Quite the opposite of being a defense of German citizenry, as some have argued, *Schindler's List* explicitly indicts those who had opportunities to alter the fate of those who perished but did nothing. The film is not a hagiography, and Oskar Schindler was not a saint. He held few deep convictions about anything; he profited from the misery of war and the suffering of others. Yet even such an obviously flawed person eventually recognized the evil that surrounded him and risked his life and fortune to help prevent even a little bit of it. What excuses, then, did the "good" people have, the churchgoing, morally responsible, ethically high-minded individuals who looked down on such a brash social climber? And, most importantly, what were they doing while Oskar Schindler was saving eleven hundred people?

GOETH

Yet another problematic critique focuses on the evil of Amon Goeth. While Spielberg offers at least a few clues about Oskar's evolution, Goeth remains a motiveless malignancy throughout the movie. The director offers no psychoanalytical analysis to account for his sadism and no broad explanation for the genocide instituted by leaders of the Third Reich and their willing henchmen. Perhaps we should expect none or, more accurately, no explanation is possible. Primo Levi, when asked to explain the Nazis' fanatical hatred of the Jews, wrote: "I must admit that I prefer the humility with which some of the most serious historians . . . confess to *not understanding* the furious anti-Semitism of Hitler and of Germany behind him" (*Reawakening* 227–28). Yet, despite his heinous actions, some commentators claim that Goeth actually becomes "the most compelling figure in the film" (Bernstein 430), a fascinating character to stand alongside Milton's Satan and Shakespeare's Iago. Take, as a representative example, Yosefa Loshitzky's contention that

Goeth attains a "tragic grandeur" that demonstrates how Spielberg finds "evil more interesting than suffering, and the oppressor more titillating that the victim" (5). This argument is repeated throughout the writing of those who see *Schindler's List* as fundamentally misrepresenting crucial aspects of the Holocaust, including its depiction of Nazis and Jews.

This assertion is unsupported by anything in the movie. To attain "tragic grandeur," at least in the classical sense, a character must demonstrate change and complexity; he or she must show how the capacity for greatness, however loosely defined, has been overwhelmed by some uncontrollable tragic flaw or, at the very least, how an initially noble figure is undone by fundamental defects in his or her psychological makeup. Oedipus, Othello, Lear, Lord Jim, Jay Gatsby, Raskolnikov, Charles Foster Kane, Heathcliff, and even the more mundane Willy Loman personify these qualities, and therefore their falls provide a catharsis for the audience, an abiding sense of fear and pity. Such is not the case with Goeth. Throughout the film, he remains a one-dimensional, static, and middle-management figure, not a man capable of nobility, courage, or change. He is neither appealing nor particularly engaging, especially when compared with the suave and charming Schindler or the ethical Stern. A murderous brutality dominates his presentation from the moment he appears until he dies: his slaying of the building supervisor Diana Reiter, his arbitrary shooting of Jews from the balcony, his savage "cleansing" of the Krakow ghetto, his murdering of Lisiek, his slaughtering of twenty-five men in payment for an escaped prisoner, his vicious beating of Helen Hirsch. Nothing places him even remotely within the realm of "tragic grandeur," beyond the faint allure of power and sadism, since we see no development in his character and no hint of greatness.

THE VISUAL ELEMENTS

Around the time of the film's release, much was written in the popular press about how *Schindler's List* evidenced a distinct alteration in Spielberg's working method and visual style. *Newsweek,* for example, described how Spielberg deflates his style: "[G]one are the majestic boom shots, the pearly-slick sheen, the push-button sense of wonder" (Ansen 113). Spielberg fueled this reaction, claiming, "'I threw my toolbox away. I canceled the crane. I tore out the dolly track. I didn't really plan a style. I didn't say I'm going to use a lot of handheld camera. I simply tried to pull events closer to the audience by reducing the artifice'" (qtd. in Ansen 114). Indeed, he went even further. Abandoning his beloved storyboards and refusing to draw up lists of specific shots to be done each day, he made *Schindler's List* with what he described as a "'passionate urgency,'" a method born out of his desire "'to give the film a spontaneity, an edge that serves the subject'" (qtd. in McBride 432). Out went what Spielberg called his "safety nets," the cranes, zoom lens, and Steadicams (McBride 432). Some 40 percent of the movie was shot with handheld cameras (a technician even held the camera during most of the dolly shots) whose unsteadiness provides a distinctly documentary feel, a jittery sense of authenticity bolstered by Spielberg's use of overexposed images, flares left in the frame, and out-of-focus moments.

While Spielberg's visual artistry and technical mastery have been justly praised by most commentators, even those who intensely dislike the film, his skillful use of sound to reinforce the physical chaos, psychological turmoil, and sheer terror has been almost totally ignored, but for Miriam Hansen's analysis. Sound plays a key role throughout the film by working, often in counterpoint, with images to dislodge viewers from the traditional conventions of narrative progression, and to generate an almost surrealistic sense of reality as experienced by the characters. To accomplish this, the director employs

> an abundance of sound bridges and other forms of nonmatching (such as a character's speech or reading turning into documentary style voice-over); and there are numerous moments when the formal disjunction of sound and image subtends rhetorical relations of irony and even counterpoint. . . . [T]he persistent splitting of the image track by means of displaced diegetic sound still undercuts the effect of an immediate and totalitarian grip on reality—such as that produced by perfect sound/image matching in numerous World War II films. (Hansen 86)

Such techniques reach their culmination in scenes of rapid movement and mass confusion, such as the liquidation of the Krakow ghetto. Here Spielberg employs various sounds, sometimes not tethered to the images from where they came, to reinforce his Jewish characters' terror: droning motor engines, marching boots, spastic gunfire, snarling dogs, haunting classical piano music, shrieking whistles, crying babies, echoing rifle shots, sobbing women, and so on. Hansen rightly notes that this pounding sequence is bound together by Goeth's speech ("Today is history") and "symbolically closed by reattaching Goeth's voice to his body, thus sealing the fate of the majority of the ghetto population" (93). While certainly not unique in cinema history, Spielberg's use of sound demonstrates a level of craftsmanship and creativity seldom matched in mainstream films.

No moving pictures exist that document the murders and other atrocities suffered by the prisoners in the Plaszow Labor Camp, though Raimund Titsch (the factory supervisor who helped Schindler write his list) did take some photographs that survived. More importantly, the cinematographer Januz Kaminski studied the poignant photographs of Roman Vishniac, who recorded the inhabitants of Eastern European Jewish *shtetls* between 1920 and 1939 and eventually published his pictures in a collection called *A Vanished World*. Kaminski "'found inspiration in that book'" and "'tried to follow his style in working with light. His pictures felt real: they're not silhouetted or heavily contrasted as in other photos of the period and not art-directed or organized. I liked the softness and fading around the edges and what he was doing with faces—always half light, half dark'" (qtd. in Freer 226). Kaminski consciously approached filming *Schindler's List* as if he "'had to photograph it fifty years ago, with no lights, no dolly, no tripod. . . . Naturally, a lot of it would be handheld, and a lot of it would be set on the ground where the camera was not level. It was simply more real to have certain imperfections in the camera movement'" (qtd. in McBride 431–32). The result is a highly constructed work that gives the impression of having been shot at the time the events transpired.

Spielberg made one crucial decision early on: to shoot the film in black and white. Resisting appeals by Tom Pollack, the chairman of Universal, to make a color version for the home-video market, the director believed that black and white better conveyed a sense of documentary authenticity; he also worried that if he made the movie in color, he might "'accidentally and subconsciously beautify events'" (qtd. in McBride 432). Some cynics claim that Spielberg purposely "Europeanized" his film, evident in this aesthetic choice of black and white, because he knew that was the way to gain artistic legitimacy and that such "high art" stylistics would pave the path toward one of his most cherished goals, an Oscar for Best Director. Though Loshitzky concludes that "the 'Americanization of the Holocaust' was paradoxically achieved through the 'Europeanization' of the film" (5), Thomas Elsaesser's more nuanced position sees Spielberg's film as part of "the ongoing dialogue between so-called post-classical American cinema and the art and auteur cinema of Europe" ("Subject" 165). Spielberg certainly knew that the world viewed his work as all bright lights and breathless action—impressive special effects, manipulative music, and mindless content. "It was good that the word 'Spielbergian' was hanging out there because it haunted me and it kept me from being myself," he told Susan Royal. "And to do this story . . . I had to be myself as a Jew, but I couldn't be myself as a filmmaker" (Royal, "Interview" 6). Whether or not Spielberg's artistic choices were a calculated gambit to achieve artistic acceptance, an instinctive aesthetic decision, or some combination of the two remains unknown, perhaps even to the director himself.

Other things are more clear. An ardent student of film history, Spielberg was influenced by previous Holocaust productions, particularly European productions such as *Night and Fog* (1955), *The Shop on Main Street* (1965), *The Sorrow and the Pity* (1969), and *Shoah* (1985), and he cited influences from David Lean's *Lawrence of Arabia* (1962) as well as from American films such as *The Grapes of Wrath* (1940), *Dr. Strangelove* (1964), and *In Cold Blood* (1967). (For a fascinating study of *Schindler's List* in relation to its European counterparts, see Elsaessar's "Subject Positions, Speaking Positions.") In addition, *Schindler's List* continually references that towering achievement in American film history, *Citizen Kane* (1942), not only in its similar use of lighting, sound, construction of mise-en-scène, and editing, but also in its focus on a complex central character who combines elements of saint and sinner. From this melange of sources evolved a visual style that Kaminski described as a mixture of two prominent cinematic traditions, German expressionism and Italian neorealism (McBride 432). Throughout most of the film, the Germans are filmed in the expressionistic mode, with high-contrast chiaroscuro lighting, and the Jews in the neorealist manner, with more natural lighting. Insdorf notes that "during the first hour, many shots present Schindler's face in half light, half shadow . . . at least until he makes a decisive choice" (261). Look, too, at the liquidation of the Krakow ghetto scene, where Spielberg juxtaposes different types of lighting, mixed with quick cuts and dazzling camera movement, to force viewers inside the Aktion.

CONCLUSION

I have contended throughout this book that it is fair to hold Spielberg accountable for the films he makes, but not for the uses others make of them. One cannot reasonably expect any director to hope that only a few people will see his work, though the financial success of one film usually spawns a gaggle of pale imitations. Subsequent history should also allay the concerns of critics like Les White, who worried that by "being held up as the ultimate expression" of this subject Spielberg's film will "prevent Hollywood from producing more credible and daring films on the Holocaust" (5). The success of *The Pianist* and Insdorf's calculations about the numerous film productions in the post-*Schindler* era demonstrate that one film need not foreclose critical opinions on the achievements of other, often very different, approaches to the same subject matter. In fact, some of the credit for this upsurge in attention to films about the Holocaust can be attributed to the broad acceptance of Spielberg's movie and his financial support of the Shoah Visual History Foundation's taping of survivor testimony.

Stephen Schiff reminds us that "the almost unmentionable secret of *Schindler's List* is that it does entertain—that it is not, in short, a lecture but a work of art" (176). For some critics, this notion that Spielberg's story about the Holocaust "entertains" immediately casts the film into the realm of cheap amusement; the fact that "it might offer us something not possible in academic historical studies" and that for the present generation it has become "the most important source of information affecting popular perceptions of the Holocaust" (Manchel 84) turns it into downright sacrilege. His detractors resolutely maintain that Spielberg can never overcome the limitations that condemn him to the status of a mere entertainer "not interested in expanding viewers' minds, in challenging their views or unsettling their emotions, but in reinforcing their received ideas of history and the world, in reconfirming their prejudices" (Cardullo 123). For such critics, Spielberg remains frozen in time, a technical wizard who conjures up sentimental movies with upbeat, optimistic endings. Nothing of substance exists behind the curtain. As a consequence of its creator's immature imagination, *Schindler's List* cannot rise above the level of sentimental melodrama, a trivial work that offers an "appealingly facile articulation" (Bernstein 431) of the Holocaust and replaces "ethics with spectacle and history with fantasy" (Nichols 11). I have few illusions that anything I have written about *Schindler's List*—or indeed about any of Spielberg's movies—will affect such immutable opinions of his work.

All the stories written by those who survived the Holocaust are anomalies; they all end with life amidst the ashes of the dead, as do many stories in Hebrew scriptures and Jewish history. *Schindler's List* tells of those who endured persecution and outlasted oppression. Elie Wiesel recently acknowledged that "hope is a key word in the vocabulary of men and women like myself and so many others who discovered in America the strength to overcome cynicism and despair. In the bottom of Pandora's box is hope" (7). This sense of "hope" in the midst of despair is precisely what *Schindler's List* presents. It is therefore unfair to criticize Spielberg for the same philosophy or because he did not cover all of the issues and situations others believe to be important. It is true, as Jim Hoberman claims, that "virtually every character in whom the audience has emotionally invested lives" (31), but so did Elie Wiesel and Primo Levi, among others. So did the Schindlerjuden and the eighty to ninety thousand Jews who emigrated to the United States after being liberated from the death camps. No single story of the Holocaust can be typical, however bleak and horrifying, and Spielberg's "happy ending" does not ignore the death of millions or the suffering of those who survived. It suggests that even after the Holocaust there exists sufficient reason to believe in and continue to bring hope into the world. *Schindler's List* does not displace other films about the Holocaust or subsume other narratives; it does not eliminate the necessity for studying history. The film requires us to see and to read them in order to fully grasp what occurs within its frames. It is one important document among many, but an impressive one that artistically balances formidable narrative and technical skills in the service of a profound theme and, in so doing, brings a powerful story to life.

Filmography

Duel (1971)
Cast: Dennis Weaver (David Mann), Jacqueline Scott (Mrs. Mann), Eddie
    Firestone (café owner)
Written by Richard Matheson
Produced by George Eckstein
Original music by Billy Goldenberg, James Lee
Cinematography by Jack A. Marta
Film editing by Frank Morriss
Art direction by Robert S. Smith

The Sugarland Express (1974)
Cast: Goldie Hawn (Lou Jean Poplin), Ben Johnson (Capt. Harlin Tanner),
    Michael Sacks (Patrolman Maxwell Slide), William Atherton (Clovis Michael
    Poplin)
Written by Steven Spielberg, Hal Barwood, Matthew Robbins
Produced by David Brown, Richard D. Zanuck
Original music by John Williams
Cinematography by Vilmos Zsigmond
Film editing by Edward M. Abroms, Verna Fields
Art direction by Joe Alves

Jaws (1975)
Cast: Roy Scheider (Police Chief Martin Brody), Robert Shaw (Quint), Richard
    Dreyfuss (Matt Hooper), Lorraine Gary (Ellen Brody), Murray Hamilton
    (Mayor Larry Vaughn)
Written by Peter Benchley, Carl Gottlieb

Produced by David Brown, Richard D. Zanuck
Original music by John Williams
Cinematography by Bill Butler
Film editing by Verna Fields
Production design by Joe Alves

Close Encounters of the Third Kind (1977)
Cast: Richard Dreyfuss (Roy Neary), François Truffaut (Claude Lacombe), Teri
  Garr (Ronnie Neary), Melinda Dillon (Jillian Guiler), Bob Balaban (David
  Laughlin), Cary Guffey (Barry Guiler)
Written by Steven Spielberg
Produced by Clark L. Paylow, Julia Phillips, Michael Phillips
Original music by John Williams
Cinematography by William A. Fraker, Douglas Slocombe, Vilmos Zsigmond
Film editing by Michael Kahn
Art direction by Daniel A. Lomino

1941 (1979)
Cast: Dan Aykroyd (Sgt. Frank Tree), Ned Beatty (Ward Douglas), John Belushi
  (Capt. Wild Bill Kelso), Lorraine Gary (Joan Douglas), Murray Hamilton
  (Claude Crumn), Christopher Lee (Capt. Wolfgang von Kleinschmidt), Tim
  Matheson (Capt. Loomis Birkhead), Toshirô Mifune (Cmdr. Akiro Mitamura),
  Robert Stack (Maj. Gen. Joseph W. Stilwell), Treat Williams (Cpl. Chuck
  "Stretch" Sitarski), Nancy Allen (Donna Stratton), Bobby Di Cicco (Wally
  Stephens), Dianne Kay (Betty Douglas)
Written by Robert Zemeckis, Bob Gale, John Milius
Produced by Buzz Feitshans, Janet Healy, Michael Kahn, John Milius
Original music by Johnny Mandel, John Williams
Cinematography by William A. Fraker
Film editing by Michael Kahn
Art direction by William F. O'Brien

Raiders of the Lost Ark (1981)
Cast: Harrison Ford (Indiana Jones), Karen Allen (Marion Ravenwood), Paul
  Freeman (Dr. Rene Belloq), Ronald Lacey (Major Toht), John Rhys-Davies
  (Sallah), Denholm Elliott (Dr. Marcus Brody)
Written by George Lucas, Philip Kaufman, Lawrence Kasdan
Produced by Howard G. Kazanjian, George Lucas, Frank Marshall, Robert Watts
Original music by John Williams
Cinematography by Douglas Slocombe
Film editing by Michael Kahn
Art direction by Leslie Dilley

E.T. the Extra-Terrestrial (1982)
Cast: Henry Thomas (Elliott), Dee Wallace-Stone (Mary), Robert MacNaughton
   (Michael), Drew Barrymore (Gertie), Peter Coyote (Keys)
Written by Melissa Mathison
Produced by Kathleen Kennedy, Melissa Mathison, Steven Spielberg
Original music by John Williams
Cinematography by Allen Daviau
Film editing by Carol Littleton
Set design by William James Teegarden

Indiana Jones and the Temple of Doom (1984)
Cast: Harrison Ford (Indiana Jones), Kate Capshaw (Wilhelmina "Willie" Scott),
   Jonathan Ke Quan (listed as Ke Huy Quan: Short Round), Amrish Puri (Mola
   Ram)
Written by George Lucas, Willard Huyck, Gloria Katz
Produced by Kathleen Kennedy, George Lucas, Frank Marshall, Robert Watts
Original music by John Williams
Cinematography by Douglas Slocombe
Film editing by Michael Kahn
Art direction by Roger Cain, Alan Cassie

The Color Purple (1985)
Cast: Danny Glover (Albert), Whoopi Goldberg (Celie), Margaret Avery (Shug
   Avery), Oprah Winfrey (Sofia), Willard E. Pugh (Harpo), Akosua Busia (Nettie),
   Adolph Caesar (Old Mister), Rae Dawn Chong (Squeak)
Written by Alice Walker, Menno Meyjes
Produced by Peter Guber, Carole Isenberg, Quincy Jones, Kathleen Kennedy,
   Frank Marshall, Jon Peters, Steven Spielberg
Original music by Andraé Crouch, Quincy Jones, Jeremy Lubbock, Caiphus
   Semenya, Rod Temperton
Cinematography by Allen Daviau
Film editing by Michael Kahn
Art direction by Bo Welch

Empire of the Sun (1987)
Cast: Christian Bale (Jim), John Malkovich (Basie), Miranda Richardson (Mrs.
   Victor), Nigel Havers (Dr. Rawlins), Joe Pantoliano (Frank Demarest), Leslie
   Masatô Ibu (Sgt. Nagata)
Written by J.G. Ballard, Tom Stoppard
Produced by Kathleen Kennedy, Chris Kenny, Frank Marshall, Robert Shapiro,
   Steven Spielberg
Original music by John Williams

Cinematography by Allen Daviau
Film editing by Michael Kahn
Art direction by Fred Hole

Always (1989)
Cast: Richard Dreyfuss (Pete Sandich), Holly Hunter (Dorinda Durston), Brad
    Johnson (Ted Baker), John Goodman (Al Yackey), Audrey Hepburn (Hap)
Written by Frederick Hazlitt Brennan, Jerry Belson
Produced by Kathleen Kennedy, Frank Marshall, Steven Spielberg, Richard Vane
Original music by John Williams
Cinematography by Mikael Salomon
Film editing by Michael Kahn
Art direction by Christopher Burian-Mohr

Indiana Jones and the Last Crusade (1989)
Cast: Harrison Ford (Indiana Jones), Sean Connery (Professor Henry Jones),
    Denholm Elliott (Dr. Marcus Brody), Alison Doody (Dr. Elsa Schneider), John
    Rhys-Davies (Sallah), Julian Glover (Walter Donovan), River Phoenix (Young
    Indy)
Written by Jeffrey Boam
Produced by George Lucas, Frank Marshall, Arthur F. Repola, Robert Watts
Original music by John Williams
Cinematography by Douglas Slocombe
Film editing by Michael Kahn
Art direction by Stephen Scott

Hook (1991)
Cast: Dustin Hoffman (Capt. James S. Hook), Robin Williams (Peter Banning/
    Peter Pan), Julia Roberts (Tinkerbell), Bob Hoskins (Smee), Maggie Smith
    (Granny Wendy/middle-aged Wendy), Caroline Goodall (Moira Banning),
    Charlie Korsmo (Jack "Jackie" Banning), Amber Scott (Maggie Banning)
Written by J. M. Barrie, James V. Hart, Nick Castle, James V. Hart, Malia Scotch
    Marmo
Produced by Gary Adelson, Craig Baumgarten, Bruce Cohen, Dodi Fayed, James
    V. Hart, Kathleen Kennedy, Malia Scotch Marmo, Frank Marshall, Gerald R.
    Molen
Original music by John Williams
Cinematography by Dean Cundey
Film editing by Michael Kahn
Art direction by Andrew Precht, Thomas E. Sanders

Jurassic Park (1993)
Cast: Sam Neill (Dr. Alan Grant), Laura Dern (Dr. Ellie Sattler), Jeff Goldblum
(Dr. Ian Malcolm), Richard Attenborough (John Hammond), Bob Peck (Robert
Muldoon), Martin Ferrero (Donald Gennaro), Joseph Mazzello (Tim Murphy),
Ariana Richards (Lex Murphy), Samuel L. Jackson (Ray Arnold), B. D. Wong
(Henry Wu), Wayne Knight (Dennis Nedry)
Written by Michael Crichton, David Koepp
Produced by Kathleen Kennedy, Gerald R. Molen, Lata Ryan, Colin Wilson
Original music by John Williams
Cinematography by Dean Cundey
Film editing by Michael Kahn
Art direction by John Bell, William James Teegarden

Schindler's List (1993)
Cast: Liam Neeson (Oskar Schindler), Ben Kingsley (Itzhak Stern), Ralph Fiennes
(Amon Goeth), Caroline Goodall (Emilie Schindler), Jonathan Sagall (Poldek
Pfefferberg), Embeth Davidtz (Helen Hirsch)
Written by Thomas Keneally, Steven Zaillian
Produced by Irving Glovin, Kathleen Kennedy, Branko Lustig, Gerald R. Molen,
Robert Raymond, Steven Spielberg
Original music by John Williams
Cinematography by Janusz Kaminski
Film editing by Michael Kahn
Art direction by Ewa Skoczkowska, Maciej Walczak

The Lost World: Jurassic Park (1997)
Cast: Jeff Goldblum (Dr. Ian Malcolm), Julianne Moore (Dr. Sarah Harding), Pete
Postlethwaite (Roland Tembo), Richard Attenborough (John Hammond), Vince
Vaughn (Nick Van Owen), Arliss Howard (Peter Ludlow), Vanessa Lee Chester
(Kelly Curtis Malcolm), Peter Stormare (Dieter Stark)
Written by Michael Crichton, David Koepp
Produced by Bonnie Curtis, Kathleen Kennedy, Gerald R. Molen, Colin Wilson
Original music by John Williams
Cinematography by Janusz Kaminski
Film editing by Michael Kahn
Art direction by Lauren E. Polizzi, Paul M. Sonski, William James Teegarden

Amistad (1997)
Cast: Morgan Freeman (Joadson), Nigel Hawthorne (Martin Van Buren),
Anthony Hopkins (John Quincy Adams), Djimon Hounsou (Cinque), Matthew
McConaughey (Baldwin), David Paymer (Secretary Forsyth), Pete Postlethwaite
(Holabird), Stellan Skarsgård (Tappan)

Written by David Franzoni
Produced by Debbie Allen, Robert Cooper, Bonnie Curtis, Paul Deason, Laurie
    MacDonald, Walter F. Parkes, Tim Shriver, Steven Spielberg, Colin Wilson
Original music by Debbie Allen, John Williams
Cinematography by Janusz Kaminski
Film editing by Michael Kahn
Art direction by Christopher Burian-Mohr, Tony Fanning, William James
    Teegarden

Saving Private Ryan (1998)
Cast: Tom Hanks (Capt. Miller), Tom Sizemore (Sgt. Horvath), Edward Burns
    (Pvt. Reiben), Barry Pepper (Pvt. Jackson), Adam Goldberg (Pvt. Mellish), Vin
    Diesel (Pvt. Caparzo), Giovanni Ribisi (T-4 Medic Wade), Jeremy Davies (Cpl.
    Upham), Matt Damon (Pvt. Ryan)
Written by Robert Rodat
Produced by Ian Bryce, Bonnie Curtis, Kevin De La Noy, Mark Gordon, Mark
    Huffam, Gary Levinsohn, Allison Lyon Segan, Steven Spielberg
Original music by John Williams
Cinematography by Janusz Kaminski
Film editing by Michael Kahn
Casting by Denise Chamian
Art direction by Tom Brown, Ricky Eyres, Chris Seagers, Alan Tomkins

Artificial Intelligence: AI (2001)
Cast: Haley Joel Osment (David), Frances O'Connor (Monica Swinton), Sam
    Robards (Henry Swinton), Jude Law (Gigolo Joe), William Hurt (Prof. Hobby)
Written by Ian Watson, Brian Aldiss, Steven Spielberg
Produced by Bonnie Curtis, Jan Harlan, Kathleen Kennedy, Walter F. Parkes,
    Steven Spielberg
Original music by Paul Barker, Max Brody, Deborah Coon, Al Dubin, Al
    Jourgensen, John Williams
Cinematography by Janusz Kaminski
Film editing by Michael Kahn
Art direction by Richard L. Johnson, William James Teegarden, Tom Valentine

Minority Report (2002)
Cast: Tom Cruise (Det. John Anderton), Colin Farrell (Det. Danny Witwer),
    Samantha Morton (Agatha), Max von Sydow (Director Lamar Burgess),
    Kathryn Morris (Lara Anderton), Mike Binder (Leo F. Crow)
Written by Philip K. Dick, Scott Frank, Jon Cohen
Produced by Jan de Bont, Bonnie Curtis, Michael Doven, Sergio Mimica-Gezzan,
    Gerald R. Molen, Walter F. Parkes, Ronald Shusett

Original music by Paul Haslinger, John Williams
Cinematography by Janusz Kaminski
Film editing by Michael Kahn
Art direction by Ramsey Avery, Leslie McDonald, Seth Reed, Paul M. Sonski

Catch Me If You Can (2002)
Cast: Leonardo DiCaprio (Frank Abagnale Jr.), Tom Hanks (Carl Hanratty),
    Christopher Walken (Frank Abagnale Sr.), Martin Sheen (Roger Strong),
    Nathalie Baye (Paula Abagnale)
Written by Frank Abagnale Jr., Stan Redding, Jeff Nathanson
Produced by Barry Kemp, Daniel Lupi, Laurie MacDonald, Sergio Mimica-
    Gezzan, Devorah Moos-Hankin, Walter F. Parkes, Anthony Romano, Michel
    Shane, Steven Spielberg
Original music by John Williams
Cinematography by Janusz Kaminski
Film editing by Michael Kahn
Art direction by Sarah Knowles, Michele Laliberte

The Terminal (2004)
Cast: Tom Hanks (Viktor Navorski), Catherine Zeta-Jones (Amelia Warren),
    Stanley Tucci (Frank Dixon), Chi McBride (Mulroy), Diego Luna (Enrique
    Cruz), Barry Shabaka Henley (Thurman), Kumar Pallana (Gupta Rajan), Zoe
    Torres (Zoë Saldana)
Written by Andrew Niccol, Sacha Gervasi, Jeff Nathanson
Produced by Jason Hoffs, Laurie MacDonald, Sergio Mimica-Gezzan, Andrew
    Niccol, Walter F. Parkes, Steven Spielberg, Patricia Whitcher
Original music by John Williams
Cinematography by Janusz Kaminski
Film editing by Michael Kahn
Art direction by Isabelle Guay

War of the Worlds (2005)
Cast: Tom Cruise (Ray Ferrier), Dakota Fanning (Rachel Ferrier), Justin Chatwin
    (Robbie Ferrier), Tim Robbins (Harlan Ogilvy), Miranda Otto (Mary Ann),
    David Alan Basche (Tim)
Written by H. G. Wells, David Koepp, Josh Friedman
Produced by Kathleen Kennedy, Paula Wagner, Colin Wilson
Original music by John Williams
Cinematography by Janusz Kaminski
Film editing by Michael Kahn
Art direction by Tony Fanning, Andrew Menzies, Edward Pisoni, Tom Warren

Munich (2005)

Cast: Eric Bana (Avner), Daniel Craig (Steve), Ciarán Hinds (Carl), Mathieu
Kassovitz (Robert), Hanns Zischler (Hans), Michael Lonsdale (Papa), Mathieu
Amalric (Louis), Ayelet Zorer (Daphna), Geoffrey Rush (Ephraim), Lynn
Cohen (Golda Meir)

Written by George Jonas (book) and Tony Kushner (screenplay)

Produced by Kathleen Kennedy, Barry Mendel, Steven Spielberg, Colin Wilson

Original music by John Williams

Cinemetography by Janusz Kaminski

Film editing by Michael Kahn

Art direction by Ino Bonello, Tony Fanning, Andrew Menzies, David Swayze,
János Szabolcs, Karen Wakefield

Works Cited

Abramowitz, Rachel. "Regarding Stanley." *Los Angeles Times,* May 6, 2001, 1, 7.

Adorno, Theodor. "Engagement." *Noten zur Literatur* 3 (1965): 109–35.

Allende, Isabel. *Portrait in Sepia.* New York: HarperCollins, 2001.

Amistad. Dir. Steven Spielberg. DVD. Dreamworks SKG, 1999.

Andrews, Nigel. *Nigel Andrews on Jaws.* London: Bloomsbury Publishing, 1999.

Ansen, David. "Spielberg's Obsession." *Newsweek,* December 20, 1993, 113–16.

Arnold, Matthew. "Dover Beach." In *The Norton Anthology of English Literature.* 3d ed. 1355–56. Ed. M. H. Abrams. New York: W. W. Norton, 1962.

Aronstein, Susan. "Not Exactly a Knight: Arthurian Narrative and Recuperative Politics in the *Indiana Jones* Trilogy." *Cinema Journal* 34.4 (Summer 1995): 3–30.

Arthur, Paul. "Spielberg and Kubrick's Love Child." *Film Comment* 37.4 (July/August 2001): 20–25.

Auster, Albert. "*Saving Private Ryan* and American Triumphalism." *Journal of Popular Film and Television* 30 (Summer 2002): 98–104.

Avisar, Ilan. *Screening the Holocaust: Cinema's Images of the Unimaginable.* Bloomington: Indiana University Press, 1988.

Bahania, Ana Maria. "Hook." *Steven Spielberg: Interviews.* Ed. Lester D. Friedman and Brent Notbohm. 193–206. Jackson: University of Mississippi Press, 2000.

Balides, Constance. "Jurassic Post-Fordism: Tall Tales of Economics in the Theme Park." *Screen* 41.2 (Summer 2000): 139–60.

Ballard, J. G. *Empire of the Sun.* New York: Simon and Schuster, 1984.

Bartov, Omer. "Spielberg's Oskar: Hollywood Tries Evil." In *Spielberg's Holocaust: Critical Perspectives on "Schindler's List."* Ed. Yosefa Loshitzky. 41–60. Bloomington: Indiana University Press, 1997.

Basinger, Jeanine. "Translating War: The Combat Film Genre and *Saving Private Ryan.*" *Perspectives* (American Historical Association Newsletter) 36.7 (October 1998): 42–47.

————. *The World War II Combat Film: Anatomy of a Genre.* New York: Columbia University Press, 1986.

Bawer, Bruce. "Ronald Reagan as Indiana Jones." *Newsweek,* August 27, 1984, 14.

Baxter, John. *Steven Spielberg: The Unauthorized Biography.* London: HarperCollins, 1996.

Bernstein, Michael Andre. "The *Schindler's List* Effect." *American Scholar* 63.3 (Summer 1994): 429–32.

Biskind, Peter. "Blockbuster: *The Last Crusade*". In *Seeing through Movies.* Ed. Mark Crispin Miller. 112–49. New York: Pantheon Books, 1990.

————. *Easy Riders, Raging Bulls: How the Sex-Drugs-and-Rock 'n' Roll Generation Saved Hollywood.* New York: Simon and Schuster, 1998.

————. "A 'World' Apart." In *Steven Spielberg: Interviews.* Ed. Lester D. Friedman and Brent Notbohm. 193–206. Jackson: University of Mississippi Press, 2000.

Blake, Edith. *On Location on Martha's Vineyard: The Making of the Movie "Jaws."* New York: Ballantine Books, 1975.

Bobo, Jacqueline. *Black Women as Cultural Readers.* New York: Columbia University Press, 1993.

Bobrow, Andrew C. "Filming *The Sugarland Express:* An Interview with Steven Spielberg." In *Steven Spielberg: Interviews.* Ed. Lester D. Friedman and Brent Notbohm. 18–29. Jackson: University of Mississippi Press, 2000.

Bogle, Donald. *Toms, Coons, Mulattoes, Mammies, and Bucks: An Interpretive History of Blacks in American Films.* New York: Continuum, 1986.

Braudy, Leo. "The Genre of Nature: Ceremonies of Innocence." In *Refiguring American Film Genres: Theory and History.* Ed. Nick Browne. 278–309. Berkeley: University of California Press, 1998.

Breznican, Antony. "Spielberg's Family Values." *USA Today,* June 24–26, 2005, 1A-2A.

Britton, Andrew. "Blissing Out: The Politics of Reaganite Entertainment." *Movie* 31–32 (1986): 1–42.

Brode, Doug. *The Films of Steven Spielberg.* New York: Citadel Press, 1995.

Browne, Nick, ed. *Refiguring American Film Genres: Theory and History.* Berkeley: University of California Press, 1998.

Brownlow, Kevin. *Behind the Mask of Innocence: Sex, Violence, Prejudice, and Crimes; Films of Social Conscience in the Silent Era.* New York: Alfred A. Knopf, 1990.

Calwell, Christopher. "Spielberg at War." *Commentary* 106.4 (October 1998): 48–51.

Campbell, Russell. "The Ideology of the Social Consciousness Movie: Three Films of Darryl F. Zanuck." *Quarterly Review of Film Studies* 37 (Winter 1978): 49–71.

Cardullo, Bert. "Schindler's Miss." *Hudson Review* 48.1 (Spring 1995): 121–27.

Caro, Mark. "Spielberg's and Cruise's Risky Business: Another Trip to the Dark Side." *Chicago Tribune,* June 16, 2002, 1.

Carroll, Noel. *The Philosophy of Horror, or Paradoxes of the Heart.* New York: Routledge, 1990.

Catch Me If You Can. Dir. Steven Spielberg. DVD. Dreamworks SKG, 2003.

Caughie, John. *Theories of Authorship*. London: Routledge, 2001.

Cawelti, John G. *Adventure, Mystery, and Romance: Formula Stories as Art and Popular Culture*. Chicago: University of Chicago Press, 1976.

Clarke, James. *The Pocket Essential Steven Spielberg*. North Pomfret, Vt.: Trafalgar Square Publishing, 2001.

Cohen, Arthur A. *The Tremendum: A Theological Interpretation of the Holocaust*. New York: Crossroads, 1981.

Cole, Tim. *Selling the Holocaust: From Auschwitz to Schindler, How History Is Bought, Packaged, and Sold*. New York: Routledge, 1999.

Coleridge, Samuel Taylor. "The Rime of the Ancient Mariner." In *English Romantic Writers*. Ed. David Perkins. 404–13. New York: Harcourt, Brace, and World, 1967.

Collins, Glenn. "Spielberg Films *The Color Purple*." In *Steven Spielberg: Interviews*. Ed. Lester D. Friedman and Brent Notbohm. 120–25. Jackson: University of Mississippi Press, 2000.

The Color Purple. Dir. Steven Spielberg. DVD. Warner Brothers, 1997.

Corliss, Richard. "A Studio Is Born." *Time*, October 24, 1994, 68–70.

Davies, Kevin. "Simulated Shades of *Jurassic Park*?" Bio-IT World. December 1, 2004 www.bio-itworld.com/news/120104_report6804.html.

Davis, Natalie Zemon. *Slaves on the Screen: Film and Historical Vision*. Cambridge, Mass.: Harvard University Press, 2000.

Denne, John D. "Society and the Monster." In *Focus on the Horror Film*. Ed. Roy Huss and T. J. Ross. 125–31. Englewood Cliffs, N.J.: Prentice Hall, 1972.

Desser, David, and Lester D. Friedman. *American Jewish Filmmakers*. 2d ed. Urbana: University of Illinois Press, 2004.

Dick, Philip K. *The Minority Report and Other Classic Stories*. New York: Citadel Press, 2002.

Dickstein, Morris. "The Aesthetics of Fright." In *Planks of Reason: Essays on the Horror Film*. Ed. Barry Keith Grant. 65–78. Metuchen, N.J.: Scarecrow Press, 1984.

Dillard, R. H. W. "The Pageantry of Death." In *Focus on the Horror Film*. Ed. Roy Huss and T. J. Ross. 36–41. Englewood Cliffs, N.J.: Prentice Hall, 1972.

Dixon, Wheeler Winston. "Twenty-Five Reasons Why It's All Over." In *The End of Cinema as We Know It: American Film in the Nineties*. Ed. Jon Lewis. 356–66. New York: New York University Press, 2001.

———, ed. *Film Genre 2000: New Critical Essays*. Albany: State University of New York Press, 2000.

Doherty, Thomas. *Projections of War: Hollywood, American Culture, and World War II*. New York: Columbia University Press, 1999.

Dubner, Stephen J. "Steven the Good." In *Steven Spielberg: Interviews*. Ed. Lester D. Friedman and Brent Notbohm. 223–41. Jackson: University of Mississippi Press, 2000.

Early, Gerald. "*The Color Purple* as Everybody's Protest Art." In *The Films of Steven Spielberg: Essays*. Ed. Charles Silet. 91–106. Lanham, Md.: Scarecrow Press, 2002.

Edelstein, David. "Philip K. Dick's Mind-Bending, Film-Inspiring Journeys." *New York Times,* June 16, 2002, 17.

Elsaesser, Thomas. "Subject Positions, Speaking Positions: From *Holocaust, Our Hitler,* and *Heimat* to *Shoah* and *Schindler's List.*" In *The Persistence of History: Cinema, Television, and the Modern Event.* Ed. Vivian Sobchack. 145–86. New York: Routledge, 1996.

———. "Tales of Sound and Fury: Observations on the Family Melodrama." In *Film Genre Reader II.* Ed. Barry Grant. 350–80. Austin: University of Texas Press, 1995.

Entman, Robert, and Francie Seymour. "Close Encounters with the Third Reich." *Jump Cut* 18 (August 15, 1978): 3–5.

Fackenheim, Emil. *The Jewish Return into History: Reflections of the Age of Auschwitz and Jerusalem.* New York: Schocken Books, 1978.

Fine, Larry. "Are We Ready for *War of the Worlds?*" *Syracuse Post Standard,* June 28, 2005, E1, E4.

Fordham, Joe. "Mecha Odyssey." *Cinefex* 87 (October 2001): 64–93.

Forsberg, Myra. "Spielberg at Forty: The Man and the Child." In *Steven Spielberg: Interviews.* Ed. Lester D. Friedman and Brent Notbohm. 126–32. Jackson: University of Mississippi Press, 2000.

Frayling, Christopher. "*Hook.*" In *Action/Spectacle Cinema: A Sight and Sound Reader.* Ed. Jose Arroyo. 219–21. London: BFI Publishing, 2000.

Freer, Ian. *The Complete Spielberg.* London: Virgin Publishing, 2001.

Freud, Sigmund. "Screen Memories." In *The Standard Edition of the Complete Works of Sigmund Freud,* vol. 3. Trans. James Strachey. 303–22. London: Hogarth, 1960.

Friedlander, Saul, ed. *Probing the Limits of Representation: Nazism and the "Final Solution."* Cambridge, Mass.: Harvard University Press, 1992.

Friedman, Lester D. "The Blasted Tree: Mary Shelley and James Whale." In *The English Novel and the Movies.* Ed. Michael Klein and Gillian Parker. 52–66. New York: Frederick Ungar, 1981.

———. "Darkness Visible: Images of Nazis in American Films." In *Bad: Infamy, Darkness, Evil, and Slime on the Screen.* Ed. Murray Pomerance. 255–71. Albany: State University of New York Press, 2004.

———. "Mother Cutter as Producer: An Interview with Verna Fields." *Mise-en-scène* 2 (Spring 1980): 49–57.

Friedman, Lester D., and Brent Notbohm, eds. *Steven Spielberg: Interviews.* Jackson: University of Mississippi Press, 2000.

Gabler, Neal. "Seeking Perspective on the Movie Front Lines." *New York Times,* January 27, 2002, 4.

Gellately, Robert. "Between Exploitation, Rescue, and Annihilation: Reviewing *Schindler's List.*" *Central European History* 26.4 (1993): 475–89.

Gelley, Ora. "Narration and Embodiment of Power in *Schindler's List.*" In *The Films of Steven Spielberg: Essays.* Ed. Charles Silet. 215–36. Lanham, Md.: Scarecrow Press, 2002.

Geng, Veronica. "Spielberg's Express." *Film Comment* 17.4 (July 1981): 57–59.

Gerstner, David, and Janet Staiger. *Authorship and Film.* London: Routledge, 2003.

Giles, Jeff. "Catch Them If You Can: A Candid Conversation with Three Superstars." *Newsweek,* December 23, 2002, 58–61.

Goldstein, Warren. "Bad History Is Bad for a Culture." *Chronicle of Higher Education,* April 10, 1998, A64.

Gordon, Andrew. "*E.T.* as Fairy Tale." *Science Fiction Studies* 10 (1983): 298–305.

———. "*Raiders of the Lost Ark:* Totem and Taboo." *Extrapolation* 32.3 (Fall 1991): 256–66.

———. "Steven Spielberg's *Empire of the Sun:* A Boy's Dream of War." *Literature/Film Quarterly* 19.4 (1991): 210–21.

Gottlieb, Carl. *The Jaws Log.* New York: Dell, 1975.

Gourevitch, Philip. "A Dissent on *Schindler's List.*" *Commentary* 97.2 (February 1994): 49–52.

Grainge, Paul. Introduction to *Memory and Popular Film.* Ed. Paul Grainge. 1–20. Manchester: Manchester University Press, 2003.

Grant, Barry Keith, ed. *Film Genre Reader III.* Austin: University of Texas Press, 2003.

Grayson, Todd. "*Schindler's List*" *Shofar* (April 1994): 2–5.

Greenaway, Peter. "The *Tulse Luper Suitcase.*" Lecture delivered at Chicago Humanities Festival, Northwestern Law School, November 9, 2004.

Greenberg, Harvey R. *The Movies on Your Mind: Film Classics on the Couch from Fellini to Frankenstein.* New York: E. P. Dutton, 1975.

———. "Raiders of the Lost Text: Remaking as Contested Homage in *Always.*" In *Play It Again, Sam: Retakes on Remakes.* Ed. Andrew Horton and Stuart Y. McDougal. 115–30. Berkeley: University of California Press, 1998.

Griffin, Nancy. "In the Grip of *Jaws.*" *Premier* 9.2 (October 1995): 88–101.

Gross, Larry. "Big and Loud." In *Action/Spectacle Cinema: A Sight and Sound Reader.* Ed. Jose Arroyo. 3–9. London: BFI Publishing, 2000.

Habermas, Jurgen. *Religion and Rationality: Essays on Reason, God, and Modernity.* Ed. Eduardo Mendieta. Cambridge: Massachusetts Institute of Technology Press, 2002.

Hammond, Michael. "Some Smothering Dreams: The Combat Film in Contemporary Hollywood." In *Genre and Contemporary Hollywood.* Ed. Steve Neale. 62–76. London: BFI Publishing, 2002.

Hansen, Miriam Bratu. "*Schindler's List* Is Not *Shoah:* The Second Commandment, Popular Modernism, and Public Memory." In *Spielberg's Holocaust: Critical Perspectives on "Schindler's List."* Ed. Yosefa Loshitsky. 77–103. Bloomington: Indiana University Press, 1997.

Hartman, Geoffrey H. "The Book of the Destruction." In *Probing the Limits of Representation: Nazism and the "Final Solution."* Ed. Saul Friedlander. 318–34. Cambridge, Mass.: Harvard University Press, 1992.

———. *Holocaust Remembrance: The Shapes of Memory.* Oxford: Blackwell, 1994.

Hawkins, Harriet. "Paradigms Lost: Chaos, Milton, and *Jurassic Park.*" *Textual Practice* 8.2 (1994): 255–67.

Helpern, David. "At Sea with Steven Spielberg." In *Steven Spielberg: Interviews.* Ed. Lester D. Friedman and Brent Notbohm. 3–17. Jackson: University of Mississippi Press, 2000.

Hill, John. "The British Social Problem Film: *Violent Playground* and *Sapphire.*" *Screen* (February 1985): 34–48.

Hillberg, Raul. *The Destruction of the European Jews.* New York: Holmes and Meier, 1985.

Hirschman, Elizabeth. *Heroes, Monsters, and Messiahs: Movies and Television Shows as the Mythology of American Culture.* Kansas City: Andrews McMeel Publishing, 2000.

Hoberman, Jim. "*Schindler's List:* Myth, Movie, and Memory." *Village Voice,* March 29, 1994, 24, 31.

Hodenfield, Chris. "*1941:* Bombs Away!" In *Steven Spielberg: Interviews.* Ed. Lester D. Friedman and Brent Notbohm. 70–83. Jackson: University of Mississippi Press, 2000.

Holden, Stephen. "Holiday Movies' Somber Embrace." *New York Times,* January 2, 2004, B1, B14.

Horowitz, Sara R. "But Is It Good for the Jews? Spielberg's Schindler and the Aesthetics of Atrocity." In *Spielberg's Holocaust: Critical Perspectives on "Schindler's List."* Ed. Yosefa Loshitzky. 119–39. Bloomington: Indiana University Press, 1997.

Insdorf, Annette. *Indelible Shadows: Film and the Holocaust.* 3d ed. New York: Cambridge University Press, 2003.

Jaehne, Karen. Review of *Saving Private Ryan. Film Quarterly* 53.1 (Fall 1999): 39–41.

Jaws. Dir. Steven Spielberg. Anniversary ed. DVD. Universal, 2000.

Jeffrey, Julie Roy. "*Amistad:* Steven Spielberg's 'True Story.'" *Historical Journal of Film, Radio, and Television* 21 (March 2001): 1–24.

Jennings, Wade. "Fantasy." In *Handbook of American Film Genres.* Ed. Wes D. Gehring. 249–65. New York: Greenwood Press, 1988.

Jones, Howard. *Mutiny on the Amistad: The Saga of a Slave Revolt and Its Impact on American Abolition, Law, and Diplomacy.* New York: Oxford University Press, 1987.

Junker, Detlef. "No Business Like Shoah Business." *Sydney Morning Herald,* March 31, 2001, 1, 8.

Kael, Pauline. *For Keeps.* New York: Plume, 1996.

Kaes, Anton. "Holocaust and the End of History: Postmodern Historiography in Cinema." In *Probing the Limits of Representation: Nazism and the "Final Solution."* Ed. Saul Friedlander. 206–22. Cambridge, Mass.: Harvard University Press, 1992.

Kane, Kathryn. *Visions of War: Hollywood Combat Films of World War II.* Ann Arbor, Mich.: UMI Research Press, 1982.

Kauffmann, Stanley. "Epiphany." *New Republic,* December 10, 1977, 20–21.

Kawin, Bruce. "Children of the Light." In *Film Genre Reader II.* Ed. Barry Keith Grant. 308–29. Austin: University of Texas Press, 1995.

Kennedy, Lisa. "Spielberg in the Twilight Zone." *Wired* 10.6 (June 2002): 104–13, 146.

Kerr, David. "Mother Love, Too Little or Too Much." *New York Times,* July 29, 2001, AR9.

Klein, Charlotte. *Anti-Judaism in Christian Theology.* Philadelphia: Fortress Press, 1975.

King, Geoff. *Spectacular Narratives: Hollywood in the Age of the Blockbuster.* London: I. B. Tauris, 2000.

Kodat, Catherine Gunther. "Saving Private Property: Steven Spielberg's American DreamWorks." *Representations* 71 (Summer 2000): 77–105.

Kolker, Robert. *A Cinema of Loneliness.* 3d ed. New York: Oxford University Press, 2000.

Kurzman, Dan, *Fatal Voyage: The Sinking of the USS Indianapolis.* New York: Broadway Books, 2001.

Langer, Lawrence L. *Admitting the Holocaust: Collected Essays.* New York: Oxford University Press, 1995.

Landsberg, Alison. "America, the Holocaust, and the Mass Culture of Memory: Toward a Radical Politics of Empathy." *New German Critique* 71 (Spring 1997): 63–86.

———. "Prosthetic Memory: The Ethics and Politics of Memory in an Age of Mass Culture." In *Memory and Popular Film.* Ed. Paul Grainge. 144–61. Manchester: Manchester University Press, 2003.

Lerner, Neil. "Nostalgia, Masculinist Discourse, and Authoritarianism in John Williams' Scores for *Star Wars* and *Close Encounters of the Third Kind.*" In *Off the Planet: Music, Sound, and Science Fiction Cinema.* Ed. Philip Hayward. 96–108. Eastleigh, U.K.: John Libbey, 2004.

Levi, Primo. *The Reawakening:* New York: Touchstone, 1965.

———. *Survival in Auschwitz: The Nazi Assault on Humanity.* New York: Macmillan, 1993.

Levinas, Emmanuel. *Entre nous: On Thinking-of-the-Other.* Trans. Michael B. Smith and Barbara Harshav. New York: Columbia University Press, 1998.

Lewis, Jon. "The Perfect Money Machine(s): George Lucas, Steven Spielberg, and Auteurism in the New Hollywood." *Film International* 1 (2003): 13–26.

———, ed. *The End of Cinema as We Know It: American Film in the Nineties.* New York: New York University Press, 2001.

Lipsitz, George. *Time Passages: Collective Memory and American Popular Culture.* Minneapolis: University of Minnesota Press, 1990.

Lopat, Phillip. "Resistance to the Holocaust." *Tikkun* 4 (May–June 1989).

Loshitzky, Yosefa, ed. *Spielberg's Holocaust: Critical Perspectives on "Schindler's List."* Bloomington: Indiana University Press, 1997.

Lyman, Rick. "Spielberg Challenges the Big Fluff of Summer" *New York Times,* June 16, 2002 (Arts and Leisure), 17.

Lyotard, Jean-Francois. *The Differend: Phrases in Dispute,* Trans. Georges Van Den Abbeele. Minneapolis: University of Minnesota Press, 1988.

Maland, Charles J. "The Social Problem Film." In *Handbook of American Film Genres.* Ed. Wes D. Gehring. 305–29. New York: Greenwood Press, 1988.

———. E-mail correspondence with the author. February 22, 2004.

Manchel, Frank. "A Reel Witness: Steven Spielberg's Representation of the Holocaust in *Schindler's List.*" *Journal of Modern History* 67 (March 1995): 83–100.

Margalit, Avishai. *The Ethics of Memory.* Cambridge, Mass.: Harvard University Press, 2002.

Maslin, Janet. "Panoramic and Personal Visions of War's Anguish." *New York Times,* July 24, 1998, E1, E28.

McBride, Joseph. *Steven Spielberg: A Biography.* New York: Simon and Schuster, 1997.

Meacham, John. "Caught in the Line of Fire." *Newsweek,* July 13, 1998, 48–55.

Menand, Louis. "Jerry Don't Surf." In *The Films of Steven Spielberg: Critical Essays.* Ed. Charles Silet. 251–56. Lanham, Md.: Scarecrow Press, 2002.

Miller, Arthur. *Death of a Salesman.* In *Masters of Modern Drama.* Ed. Haskell M. Block and Robert G. Shedd. 1020–54. New York: Random House, 1964.

Mintz, Alan. *Popular Culture and the Shaping of Holocaust Memory in America.* Seattle: University of Washington Press, 2001.

Morrison, Toni. *Toni Morrison: Profile of a Writer.* Television special. Public Broadcasting Service, 1987.

Mott, Donald R., and Cheryl McAllister Saunders. *Steven Spielberg.* Boston: Twayne Publishers, 1986.

Mounteer, Carl A. "The Religious Experience of Modern American Film." *Journal of Psychohistory* 20.1 (Summer 1992): 53–63.

Nathan, Ian. "The Fortunes of War." In *Empire: The Directors Collection.* 115–120. London: Endeavour House, 1999.

Neale, Steve, ed. *Genre and Contemporary Hollywood.* London: BFI Publishing, 2002.

Nichols, Bill. "The Ten Stations of Spielberg's Passion: *Saving Private Ryan, Amistad, Schindler's List.*" *Jump Cut* 43 (2000): 9–11.

1941. Dir. Steven Spielberg. Collector's ed. DVD. Universal, 1999.

Novick, Peter. *The Holocaust in American Life.* Boston: Houghton Mifflin, 1999.

O'Brien, Tim. *The Things They Carried.* New York: Broadway Books, 1990.

Owens, Susan A. "Memory, War, and American Identity: *Saving Private Ryan* as Cinematic Jeremiad." *Critical Studies in Media Communication* 19.3 (September 2002): 249–82.

Owens, William A. *Black Mutiny: The Revolt on the Schooner Amistad.* New York: Black Classic Press, 1997.

Peebles, Stacey. "Gunning for a New Slow Motion: The 45–Degree Shutter and the Representation of Violence." *Journal of Film and Video* 56.2 (Summer 2004): 45–54.

Perry, George. *Steven Spielberg Close Up: The Making of His Movies.* New York: Thunder's Mouth Press, 1998.

Phillips, Caryl. "Another Course Change toward Seriousness." *New York Times,* September 7, 1997, 39, 42.

Pizzello, Stephen. "Five-Star General." In *Steven Spielberg: Interviews.* Ed. Lester D. Friedman and Brent Notbohm. 207–14. Jackson: University of Mississippi Press, 2000.

Place, J. A. "Some Visual Motifs of *Film Noir.*" In *Movies and Methods.* Ed. Bill Nichols. 325–38. Berkeley: University of California Press, 1976.

Polan, Dana. *Power and Paranoia: History, Narrative, and the American Cinema, 1940–1950.* New York: Columbia University Press, 1986.

Pomerance, Murray. "The Man-Boys of Steven Spielberg." In *Where the Boys Are: Cinemas of Masculinity and Youth.* Ed. Murray Pomerance and Frances Gateward. 133–54. Detroit: Wayne State University Press, 2004.

Prager, Dennis, and Joseph Telushkin. *Why the Jews?* New York: Simon and Schuster, 1985.

Prawer. S. S. *Caligari's Children: The Film as Tale of Terror.* New York: Oxford University Press, 1980.

Prince, Stephen. *A New Pot of God: Hollywood under the Electronic Rainbow, 1980–1989.* Berkeley: University of California Press, 2000.

———. *Visions of Empire: Political Imagery in Contemporary American Film.* New York: Praeger, 1992.

Probst, Christopher. "The Last Great War." *American Cinematographer* 79.8 (August 1998): 31–42.

Rafferty, Terrence. "The Movie That Created the 'Summer Movie.'" *New York Times,* April 30, 2000, 30, 36.

Richardson, John H. "Steven's Choice." In *Steven Spielberg: Interviews.* Ed. Lester D. Friedman and Brent Notbohm. 156–69. Jackson: University of Mississippi Press, 2000.

Roffman, Peter, and Jim Purdy. *The Hollywood Social Problem Film: Madness, Despair, and Politics from the Depression to the Fifties.* Bloomington: Indiana University Press, 1981.

Rosen, Gary. "*Amistad* and the Abuse of History." In *The Films of Steven Spielberg: Critical Essays.* Ed. Charles Silet. 239–48. Lanham, Md.: Scarecrow Press, 2002.

Rosenfeld, Alvin H. "The Holocaust in American Popular Culture." *Midstream* 29–30 (June 1983): 53–59.

Roskies, David G. *Against the Apocalypse: Responses to Catastrophe in Modern Jewish Culture.* Cambridge, Mass.: Harvard University Press, 1984.

Roth, Lane. "Raiders of the Lost Archetype: The Quest and the Shadow." *Studies in the Humanities* 10.1 (June 1983): 13–21.

Royal, Susan. "*Always:* An Interview with Steven Spielberg." In *Steven Spielberg: Interviews.* Ed. Lester D. Friedman and Brent Notbohm. 133–50. Jackson: University of Mississippi Press, 2000.

———. "An Interview with Steven Spielberg, 1997–2003." *Inside Film Magazine,* October 28, 2004, 2–7.

———. "Steven Spielberg in His Adventures on Earth." In *Steven Spielberg: Interviews.* Ed. Lester D. Friedman and Brent Notbohm. 84–106. Jackson: University of Mississippi Press, 2000.

Rubin, Susan Goldman. *Steven Spielberg: Crazy for Movies.* New York: Harry N. Abrams, 2001.

Russell, David J. "Monster Roundup: Reintegrating the Horror Genre." In *Refiguring American Film Genres: Theory and History.* Ed. Nick Browne. 233–54. Berkeley: University of California Press, 1998.

Salisbury, Mark. "Spielberg." *Empire* 51 (March 1994): 82–91.

Sanello, Frank. *Spielberg: The Man, the Movies, the Mythology.* Dallas: Taylor Publishing Co., 1996.

Santner, Eric L. "History beyond the Pleasure Principle: Some Thoughts on the Representation of Trauma." In *Probing the Limits of Representation: Nazism and the "Final Solution."* Ed. Saul Friedlander. 143–54. Cambridge, Mass.: Harvard University Press, 1992.

Sanz, Jose Luis. *Staring T. Rex! Dinosaur Mythology and Popular Culture.* Bloomington: Indiana University Press, 2002.

Schatz, Thomas. *Hollywood Genres: Formulas, Filmmaking, and the Studio System.* Philadelphia: Temple University Press, 1981.

———. "The New Hollywood." In *Film Theory Goes to the Movies.* Ed. Jim Collins, Hilary Radner, and Ava Preacher Collins. 8–36. New York: Routledge, 1993.

———. "World War II and the Hollywood War Film." In *Refiguring American Film Genres: Theory and History.* Ed. Nick Browne. 89–128. Berkeley: University of California Press, 1998.

Schiff, Stephen. "Seriously Spielberg." In *Steven Spielberg: Interviews.* Ed. Lester D. Friedman and Brent Notbohm. 170–92. Jackson: University of Mississippi Press, 2000.

Scott, A. O. "The Studio-Indie, Pop-Prestige, Art-Commerce King." *New York Times,* November 9, 2003, 60–63.

Selizer, Barbie. *Remembering to Forget: Holocaust Memory through the Camera's Eye.* Chicago: University of Chicago Press, 1998.

Shattuc, Jane. "Having a Good Cry over *The Color Purple:* The Problem of Affect and Imperialism in Feminist Theory." In *Melodrama: Stage, Picture, Screen.* Ed. Jacky Bratton, Jim Cook, and Christine Gledhill. 147–56. London: BFI Publishing, 1994.

Shay, Don, and Jody Duncan. *The Making of "Jurassic Park."* New York: Ballantine, 1993.

Sheehan, Henry. "The PANning of Steven Spielberg." *Film Quarterly* 28.3 (May–June 1992): 54–60.

———. "Spielberg II." *Film Quarterly* 28.4 (July–August 1992): 66–71.

Shohat, Ella, and Robert Stam. *Unthinking Eurocentrism: Multiculturalism and the Media.* New York: Routledge, 1994.

Silet, Charles, ed. *The Films of Steven Spielberg: Critical Essays.* Lanham, Md.: Scarecrow Press, 2002.

Slade, Darren, and Nigel Watson. *Supernatural Spielberg.* London: Valis Books, 1992.

Sloan, Kay. "The Loud Silents: Origins of the Social Problem Film." In *Movies and American Society.* Ed. Steven I. Ross. 42–63. Oxford: Blackwell, 2002.

Sobchack, Vivian. "Science Fiction." In *Handbook of American Film Genres.* Ed. Wes D. Gehring. 228–47. New York: Greenwood Press, 1988.

———. *Screening Space: The American Science Fiction Film.* New York: Frederick Ungar, 1987.

Solomon, Stanley J. *Beyond Formula: American Film Genres.* New York: Harcourt Brace Jovanovich, 1976.

Sontag, Susan. "Fascinating Fascism." In *Movies and Methods.* Vol. 1. Ed. Bill Nichols. 31–43. Berkeley: University of California Press, 1976.

———. "The Imagination of Disaster." In *Against Interpretation.* 209–25. New York: Delta Book, 1961.

Spielberg, Steven. "Dialogue on Film." *American Film* 13.8 (June 1988): 12–16.

Stanton, Doug. *In Harm's Way: The Sinking of the USS Indianapolis and the Extraordinary Story of Its Survivors.* New York: Henry Holt, 2001.

Storey, John. "The Articulation of Memory and Desire: From Vietnam to the War in the Persian Gulf." In *Memory and Popular Film.* Ed. Paul Grainge. 99–119. Manchester: Manchester University Press, 2003.

Sturken, Marita. *Tangled Memories: The Vietnam War, the AIDS Epidemic, and the Politics of Remembering.* Berkeley: University of California Press, 1997.

Tarratt, Margaret. "Monsters from the Id." In *Film Genre Reader II.* Ed. Barry Keith Grant. 330–49. Austin: University of Texas Press, 1995.

Taylor, Philip. *Steven Spielberg: The Man, His Movies, and Their Meaning.* New York: Continuum, 1994.

Telotte, J. P. *Science Fiction Film.* New York: Cambridge University Press, 2001.

The Terminal. Press kit. Dreamworks SKG, 2004.

Thomson, David. "Who Killed the Movies?" *Esquire* 25.6 (December 1996): 56–60.

Todorov, Tzvetan. *The Fantastic: A Structural Approach to a Literary Genre.* Ithaca, N.Y.: Cornell University Press, 1975.staz

Tomasulo, Frank P. E-mail correspondence with the author. March 18, 2004.

———. "Empire of the Gun: Steven Spielberg's *Saving Private Ryan* and American

Chauvinism." In *The End of Cinema as We Know It: American Film in the Nineties*. Ed. Jon Lewis. 115–30. New York: New York University Press, 2001.

———. "The Gospel According to Spielberg in *E.T. the Extra-Terrestrial*." *Quarterly Review of Film and Video* 18.3 (2001): 273–82.

———. "Mr. Jones Goes to Washington: Myth and Religion in *Raiders of the Lost Ark*." *Quarterly Review of Film Studies* 7.4 (1982): 331–40.

Toplin, Robert Brent. *Reel History: In Defense of Hollywood*. Lawrence: University Press of Kansas, 2002.

Torry, Robert. "Politics and Parousia in *Close Encounters of the Third Kind*." *Film/ Literature Quarterly* 19.3 (1991): 188–95.

Tuchman, Mitch. "Close Encounter with Steven Spielberg." In *Steven Spielberg: Interviews*. Ed. Lester D. Friedman and Brent Notbohm. 37–54. Jackson: University of Mississippi Press, 2000.

Tudor, Andrew. "From Paranoia to Postmodernism? The Horror Movie in Late Modern Society." In *Genre and Contemporary Hollywood*. Ed. Steve Neale. 105–16. London: BFI Publishing, 2002.

———. *Monsters and Mad Scientists: A Cultural History of the Horror Movie*. Oxford: Blackwell, 1989.

Underwood, Tim, and Chuck Miller, eds. *Bare Bones: Conversations on Terror with Stephen King*. New York: McGraw Hill, 1988.

Walker, Alice. *The Color Purple*. New York: Harcourt Brace Jovanovich, 1983.

———. *The Same River Twice: Honoring the Difficult*. New York: Washington Square Press, 1996.

Wallerstein, Andrew. "Shoah Business: A Conversation on Jewish Culture, Politics, and Religion." *Moment*, April 2, 2002, 1–5.

War of the Worlds. Press kit and Production notes. Dreamworks SKG, 2005.

Wells, H. G. *The War of the Worlds: The Deluxe Illustrated Edition*. Naperville, Ill.: Sourcebooks, 2005.

Wells, Paul. *The Horror Genre: From Beelzebub to Blair Witch*. London: Wallflower, 2000.

Wexman, Virginia Wright, ed. *Film and Authorship*. New Brunswick, N.J.: Rutgers University Press, 2003.

White, Les. "My Father Is a Schindler Jew." *Jump Cut* 39 (1994): 3–6.

Wiesel, Elie. "The America I Love." *Parade*, July 4, 2003, 5–7.

———. *From the Kingdom of Memory: Reminiscences*. New York: Summit, 1990.

———. *Memoirs: All Rivers Run to the Sea*. New York: Shocken, 1995.

———. *Night*. Trans. Stella Rodway. New York: Bantam, 1982.

———. "Some Measure of Humility." *Sh'ma* 5.100 (October 31, 1975): 314–16.

Wieseltier, Leon. "Close Encounters of the Nazi Kind." *New Republic*, January 24, 1994, 42

Will, George F. "A Summons to Gratitude." *Newsweek*, August 17, 1998), 70.

Williams, Linda. "Melodrama Revisited." In *Reconfiguring Film Genres: Theory and History*. Ed. Nick Browne. 42–88. Berkeley: University of California Press, 1998.

Williams, Mark. "Real-Time Fairy Tales: Cinema Prefiguring Digital Anxiety." In *New Media: Theories and Practices of Digitextuality*. Ed. Anna Everett and John T. Caldwell. 159–78. New York: Routledge, 2003.

Williams, Tony. "Close Encounters of the Authoritarian Kind." *Wide Angle* 5.4 (1983): 22–29.

Wollen, Peter. "Theme Park and Variations." In *Action/Spectacle Cinema: A Sight and Sound Reader*. Ed. Jose Arroyo. 182–87. London: BFI Publishing, 2000.

Wordsworth, William. "Ode: Intimations of Immortality from Recollections of Early Childhood." In *English Romantic Writers*. Ed. David Perkins. 279–82. New York: Harcourt, Brace, and World, 1967.

Wood, Robin. *Hollywood from Vietnam to Reagan*. New York: Columbia University Press, 1986.

Wright, Judith Hess. "Genre Films and Status Quo." In *Film Genre Reader II*. Ed. Barry Keith Grant. 41–49. Austin: University of Texas Press, 1995.

Yule. Andrew. *Spielberg: Father of the Man*. London: Warner Books, 1996.

Zelizer, Barbie. *Remembering to Forget: Holocaust Memory through the Camera's Eye*. Chicago: University of Chicago Press, 1998.

Zimmermann, Patricia. "Soldiers of Fortune: Lucas, Spielberg, Indiana Jones, and *Raiders of the Lost Ark*." *Wide Angle* 6.2 (1984): 34–39.

Index

Abagnale, Frank Jr. (*Catch Me*), 6, 23, 66, 70–76, 73, 98, 118
Abagnale, Frank Sr. (*Catch Me*), 70–76, 98
Abramowitz, Rachel, 48
Abyss, The, 133
Action/adventure melodramas: *Catch Me,* 66, 70, 118; costumes in, 79–80; female figures in, 85; genre expectations in, 78, 112–18, 125; hero's moral education in, 65, 78, 81, 82, 90, 116, 118; *Indiana Jones* trilogy, 66, 85, 108, 118; physical exploits in, 64, 77, 78; social codes as barriers in, 64, 65, 66; by Spielberg, 65–66, 118; stereotypes of, 92, 109, 110; *Sugarland Express,* 66, 118; tension in, 63–65
Adams, Amy, 72
Adams, John, 272, 276, 277
Adams, John Quincy (*Amistad*), 271, 272, 273, 276–80, 277
Adorno, Theodor, 298–99
Age of Aquarius, 109
Aldiss, Brian, 47
Alien series, 64
Allen, Debbie, 269, 272, 273
Allen, Karen, 78, 87
Allen, Nancy, 193
Allen, Woody, 48
Allende, Isabel, 186
All Quiet on the Western Front, 229
Althusser, Louis, 257

Altman, Robert, 58, 67, 68, 306
Always, 14–17; audience expectations frustrated by, 17, 25; characters in, 8, 16, 141; commercial failure of, 17, 65, 220; counternarrative in, 5, 16; as fantasy film, 12, 13, 243; flying as theme in, 7, 14, 16, 25, 283; gross earnings of, 270; male angst in, 130; music for, 175; source material for, 14, 17; visual hallmarks in, 25
Ambrose, Steven, 221
American Cinematographer, 232
American Dream: debasement of, 33, 64, 70; siren song of, 76
American Film Institute, 3, 4, 65
American Jewish Filmmakers (Desser and Friedman), 297
American Tail, An, 297–98
America Online (AOL), 221
Amistad, 269–82; author's conclusion, 282; characters in, 6, 8, 272, 275, 276–78, 277, 279–80; ending of, 275–76; and *E.T.,* 275–76; gross earnings of, 270; as historical drama, 48, 245, 269, 271–75, 276–78; music for, 175, 270; opening scene of, 281–82; Oscar nominations for, 270; social issues addressed in, 9, 10, 23, 108, 195, 244, 245–47, 252, 270, 276, 282, 289, 305; source material for, 269; visual elements in, 278–82, 286
Anderson, Carl, 249

Anderton, John (*Minority*), 6, 31, 32, 35–36, 46, 50–54, 55, 108, 158
Andrews, Nigel, 175
"Anne Frank" (TV), 295
Anne Frank Remembered, 295
Ansen, David, 252
Apocalypse Now, 185, 193
Armstrong, Neil, 56
Arnold, Edward, 278
Arnold, Gary, 190
Aronstein, Susan, 77, 83, 84, 110, 117
Arthurian legends, 77
Artificial Intelligence: AI: on assuming adult responsibilities, 28; characters in, 6, 30, 31, 35, 38–39, 46; children in, 23, 30, 31, 32–34, 35, 36, 44; darkness of, 46, 69; flying as metaphor in, 7; happy ending of, 152; and Kubrick, 48–49, 198; public reception of, 49, 62; religious aspects of, 43–45; robots in, 30, 44–45; as science fiction, 26, 28; social issues addressed in, 9, 10, 108; source material for, 47; special effects in, 30, 47, 145; structure and point of view, 29, 30, 31; as unconventional film, 62, 252
Assault, The, 295
Atherton, William, 66
Atswhatimtalknbout (horse), 4
Attenborough, Richard, 134, 135, 137
Au Revoir les enfants, 295
Avery, Margaret, 249
Aykroyd, Dan, 195, 196, 197

Baby Boomers, 99, 221, 222
Backlinie, Susan, 170, 195
Baker, Chris, 47, 48
Bale, Christian, 197, 208, 213
Balides, Constance, 133–34, 223
Ballard, J. G., 197–98, 199, 201, 202, 204, 209, 212, 219, 248
Bambi, 14
Bana, Eric, 10
"Band of Brothers" (TV), 3
Banning, Peter (*Hook*), 6, 13, 18–22, 21, 23, 25
Barrie, Sir James, 18, 21
Barry (*Close Encounters*), 31, 32–33
Barry, Gene, 150
Barry Lyndon, 48
Barrymore, Drew, 33
Bartov, Omer, 300, 314, 315, 317, 318
Basche, David Alan, 151

Basco, Dante, 21
Basie (*Empire*), 205, 206, 207, 209–15
Basinger, Jeanine, 180, 181, 184, 185, 190, 240
Bates, Norman (*Psycho*), 38, 59, 119
Battleground, 229
Battle of Midway, The, 229
Battle of San Pietro, The, 229
Bawer, Bruce, 100
Baxter, John, 297
Baye, Nathalie, 70
Belloq, Rene (*Raiders*), 78, 88, 90, 92–95, 94, 97, 114, 115
Beloved (Morrison), 281
Belushi, John, 195, 196, 197
Benchley, Peter, 169, 248
Berenbaum, Michael, 296
Bergman, Ingrid, 93
Bernstein, Melvin, 291
Binder, Mike, 55
Birds, The, 124
Birth of a Nation, The, 273, 274
Biskind, Peter, 32, 76, 99, 106, 109, 110, 116, 176, 177
Black Mutiny (Owens), 269
Black Women as Cultural Readers (Bobo), 253
Blade Runner, 49, 119
Blue Fairy, quest for (*AI*), 29, 43–44
Bluth, Don, 297
Boat Is Full, The, 295
Bobo, Jacqueline, 253, 255–59, 267–68
Bogart, Humphrey, 93, 195
Bogle, Donald, 252
Bond, James, movies about, 111, 112
Bonnie and Clyde, 177, 232
"Book of Destruction, The" (Hartman), 299–300
Boorman, John, 68
Braudy, Leo, 147
Breakout, 177
Bricusse, Leslie, 24
Bridge on the River Kwai, The, 198
Britton, Andrew, 33, 40, 58, 76, 86, 110, 111, 275
Brode, Doug, 24, 83, 86, 87, 195, 220
Brody, Chief Martin (*Jaws*), 6, 22, 108, 132, 164–65, 165, 166–73, 174, 175
Brokaw, Tom, 221
Brolin, James, 70
Brown, Tony, 253, 254, 259

Browne, Nick, 9
Brownlow, Kevin, 244
Buffett, Jimmy, 24
Burgess, Lamar (*Minority*), 35–36, 53
Burning Bed, The, 244
Burns, Edward, 234, 237
Butler, Bill, 162
Byron, Kathleen, 238

Cabaret, 295
Cameron, James, 133
Campbell, Joseph, 77
Campbell, Russell, 245
Campion, Jane, 305
Capa, Robert, 229
Cape Fear, 302
Capra, Frank, 61, 235, 278
Capshaw, Kate, 85, 97, 270
Carlyle, Thomas, 3
Caro, Mark, 43
Carroll, Noel, 119, 121
Carter, Rick, 148
Carter, Ruth, 270
Casablanca, 16–17, 93, 183–84, 306
Cassidy, Hopalong, 78
Castro, Fidel, 4
Catch Me If You Can, 69–76, 288; as action/
    adventure melodrama, 66, 70, 118; broken
    family in, 71, 72–76; characters in, 6, 8,
    72–75, 73; counternarrative in, 5; dark side
    of, 70–71; flying as metaphor in, 7, 283;
    personal identity as issue in, 9, 74, 130;
    visual approach in, 69, 108
Caughie, John, 9
Celie (*Color Purple*), 6, 108, 248, 249–52, 255,
    258, 258, 260–63, 266–67, 268
CGI, 133, 134, 156, 219
Champlin, Charles, 190
Chatwin, Justin, 151
Chen, Renee Shin-Yi, 103
Chester, Vanessa Lee, 149
Chiaq, Roy, 86
China, 79
China Syndrome, The, 244
Chong, Rae Dawn, 255
"Christmas Song, The," 75
Ciccolella, Jude, 285
Cinque (*Amistad*), 271, 272–73, 272, 275–82,
    277
Citizen Kane, 316, 322

Citizen Soldiers (Ambrose), 221
Clairmont Camera Image Shaker, 232
Clark, Spencer Treat, 51
Clarke, James, 195, 203
Clockwork Orange, A, 54
Close Encounters of the Third Kind: aliens in,
    27, 29, 30, 31, 34, 37, 40, 56, 58, 59, 61–62,
    306; American culture emphasized in,
    56, 58, 61; characters in, 6, 22, 31, 35, 36,
    37–38, 37, 141; children threatened in, 23,
    33, 34, 35, 276; counternarrative in, 5, 62;
    fascist model assigned to, 58–62; flying as
    theme in, 283; influence of, 4, 62; on the
    innocence of childhood, 28; optimism of,
    46, 61–62, 150; popular success of, 62, 190;
    religious aspects of, 39–40, 42–43, 44; as
    science fiction, 26, 27, 28, 48; Spielberg's
    personal connection to, 9; structure and
    point of view, 28, 29–31, 60, 155, 285; tech-
    nology in, 42–43, 198
Close, Glenn, 24
Cohen, Arthur A., 301
Cold Mountain, 223
Cole, Nat "King," 75
Cole, Tim, 291
Collins, Phil, 24
Color Purple, The, 247–69, 276; author's
    conclusion, 267–69; awards for, 269; Black
    women's favorable response to, 257–59;
    characters in, 6, 8, 23, 249–52, 256, 258,
    259–67; controversies around, 252–67;
    flying as metaphor in, 7; gross earnings
    of, 270; music for, 174, 192, 248, 250, 268;
    negative depiction of Blacks charged to,
    252, 253–59, 270; PG-13 rating of, 261;
    social issues addressed in, 10, 23, 100, 108,
    195, 244, 245–46, 289; source material for,
    248, 249, 251, 252, 254–56, 258, 259–61, 263,
    267–68, 297; as transitional film, 24, 220,
    251, 268; and Walker, 248–52, 259–61, 267
Columbus, Chris, 100
Connery, Sean, 81, 89, 112
Conrad, Joseph, 198
Cooper, Gary, 15, 286
Coppola, Francis Ford, 270
Corliss, Richard, 137
Corner in Wheat, A, 244
Coyote, Peter, 29
Creature from the Black Lagoon, The, 128
Crewdson, Gregory, 4

Crichton, Michael, 132, 137, 138, 148
Crockett, Davy, 161
Crosby, David, 24
Crow, Ashley, 53
Cruise, Tom, 31, 32, 151, 154, 155–56, 284
Cry Freedom, 272
Curtis, Bonnie, 48
Curtiz, Michael, 17, 306

Dagan, Ezra, 307
Dandourian, Magdalena, 314
David (*AI*), 6, 30, 31, 32, 33–34, 36, 38–39, 43–45, 46, 108
Davidson, Bill, 195
Davidtz, Embeth, 306
Davies, Jeremy, 237
Day After, The, 244
Day the Earth Stood Still, The, 27
Death Becomes Her, 197
Deer Hunter, The, 185
Deisel, Vin, 228, 237
Deliverance, 68
Denby, David, 16
Denne, John D., 122
Dent, Bobby and Ila Faye, 66
Dern, Laura, 135, 135
Desser, David, 297
Diary of Anne Frank, The, 295
Diary of a Young Girl (Frank), 292, 301
DiCaprio, Leonardo, 70, 73
Di Cicco, Bobby, 193
Dick, Philip K., 49, 248
Dickstein, Morris, 121, 122
Die Hard series, 64
Dietrich, John, 87
Dillard, R. H. W., 122
Dixon, Frank (*Terminal*), 283, 285–88
Dixon, Wheeler Winston, 9, 106
Doherty, Thomas, 180, 181, 229, 239–40
Donovan, Walter (*Last Crusade*), 78, 95, 114, 115
Doody, Alison, 78, 89
Doom 2, 192
Dracula, 123, 125
Dragonslayer, 111
Dreamworks SKG, 3, 270, 274
Dreyfuss, Richard, 13, 25, 37, 162, 165, 173, 297
Dr. Strangelove, 322
Dr. Zhivago, 198
Duck Soup, 191

Duel, 127–32, 131, 195; author's conclusion, 132; awards won by, 128; box-office success of, 128; characters in, 6, 22, 127, 141; expanded theatrical release of, 127; male anxiety in, 129–32; as monster movie, 123–26; as television movie, 127; truck as monster in, 125, 127, 132; use of sound vs. dialogue in, 128–29; visualization of, 108, 128–29
Dumbo, 195

Early, Gerald, 253, 254, 255, 259
Easy Rider, 177
Eckstein, George, 127
Eichmann, Karl Adolf, 292
Eisenhower, Dwight D., 155
Ejiofor, Chiwetel, 277
Elliott (*E. T.*), 6, 29, 31, 32–33, 35, 36, 37, 41, 155, 275
Elsaesser, Thomas, 321
"Embraceable You," 71, 72
Emerson, Ralph Waldo, 237
Empire of the Sun, 197–220, 286; author's conclusion, 220; characters in, 6, 8, 100, 141, 199; counternarratives in, 5; ending scene of, 152, 202–3, 216, 219; father figures in, 199–215; flying as theme in, 7, 199, 208, 283; gross earnings of, 220, 270; lost child in, 23, 35, 45, 72, 199, 202, 204, 211, 213, 216, 235, 243, 276; male angst in, 130, 199, 201; mother figures in, 215–19; music for, 219; source material for, 197–98, 199, 201, 248; technical note, 219–20; as transitional film, 24, 198–99, 220, 252; in World War II combat film genre, 180, 190, 243
English heritage films, 80
Entman, Robert, 58
"E.R." (TV), 3
Erin Brockovitch, 244
Escape to Nowhere, 189
E. T. the Extra-Terrestrial: and aliens, 27, 29, 31, 40, 41, 57–58, 57, 241, 275–76, 297, 306; characters in, 6, 31, 35, 36–37; children in, 31, 32–33, 36; as conservative film, 57–58, 62, 111, 240; flying as theme in, 7; on the innocence of childhood, 28, 192, 276; and Peter Pan, 24; popular success of, 62, 133, 162, 163, 220; promotion of, 4; religious aspects of, 40–42, 41, 43, 44; as science fiction, 26, 27, 28; Spielberg's personal

connection to, 9, 162; structure and point of view, 29, 155, 285; technology in, 42–43; warmth of, 46, 57, 58, 108, 150, 275

Ethics of Memory, The (Margalit), 187

European art cinema, 106, 321, 322

Fabian, Miri, 307

Fabian Society, 159

Fackenheim, Emil, 300

Fahrenheit 9/11, 284

Fangorn (Baker), 47, 48

Fanning, Dakota, 151, 154

Fantastic, The: A Structural Approach to a Literary Genre (Todorov), 12

Fantasy films, 11–13; *Always*, 12, 13, 243; amazement evoked by, 119; audience expectations in, 125; character development in, 13; character types in, 13; distance maintained in, 120; evil forces in, 120; *Hook*, 12, 13; narrative structures in, 12; quest for "home" in, 13; science fiction vs., 12, 26; by Spielberg, 13, 106; stereotypes in, 110–11

Farrell, Colin, 45

"Fascinating Fascism" (Sontag), 58, 59, 60

Ferrero, Martin, 135–36

Ferrier, Ray (*War of Worlds*), 6, 23, 108, 130, 132, 151, 152, 153–56, 154, 158

Fields, Verna, 68, 162–63

Fiennes, Ralph, 300, 303, 304, 312

Fighter Squad, 189

Film industry, *see* Hollywood

Fine, Larry, 158

Fingesten, Peter, 39

Firelight, 189–90

Fisher, Carrie, 24

Flaubert, Gustave, 33

Flemming, Victor, 14

Flowers, A. D., 193

Folklore, in monster movies, 121, 123

Fonda, Henry, 15

Forbidden Planet, 27

Ford, Harrison, 64, 89, 94, 97, 102

Ford, Henry, 305

Ford, John, 81, 112, 113, 162–63

Frank, Anne, 292, 295, 301

Frankenstein, Victor, 134–35, 136, 138, 143

Frankenstein films, 123, 125, 144

Franzoni, David, 272

Frazer, Robert, 200

Freedom from Fear (Rockwell), 203–4, 213, 217, 219

Freeman, Morgan, 150, 276

Freeman, Paul, 78, 94

Freer, Ian, 79, 191, 198, 219, 278

French, Michael, 79

French New Wave, 56

Freud, Sigmund, 39, 121, 186

Friedman, Josh, 151

Friedman, Les, personal history, 290–91

Fugitive, The, 305

Fuller, Sam, 50, 103, 229

Full Metal Jacket, 48

Gabler, Neal, 222

Gale, Bob, 191, 193, 194

Gale, Peter, 216

GameWorks, 4

Garden of the Finzi-Continis, The, 295

Garland, Judy, 71, 72

Garner, Jennifer, 74

Garr, Teri, 36, 37

Gary, Lorraine, 172

Geffen, David, 3, 270

Geiggar, Kwazi, 253

Gelley, Ora, 311, 313

Generation X, 222

Geng, Veronica, 191

Gerstner, David, 9

Gervasi, Sacha, 288

Ghost, 17

Ghostbusters, 111

Giles, Jeff, 75

Gilmore, William S. Jr., 68

Gladiator, 231

Glory, 272

Glover, Danny, 249, 259

Glover, Julian, 78

Godfather, The, 108, 161, 177, 178, 193

Godzilla series, 123

Goeth, Amon (*Schindler*), 308, 309, 311–14, 312, 316, 318–19, 320

Goldberg, Adam, 228, 237

Goldberg, Whoopie, 248, 249, 258, 259, 268

Goldblum, Jeff, 135, 136, 149

Golden Voyage of Sinbad, The, 177

Goldfinger, 74

Goldman, William, 222

Goldstein, Warren, 271, 273

Gone with the Wind, 177

Goodall, Caroline, 19, 315
Goodman, Benny, 192
Goodman, John, 14
Gordon, Andrew, 40, 77, 93
Gordon, Flash, 78, 88
Gordon, Michael, 307
Goya y Lucientes, Francisco de, 279
Graduate, The, 177
Graham, Billy, 62
Graham, Jim (*Empire*), 6, 45, 108, 197, 199–219, 208, 213, 235
Graham, John (*Empire*), 199–204, 215
Granger, Stewart, 79
Grant, Alan, (*Jurassic*), 6, 132, 135, 135, 138–40, 141–43, 142, 145, 146
Grant, Barry Keith, 9
Grapes of Wrath, The, 162, 322
Greatest Generation, The (Brokaw), 221
Greatest Show on Earth, The, 79
Greenaway, Peter, 188
Greenberg, Harvey R., 121
Gregoire, Dan, 157
Gremlins, 103
Griffith, D. W., 244, 274
Grochal, Aldona, 307
Gross, Arye, 53
Gross, Larry, 106
Guffey, Cary, 32
Guillory, Bennet, 250
Guinness, Alec, 198
Guy Named Joe, A, 14

Haggard, Rider, 116
Halbwachs, Maurice, 186
Hamilton, Murray, 170
Hammond, John, 134–38, 135, 140, 142, 143, 144, 147, 149–50
Hanks, Tom, 70, 73, 149, 224, 236, 283, 284, 288, 288, 304
Hanratty, Carl (*Catch Me*), 70, 73–75, 73, 118
Hansen, Miriam, 308, 320
Harlan, Jan, 47
Harmetz, Aljean, 191
Harper, Jessica, 51
Hartman, Geoffrey H., 299–300
Haskin, Byron, 151
Hauberger, Rami, 311
"Haven" (TV), 295
Havers, Nigel, 204
Hawks, Howard, 50, 69, 87, 165

Hawn, Goldie, 66
Hawthorne, Nigel, 278
Hell Is for Heroes, 229
Henley, Barry Shabaka, 285
Hepburn, Audrey, 16
Hero with a Thousand Faces, The (Campbell), 77
Heston, Charlton, 79
High Noon, 287
Hill, John, 245
Hillberg, Raul, 300
Hirsch, Helen (*Schindler*), 306, 307, 311–14, 319
Hirschman, Elizabeth, 40
Hiser, Tim, 115
Hitchcock, Alfred, 2, 7, 34, 60, 112, 124, 130–31, 132, 169, 170, 172, 226
Hitler, Adolf, 95, 114, 297, 318
Hoberman, Jim, 323
Hoffman, Abbie, 56
Hoffman, Dustin, 18
Holden, Stephen, 223
Holinshed Chronicles, 268
Hollywood: art vs. commerce in, 177–78, 199, 298, 315; blockbuster mentality in, 2, 176–78, 317; censorship in, 229; cinema of immersion, 223; and collective memory, 185–88, 296; economic decline of, 110; elements of film construction in, 169–70; escapist fantasies of, 245; excesses of, 23, 106; films as cultural events in, 177, 243; fiscal demands of, 298; genre formats in, 112, 245; Holocaust treated by, 294–97, 298, 301, 315, 318, 322–24; infantalization of movies by, 2, 105, 106, 317; marketing strategies in, 177–78; "masculine" genres of, 183, 233; and movies in war years, 181–84, 229, 242; New Hollywood cinema (1970s), 106, 176; racism in, 256, 272; source materials for, 268; Spielberg's influence on, 5, 105–7, 126–27, 133, 148, 176–78; treatments of history by, 187–88, 273–75; word of mouth in, 177; and World War II, 180–84, 221, 229, 242; youth market for, 177; and youth rebellion (1960s and 1970s), 181, 184
Holocaust: emergence in U.S. life, 291–92, 296, 318, 321; evil depicted in, 292, 299, 300, 306, 309, 314, 315, 318–19; and Hollywood storytelling, 186, 298, 323; and Jew-

ish identity, 44, 293, 297–98, 305; learning from the past, 301; media treatments of, 294–97, 298, 301, 315, 318, 322–24; memorials of, 292, 294, 304, 323; and national identity, 293–97; as outside history, 298–99; representational issues in, 298–301; and role of *Schindler's List*, 294, 296–97, 301, 317–18, 323–24; survivors' stories of, 296, 299, 300–301, 323–24; as universalized symbol, 294; visual re-creation of, 186, 299–301

"Holocaust" miniseries (TV), 292, 294, 295, 301, 306

Hook, 18–25, 21; on assuming adult responsibilities, 19–22, 23, 276; audience expectations frustrated by, 24, 25; cameos in, 24; characters in, 6, 19–21, 141; as critical flop, 23–25, 65, 220; death motif in, 21–22; elegy for childhood in, 20, 23, 72; as fantasy film, 12, 13; flying as theme in, 22, 24, 25; gross earnings of, 17, 23; lost time as theme in, 18–19, 20, 22; male angst in, 22–23, 130, 200; as musical, 24, 175; and Peter Pan myth, 18, 19–20, 24, 25; source material for, 18, 20, 21; special effects in, 23–24, 147; as transitional film, 23, 24–25

Hooper, Matt (*Jaws*), 164–65, 165, 166–69, 168, 174, 175

Hooper, Tobe, 14

Hopkins, Anthony, 270, 276, 277

Horror films, *see* Monster movies

Hoskins, Bob, 21

Hounsou, Djimon, 272, 275, 277

House of Rothschild, The, 61

Howard, Arliss, 149, 278

How Green Was My Valley, 162

Hudlin, Warrington, 270

Human Genome Project, 55

Hunter, Holly, 15

Hunter, Stephen, 222

Hurricane Iniki, 147

Hurt, William, 30

Huston, John, 50

Huyck, Willard, 103

Huyssen, Andreas, 301

I Am a Fugitive from a Chain Gang, 244

Ibu, Masato, 207

Imitation of Life, 246

In Cold Blood, 322

Indelible Shadows (Insdorf), 295

Indiana Jones and the Last Crusade: characters in, 8, 72, 78, 89, 100, 101; chronology of, 76; father and son in, 78, 83, 84–85, 86, 89–92, 89, 97–99, 114, 118, 276, 283; father figures in, 97, 101; female figure in, 85, 89–93; gun used in, 80; Nazis in, 95, 98, 116; opening vignette of, 80–81, 112–13; quest in, 77, 78, 82–85, 90–91, 97, 98–99, 101, 105, 114, 115, 116; revisionism in, 113; western arrogance in, 104–5, 112, 115–18

Indiana Jones and the Temple of Doom: characters in, 97, 100, 101–5, 102; children threatened in, 23, 96, 101, 103; chronology of, 76; and ethnic stereotypes, 101–5; father figures in, 96, 97; female figure in, 85–87, 89, 96; gun used in, 79; opening vignette of, 80–82, 192; PG-13 rating for, 103; quest in, 77, 78, 82–84, 105, 114, 116; religious elements in, 101–2

Indiana Jones trilogy, 76–118, 317; as action/adventure melodramas, 66, 85, 108, 118; alternative reading of, 112–18; antagonists of, 92–95; chronology of, 76; commercial success of, 112, 220; and conservative ideology, 106, 109–12, 113, 117–18; costumes in, 79–80; counternarratives in, 5; dark Other and ethnic figures in, 85, 100–105, 111, 116–17; father figures in, 95–100; female figures in, 85–92, 111; and macho codes, 6, 7, 113–15; music for, 175; narrative structure of, 76, 77–79; objects of the quests, 82–85; opening vignettes of, 80–82, 116; popularity of, 66; religious aspects of, 82–83, 116–18; and Spielberg-Lucas collaboration, 105–9; themes and elements in, 77, 113; as transitional films, 99; war as backdrop for, 180, 243; *see also specific films*

Industrial Light and Magic (ILM), 48, 133, 145, 157, 231, 304

Informer, The, 162

Insdorf, Annette, 295, 296, 322

Into the Arms of Strangers, 296

Invaders from Mars, 27

Invasion of the Body Snatchers, 27

Irving, Amy, 17, 99, 112

Ishimatsu, Guts, 204

It's a Wonderful Life, 221

Ivanir, Mark, 307

Jackson, Leonard, 249

Jackson, Michael, 24

Jackson, Samuel L., 141

Jaehne, Karen, 305

Jagger, Mick, 4

Jaws, 161–79, 193; awards won by, 172, 173, 174; beach sequence of, 68, 170–73; characters in, 6, 22, 108, 164, 165, 173; commercial success of, 105, 107, 127, 161, 175–76, 190, 220, 317; critical interpretations of, 162, 163–65; editing pattern of, 172–73; flying as leitmotif in, 7; happy ending of, 152, 175; impact of, 127, 161, 162, 176–78; *Indianapolis* speech in, 166–69; male angst in, 130, 168, 176; male bonding in, 165–69, 168; message of, 175; as monster movie, 123–26, 178; music for, 174–75; narrative flow of, 170; precursors to, 126–27, 128, 132; production events of, 161–62; promotion of, 161, 177–78; sequels to, 148, 178; shark as monster in, 125, 168, 170–73, 174, 175–76, 306; source material for, 169, 248; visual highlights of, 169–73, 280; as watershed in Spielberg's career, 126–27, 132, 162–63

Jeffrey, Julie Roy, 270

Jein, Gregory, 193

Jennings, Wade, 12

Johnson, Ben, 67

Jones, Chuck, 192

Jones, Howard, 278

Jones, Indiana, 94, 97; bullwhip of, 79, 80, 81; character development of, 97, 118; emotionally stunted, 23; fear of snakes, 6, 78, 81, 113; guns of, 79–80; and his father, 78, 83, 84–85, 86, 89–92, 89, 96, 97–99, 283; and "Indy Boot," 79; male angst of, 7, 78, 82, 92, 98, 113–14; moral education of, 78, 116–17; as suffering hero, 64; and women, 85–92, 111, 113, 114; *see also specific films*

Jones, Quincy, 24, 174, 248, 250, 260

Jones, Tommy Lee, 304–5

Judgment at Nuremberg, 295

Jung, C. G., 121

Jurassic Park, 108, 132–48; awards won by, 133; box-office success of, 133; characters in, 6, 8, 133, 134–38, 135, 141, 142; children threatened in, 136, 137–38, 141, 276; dinosaurs in, 125, 132, 139, 144–45, 146; father figure in, 137, 138–40, 141, 142; flying as metaphor in, 7; ideology of reconstituted family in, 126, 138–43, 142, 179; impact on film industry, 133; merchandising of, 133–34, 148; as monster movie, 123–26; mother figure in, 140–41; music for, 134, 175; narrative space of, 132–33; nature and technology in, 143–46; nature's brutality portrayed in, 124, 134, 144; parallel editing in, 146; past incorporated into present in, 146–48; production demands of, 147; sequel to, *see Lost World*; source material for, 132, 137, 138, 148, 150; special effects in, 132–33, 145–46, 156, 219; visual hallmarks of, 146, 280

Kael, Pauline, 40, 69, 232

Kaes, Anton, 298

Kafka, Franz, 49

Kahn, Michael, 68

Kaminski, Janusz, 69, 157, 230, 231–32, 270, 278–79, 321, 322

Kane, Kathryn, 180, 182

Kataoka, Takatoria, 212

Katz, Gloria, 103

Katzenberg, Jeffrey, 3, 270

Kauffmann, Stanley, 40

Kawin, Bruce, 121

Ke Huy Quan, 86, 97

Kempley, Rita, 252

Keneally, Thomas, 248, 302, 305, 315, 316

Kennedy, John F., 305

Kennedy, Kathleen, 260

Kennedy, Lisa, 145

Kennedy era, 56

Kerr, David, 43

"Kick the Can" (*Twilight Zone*), 103

King, Geoff, 132, 139, 142

King, Stephen, 126

King Kong, 123, 125, 149

Kingsley, Ben, 39, 306, 310, 317

King Solomon's Mines, 79

Kinsaka, Peto, 249

Kipling, Rudyard, 116

Klein, Charlotte, 44

Knight, Wayne, 144

Koch, Howard, 151

Kodat, Catherine, 273, 275

Koepp, David, 149, 151, 155

Kolker, Robert, 58–61, 62, 110, 235

Korean conflict, 80, 182, 221

Korsmo, Charlie, 18
Kramer vs. Kramer, 111
Kubrick, Christiane, 47
Kubrick, Stanley, 46–49, 54, 58, 60, 198, 241
Kurosawa, Akira, 268

Ladd, Alan, 79
Landis, John, 103
Landsberg, Alison, 186
Lang, Helmut, 221
Langer, Lawrence L., 294, 316
Lantieri, Michael, 133
Lanzmann, Claude, 300
La Rue, Lash, 79
Last Days, The, 296
Law, Jude, 45, 46, 48
Lawrence of Arabia, 80, 198, 322
Lean, David, 197–98, 322
Leigh, Janet, 226
Lenehan, Nancy, 72
Lerner, Neil, 40
Levi, Primo, 299, 318, 323
Levinas, Emmanuel, 292
Lewis, Jon, 108, 109
Life Is Beautiful, 295
Lindsay, Vachel, 181
Lipsitz, George, 185
Loman, Willy (*Salesman*), 70
Long Goodbye, The, 68
Long Way Home, The, 295
Looney Tunes cartoons, 192
Lord of the Rings trilogy, 12, 119
Loshitzky, Yosefa, 1, 318, 321
Lost Horizon, 12
Lost World, The: Jurassic Park, 148–50; characters in, 149–50; dinosaurs in, 125, 132, 150; and merchandising, 148; moments of terror in, 149; as monster movie, 123–26; as sequel, 148, 149–50, 269
Lucas, George, 2, 24, 81, 105, 176; and ILM, 133, 145; and *Indiana Jones* trilogy, 100, 105–9, 110, 111; and *Jurassic Park,* 134; and previsualization, 156
Luna, Diego, 285, 288
Lyotard, Jean-François, 299

Macbeth (Shakespeare), 268
MacNaughton, Robert, 33
Maland, Charles J., 244–45, 246–47
Malcovich, John, 198

Manchel, Frank, 2
Mandell, Siegfried, 39
Manifest Destiny, 56, 116
Mann, David (*Duel*), 22, 74, 127, 129–31, 131, 132
Man Who Shot Liberty Valence, The, 162
Marcuse, Herbert, 121
Margalit, Avishai, 187
Marshall, George, 181, 234
Mary Poppins, 12
Masamba, Lelo, 249
Matheson, Richard, 127
Matheson, Tim, 193
Mazzello, Joseph, 136, 142
McBride, Chi, 284, 288
McBride, Joseph, 17, 23, 96, 99, 100, 115, 197, 259, 303, 309
McCabe and Mrs. Miller, 67
McCarthy, Joseph, 62
Melodrama genre: action and feelings combined in, 118; all Spielberg films in, 118, 247; political power of affect in, 247; tension in, 63–65; *see also* Action/adventure melodrama
Memphis Belle, The, 229
Meyjes, Menno, 248, 260
Milestone, Lewis, 229, 268
Milius, John, 167, 191
Miller (*Pvt. Ryan*), 6, 155, 224–27, 228, 234–35, 236, 237–39, 240–41
Miller, Mitch, 72, 74
Minnelli, Vincent, 63–64, 266
Minority Report: alternate endings for, 52; on assuming adult responsibilities, 28, 36, 252, 276; camerawork in, 50, 108; characters in, 6, 8, 32, 35–36, 50–51; counternarratives in, 5; darkness of, 46, 50, 69; eye imagery in, 53–54, 55; government intrusion as issue in, 9, 51–54, 55, 158, 286; happy ending of, 152; kidnapped child in, 23, 31, 55; lost children (Pre-Cogs) in, 30–31, 32, 45–46, 50, 52, 53, 54, 55; male angst in, 35, 130; perception blurred in, 53, 55; on personal level, 50–51; on philosophical level, 50, 55–56; on political level, 50, 51–54, 62, 284; public reception of, 49, 62; religious aspects of, 45–46; as science fiction, 26, 28, 49; source material for, 49, 248; spider-hunt scene, in, 54; structure and point of view, 29, 30–31; technol-

ogy in, 49–50, 108, 145; water images in, 50–51, 53

Misak, Albert, 307

"Miss Celie's Blues" (Jones), 262

Mississippi Burning, 272

Mister (*Color Purple*), 6, 23, 249–51, 261, 262–65, 266–67, 268

Moby Dick, 59

Modern Problems, 111

Mola Ram (*Temple*), 77–78, 92, 96, 101, 102, 114, 115

Monster movies, 119–23; accountability assigned in, 125; audience responses to, 119–20; basic formula for, 119, 126; categories of, 124–25; cathartic function of, 123; communal values triumphant in, 179; cultural history of, 124; dark side of life in, 122–23; *Duel*, 123–26; and fairy tales, 120; fears evoked by, 119, 122–23, 146–47, 159, 160–61, 178, 179; *Jaws*, 123–26, 178; *Jurassic Park*, 123–26; *Lost World*, 123–26; narratives of, 119, 121; "otherness" confronted in, 119, 122; and psychoanalysis, 121–23; revenge of nature in, 124; science fiction vs., 120–21; source materials for, 121; by Spielberg, 123–26, 178–79; "surplus repression" analysis of, 121–22; *War of the Worlds*, 123–26

Monsters: as emotional center of films, 125; taxonomy of, 123–24

Monsters and Mad Scientists (Tudor), 124

Moore, Demi, 17

Moore, Julianne, 149

Moore, Michael, 284

Morris, Kathryn, 36

Morrison, Toni, 281

Morrow, Vic, 103

Morton, Samantha, 31, 32

Mounteer, Carl A., 40

Mr. Smith Goes to Washington, 195, 278

Muchar, Anna, 307

Munich, 10

Muren, Dennis, 30, 48, 133

My-Ca Dinh Le, 103

My Darlin' Clementine, 162

Mythology, and monster movies, 121

NAACP, 4, 253

Napier, John, 24

Nasseri, Merhan Karimi, 283

Nasty Girl, The, 295

Nathanson, Jeff, 288

Navorski, Viktor (*Terminal*), 23, 155, 158, 283–88, 288

Nazi Germany: *Last Crusade*, 95, 98, 116; *Pvt. Ryan*, 23, 241–42; *Raiders*, 78, 80, 83, 84, 88, 90, 95, 114; *Schindler*, 23, 25, 44, 95, 305–6, 311–14, 315, 318–19; *Triumph of the Will*, 58, 61; and *War of the Worlds*, 159

Neale, Steve, 9

Neary, Ronnie (*Close Encounters*), 36, 37–38, 37

Neary, Roy (*Close Encounters*), 22, 29, 31, 34, 36, 37–38, 37, 40, 59, 60, 108, 155

Neeson, Liam, 304, 305, 310, 312

Neill, Sam, 135, 135, 142

New Hollywood cinema (1970s), 106, 176

Nichols, Bill, 305

Night and Fog, 322

Night Porter, The, 314

Nikolaev, Valera, 286

1941, 190–97, 196; characters in, 6, 141; as commercial failure, 65, 107, 190–91; as cult classic, 191; "cut time" in, 192–93, 195, 196; flying as metaphor in, 7, 283; gross earnings of, 17, 191; historical background of, 194–95; music for, 191–92; as satire, 190, 192–93, 243; special effects in, 193–94, 219; Spielberg overwhelmed by, 147, 192, 195–97, 243; in World War II combat film genre, 180, 185, 190, 243

Nitzan, Adi, 307

Nixon, Richard M., 62

Norris, Frank, 244

Northam, Jeremy, 280

North by Northwest, 34

Nostromo (Conrad), 198

Novick, Peter, 293

Nowak, Beata, 311

O'Brien, Tim, 223

O'Connor, Frances, 36

Officer and a Gentleman, An, 111

O'Hara, Maureen, 35

Oliver Twist, 198, 250

One Survivor Remembers, 295

Oppenheimer, Robert, 144

Ortiz, John, 282

Orzech, Stanley, 316

Osment, Haley Joel, 32, 46

Otto, Mirando, 151
Our Daily Bread, 244
Out of Africa, 269, 302
Owens, William, 269

Pal, George, 150, 151, 159
Pallana, Kumar, 284–85
Paltrow, Gwyneth, 4, 24
Paluch, Beata, 307
Panaflex camera, 68
Pantoliano, Joe, 210
Passage to India, A, 198
Patriot, The, 231
Patton, George, 155
Patton, John Jr., 261
Pawnbroker, The, 294
Paymer, David, 280
Pearson, Roberta, 9
Peck, Bob, 140
Peckinpah, Sam, 48, 129, 232
Peebles, Stacey, 231
Penn, Arthur, 58
Pepper, Barry, 227–28, 237
Peter Pan, *Empire* as reverse of, 199
Peter Pan (Barrie), 18, 20, 21
Peter Pan (*Hook*), 18, 19–20, 21–22, 24, 25,
  31, 141
Philadelphia, 244, 304
Phillips, Leslie, 200
Phoenix, River, 81
Pianist, The, 295, 302, 322
Piano, The, 305
"Pick 'em Up" (*Hook*), 24
Pinky, 246
Pinocchio, 44
Plaszow Labor Camp, 321
Plato, 28
Playboy, 127
"Playing for Time" (TV), 294
Polan, Dana, 183
Polanski, Roman, 302, 303
Polk, Piotr, 307
Pollack, Sydney, 302
Pollack, Tom, 321
Poltergeist, 14, 111
Pomerance, Murray, 6
Poplin, Clovis (*Sugarland*), 22, 66, 67, 69, 127
Poplin, Lou Jean (*Sugarland*), 66, 67, 118, 127
Pork Chop Hill, 229
Posner, Philip, 297

Postelthwaite, Pete, 149
Powell, Dilys, 128
Powers, John, 252
Prager, Dennis, 44
Prawer, S. S., 122
Presnell, Harve, 234
Prince, Stephen, 110
Probst, Christopher, 232
Psycho, 38, 59, 119, 123, 226
Pugh, Willard, 249
Puri, Amrish, 77, 102

Quiet Man, The, 35, 162
Quint (*Jaws*), 164–65, 165, 166–69, 168, 175

Rafferty, Terrence, 178
Raiders of the Lost Ark, 240; characters in,
  6, 92–95, 94, 100–101, 104; chronology of,
  47, 76, 107, 110; as entertainment, 110, 192;
  father figures in, 96–97; female figure in,
  78, 85, 87–89, 140, 141; flying as leitmotif
  in, 7; government institutions in, 114–15;
  guns used in, 79–80; Nazis in, 78, 80, 83,
  84, 88, 90, 95, 114; opening vignette of,
  80–82; quest in, 77, 78, 82–85, 88, 92, 101,
  105, 114–15, 116; *see also Indiana Jones* tril-
  ogy
Rains, Claude, 278
Ramer, Bruce, 162
Ravenwood, Abner (*Raiders*), 87–88, 96
Ravenwood, Marion (*Raiders*), 85, 87–89,
  90, 93, 96–97, 114, 140, 141
Rawlins (*Empire*), 204–9, 212, 215
Ray, Nicholas, 64
Reagan, Ronald, 96, 99–100, 112
Reaganite entertainment, 33, 40, 76, 83, 99,
  109–11, 115–16, 240
Rear Window, 34
Red River, 59
Ribisi, Giovanni, 227, 237
Rice, Condoleezza, 221
Richard, Emily, 215
Richards, Ariana, 136, 142
Richardson, Miranda, 216–19
Riefenstahl, Leni, 58, 60
Ritchie, Lionel, 250
Riva, J. Michael, 249
Road Runner series (TV), 192
Robards, Sam, 33–34
Robbins, Tim, 151

Roberts, Julia, 19
Robinson, Ann, 150
RoboCop, 120–21
Rockwell, Norman, 203–4, 213, 217, 219
Roosevelt, Franklin D., 203
Rosen, Gary, 271, 273
Rosenfeld, Alvin H., 294
Roskies, David G., 300
Roth, Lane, 77, 93
Royal, Susan, 316, 321
Rubin, Susan Goldman, 203
Russell, David J., 123, 124

Sachar, Howard, 167
Sack, Michael, 66
Sagalle, Jonathan, 307
Sahara, 195
Saldana, Zoe, 285, 288
Same River Twice, The (Walker), 248, 266
Sanz, Jose Luis, 144
Sattler, Ellie (*Jurassic Park*), 135, 135, 136–37, 138, 139–41, 142, 145, 146
Saturday Evening Post, 203, 204, 217
Saturday Night Live (TV), 197
Saving Private Ryan, 220–43, 236, 269, 274; author's conclusion, 242–43; characters in, 6, 8, 72, 237; commercial success of, 185, 220–21; critical attacks on, 240–42, 305; flying as leitmotif in, 7; history treated in, 9, 48, 108, 155, 188, 243; impact of, 220–21, 223, 243; masculine codes in, 130, 235; as Memorial Day tradition, 221; moral values in, 190, 222, 233–35, 237–40, 241, 242; Nazis in, 23, 241–42; opening Omaha Beach scene of, 68, 184, 222–28, 224, 229–30, 232, 233, 242; as sacramental rite, 239–40, 243; technical elements in, 68, 198, 229–33; in World War II combat film genre, 180, 184, 190, 243
Schatz, Thomas, 65, 176, 177
Scheider, Roy, 172, 173
Schepisi, Fred, 302
Schiff, Richard, 149
Schiff, Stephen, 323
Schindler, Oskar (*Schindler's List*), 305–6, 308–10, 310, 312–14, 312, 315–18, 319, 322
Schindler's List, 301–24, 317; Aktion (Krakow ghetto destruction) portrayed in, 309, 316, 319, 320, 322; author's conclusion, 322–24; awards for, 295, 304–5, 321; characters in, 6, 8, 306–14, 310, 312, 316–19; critical attacks on, 300, 303, 305–6, 307, 311, 316–18, 319, 323; critical success of, 163, 220, 269, 290, 295, 323; editing patterns in, 311–14; as emotionally draining project, 134, 148, 303, 304; evil addressed in, 25, 134, 292, 306, 315, 318–19; external threat resisted in, 276, 286; financial achievements of, 295, 305; and Holocaust, *see* Holocaust; impact of, 162, 269, 290, 295, 296–97, 301, 317, 322, 324; Jews in, 305–14; movie rights to, 302–3; music for, 175; narrative breadth of, 307; Nazis in, 23, 25, 44, 95, 305–6, 311–14, 315, 318–19; scholarly studies of, 1, 162; sense of hope in, 323–24; sex and violence in, 314–15; shooting, 304; social issues addressed in, 9, 108, 195, 243, 252, 290, 292; source material for, 248, 302; and Spielberg's Jewish identity, 303–4; structural sophistication in, 307; television presentation of, 305; use of sound in, 320; visual elements in, 68, 156, 198, 280, 307, 319–22; war as backdrop for, 180; as watershed in Spielberg's development, 43, 44, 95, 99, 148, 162, 252, 303, 319; as work of art, 307, 316, 321–22, 323
Schindler's List (Keneally), 248
Schneider, Elsa (*Last Crusade*), 78, 85, 89–92, 89, 95, 98, 114, 115
Schwarzenegger, Arnold, 149
Science-fiction films, 11–12, 25–27; *A.I.*, 26, 28; alien creatures in, 26–27; audience expectations in, 125; children in, 31–32; *Close Encounters*, 26, 27, 28, 48; concepts in, 26, 121; conservative label affixed to, 56–62; cultural anxieties mirrored in, 26; *E.T.*, 26, 27, 28; fantasy vs., 12, 26; happy endings in, 27; *Minority Report*, 26, 28, 49; monster films vs., 120–21; narrative trajectory of, 121; of 1940s and 1950s, 61; religious components in, 39–46; science in, 25, 26; social implications explored in, 28, 284; special effects in, 27, 28; speculation evoked by, 119, 120–21; by Spielberg, 27–28; structure and point of view in, 29–31
Scorsese, Martin, 9, 58, 198, 241, 270, 302, 303
Scott, Amber, 19
Scott, Jacqueline, 127
Scott, Ridley, 49

Scott, Willie, (*Temple*), 85–87, 90, 96, 97
Searchers, The, 59, 155, 162
Secret of the Incas, 79
September 11 attacks, 51, 158, 159
Seven Beauties, 314
Seymour, Francie, 58
Shakespeare, William, 268
Shattuc, Jane, 247
Shaw, Robert, 162, 165, 167, 173
Sheard, Michael, 95
Sheehan, Henry, 7, 22–23, 25, 117, 195
Sheen, Martin, 72
Sheinberg, Sid, 302
Shelley, Mary, 135
Shining, The, 47
Ship of Fools, 295
Shoah, 300, 322
Shohat, Ella, 76, 104, 110, 116
Shop on Main Street, The, 295, 322
Short Round (*Temple*), 6, 78, 86, 87, 96, 97, 101, 103
Shug (*Color Purple*), 248, 249–51, 255, 259–66, 267
Siegel, Don, 229
Siemion, Adam, 307
Silet, Charles, 1
Silkwood, 244
Silva, Geno, 282
Sinclair, Upton, 244
"Sing, Sing, Sing" (Goodman), 192
Singh, Raj, 101
Singin' in the Rain, 24
Sirk, Douglas, 63
"Sister" (Jones), 250, 263, 264
Sizemore, Tom, 225, 237
Skarsgard, Stellan, 279
Slade, Darren, 195
Smith, Lois, 50
Smith, Maggie, 18
"Smoke Gets in Your Eyes," 25
Sobchack, Vivian, 25, 39, 56, 58
Social problem films, 244–46; *Amistad,* 244–47, 289; *Color Purple,* 244, 245–46, 289; happy endings in, 245; narrative structure of, 245, 289; "otherness" addressed in, 275–76; *Schindler's List,* 290, 292; by Spielberg, 246–47, 289, 297; stereotypes in, 246, 255, 260, 272; *Terminal,* 244, 289
Sofia (*Color Purple*), 249–50, 255, 256, 266, 268

Something about Amelia, 244
Sontag, Susan, 58, 59, 60
Sorrow and the Pity, The, 322
Spielberg, Arnold, 34, 99, 112, 145, 189, 240, 243
Spielberg, Max, 18, 252
Spielberg, Mikaela George, 270
Spielberg, Steven, 173; audience seduced by, 48, 111, 251, 266; and business of filmmaking, 3–4, 111; career evolution of, 5, 10, 23, 24–25, 43, 69, 99, 108, 126, 127, 128, 132, 148, 162, 192, 220, 242, 243, 252, 276, 289, 290, 302–3, 319; career longevity of, 9–10, 118; children of, 18, 100, 252, 270; commercial successes of, 1–2, 4–5, 58, 105, 109, 111, 112, 118, 148, 178, 251; control exercised by, 48, 137; creativity of, 41–42, 43, 108, 109, 251, 307, 320, 321–22; desire to produce a musical, 24, 191–92; as director vs. producer, 108–9; divorce of, 17, 99, 112; films of, *see* Spielberg, Steven, films of; *specific films;* independence of, 9–10; influence of, 3–5, 105–7, 126–27, 133, 176–78, 220–21; Jewish identity of, 44, 297–98, 303–4; and Kubrick, 46–49; liberal humanism of, 288–89; and Lucas, 105–9, 105; and parents' divorce, 34, 35, 47, 96, 99; and postproduction, 108, 109; reputation of, 5, 107, 251, 317, 319; as storyteller, 220, 265, 314; and Walker, 248–52, 297
Spielberg, Steven, films of: characters in, 6–7; as closed universes, 125–26; conservative label attached to, 56–62, 96, 99, 106, 109–12, 113, 117, 222, 240, 267; counternarratives in, 5, 16, 33, 112, 117–18, 125, 155–56, 160–61, 199, 203, 233, 242, 311; eternal childhood in, 31–32, 106; ethnic stereotypes in, 85, 100–105, 111, 116–17, 253–59; families reconstituted in, 112, 118, 126, 141–43, 179, 276, 285; father figures in, 33–36, 47, 95–96, 112, 137; female characters in, 8, 36–39, 85–86, 96, 111–12, 140–41; flying as leitmotif in, 7, 189; gender stereotypes in, 142; genre conventions twisted in, 16, 108, 112–18, 125; happy endings of, 76, 152, 241, 282; influences on, 50, 79, 85, 87, 130–31, 165, 184, 192, 195, 198, 243, 322; lost children in, 20, 23, 31, 32–33, 141–42; male angst in, 7–8, 22–23, 129–30, 153, 286; male bonding in, 165–69; masculine

code of behavior in, 15–16, 35, 113–15, 130; and merchandising, 112, 133–34; special effects of, 106, 108, 145–46, 156–58, 220; Spielberg reflected in, 137; visual dexterity in, 5, 67–68, 108, 157–58, 169–73, 178, 194, 198, 220, 229, 230, 251, 280, 319–20; *see also specific films*
Spielberg, Theo, 270
"Spielbergian," use of term, 4
Springfield, Dusty, 74
Stack, Robert, 195
Stadler, Joerg, 238
Stagecoach, 162
Staiger, Janet, 9
Stallone, Sylvester, 64
Stam, Robert, 76, 104, 110, 116
Star Wars, 105, 107, 108, 111, 161
Steel Helmet, The, 103, 229
Steffens, Lincoln, 244
Steiner, George, 298
Stephens, Robert, 200
Stern, Itzhak (*Schindler*), 6, 306, 307, 308–11, 310, 316, 317, 319
Stevens, George, 229
Stewart, James, 278
Stilwell, Joseph W., 194, 195
Stoppard, Tom, 197, 199
Stormare, Peter, 54, 149
Straw Dogs, 129
Sturken, Marita, 187–88
Sugarland Express, The, 66–69, 127, 248; as action/adventure melodrama, 66, 118; basic structure of, 67; characters in, 6, 22, 66; limited success of, 69; lost children in, 23; music for, 68, 174; source material for, 66; time frozen in, 68–69; visual analysis of, 67–69, 108, 172
"Suo Gan" (Welsh melody), 219
Superman films, 111
"Super-Toys Last All Summer Long" (Aldiss), 47
Swayze, Patrick, 17
Sydow, Max von, 35

"Taken" (TV), 4
Tarantino, Quentin, 232
Tarbel, Ida, 244
Tarratt, Margaret, 121
Tarzan, 78
Tati, Jacques, 191
Telotte, J. P., 26

Teluskin, Joseph, 44
Temes, Delia, 281
Temperton, Rod, 250
Terminal, The, 283–89; author's conclusion, 287–89; characters in, 6, 23, 141, 283, 285, 288; flying as theme in, 7, 283; music for, 287; point of view in, 155; political implications in, 9, 158, 284–86, 287; scenes eliminated from, 287–88; as social problem film, 244, 289; themes and motifs in, 283–84, 285; visual stylistics of, 286–87
Terminator films, 133
"There Are No Cats in America" (American Tail), 297
Thing, The, 27
This Island Earth, 27
Thomas, Henry, 32, 41
Thomas, Jake, 45
Thomson, David, 106, 110
Three Kings, 231
Throne of Blood, 268
Tiananmen Square, 287
Tin Drum, The, 95
Tinker Bell (*Hook*), 19, 20, 21, 22
Tippett, Phil, 133
Titsch, Raimund, 321
Todorov, Tzvetan, 12
Tomasulo, Frank P., 40, 58, 76, 77, 87, 110, 116, 240–42
Tootsie, 302
Toplin, Robert Brent, 274, 282
Tora! Tora! Tora!, 193
Torry, Robert, 39
Tragedy, classical, 121
Treasure of the Sierra Madre, 107
Triumph of the Will, 58, 61
Truffaut, François, 29, 56
Tucci, Stanley, 283
Tudor, Andrew, 122, 123, 124, 125
Turner, Tina, 248
Twilight Zone: The Movie, 103
2001: A Space Odyssey, 48, 59, 120

Universal Studios, 4, 127, 137, 173, 302, 303
"Uprising" (TV), 295
Used Cars, 197

Van Buren, Martin (*Amistad*), 271, 275, 278, 280
Van Der Beek, James, 4
Vanished World, A (Vishniac), 321

Vaughn, Vince, 149
Vertigo, 34, 172
Vietnam War: aftereffects of, 56, 109, 175, 185, 187, 221–22, 292; effects on filmmaking, 56, 221–22, 223, 242; images from, 80, 158, 176; as turning point in U.S. history, 80, 292; World War II contrasted to, 182, 184–85, 223, 242
Visas and Virtues, 295
Vishniac, Roman, 321

Walken, Christopher, 70
Walker, Alice, 248–52, 253–56, 258, 259–61, 266, 268, 297
Walk in the Sun, A, 229
Wallace, Dee, 36
War of the Worlds, 150–61; aliens in, 125, 132, 150–52, 158, 159, 160; box-office success of, 151; characters in, 6, 8, 23, 72, 151, 153–56, 154; counternarrative reading of, 158–61; dysfunctional family in, 151, 153, 155, 179; ending of, 152; invasion and annihilation as issues in, 9, 130, 151, 152, 156, 158–59; male angst in, 153–55, 156; as monster movie, 123–26; narrative structure of, 152, 155–56; sources of, 150, 158, 159; technical and visual elements in, 156–58
Watson, Nigel, 195
Wayne, John, 15, 17, 35, 113, 155, 235, 241
Weaver, Dennis, 127, 131
Weaver, Sigourney, 64
Webber, Jonathan, 294
"We Don't Wanna Grow Up" (Hook), 24
Welles, Orson, 68, 150, 151, 159
Wellman, William, 229
Wells, H. G., 150, 151, 152, 158, 159–61
Wells, Paul, 122
Westworld, 132
Wexman, Virginia Wright, 9
"When You're Alone" (Hook), 24
White, Les, 322
Who Framed Roger Rabbit?, 109
Why We Fight series, 61, 229
Wiesel, Elie, 294, 299, 301, 323
Wilder, Billy, 302
Will, George F., 221
Williams, John: Always, 175; Amistad, 175, 270; Close Encounters, 40; Empire, 219; Hook, 24, 175; Indiana Jones trilogy, 175; Jaws (Academy Award), 174–75; Jurassic Park, 134, 175; and 1941, 191–92;

Schindler's List, 175; Sugarland, 68, 174; Terminal, 287
Williams, Linda, 65
Williams, Robin, 13, 21, 149, 303
Williams, Tony, 40, 42, 58
Williamson, Bruce, 190
Willis, Bruce, 64
Winfrey, Oprah, 249, 256, 259, 269
Winston, Stan, 133
Wizard of Oz, The, 12, 24, 157
Wojcicki, Jacek, 307
Wollen, Peter, 141, 147
Wong, B. D., 143
Wood, Robin, 76, 110, 119, 121, 122, 125
Wordsworth, William, 20, 81, 141
World War II: debt owed for, 239–40; effect on filmmaking, 180–84; failures in, 114; heroism in, 14–15, 239–40, 241; looking back to, 27, 80, 155, 184–85; masculine code in, 15–16, 17, 235; mass media and collective memory of, 185–88, 243; modern depictions of, 17, 188, 190, 242; moral certainty in, 182–83, 185, 242; movies in war years (1941–1945), 182–84, 221, 229, 242; propaganda films in, 181; renewed interest in, 221; self-sacrifice in, 16–17, 182, 240; Spielberg's father and, 189, 240, 243
World War II combat films, 180–243; cultural memory formed by, 188; Empire of the Sun, 180, 190, 243; enduring issues of, 184, 239–40; Escape to Nowhere, 189; genre of, 180–85; individualism sacrificed for community, 183–84, 233–34; 1941, 180, 185, 190, 243; popularity of, 184; Saving Private Ryan, 180, 184, 190, 243; special effects in, 184; by Spielberg, 185, 189–90; Vietnam era vs., 182, 184–85, 221–22, 223, 242

Young, Harrison, 223
Young, Richard, 81

Zaillian, Steven, 305, 306, 308
Zanuck, Richard, 173, 177
Zemeckis, Robert, 109, 191, 193, 194, 197
Zeta-Jones, Catherine, 283
Zika, Christian, 195
Zimmermann, Patricia, 76, 87, 110–11, 114
Zinnemann, Fred, 287
Zorro, 78, 79
Zsigmond, Vilmos, 67–68
Zucker, Jerry, 17

LESTER D. FRIEDMAN is scholar-in-residence at Hobart and William Smith Colleges. Previously he has taught in the media studies programs at Syracuse and Northwestern Universities. He is the author of numerous books and articles, including works on multiculturalism, medicine and media, British film during the Thatcher era, and post–World War II American cinema. Friedman won the National Jewish Book Award for *The Jewish Image in American Film*.

The University of Illinois Press
is a founding member of the
Association of American University Presses.

University of Illinois Press
1325 South Oak Street
Champaign, IL 6182006903
www.press.uillinois.edu